Unschooling To University

Relationships matter most in a world crammed with content

Judy Arnall

Professional
Parenting

Library and Archives Canada Cataloguing in Publication

Arnall, Judy, 1960-, author

Unschooling to university / Judy Arnall. -- First edition.

Issued in print and electronic formats.

ISBN 978-0-9780509-9-3 (Soft cover).--ISBN 978-1-77517-860-6 (PDF)

1. Home schooling--Canada. 2. Alternative education--Canada.

3. Education--Parent participation--Canada. 4. Universities and

colleges--Canada--Admission. I. Title.

LC40.A66 2018   371.04'20971   C2018-904386-5

C2018-904387-3

Published by Professional Parenting, Calgary, Alberta, Canada

www.professionalparenting.ca

www.unschoolingtouniversity.com

First edition 2018

Edited by Beverley Kroeker, www.betterword.ca

Printed and bound in Canada

To Elizabeth Grace,
for believing in the power of children's curiosity,
for trusting parent's knowledge of their children,
for facilitating families learning together,
thank you.
We could not have been what we are today without you.

To the Team of Thirty,
thank you for your stories, inspiration, and friendship.

To my loving family,
thank you for your love, support and encouragement for this project.
I'm so proud of the wonderful people you have become.

Advance Praise for *Unschooling To University*

"Concise parenting advice that presents alternative ways to help children grow, learn, and get into college or work. Arnall's stage-by-stage descriptions, supporting documentation, and personal stories create a useful handbook for families interested in self-directed education."

— Patrick Farenga, John Holt / Growing Without Schooling

Table of Contents

PART 1:
WHAT IS UNSCHOOLING/SELF-DIRECTED EDUCATION?

Chapter 1 - The Problem: You Can Lead a Child to School but You Can't Make Him Think

Chapter 2 - The Solution: Self-Directed Education and Adult Facilitation

Chapter 3 - What Unschooling is and What It is Not

Chapter 4 - Play is the Primary Learning Vehicle of Children

Chapter 5 - Unschooling at School

PART 2:
WHY UNSCHOOLING? THE DIGITAL GENERATION NEEDS ADULTS AND SELF-DIRECTION MORE THAN PEERS AND CURRICULUM

Chapter 6 - A Brief History of Education

Chapter 7 - Academic Benefits of Unschooling

Chapter 8 - Social Benefits of Unschooling

Chapter 9 - Emotional Benefits of Unschooling

Chapter 10 - Physical Benefits of Unschooling

Chapter 11 - Benefits to Society

PART 3:
HOW TO UNSCHOOL - 3 CRITICAL COMPONENTS OF A PERSONALIZED EDUCATION

Chapter 12 - Adult/Facilitator

Chapter 13 - Resources

Chapter 14 - Unstructured Time

Chapter 15 - Assessment

PART 4:
UNSCHOOLING AND CHILD DEVELOPMENT STAGES

Chapter 16 - Brain Basics

Chapter 17 - Babies, Toddlers, and Preschoolers Ages 0-5: Explore and Build the Bond

Chapter 18 - Elementary Ages 6-11: Play, Read, and Learn Together

Chapter 19 - Junior High Ages 12-14: Create, Experiment, and Travel

Chapter 20 - High School Ages 15-18: Investigate, Problem Solve, and Explore Careers

Chapter 21 - Postsecondary School Ages 18-25: Follow Passions

Introduction

*"People own their education from the first day of life. We are never **not** learning. If one breathes, one learns."*

In developed countries, children do not suffer from lack of schools, teacher expertise or resources. The 30 percent dropout rate in high schools indicates a problem that no amount of funding can solve: disengagement. Clearly, for a significant proportion of today's children, school does not work. Many withdraw from school as soon as they are legally able to. Traditionally, stay-in-school initiatives have been aimed at fixing children rather than at fixing the system. School staff often contact teens who have left to invite them back. But in the root cause of disengagement—relevancy to children's lives—little has changed. Children don't see relevance in memorizing the facts and theories that can be attained in seconds simply by consulting their phones.

What children need in their education is passion—the kind of motivation they bring to their play. Passion cannot be taught, nor coaxed. It must be intrinsically motivated. Today's children can learn most preschool, elementary, junior high, and even some high school content by following their interests. They don't need the mandated government curriculum. All children are born self-directed learners. They just need adults, free time, and access to resources.

We must consider education outside of the monopoly of government; children are no longer limited to a physical school that serves a specific community. Education today is globalized and borderless. Learners can take courses from anywhere in the world. They can sidestep the entire government education system and write the SATs (Scholastic Aptitude Tests), ACTs (American College Tests) or Grade 12 equivalent exams to qualify for postsecondary entrance.

Education encompasses all the learning in a person's life. Parenting is a major factor in education, guiding the whole child in all four developmental domains: social, physical, cognitive, and emotional. Teaching a child to become a productive and caring member of society is the goal of parenting. We want our children to be engaged citizens, hold down jobs, and sustain caring relationships. That is the goal of education as well. Thus, teaching is inherent in parenting. Teaching does not have to be coercive—in fact, coercion breaks relationships. Parenting and teaching are about building relationships because relationships are the foundation of our society. Parenting and teaching begin the day your child is born, and do not end on September 1 of your child's sixth year. Parents do not suddenly become incompetent at teaching and kids do not suddenly stop learning when there are six candles on the cake. Your child can continue to learn in the same way, and you can continue to build your bonds. Children can learn math any old time, but they have only a few short years to cement relationships with those who will accompany them on their journey through life—siblings and family.

I am not anti-school. I recognize that parents will always require schools, especially if they wish to work full-time and need childcare. I do believe, however, that school is not the only place to get an education.

School should be voluntary, not mandatory. Children should spend their time being inventors, designers, researchers, entrepreneurs, innovators and scientists, in areas that interest and challenge them. If their school provides that, great. If not, children can pursue those topics and interests outside of a school framework. Children should read, write, play, volunteer, work, build projects, travel; see new places and do new things. In exploring their interests, children develop the contextual language arts of reading, writing, speaking, and representing, as well as numeracy skills. They *experience* social studies, history, geography and sciences, instead of reading about them and memorizing facts and figures.

If children then choose a more formal high school experience when they reach the age of 15, they will approach it with creativity, motivation, and a well-rounded educational base. In contrast, children educated in a government-mandated curriculum endure 16 years of rote learning, and stress caused by their lack of control in the content and delivery of their education. Children who enter preschool at age two and finish high school after Grade 12 have attended an institution for 16 of their 18 years. Is it any wonder many kids do not want to spend four to seven years in postsecondary education? They want control and relevancy, and often quit school to get it. (Gavel, 2017)

Today, age 13, or Grade 8, marks the average burnout point for most children, a result of too much formal school and too early a start. Research from the Alberta Education Survey, "Tell Them From Me," shows that the percentage of students classified as engaged drops dramatically between Grades 7 and 12, or age 12 – 18 years. (Gavel, 2014) In contrast, children who have never been to a bricks-and-mortar school or completed a formal homeschool program are gearing up to enter high school eagerly and with passion. Research shows that the longer children avoid formal schooling and instead determine their own education, the more likely they are to attend postsecondary education and love it. (Gray, 2014)

Children need to be out in the world, not sitting inside of four walls. We are so used to being raised in boxes called classrooms that we no longer question their effectiveness. Instead of asking how to make the boxes more relevant for today's lifestyles, why don't we ask why children even need the boxes, or whether the boxes make for their best learning environment? Parents and employers need schools. Do children?

Children need relationships, and especially, adult relationships. "Contrary to common assumptions, scientific evidence shows that the influence of relationships on development continues throughout the lifespan. These relationships are not more important at a particular stage of a child's life compared to another, but the nature of those impacts does vary by age and developmental status." (Palix, 2017)

Through curiosity and creative exploration of the world around them, with adults at their side who mentor instead of teaching, children acquire passion and motivation and absorb knowledge in the areas they want to study and that could become their life's work. This new breed of creative problem solvers, those who have grown up outside of the box, will find the answers to society's problems of unemployment, pollution, global warming, political unrest, economic crisis, social problems, and global conflict.

This book is for parents

Are you the worried parent of an unmotivated, scared, unhappy, or disengaged learner? Relax! Your child will learn. Don't worry about the need for or the quality of preschool, homework, educational daycare, enrichment activities, get-ahead tutoring, or public or private schooling. You can't make your children learn—and you can't stop them from learning!

Yes, we live in a competitive world. Like all parents, you want your child to do well academically. But formal school may not be the right educational path for your child. Your child doesn't have to go to school in order to attend university or postsecondary institutions. All your child needs to do is demonstrate competency; skills and content can be learned, and learned well, outside of government-provided education systems. Content is everywhere. Children find the motivation to seek out their passions when they are ready, and when it really counts—as teenagers or as emerging adults.

This book is for kids

Play. Explore. Read. Experience. Discover your passions and interests. Find what you love to do. Do not fear boredom: it is a gift that will spur you to learn more. Be creative. Get messy. Find out. Don't be afraid of mistakes. Always ask Why? How? When? Be respectful but challenge conventional thinking; be sure to question everything you don't understand. Listen. Work hard. Play hard at your passions. Help others. Leave your mark in the world to make it a better place. Explore your interests—then get the best possible education for pursuing your passions: either self-taught or through the many resources available. Go as far as you can go.

This book is for teachers and homeschooling parents

You are saints! You juggle kids, parents, curriculum, testing, outcomes, principals, school boards, and administrations as well as community stakeholders. You deserve children who want to explore and learn. You deserve to interact with children who are as passionate about learning as you are. Relax! Children need you more than they need content. Human contact can't be replaced by technology. They don't need you as a lecturer, but rather as a facilitator who helps them find what they need and discover the answers to the questions they ask. Their questions—not yours. Help them discover what they want to know, not what the system thinks they need to know.

I realize that in government schooling, both teachers and students have little input. But we need to push for a better educational experience for everyone—teachers and students. If you are not confident in your ability to homeschool or are already a homeschooling parent whose children don't listen to you or take direction, don't worry! You don't have to teach your children like a school does. Trust in their passions. They will capture what they need along the way, when they need it. Join their journey on their chosen path of learning.

This book is for principals, administrators, and government

There are alternative methods of education; for the sake of our future, we need to acknowledge and support them rather than compete with them. Not everyone will be comfortable with this new model or agree with it, but everyone should be informed that it exists, and that it produces amazing results. If it needs further research, so be it. We cannot deny that children can learn and succeed without school as we know it.

This book is for members of society

The unrelenting, stress-inducing competition of institutional academic supremacy requires a backlash, and that is self-directed education. We need to step back from coerced learning, and bring joy back into the learning process. I've attended many education- and government-sponsored symposiums on what "education" and "school" should be, in light of today's huge advancements in technology. Most stakeholders still think inside the box—the traditional model of children starting school at age five and stepping off the educational assembly line at 18, with certain anticipated outcomes. Textbooks, classrooms, curriculum, and control of scope and sequence are not even questioned. Question it! We need to nurture our children's passions and creativity. Our society desperately needs future problem solvers. We can't let them drop out!

This book is for all countries

Although many of the examples in this book reference Canada and the province of Alberta, they are useful for other countries and governments in developing policy around self-directed education and balancing the needs of families' autonomy and public interest in education.

The Team of Thirty study

I do not have a stake in the "school industry." I only have a small research project with my Team of Thirty and the anecdotal experiences of 1500 unschooling families across Canada, but I believe we must commit ourselves to exploring and researching the outcomes of alternative education. If we all truly and honestly want the best education for each child, it follows that corporate profits and government jobs in the school industry will be impacted. And that is a small price to pay in order to grow global problem solvers.

The stories in this book are drawn from thirty unique unschooled individuals from my personal circle of family and friends. The children are either my kids' friends or my friends' kids. The parents and I laughed together, commiserated together; we got together for coffee or visits online. The kids played together, supervised each other, and had sleepovers (sometimes double-headers!). They all unschooled as children, following their own passions for at least three and up to all 12 years of the time they would otherwise have spent in school.

While most children spent those years within school walls, the Team of Thirty played, explored, and learned—without imposed structure, intentional targets or predetermined outcomes. By simply living life, they developed creativity and innovation, critical thinking, and problem-solving and decision-making skills. They acquired literacy and numeracy skills. They developed general and interpersonal communication skills, collaboration and leadership skills, digital and technological fluency, and a love of lifelong learning.

They were all accepted at various universities, colleges and postsecondary schools and most have graduated with degrees, certificates, or diplomas. The rest are still working on them, demonstrating grit, perseverance, and a healthy work ethic.

The team members followed various pathways to acceptance from postsecondary institutions. They adjusted to deadlines, requirements, and exams. Some received scholarships.

They take personal management and well-being, and social, cultural, global and environmental responsibility seriously.

They are engaged thinkers and ethical citizens; they have enterprising spirits. They are equipped to lead productive and satisfying lives. Their names have been changed to protect their identities as they make their way in the world, getting jobs—or making jobs! —and solving the world's problems.

You don't have to send your children to school or homeschool for them to get an education and attend university, college or technical schools. Children can acquire an education by living life.

Welcome to unschooling!

Author's notes:

Many commercial products are mentioned in this book. To eliminate text distraction, the symbols ™ and ® are not used.

The terms "he" and "she," "him" and "her" are used interchangeably and are not mean to exclude non-binary genders.

All names have been changed to protect the privacy of the Team of Thirty.

PART 1:
WHAT IS UNSCHOOLING/ SELF-DIRECTED EDUCATION?

1

The Problem — You Can Lead a Child to School But You Can't Make Him Think

"Google is our curriculum and the world is our classroom."

Adults can choose, but children cannot

Imagine that you are at a conference. You have spent the last three days listening to a lecturer and looking at 600 PowerPoint slides. You are tired, bored, and lectured out. It's not a topic you would have chosen, but your employer required you to go. The last presenter is putting you to sleep. You decide to either tune out and check your social media feeds or walk out and go to your hotel room to answer emails. As an adult, you have that choice.

The day after the conference, you are getting your son ready for school. It's his first day of Kindergarten. He gets up and eagerly packs his huge backpack with his snack, a notebook, and a pencil. He dresses in his new clothes and heads out the door with you. You drive him to the big school building a few blocks away. He sees a few hundred other children looking as scared as he is, and he hesitantly opens the door. He walks into the building. Two hours later, you drive back to the school to pick him up. As he comes running to the car, you excitedly ask him, "How was your day at school?" He proudly announces that he had a really great day and that it is now done. He finished school. He wants to go back to spending his days playing. What do you say? As a child, he has no choice.

Every day in Canada, seven million children (Hildebrandt, 2014) get up earlier than they probably want to; they eat breakfast, get dressed, and board a bus to go to a building where they spend the next six hours, most of their day, in a room with one adult and 30 peers. Going to school is their single most common activity for most of their childhood. Throw in an hour of bussing and kids spend 18,720 hours of childhood not feeding their curiosity, but following a rigid, often outdated, government-mandated agenda.

When adults do not choose their education, they have the ability to leave. Unfortunately, children do not. In North America, 20 to 50 percent of children drop out of school before graduating from high school. Many more who can't leave because of truancy laws simply tune out instead. Wouldn't it be great if kids could choose what they would like to learn, and be excited about their education?

Parents and children have been doing "school" for the past 150 years and although society and technology has changed most other aspects of our lives and cultures, not many people question whether this model of education still serves our children best, especially in the light of the borderless education delivery made possible by the internet.

A high dropout rate indicates a need for real change in education

Alberta has one of the highest dropout rates in Canada. Only 74 percent of Alberta's high school-age children finish and graduate from high school within three years. Of those who do not, some make it back, and another six percent graduate within five years. (Harvaardsrud, 2013) That means that 20 percent of children don't make it back at all while they are still young and unencumbered by mortgages, jobs, and children. It means that one out of every five brains is not reaching its full potential, yet society accepts this. I cannot imagine a brain surgeon saying, "Well, we lose about one out of every five patients on the operating table, but that is an acceptable loss." Our society would be outraged. Yet we don't question the efficiency of a system that loses one-fifth of its clients annually? There are points of progress, but as pointed out in my Introduction, most stay-in-school programs focus on fixing students rather than on fixing the school system. (Gavel, 2014)

We may think that if a child quits school, he is the only one who suffers the consequences. Not true. In addition to the financial repercussions that high school dropouts face personally, they place a financial burden on society. In Alberta, 9000 high school students drop out every year. This drains our economy—every year—of $142 million in unemployment, healthcare, social assistance, and judicial costs, as well as lost tax revenue. The Canadian Council on Learning 2008 cites a cost to society of $15,850 per dropout, per year, for the rest of their lives. (Hankivsky, 2008) Multiply that by 3000 students and the cost to society in the city of Calgary alone is $48 million per year. (Miller, 2013)

Schools were first established around 1850 to keep children busy while their parents went off to work in factories during the upswing of the second industrial revolution, which demanded ever greater numbers of obedient, non-thinking workers. Schools were structured, inflexible, and routine; coerced curriculum rewarded conformity and reinforced the mindset required by industry, and later, by the military. There was no questioning the status quo. Schools are institutions.

Undoubtedly schools improved since industrialization, allowing more interesting curriculum content, but rigidity and the demand for obedience remained with bells to signal the start and end of classes; enforced subject and topic divisions; grading systems; and punishments and bribery.

Many critics have spoken about the "hidden curriculum" of schooling; most notably, John Taylor Gatto, a New York Teacher of the Year whose distaste for the schooling industry led him to write the bestselling book titled *Dumbing Us Down*. Teaching children values, attitudes, and beliefs has always been the hidden curriculum of schooling. The problem is: Whose values? Whose attitudes? Whose beliefs? Who determines what is taught? Companies? Parents? Teachers? Universities? Governments? Politicians? The church? Community? And then—which companies? Whose parents? And so on.

In the 1850s, school was an extension of parenting. Nowadays, schools have taken the place of parenting. They are tasked with teaching values—possibly contradictory or contrary to those held by their students' parents. Many schools have tried to become value neutral. But institutions must run efficiently and to do so, certain values are embedded and promoted: obedience, conformity, unquestioning acceptance of ideas. Some parents who have disagreed with this hidden curriculum have started charter schools or placed their children in private schools whose values and beliefs are more in line with their own; or they have homeschooled. But not all parents can opt out of the public system, as there may be financial, geographical, or admission barriers.

Students are borderless in a digital world

Other sectors of our society have changed along with the digital revolution. Mostly, school has not. The digital revolution of the past twenty years has disrupted so many industries: music, movies, television, conferences, books, hotels, taxis, travel, dating, shopping—even dying. The internet has allowed us to birth at home, educate at home, work at home, shop at home, retire at home, and die at home. Services and products to help us do all that are available even on our mobile devices!

With a whole library at our fingertips on our mobile phones, we no longer even have to purchase books, music, movies, or classes. All are available free or for a nominal cost and are accessible instantly. We can subscribe to services that supply us with more content than we could ever absorb. Google promotes learning anytime, anywhere. Kids do not need to take local government or school board courses online just because they are government-approved, or local, or free. Countries across the world offer amazing courses! Parents do not have to be the teachers. They can direct their children's education with resources from around the world.

Even universities now have open courses, accessible anytime. Research studies on every conceivable topic are available to everyone. Resources and knowledge are everywhere.

So. With information available twenty-four hours a day, every day, why do children still go to school at fixed times, on fixed days, and attend fixed classes and subjects? Why is the school format so unchanged? Even homeschooling departments of major school boards are still run on the traditional September-to-June school model, a remnant from the time when children had to be free in the summer to work the farms. Learning now takes place 24 hours a day, seven days a week, 365 days a year.

The answer is that traditional schooling maintains the traditions that sustain it as an industry, rather than changing to grow along with the clients it serves.

The single major change generated by the digital age is the visual and aural forms in which courses are taught: much educational content is now being read from a screen instead of being read in a textbook or heard in a lecture. But although the delivery method may have changed greatly, course content has changed very little. Overhauls of government-mandated curriculum are far too infrequent, occurring approximately every 15 years—and far too inadequate in today's fast-paced world. My kids have been studying Social Studies from a ten-year-old textbook, written before smartphones literally changed our way of living, communicating, and educating. I remember reading the book *Animal Farm* by George Orwell when I was in high school 35 years ago, and now my children have to study it. The words, storylines, and concepts in the book are so far removed from our children's reality that it is difficult for them to relate to life in the 1940s when people lived on farms and didn't have TV, let alone mobile phones. Have no great books been written since then that would have more relevance?

Information is available all day, every day, and everywhere; why not let children loose to choose their own program of study based on their interests? Why do we keep slotting them into the government agendas, rather than letting them create their own? Do we think they will stop learning? Not a chance! Kids are very good at learning—we just need to get out of the way. Why don't we trust that our learners will self-acquire knowledge, outside of the government-controlled education system?

There is one big reason: Education is an industry and it is driven by economics. The school industry both costs and generates billions of dollars. It's big business. Directly and indirectly, it employs millions of people, all of whom have a vested interest in maintaining the status quo.

Which sectors would be affected if children were allowed to study whatever they wish? What kinds of jobs would change drastically, or be sacrificed?

Teachers—we will always need teachers but teaching methods and delivery would change. To name just one, an exciting new online industry is emerging, in which teachers develop and sell learning modules over the Internet.

Textbook and curriculum producers would lose lucrative contracts for print and online material. Today, textbooks are sold and distributed as government curricula mandates—whether they are actually used or not. How many textbooks would they sell if we allowed our children to explore subjects based on their interests? And to take this one step further, what if parents knew that their kids could learn just as much from video games as they do from textbooks?!

Bussing and transportation—bus manufacturers, drivers, mechanics, gasoline suppliers and maintenance workers, administration. Even within the school system, many kids are online on a parent-supplied laptop, in a school building—how is it we do not question why they even have to physically move from home to a school building? Bussing companies would suffer. But in addition to benefitting our children, imagine the benefits to our environment if millions of children did not spend an average of one and a half hours commuting to and from school every day—only to do their work on the same laptop screen they could use at home!

Buildings—architects, contractors, tradespeople, building maintenance employees—all who design, plan, build, maintain, clean, and in general, keep schools in shape.

Materials providers such as printers, paper products, book manufacturers, designers, editors, distributors, libraries, computer and internet suppliers, cafeteria provisioners, manipulative suppliers, art, music and theater suppliers, and many more. Even toilet paper needs to be supplied by someone!

Professionals and support staff—psychologists, police officers, nurses, guidance counselors, secretaries, janitors and social workers working in schools. Museum docents, artists- and writers-in-residence, speakers, musicians, and actors that visit classrooms.

School board administrators, superintendents, curriculum developers and testers, assessment and exam departments, directors, managers, and clerical staff in education departments.

If personalized learning is truly in the best interests of every child, why is society not prioritizing that? Why are we still institutionalizing children? By definition, public schooling cannot be personalized for each child. The system must be consistent in its policies, rules, and treatment. And the status quo remains. The schooling industry needs a disruptor to its gatekeepers of knowledge. Think UBER, which provides rides but no cars; Amazon, which sells everything but carries no stock; and Airbnb, which sells accommodation but doesn't own hotels.

So, do we need a school with no buildings and books? Yes! Think Google! Think Life!

There will always be a need for schools because of society's need for child supervision. But what we don't need is today's formula with its universally prescribed programs. People must know that attending a school is but one out of many options.

Clark Aldrich, author of *Unschooling Rules*, stated in a conference session that change in a monopoly never happens from within. Reforms occur when outside forces change. The homeschooling and unschooling movement is one huge external pressure on today's school system (Aldrich, 2015), growing exponentially every year. When homeschooling reaches 30 percent of the education demographics, it will be considered mainstream.

For many years, our local public school board had a small home-education department. Its employees' mandate, it seemed, was to dissuade callers from even considering homeschooling. I know—I was one of those callers. The response to callers seeking information was patronizing, condescending, and offensive. We would hear comments such as "You must know you can't do as good a job as the school," or "Aren't you worried about socialization?" or the biggest heart-stabber of all, "You could wreck your child for life! It's better to just enroll them in school."

But the hostile attitude had the opposite effect. The Alberta government mandates supervision of homeschooling families; smaller private schools and non-local school boards began offering this supervision by long distance—an option that allowed families to circumvent their local public school boards. Homeschooling and unschooling families increased and flourished.

Clearly, this led to the public system losing many students and the corresponding government funding. Realizing its loss to homeschooling, unschooling, charter, and private schools, the public system hired a new department head for its homeschooling department in 2004 to update and grow the department and make it more supportive and welcoming.

School is not best for every child. Just as some people like to work in a big company, other people prefer to work in a small company or run their own business. In education, not every child wants to attend a big school. Some would prefer a private school or self-study. Children must have choices. Unschooling is one.

What is Unschooling?

First, let's define "schooling": "The process by which a predetermined, arbitrary set of outcomes is reached using predetermined, standardized curriculum administered by an authority figure to target groups of students sorted by chronological age." (Sandy K, 2002)

Parents' options to traditional schooling are homeschooling or unschooling. Most people understand homeschooling but not unschooling.

Unschooling is the philosophy of self-directed free-learning. Children decide what they want to learn, when they learn it, how they learn it, and how much they want to learn about a topic.

For example, a child has just heard about the Roman Empire because she was playing a computer game called *Age of Empires*. She wants to know more about the Romans, so her parent might check books out of the library, scour Netflix for movies about Rome, and suggest they build a model of the Coliseum. The child may choose to do some or all of those things—and the parent is okay with her choices. She may wish to explore the Roman empire in depth—or not. Perhaps the family goes so far as to plan a trip to Rome in a few months. Or, the child may be happy simply looking at picture books! Whatever the case, the child directs how deeply she wants to study about Rome. The learner takes total responsibility for her learning. Practiced around the world, unschooling is one of the fastest-growing trends in education today. Unschooling produces children who love learning. Unschooling capitalizes on children's curiosity and their drive to find out the answers to their questions—their motivation to learn.

If children could do this in school, would they drop out? Research shows they wouldn't. Summerhill School in the U.K. has been allowing children to choose their own learning path and curriculum for the past 97 years, with tremendous success.

As in the example above, curriculum is determined by the learner. Traditional curriculum is often defined as "packaged programs a school purchases for its teachers to use in their classes" and most people indeed think of curriculum as a canned package. In the broader sense, curriculum can be defined as "what schools, parents, and individual teachers do in their encounters with the child." (SAPTA, 2013) In this context, "curriculum" is present from the time the newborn emerges from the birth canal until the child walks in the front door of the Kindergarten—and far beyond. Curriculum is all around us in every conceivable form. Curriculum encompasses interactive and experiential learning, something all unschoolers do. But instead of learning from texts and workbooks, they might use a park, a video game, or a discussion. In whatever form, the learning is always self-directed.

If adults were to trust that a child knows what he needs to learn, they would be surprised to see that most of the child's choices coincide with established curriculum! In their play, children naturally gravitate to experimenting with water, sand, magnets, blocks, boats, worms, planes, rocks, motors—an infinity of objects and subjects. Children are natural scientists; they want to know about everything they encounter in their world!

In a way, children choose their curriculum even in traditional schools. When they deem the subject boring or irrelevant, they tune out; when the subject is of interest, they listen! Long periods of studying uninteresting or irrelevant subject matter can lead to children eventually dropping out of school. Meanwhile, since they are not engaged, they act up and waste everyone's time and effort: parents, bus drivers, teachers, principals, and fellow classmates.

A positive result of traditional schools is the development of additional adult-child relationships outside of the family. The central relationship is the teacher-child bond. Without a doubt, teachers are the best part of traditional schooling. Children always need adults, and even more so with the inherent isolation that is a product of the digital revolution. With so much information at children's fingertips, they need a caring adult—whether teacher or parent—to help them make sense of the information and interpret its significance; to connect the dots between random bits of information.

In traditional schooling, the biggest challenge is reaching children that don't want to learn. Thousands of books are written on how to engage unmotivated students. Yet motivation is ultimately up to the learner and no measure of tips and tricks are going to turn an uninterested student into an engaged one, if he or she doesn't want to learn what the teacher is required by the system to teach.

Parents want choices. At the same time, they can be overwhelmed by them. We have so many more choices in education now: charter schools, language schools, rote learning schools, online schools, homeschooling, and unschooling. With choice comes worry: what is the right choice? Will your choice mess up your child for the rest of his life? I can assure you, parents, that you can't mess up a child's education! Because they, as learners, are ultimately in charge of it. They own it. They will decide what and how much they learn, where they learn, and in which way they will learn. True learning is *always* self-directed.

Do children need 12 years of prescribed, government-controlled curriculum in the digital age?

No. As evidenced by the Team of Thirty, they probably only need about three years of intense study in Math and Science, and perhaps a year or two in English, History, and Writing to prepare them for university or other postsecondary choices. As the brain's pre-frontal cortex matures, it develops the abstract and critical thinking skills that promote accelerated learning of basic, intermediate, and advanced concepts. Children do not miss out if they don't have 12 years of traditional schooling; rather, they learn in a different way—through interests instead of school.

Writing an essay is a critical skill. Children learn how to write a five-paragraph essay in almost every year of Grade 1 to 12 schooling; then they go to university and are taught it again in first-year English courses. Repetitive and boring for those that catch on the first time. Those who want to know how to write an essay or need a refresher can look it up online and practice on their own or with an adult's help. Mathew was about to be tested on Grade 10 level cell components. He was to study a website, memorize the cell parts, and learn them for an exam. He told me, "If I ever need to know about cell parts, I can just find it on the internet. Why do I have to memorize this?" Good point!

2

The Solution — Self-Directed Education and Adult Facilitation

"Unschooling is self-directed, adult-facilitated, interest-based free-learning in response to intense, compelling curiosity."

We are natural learning organisms from birth to death

My children and I are shopping in a grocery store. It is eleven o'clock Monday morning, a time that most kids their age are in a school. As we approach the cashier to pay for our week's worth of food, we brace for the inevitable question: "No school today?" We are practiced with a variety of answers, such as "We homeschool," "No school today," or just plain "No." The questions keep coming until we admit that "Yes, we homeschool." Then the comments come, "Oh, I could never do that. You must be a saint to want to be around your kids all day." My kids are standing right here. They can hear you! Or, "You must miss being with your friends."—as if school is the only place to make friends. Or my favorite, "Is that legal?" No, I'm modeling criminal behavior as a form of good parenting!

More recently, such comments are fewer, as more people are homeschooling and children are becoming more visible in the real world during business hours. Still, the clerk might ask, "When are you taking a break from homeschool?" Which is like asking, "When are you taking a break from breathing?" It's only recently that I have come out of the closet and admit that we *unschool*, not homeschool. Then they ask, with extreme skepticism, "But how do your children learn?" The fact that people learn from many sources is far removed from most people's thinking. The idea that school is the only place to learn is entrenched in their brains. It is reinforced by the media, books, internet, adults, kids, and life in general. It's a huge assumption. When most adults meet a child for the first time, they ask their name, followed by what grade they are in—not their age or interests!

When babies are born, their brains are wired to learn. They don't learn how to learn; they just do it. Babies learn to walk, toddlers learn to talk, children learn to count, youths learn to read, and teens learn about sex—all without teachers. Learning is innate and motivates every action from birth to death. Our desire to learn, conscious or unconscious, never ends. Every action we take, every thought we have, every word we utter is driven by our ingrained desire to learn.

11

The primary learning vehicle during childhood is play, and it is far more important than coerced curriculum. Yet free play time for school-age children and even preschoolers and toddlers is being eroded in favor of more school, earlier school, and more academic school. No wonder kids burn out.

People cannot pursue their passions by following someone else's agenda or curriculum. Entrepreneurs tell us that they can't dedicate the necessary time and energy to grow a business while they are working for someone else. In fact, it can be done, but it is hard. The same goes for education. Time spent on the government's agenda means less time for one's own.

Through its mandated coercive curriculum and outdated rules, the school system undermines a child's confidence in his learning. When children respond to mandated curriculum with boredom or inattention, the school system resorts to bribery, punishment, shaming, and other methods of coercion to encourage cooperation. Children who have experienced this grow up to be adults who are fearful of learning. I know—I get them in my adult education classes. They are fearful of tests, marking, and being ridiculed in front of their peers. They have bad memories of school and worry that the learning atmosphere will be a repeat of their childhood experiences. I try to make learning enjoyable for them. Many rediscover the joy of learning through adult education because it treats them with respect through self-directed curriculum and goals.

We need to protect our children's primal desire to learn.

Adults provide 7 Critical Cs of education

Research shows that the two most important factors in children's well-being are stimulation in their academic environment and at least one warm, nurturing, encouraging relationship with an adult. If there is more than one such relationship, even better. (The Economist, 2014) Some children don't have a warm, caring parent, and need to develop such a relationship with a school teacher. Peers, by their very nature, are not nurturing. At best, they provide friendships, and at worst, they are sources of stress caused by bullying, competition, negative peer pressure, and classroom interruptions. Adults are nurturing.

Unfortunately, teachers are busy. They are managing classes of up to 40 children; they don't have the time to establish meaningful nurturing relationships with their students. They used to be able to cuddle children in their laps while reading to them, a practice that research shows enhanced reading enjoyment for children. (Kidspot, 2016) Homeschoolers do provide this, and it may be the biggest reason for homeschooled children's academic excellence. They are given individual attention, are not restricted to stay within a defined space, and can veer off from the course curriculum as much as they wish. Whether as parent, sibling, relative, family friend, or teacher, following are seven critical ways a supportive adult can contribute to a child's education.

The 7 Critical Cs that adults provide are:

1. **Curiosity**: Children have it, and the adults around them can lend their own. "I wonder what happens when..." is a great way for adults to share their enthusiasm for deeper exploration of a subject.

2. **Caring**: Bullying and nastiness abounds in our society, both in the real world and on the internet. More than ever, children need adult models who demonstrate caring for one another.

3. **Creativity**: Innovation is essential in finding solutions for problems large and small. When adults urge children to take risks and celebrate their successes—or their mistakes, as lessons learned—they send the message that creativity is valuable.

4. **Competencies**: The content of all the core subjects taught in school can be found online. Adults can show children how to search effectively.

5. **Context**: How do bits of information fit together? Google doesn't provide the context that adults with many years of experience can provide. Healthy adult-child relationships will make children feel comfortable in approaching adults who can explain the context. Children need to connect the dots and weave the webs between bits of scattered information; adults are in the best position to help them do that.

6. **Conversations**: Language, storytelling, and expression, whether oral or written, all involve conversations between people. Children need both the oral and the written interchanges. Children learn vocabulary, conversation etiquette, syntax, and language usage from conversing with the adults around them. We call this interaction "serve and return." The child "serves" by speaking and the adult "returns" the serve by being attentive and responsive. This is ever more critical as our society raises "the silent generation." With adults silently tapping away on their screens or keyboards, children are left in desperate need of someone to talk to them. Online courses exacerbate the problem for our children.

7. **Community**: Humans are social beings. Children need adults to demonstrate sustainable communities that work; that live together and help each other. Not only school communities, but also neighborhood ones.

The current model of 40 kids accessing a single teacher is no longer what our kids need. Teachers cannot provide all the above 7 Cs and also teach 1400 content outcomes per grade. It's impossible. I suggest that the content must go—not the adult connection. When asked what the classroom of the future would look like, Hanan Yaniv, Associate Professor in Education at the University of Calgary, replied, "Classrooms will develop into virtual classrooms in which teachers and experts will be available to provide students [with] direction when needed, but the idea of learning will become more independent of a specific location and time." (Yaniv, 2011) My response would take this one step further: that kids need answers to their questions and can find them by searching Google.

What our children truly need is the one thing that can't be delivered virtually: relationships.

Curiosity is the central driver of learning

Online government-prescribed courses are growing in popularity, but these are not homeschooling. Online courses fuel the practice called "roamschooling," which are government courses that can be accessed from anywhere. With roamschooling, a child can be sitting in front of a computer taking an online course at home, or in a classroom at school—either way, that child is still learning from someone else's agenda. This is not unschooling, nor even parent-controlled homeschooling. The difference between home education and school is not *where* the learning takes place, but *who* controls the agenda. Only in unschooling and independently funded free-schools are children allowed to self-direct their learning. Anything else is "school"—no matter how it's delivered. Like homeschooling, unschooling is most often done in the home and in the community. About 10 percent of homeschoolers self-define as unschoolers.

Unschooling is pure free-learning

Free-learning doesn't mean no-cost education. It means the freedom to learn whatever the learner chooses to learn, and is often used to describe unschooling. The term "unschooling" was first conceived by US educator John Holt of the homeschooling movement and the magazine *Growing without Schooling*, in the 1970s. Holt fashioned the term after the soft drink slogan, "7Up–The Uncola," and used it to mean "not school." (Farenga, 2003)

Unschooling is called by other names as well: andragogy, self-directed learning, self-education, self-directed education, non-curricular learning, discovery learning, constructivist learning, experiential learning, problem-based learning, self-taught, auto-didactic, child-centered learning, child-focused learning, inquiry-based learning, hack-schooling, roam-schooling, flex-schooling, immersion, adventure, child-led, or delight-directed learning. Other terms are free-schooler, free-learner, self-schooler, world-schooler or life-learner.

Some people love the word "unschooling"—because that is what it is. It is not school. It is education that doesn't have the typical elements of school; it has no coercion, timetables, subjects, bells, forced curriculum, grades, uniforms, or other elements typically associated with school. Other people dislike the word because it is negative and sounds "anti-school." Schools have a place in society and are beneficial for some people. But not for all. "Un" means "not" and "school" has become synonymous with "learning" and "education"—words that have been hijacked and twisted by schools in the last 100 years in such a way that people cannot understand that "not school" does not mean "not learning." And so, we perpetuate the myth that children who do not attend school or homeschool do not learn.

This is absolutely false. On the contrary, unschooled children are very well educated.

Personally, I love the term "self-directed education." It is more positive and inclusive than unschooling. It includes children that do want to study with teachers and books. It includes children who choose school over home. It includes children who don't self-teach, but rather self-learn. It includes parents who don't teach, but design an education program, pulling from many global resources. It includes families in which one child chooses to attend school and one chooses not to. It includes adults as well as children. The central theme is "self-chosen." Because self-chosen is a bit wordy, I will continue to use the term unschooling because most people know that unschooling means self-directed education in the home.

Self-directed education takes many forms

Self-directed education feeds a person's curiosity. But how? It manifests itself in different ways throughout the lifespan. Babies, toddlers, preschoolers and school-agers feed their curiosity mainly through exploration and play. Teens do it through study, reading, play, work, and experimentation. Adults do it through reading, work, courses, and research; and if they are lucky, continue to commit to play time.

Unschooling research: does it work?

Does unschooling "work?" There are two major types of research:

Qualitative research

Stories. This type of research deals with descriptions and data that can be observed but not measured: surveys, interviews, anecdotal examples, observations. It can be subjective and biased.

Quantitative research

Numbers. Data. It is more likely to be objective and unbiased.

The best research with the least amount of bias is quantitative, done with a large number of participants. For example, if thousands of children were unschooled for at least five years and they wrote their end-of-school leaving exams, their average marks would be a good indicator as to whether unschooling helped or hindered their educational development.

We might question what exactly we are measuring when we ask, "does it work?" How is success in unschooling defined and measured? Does one measure by a scale of happiness throughout childhood and adolescence, or at the age of 18? Does one measure by the kind of adult job one attains?

Schools measure success rate by the average mark attained in a set of Grade 12 diploma exams.

Governments measure success rates by how many students graduate with a high school diploma, yet many students don't get high school diplomas because universities do not require them.

Most universities only require marks for core subjects at the Grade 12 level for entrance.

Many unschoolers don't write exams at all, though, because the concept of comparison or ranking is so antithetical to the unschooling philosophy.

In this book, the benchmark is measured by the acceptance rates from postsecondary institutions; an impossible measure for schools. In society, a child is deemed successful if he receives an offer of acceptance into a degree, diploma, or certificate program at adult age, regardless of his measurable educational status. Our entire Team of Thirty achieved this. If I can count, within my small circle of friends and family, 30 kids I know who unschooled and all had postsecondary offers and are generally happy with their life choices, I would say they were definitely successful learners!

And if I can count 30 successful unschoolers just in my inner circle, how many more are out in the wider world? We will never know unless we acknowledge unschooling, discuss it, and measure it. Because education statistics lump unschoolers together with homeschoolers, they are represented in research but not segregated. Other than the Concordia University 2011 study, there is no distinction in any study of home education between homeschoolers and unschoolers. However, if we estimate unschoolers to represent about 10 percent of the more than two million US homeschooled children (Shultz, 2014), then in fact they are included in the statistics.

I also caution that unschooling means many things to many people. I've heard people call themselves "full" unschoolers, even when parents direct the education choices—including insisting on non-school even when children want to attend school; and "half" unschoolers, in which parents direct the math and English studies but leave the rest up to the child. I do not believe these are examples of unschooling as intended in the research. For purposes of the examination of these studies, unschoolers are defined as children who wholly self-direct their education.

Quantitative research
Team of Thirty Unschoolers Survey, by Judy Arnall, 2017

The 30 children surveyed practiced self-directed, free-learning unschooling for a minimum of three and a maximum of 12 school years. We didn't include Kindergarten as it is not mandatory. All 30 children were accepted to postsecondary schools. Twenty will have graduated by the time this book goes to print. Twenty went to university, seven to college, two to technical schools, and one is undecided. Of the 30 kids, 12 went into STEM (Science, Technology, Engineering, Mathematics) fields, four of whom were accepted into Engineering and the rest in Bio-Science, Business and Earth Science programs. Nine unschoolers chose the Humanities in various disciplines, such as Psychology, Asian Studies, and Anthropology. Nine unschoolers went into the various Arts fields of music, the culinary arts, fashion design, photography, and visual arts. Only 11 of the 30 children had attended preschool. Nine graduated with a self-designed high school diploma and 20 used a diploma to get into postsecondary schools. Although the sample size of 30 participants is extremely small, it is at least double the number in the Concordia University Study. It exhibits promise of the validity and educational capacity of unschooling and self-directed education.

The Team of Thirty

We are mainstream—not outliers! Friends in my circle who have children that unschooled and were accepted into the postsecondary school of their choice.

(SD) Self-Directed (IP) In-Progress

Name	Pre-school	Years Un-schooled	High School Diploma	Reached postsecond-ary with	Scholar-ships	Degree/Focus	Institution	Acheivement
Rosie	✓	6	✓	Diploma	✗	STEM	University	BA in Business and Economics
Joey	✓	9	✗	Mature	✓	Arts	University	BA in Music Composition
Aras	✗	8	✗	Grade 12 English, interview and portfolio	✗	Humanities	University	(IP) BA in Liberal Arts
George	✗	12	✗	Some Grade 12 Marks	✗	Arts	Technical	(IP) Diploma in Culinary Arts
Will	✓	8	✗	5 Grade 12 Marks	✗	STEM	University	(IP) BSc in Mechanical Engineering
Naomi	✗	12	✗	Portfolio	✗	Arts	Technical	Photography
Irene	✗	12	✗	Interview and application	✗	Arts	College	Fashion Design
Don	✗	6	✓	Diploma	✓	Humanities	University	BA in Philosophy and Psychology
Ross	✗	6	✓	Diploma	✓	STEM	University	BSc in Nanotechnology Engineering
Bill	✗	6	✓	Diploma	✓	STEM	University	(IP) BSc in Biochemistry
Jake	✓	10	✓	Diploma		Humanities	University	(IP) BA in History/Language
Aura	✗	7	✓(SD)	(SD) Diploma	✓	STEM	University	(IP) BSc in Mechanical Engineering
Mikko	✗	10	✓(SD)	(SD) Diploma	✓	STEM	University	(IP) BSc in Computer, Programming and Design
Phoenix	✓	9	✓(SD)	(SD) Diploma	✓	Arts	University	BA in Music, Performance

Name	Pre-school	Years Un-schooled	High School Diploma	Reached postsecond-ary with	Scholar-ships	Degree/Focus	Institution	Acheivement
Keith	✗	11	✗	5 Grade 12 marks	✗	STEM	College	EMT/EMR and Firefighter
Nolan	✓	9	✓	Diploma	✓	Humanities	University	BA in Asian Studies
Mabel	✗	7	✓(SD)	(SD) Diploma	✓	STEM	College	Nursing Diploma, (IP) BSc in Nursing
Sunny	✓	12	✗	Interview and portfolio	✗	Arts	College	Stage Manager
Lara	✓	12	✗	Interview and portfolio	✗	Humanities	College	Ship Captain
Mark	✗	8	✓(SD)	(SD) Diploma	✓	STEM	University	BSc in Nursing
Nathan	✗	11	✓(SD)	5 Grade 12 marks; no diploma when applied	✓	STEM	University	BSc in Electrical Engineering
Sara	✗	12	✓(SD)	(SD) Diploma	✓	Humanities	University	BA in English
Robert	✗	12	✓(SD)	(SD) Diploma	✓	STEM	University	(IP) BSc in Biology
Amy	✗	12	✓(SD) (IP)	(SD) Diploma	(IP)	Humanities	Applying	Undecided
Anne	✓	10	✓	Diploma	✓	Arts	University	BA in Drama
Dan	✓	3	✓	Diploma	✓	Arts	College	Art
Lan	✓	6	✓	Diploma	✓	Arts	College	Visual Art
Sandy	✗	4	✓	Diploma	✗	Humanities	University	BA in Leisure Studies
Mandy	✗	3	✓	Diploma	✗	STEM	University	BA in Architectural Design
Melody	✗	9	✓	Diploma	✗	Humanities	University	(IP) BA in Anthropology

Fraser Institute Research Reports, 2007 and 2015

In 2007, The Fraser Institute published a paper called *Homeschooling: From the extreme to the mainstream.* (Basham, 2007) The paper was a meta-analysis look at research studies on homeschooling from Canada and the US. Meta-analysis is a statistical technique used to amalgamate, summarize, and review quantitative research. Key findings showed the following results for home-educated children:

- They experienced no specific benefit if their parents were certified teachers

- They did not suffer socio-economic effects, and those of single parents fared better than their public-school counterparts.

- They scored life satisfaction as "high."

- Their families spent less than $4000 annually per household on education.

- Their primary behavior models were adults rather than peers.

The Fraser Institute published another report, more focused on Canadian studies, called *Fraser Institute: Homeschooling in Canada — the current picture 2015.* (Van Pelt, 2015) Not only were the findings similar to the 2007 report, they also indicated that homeschooling (not home-based schooling such as online and correspondence courses) enrollments in the five years from 2007 to 2012 grew 29 percent, while public school enrollments during the same period dropped 2.5 percent. The 2015 report also attested that homeschooling saved Canadian taxpayers $256 million in education funding for the 2011/2012 school year, including $95 million in Alberta.

> Home-educated children outperformed both public and private school students academically.
> Home-educated children were involved in an average of eight social activities outside of the home.

Concordia University Study, by Sandra Martin-Chang, 2011

The Concordia study comprised 74 students aged 5 - 10 (or Grades K to 5) that wrote standardized tests in Reading, Writing and Math. Thirty-seven of the students were homeschooled and 37 were public schooled. Of the 37 homeschooled, 12 were un-schooled.

The study was conducted by Chang at Concordia and Mount Allison universities and suggests that homeschooled children in New Brunswick and Nova Scotia do better aca-demically than students in public school. The homeschoolers scored a half grade higher in Math and two grades higher in Reading. The study included "a set of children" [12 kids to be exact] educated in an unstructured (unschooling) education environment and this group showed less progress, faring 1 - 4 grade levels below their structured homes-chooling counterparts. In fact, children in public school fared better than the unschool-ers in seven tests.

This study made news headlines despite having a sample size of only 12 unschooled children and is problematic in several ways. First, unschooled children, because of the very nature of unschooling, do not follow the same topics in the same sequence as children in school or homeschool. If they had no interest in the given topics at the same point in their education, they would not have covered them and it would be unfair to test them on that knowledge. It is like testing fish to see if they can climb trees.

Second, the testing was done on children under 10 years of age. Most children that young love to be physical and play. When they are allowed to do so instead of being chained to a desk, they learn through experience and interaction with the world. Unschooled children 5 - 10 years of age have that benefit—but at the same time, they manifest a deficit in paper-and-pencil classwork. That is not to say that they will not eventually learn and understand the same material or do well in life; it simply means that their early learning does not include a lot of bookwork. Most unschooled kids understand mental math but are not very practiced in paper math: how to write fractions, which way numbers face, or even how to properly line up three-digit numbers in a column for addition. Kids catch up fast when they need to, and they do just fine when they take math courses and do paper math on a regular basis. Just like late toilet trainers, or readers, once children master a concept, they advance very quickly because their brains are ready. No one can tell at what age my kids started to read, but they are voracious readers now—probably because we didn't give them complexes and insecurities by freaking out over their late reading start (although the homeschooling supervisors sure got concerned!).

A third problem with the Concordia study is the reliance on formal testing. Test-taking is a learned skill, and unschoolers often don't have it. Certainly, taking tests was a foreign concept to my children at that age. When my kids took their first online Grade 8 class, they were handed a pencil, a test book, and a Scantron form. I had to ask the exam supervisor to show them how to complete the forms and take the test so that the result would be a fair assessment of their knowledge and not an unfair test of their test-taking abilities.

In all the years we unschooled, I had my children take the PATs (Provincial Achievement Tests): Grade 6 and 9 in English and Math. They did well, scoring at either Acceptable or Excellent levels. They did not write the Social Studies and Science exams. Those exams are topic-specific; if my children had no interest in those topics, it would not have been fair to subject them to the exams. Again, this did not mean they wouldn't have that knowledge by Grade 12; it meant that their learning on those subjects did not occur according to the government-mandated timeline.

A better study with more accurate results than the Concordia one would measure diploma exam marks, or SAT results at the Grade 12 finish line. By Grade 12, most unschooled children have the same reading and writing skills as public school children. They may not have the same math skills—and not everyone will need STEM math in their career of choice. If they won't need it, and don't have the interest—why study it?

Says a mom from a Facebook group: "We unschool in all subjects except mathematics. According to this study, then, my students should be expected to do extremely well on the math part of the standardized tests, and poorly in reading and writing. I see the opposite. Their reading and writing scores consistently fall well above their respective grade level—more than two grade levels on most subtests. Their math scores, on the other hand, are more modest, falling 'only' in the grade level category or slightly below on those subtests. I have no explanation for these counterintuitive results, but they are quite consistent from year to year." (Helga R, 2015)

Qualitative research

Homeschooling's Lessons for Education, Survey by Cardus Research, by Deani Van Pelt and Beth Greene, 2017

Cardus has numerous research reports on its website regarding the benefits of home education. They strongly state that "the notion that only a provincial curriculum is sufficient to ensure a quality education is misguided."

Online Blog Survey of 74 Adult Unschoolers, Gray and Riley, 2013

In 2013, Peter Gray, a professor at Boston College, and his colleague Gina Riley surveyed 74 grown unschoolers about their educational experience. All had at least three years of unschooling and one-third had never been to school or homeschooled. Although the caveat here is that the Gray and Riley surveys most likely attracted respondents from those who regularly read Peter Gray's blog, the results are interesting.

Most of the unschooling families reported the following:

- Their children had time to pursue their passions and develop expertise.

- They had earlier exposure to career choices.

- They developed personal self-direction and motivation skills.

- Their social experiences were better than in school because of the wide diversity in their groups of friends.

- They felt ready for college, thanks to their years of self-direction.

- They had some trouble adjusting to the social immaturity of their peers in higher education, but eventually worked it out.

- Some felt they had gaps. Only11 percent articulated this and identified the gaps as mostly in math; they overcame the deficiency when the need arose.

The most interesting outcome of this study is that the less formal studies and seatwork the school-replicated, government-based curriculum homeschoolers had, the more likely they were to go on to postsecondary education. Of the 74 participants, 62 from all groups (including 18 of the 24 kids who were always unschooled) went on to some form of postsecondary study, whether vocational training, university, or college.

The participants were admitted to postsecondary schools through various means, such as taking community college courses and then transferring to a four-year program. Some wrote the SAT/ACT exams. Some had a GED (General Educational Development) diploma, and some acquired a diploma online. Following are some of the findings from the always-unschooled postsecondary students:

- Nineteen of the 24 have jobs or careers in the arts, film, theater, or writing.

- They all had gaps in test-taking, note-taking, essay writing, but quickly picked up those skills when needed.

- As college students, they had expected a more adult social life; they were disappointed in the frat parties, the immature social life, and the lack of intellectual curiosity of the peers.

- They were disappointed in the way professors treated them like children that needed to be spoon-fed. They knew how to manage their time without their professors building in structure.

Some parents were more hands-on unschoolers and strewed interesting items and experiences into their children's educational environment; some were more hands-off, totally leaving the children to their own academic devices. Both methods worked. Interestingly, in all cases but three, participants felt that their parents had met their emotional needs. This fit the healthcare community's requisite for healthy parenting, in providing physical well-being, emotional support, and intellectual stimulation to their children. Good parenting involves "scaffolding the brain" and being present and attentive; those same qualities are also essential for unschooling success.

Another trend was children's need for connection to the community. When parents acted as facilitators and involved their children in the community, learning was successful.

Brookings Institution Research Paper, by Reeves and Howard, 2013

Richard W. Reeves and Kimberley Howard of the Brookings Institute think tank wrote a paper called *The Parenting Gap*, which concludes that parenting accounts for about one-third of the gap in development between rich and poor children. The two aspects of parenting that seem to matter most are intellectual stimulation, such as talking, reading, answering "why?" questions, "serve and return interactions"; and emotional support such as bonding with infants so that they grow up confident and secure. Reeves and Howard developed a composite measure of these aspects and called it the HOME scale (Home Observation for Measurement of the Environment). They relate it to how well children do in later life, using data from a comprehensive federal survey of those born in the 1980s and '90s. "All this suggests that, when it comes to education, the best returns will come not from pumping yet more money into schools but from investing in the earliest years of life. And that includes lending a helping hand to parents who struggle." (The Economist, 2014) We need to help parents provide stimulating activities for their children, and not simply take over the institutional education of their children.

Online Blog Survey of 232 Parents of Unschoolers, Gray and Riley, 2011

In 2011, Gray and Riley surveyed 232 parents about their experiences in unschooling their children. Most parents were positive about the choices they had made.

Home Education Reason and Research, The National Home Education Research Institute (NHERI) Survey, by Brian Ray, 2009

In 2003, the National Home Education Research Institute conducted a survey of 7,300 US adults who had been homeschooled (5,000 of them for more than seven years) and found the following:

- Homeschool graduates are active and involved in their communities. Seventy-one percent participate in an ongoing community service activity such as coaching a sports team, volunteering at a school, or working with a church or neighborhood association, compared with 37 percent of US adults of similar ages from a traditional education background.

- Homeschool graduates are more involved in civic affairs and vote in much higher percentages than their peers. 76 percent of 18 – 24-year-olds surveyed voted within the last five years, compared with only 29 percent of the corresponding US populace. The statistics are even higher in older age groups, with voting levels not falling below 95 percent, compared with a high of 40 percent for the corresponding US populace.

- Almost 59 percent of homeschool graduates report that they are "very happy" with life, compared with 27.6 percent for the public-schooled US population.

Fifteen Years Later: Home-Educated Canadian Adults; A Synopsis, CCHE, by Deani Van Pelt, 2009

This study showed that homeschooled adults were more likely to study at postsecondary institutions such as trade schools, community colleges, and university bachelor's degree programs than their school counterparts.

Home Education UK Study, 2005

This study from the UK shows that parental attention is the major influence on raising test scores for children from low socio-economic sections (SES). Children with low SES were able to outdo more affluent schooled peers. (Rothermel, 2005)

Home Education in Canada: A summary of the Pan-Canadian Study on Home Education 2003 by the Canadian Center for Home Education, 2003

A random sample of 1,648 families found that among the children who reached adulthood, 40 percent participated in cross-cultural activities, 72 percent of eligible voters exercised that right, and 82 percent volunteered with one or more organizations.

The Smithsonian Report, 1960

The Smithsonian Institution's Journal, *Horizon*, published a recipe for childhood genius in 1960. The first of the three ingredients was "much time with warm, responsive parents and other adults." The second was "isolation from peers," and the third called for "much freedom for children to explore their own interests." Harold McCurdy, the study's director, contrasted that to families and schools when he stated, "...the mass education of our public school system is, in its way, a vast experiment on reducing...all three factors to a minimum; accordingly, it should tend to suppress the occurrence of genius." (Moore, 1999) The analysis further suggests that children need "more of home and less of formal school," "more free exploration with...parents, and fewer limits of classroom and books," and "more old-fashioned chores—children working with parents—and less attention to rivalry sports and amusements."

They concluded that the bonds and emotional development resulting from being at home with parents during school-age years produced critical long-term results that were cut short by enrollment in schools, and could neither be replaced nor afterward corrected in an institutional setting. Recognizing the necessity for early out-of-home care for some children—particularly special needs and starkly impoverished children, and children from exceptionally inferior homes—they maintained that the vast majority of children is far better situated at home, even with mediocre parents, than with the most gifted and motivated teachers in a school setting.

Sudbury Valley School, US

Sudbury Valley Day School was founded in 1968 in Framingham, Massachusetts. It is one of two of the most famous research-based schools that demonstrate how the unschooling model can work in a school setting.

Sudbury has extensive follow-up studies that show the school's graduates have done well. (Gray, 1986) (Greenberg, 1992). Graduates applied to and were accepted into reputable colleges; they were successful in their careers. They reported that self-directed learning had taught them to be self-disciplined and socially responsible. These results show that children can acquire their own education through curiosity, without adult coercion.

Both internal and independent studies show that Sudbury graduates are self-confident, self-motivated, resourceful, and highly self-aware. (Vangelova, 2013) Ninety-three percent have gone on to postsecondary studies (far higher than the national average of 66 percent from the same income bracket). Sudbury graduates are leaders, entrepreneurs, and role models in living examined, fulfilling, successful lives. (Groeneveld, 2014)

Summerhill Boarding School, UK

Summerhill School has operated continuously since its founding in the United Kingdom in 1921. Detractors have studied it relentlessly in the hopes of finding some kind of neglect among students that would rationalize the government closing it down. However, it has consistently turned out well-educated graduates, in spite of students being permitted to choose their own program of studies. When visiting the UK, I inquired about their graduates' postsecondary acceptance rate. They replied, "We do not keep such records, but please be assured that the vast majority of graduating Summerhillians move on to higher education or college." (Lynn, 2014)

In conclusion, research shows that unschooling works well when the whole family is on board, the parents are emotionally healthy, and the family is socially connected to the many external supports offered in their neighborhoods and communities.

3

What Unschooling is and What It is Not

"You can't force a child to learn and you can't stop a child from learning."

Unschooling is a buffet

The short definition of Unschooling is: self-directed education outside of government control. The learner chooses what to learn, when, where, how and if they are going to learn about a topic.

The long definition is that unschooling, a philosophy of educational freedom based on the natural curiosity and self-determination of a healthy child, given access to a rich and stimulating environment and a wealth of resources, and facilitated by a willing adult, will lead the child to learn what they need to know, in the time frame that they need to know it. The learner is totally self-directed, self-motivated, and often but not always, self-taught.

Imagine that a child is standing before a food-laden buffet table. The child carries an empty plate. Unschooling gives that child the opportunity to pick and choose from the wide array of "food." He decides how much of each food he will take, and if and when he will refill his plate. School offers the same buffet but with a teacher, principal, school board, government and a whole gamut of support staff putting food on that child's plate, whether he wants to eat it or not. They are deciding what type of food that child eats (subjects), how much of each food to serve him (outcomes), and whether there will be any refills (depth). In homeschooling, it's the parent filling the child's plate and making those same decisions for the child.

On the buffet table are brownies (video games) and broccoli (Shakespeare). In the school model, the government decides to put the brownies on a pedestal in order to get the child to finish his broccoli. Sometimes, in homeschooling, the same approach is taken by the parent. In contrast, the unschooling child has free rein to choose between the brownies and broccoli, which are placed at the same level on the table. Because he has never known the brownies to be judged as the wonderful food and the broccoli as "the stuff you have to slog through to get to the good stuff—the brownies," he chooses a bit of both. No one item in the buffet is deemed as "good" or "bad," as "junk" or "educational." Everything in the buffet is deemed to be of equal educational value and a starting point for further exploration.

Inquiry-based, self-directed learning in government-funded schools is still the same buffet, but the child is allowed to choose food items from a cordoned-off section of the table. This is not the same as unschooling. His inquiry is limited by the parameters of the school board- and government-dictated outcomes and it may not include what he would voluntarily choose. The system still controls what is on that child's plate.

In free-schools that are not government funded, the child can choose what is on his plate. This is unschooling in free-schools such as Sudbury and Summerhill.

School system	Homeschooling	Unschooling
Government, administrators, school boards, principals, teachers control	Government, school boards, parents control	Learner controls: What — interests When — age Where — venue If — now, later, never How much — depth and scope of topic How — method of learning
Subjects	Subjects	No division between life and learning
System sets goals for learner	Parents set goals for learner	Learner sets goals for themselves
Curriculum	Curriculum	Learn from unlimited resources and stimuli
System makes decisions	Parents make decisions	Makes own decisions
System sets pace	Parents set pace	Sets own pace
System assesses for progress proof	Parents observe progress and reports	Self-evaluates progress continuously

Comparison of education methods

"Radical" or "whole life" unschooling versus "educational" unschooling

Further, there is a division between "radical" or "whole life" unschooling and "educational" unschooling. Radical, or whole life, unschoolers incorporate the educational philosophy into their lifestyle, extending it to parenting and family life—the children identify their position in the family structure and self-direct their participation in family life. They decide when and what to eat, when to go to bed, and when and if to contribute to the family unit. Recently, the media has termed this lifestyle as *Feral Families*. Many onlookers see this negatively, as permissive parenting, but it works for many families and the children grow up healthy and well-adjusted.

Other unschoolers separate their parenting and educational philosophies and are called "educational" unschoolers. They still provide structure, or scaffolding, in their parenting—they determine the environment until children are ready to take it on themselves. They have regular family meal times, reasonable bed times, and consensual limits on technology; everyone pitches in for family chores to ensure the household functions smoothly. They have routines, rituals, and celebrations. They work and play together as a family unit within the community. This also works for many families, who have two buffet tables: one for education and one for parenting. I am one of those.

"On the parenting buffet table, some things are not on it—trying heroin, for example, or trampling on people's feelings or destroying the property of others. However, the educational buffet table holds unlimited choices; the kids are in total control of that one," says Linda, unschooling mom of two kids. Read more detail about parenting and education styles in Chapter 12.

Can a person be "a little bit unschooling," or just unschool one subject? I have seen parents loosen up a little on Social Studies and Science but insist on more structure in Math and English. Most unschoolers have an opinion on this, and there is a wide range! Labels are for jars. People become more complex as we change and grow. My stance is that if you think you are unschooling, you are probably unschooling.

Most unschoolers, whether "radical whole life" or just "educational" unschoolers, can agree on several points. Unschooling is not just another homeschooling method. It's a paradigm shift. It's not leaving kids to their own devices—it's about being with them, observing them, noticing what interests them and offering more of that, pointing out connections between their interests and the universe.

The goal of unschooling is not education. It is to help a child be who she is and blossom into who she will become. Education happens as a side effect. (Tia L, 2003)

Unschooling is ...

- Self-directed education through living life, pursuing interests and projects, satisfying curiosities, and playing.

- Parental attentiveness to indicated needs for children's learning and the ability to facilitate time and resources for that purpose.

- Determined totally by the child. A child may indicate a desire for structured activities—textbooks, courses, tutoring or direct teaching; or totally unstructured activities—playing video games all day.

- Flexible, motivating, and personal. Learning occurs anywhere, anytime; true self-directed learners never lack motivation.

- A philosophy that acknowledges a simple truth: that every person chooses what they learn, either by paying attention or by tuning out, whether in a school or homeschooling setting. Unschoolers never tune out because there is nothing to tune out of.

- Cost effective. In fact, it costs governments and taxpayers nothing.

- A philosophy that has been used in "free-schools" that are not government funded. Most schools that receive government funding are still required to meet outcomes set by the government. Free-schools funded by parents can truly be unschooling schools.

Unschooling is not ...

- **Homeschooling**, which tends to be the "school-replicated-at-home" model. Although, by law, unschooling is most easily undertaken at home because it enjoys the least government interference and is not publicly funded. It is governed by the local state or provincial homeschooling regulations.

- **Uneducated**. Every child learns to read, write, and do mathematics as well as their schooled or homeschooled counterparts. They simply obtain their knowledge in a different manner—through play and curiosity rather than curriculum and rigid agendas. As one 12-year-old unschooler said, "Comparing me to those who are conventionally schooled is like comparing the freedoms of a spirited horse drinking in all that the world has to offer to those of a lamb in a feedlot."

- **Socially isolating**. Whole families participate actively as community givers, volunteers, travelers, employees, entrepreneurs, farmers, and mentors; they function well in the community and in society. In fact, it is more unsocial to be contained all day within an institutional classroom.

- **Permissive**. Unschooling is free-learning, not permissive parenting. A parent or adult acts as a mentor, guide, coach and facilitator to provide learner-desired resources, support, and structure, when the learner shows interest in a topic. Permissiveness is neglect. Neglect is born of no adult involvement. Unschooling is the opposite—dedicated adult attentiveness to the needs of the learner.

- **Well researched yet**. Most unschoolers detest the whole idea of standardized testing, knowing and believing—as many teachers do—that testing does not adequately assess the range of learners' intelligences. Thus, measurement of how unschoolers compare to schoolers or homeschoolers is largely unstudied.

Unschooling is an education style based on the concept that learning is an integral and continuous part of life. **We're never *not* learning**. Note my use of the collective "we." Unschooling is lifelong learning that includes us adults as well as our kids. We don't start learning in preschool and stop after high school or college. We learn as we go, intrinsically motivated to master the skills and acquire the knowledge we need to pursue our dreams, accomplish our goals, and live our lives. If you are reading this book, you are learning something new!

Unschooling is never coercive, bribed, or forced learning; it is second nature to all of us. On that note, it is important that unschooling and homeschooling be a family decision. And if a child absolutely wants to attend school, that is unschooling too, in that the child is still self-directing his education.

A mom on our listserve defines it best: "Unschooling can mean doing workbooks for one child, while another might never touch them. The heart of it is trust in your child. It recognizes individual learning styles and stages of development for each child and allows them to 'go with it' rather than force the child to do what they 'should' be doing because they are a certain age. It recognizes the value of downtime—those times when the child seems to be doing nothing—and that some of the most amazing development might be happening internally, even though it is invisible and can't be measured." (Anna KB, 2000)

How to unschool

Unschooling needs three components to work: adults, resources, and time. Much like a three-legged stool, it is not stable with one of the legs missing.

1. **Adults**: A parent, another adult, or even a teacher must be available to the child for help and mentorship, but not to take over or direct. The adult facilitates but does not "teach" unless the child asks for clarification. She lets the child pick and choose what to do with his time and the materials available to him. His inner processes of curiosity, interest and concentration will guide him on whether and how much knowledge to absorb.

2. **Resources**: Provide an environment rich in resources: books, videos, cameras, computer and video games, workbooks, textbooks, projects, jobs, museums, field trips, volunteer programs, atlases and maps, science centers, zoos, museums, theaters, TV, toys, concerts, musical instruments, board games, mentor and apprenticeship programs, music, internet, libraries, instructors, living history parks, art galleries and supplies, sporting venues and equipment, science equipment, corporate venues, parks, travel, and many more.

3. **Time**: Provide lots of unstructured time for the learner.

That's it. It sounds very simple but it can be very hard. Sometimes the thought of homeschooling and working through a structured curriculum program of "five pages of workbook per day and then we are done" sounds very enticing. The reality is that interest and curiosity do not happen on a schedule. When your six-year-old son wants to see what happens when a chicken bone is soaked in vinegar for a few days and wants to begin the experiment at eight o'clock at night when you are enjoying your favorite Netflix show, it can be very hard to encourage and help him! Yet that is when his interest is fired up. So, you run with it.

Many parents already "afterschool," "flexschool," "worldschool," and "homeschool" while in the system

This is primarily why we started "homeschooling." We found we were "afterschooling" way too much. Afterschooling is the practice of parents supplementing the school curriculum at home after school hours, either to help a child who is behind or to get a child to work ahead, or simply to satisfy the child's real interests, as was our case. The oldest boys would spend six hours a day in Kindergarten and Grade 1, then come home and really want to delve into learning what they wanted to learn—which never seemed to coincide with what they were studying at school. For instance, Mathew wanted to plant an egg to see if an egg tree would grow. It was not enough for me to assure him that it wouldn't; he had to see it for himself. He nagged me so much that we went out to the back yard and planted the egg. He kept watch for two weeks! Every day after school, he would come home and learn what he really wanted to learn. The teacher told him to wait until Grade 12 to learn about eggs. He was supposed to put his curiosity on hold for 11 years? Not a chance! I discovered it was indeed possible for them to just quit school and learn what they wanted to learn.

As well, when children struggle at school, parents spend a lot of time at home trying to approach a concept in a different way in the hope that the child will catch on. Or they have to deal with supervising a lot of a child's homework. This is also called "afterschooling."

Some parents are very supportive of the homeschooling concept and yet don't wish to jump into it fulltime. They enroll their children in school, using it as the default when family plans allow. This is called "flexschooling." When they go on vacation, they pull their children out of school. If they want to take the children on a field trip outside school, they pull them out. When they want to take the kids shopping, they pull them out. School is where the kids go when nothing else is going on.

Other parents enroll their kids in school but pull them out at any time for holidays. This is called "worldschooling." It may work when children are young and won't miss much but becomes harder as they age and want to connect with peers. FOMO (fear of missing out) can result in children falling behind and missing assignments, labelling them negatively in front of their classmates at an age when peer impression is important.

Many parents of different cultures buy the same textbooks that their children are studying in school and are very involved in homework. They subject their children to a double shift: schooling and homeschooling. They review the day's curriculum, repeating it at night. But it is still the school's agenda and not their own. The risk of burn-out is real.

Philosophies of education

There are many philosophies of education: Classical (including Trivium, Quadrivium), Charlotte Mason, Christian, Montessori, Waldorf, Thomas Jefferson, Reggio Emilia, unit studies, and many more. Some are practiced in a school, some at home. Some are delivered in a traditional classroom. Some are delivered online, by correspondence, or in boxed packages. All except unschooling have specific content and delivery methods.

In the province of Alberta, public, charter, and private schools are treated equally: if the government provides its funding, its students must meet mandated outcomes, using approved resources—this is called The Alberta Programs of Study (APS). It means that each child must study English, Math, Science, Social Studies, Art, Music, Health and Physical Education subjects in each grade, with prescribed content for each grade level from one to twelve. Every child in every school in Alberta learns about rocks and minerals in Grade 3. Every child learns about Japan in Grade 6, and every child learns long division in Grade 5. Each grade has about 1400 "outcomes" from the eight subjects above that the child is expected to learn by the end of the grade. The child must get 50 percent of the outcomes correct to meet the acceptable standard.

Only in homeschooling and unschooling, considered "parent-controlled," are families free to choose the educational philosophy they wish to follow. Although homeschoolers are reimbursed for a small amount of receipted expenses, about $850 per year per student, they are not funded for operating a homeschool, nor is the parent paid for teaching. This allows the parent to control the learning program.

Homeschooling is different from schooling

Homeschooling is closer to school than it is to unschooling. The elements of school are replicated in the home, with the parent substituting for the teacher. In many countries, home education families must follow government-controlled curriculum. In our province, parents have to follow a "home education" set of outcomes, which are different and more flexible than the school outcomes. Many parents provide a faith-based program, and some just follow interest-based unit studies. Most homeschoolers use packaged curriculum of some kind, whether it is government approved or not. Some parents take their children on a field trip every day, as well as setting time for the seatwork. Some parents closely mimic the school schedule, with the same hours, days, and months; desks in rows; uniforms; official recesses. Some even give homework! There are two distinct differences, though, between homeschooling and school. One difference, and the major benefit of homeschooling, is the presence of a caring adult; the one-to-one adult-to-child ration is the single biggest factor in the success of homeschooling. The second difference is that the parent, rather than the school, controls the educational environment and content. But either way, the point is that an authority (government or parent, or both) controls the environment, the content, and the learner. Homeschooling is not unschooling.

Few people realize how little time homeschooling takes compared to school. In Grades 1 through 6, the four core subjects of English, Math, Science, and Social Studies can be taught at home in a total of 30 minutes' time. This doesn't include dawdle time! Art, gym, music and drama consume extra time, but those are fun things not usually counted as "school time." For Grades 7 to 9, it takes about one hour of actual book or textbook work to finish all four cores, and a motivated high school student can complete two core subjects and two optional courses each semester in two to three hours per day. Options such as physical education, food studies, and computer programming fill another hour. That's it. No homework, either. The rest of the day is spent playing, in leisure activities, doing projects, or reading–typical unschoolers' activities. Unschooling, therefore, eliminates the homeschoolers' dedicated time to workbook and seatwork.

If the general public knew how little time it takes for homeschoolers to "do school," they would probably flock to homeschooling! Parents of children in school who battle through three hours of homework with their child every night may think it impossible to take on the six-hour school day by homeschooling.

But instructional time of six hours a day does not mean that the teacher is actively teaching or lecturing six hours a day! "Instructional time" is the total time spent in structured classes in a school. The 20 minutes children might spend waiting their turn to use a pair of scissors, or waiting for all their classmates to get ready for the bus on a field trip, or waiting until the class clown settles down in order for the teacher to continue lecturing—are all considered instructional time. When videos such as "Frozen," or "Family Guy," are shown in class, it is considered instructional time. A teacher with 30 students who spends five days a week, six hours a day with them may only get one hour a week of one-on-one time with each student.

A good analogy is the dinner party versus eating alone. A person planning a dinner party for 10 people needs to plan the guest list, menu, decor, wine, table settings, serving pieces, and a seating plan. They need to shop, store, cook, serve, and clean up. It involves a lot of work and preparation. That is what a teacher does for a classroom of 30 students. Alternatively, a person eating alone or just with a partner might slap together a sandwich or two and eat it over the sink. That is what a homeschooler can do. Learning, just like eating, can be done on a large or a small scale.

In reality, the six-hour school day contains a lot of waiting time, time not needed by homeschoolers. Even managing a large family of five homeschooled siblings doesn't take as long as organizing a classroom of 30 children. Conversely, if one tallied the time that an unschooler ponders questions, thinks about problems and how to solve them, and formulates ideas, it would probably exceed the instructional time in a school, because it is not done in one neat, controlled, measured parcel of time.

Many homeschoolers burn out because they try to replicate school at home and they end up not finishing their planned program. Life gets in the way. Kids lose interest. Though they may start with a planned program that looks very much like a formal school day, about 80 percent of homeschoolers end up not following a school approach. They learn very quickly that what works in a classroom does not work in a home. A teacher role in the class is not the parent role at home, and it can be very difficult to wear both hats at the same time. Teachers are more of an unknown quantity for children; they are often more afraid to act up in front of teachers than they are for dear old mom or dad. They certainly listen more to teachers than to their parents.

Parents find it hard to motivate their children when they try to replicate school in the home. Says Julie, a homeschooling mom of four kids, "I loved watching my children learn, but hated, hated, teaching them 'required curriculum' when they didn't want to learn. That was the worst part of parenting and homeschooling. Fighting with the kids on the required curriculum that neither they nor I wanted to cover, but felt we had to in order to stay up to par with peers and the grade-by-grade outcomes of the program we were on. It broke my heart that I had to be the 'authority' and the 'strict parent' in order to get work done. When my kids were in tears, I felt terrible. When we both were in tears, I felt like quitting. I asked myself, 'Do teachers do this?'"

Consequently, many homeschoolers do not follow a linear, organized pattern of information delivery. It's scattered, hit-and-miss, sporadic. Many homeschoolers start the year with structure and the best of intentions and by the end of the year, scramble to "get something covered." Many homeschoolers never finish the planned school year by June, and yet research shows that the children still excel as they begin a new grade in September. (Van Pelt, 2015) Why? Because it's the adult-child relationship that is critical, not the content learned.

Government-controlled distance education is not homeschooling

When children study a government-provided online or correspondence course at home, they are not homeschooled. Homeschooling only occurs when the parents or the learner choose what is going on the child's plate at the buffet—when the course is one that the parent or child has chosen and is not mandated by the government.

Structured, government-controlled online and print courses are "school without the busses and buildings." They are directed by teachers, administrators, and principals; students and parents have little or no input into content, sequence, delivery, or assessment. This schooling-based-at-home is also called "blended" (half physical school and half online school), "distance learning," "distributed learning," "online school," "correspondence school," "teacher-directed," or "virtual school."

More of these types of schools are popping up because they get full government funding for student registrations. Content is delivered to the student via computer screen text and/or workbooks. Sometimes, recorded videos are shown. Essentially, the students teach themselves the concepts, do the work, and submit it for marking. There is limited online contact with the teacher and, rarely, in-person contact. The teacher is a name on the screen and a paid marker; the student basically reads content off a screen and writes tests. Students might do a project that's submitted online. Input and output. Read and regurgitate. Students write the final test and complete the course. The learning doesn't move into long-term memory, because the learning experience was less than memorable.

Interestingly, as these online classes get larger, with up to 100 students in one teacher-led virtual class, teachers may even offload some of their main function—marking. In the past year, I've noticed that the students are required to self-correct their work and upload it to the teacher for final assessment. The rationale is that the students learn more when they correct their own work. Now the students' workload is increased by a third. Not only do they have to teach themselves the material, they have to do the assignment, then mark it and submit it for ultimate teacher approval. Teach, work, mark. What, then, is the point of taking the class? Why not just self-study, with a lot more flexibility, without the "shell" of the course, and challenge the exam for the credential? If the emphasis is now on competencies rather than content, and if kids know the material, why should they have to go through the prescribed course to get to the exam? Thankfully, in our province, kids can challenge the Grade 12 diploma exams and get credit for knowledge they have obtained outside of government-provided education. This is good for unschoolers. It means our kids can demonstrate their knowledge in a standardized format, attaining the credentials they need for postsecondary admittance without having to slog through a boring course in which they have already mastered the content.

My children did some of these online courses in high school to get the marks and credits required by universities. I am convinced that the learning doesn't stick beyond the final exam because there is no human relationship involved; online courses are anything but experiential education. Virtual schools don't serve the various learning styles as a classroom or homeschool would. And although auditory learners may benefit from software that "speaks," and visual learners may benefit from watching videos and reading content, kinesthetic learners miss out. Kinesthetic learners have to physically move in order to learn, and very little online content can offer this form of learning. Passive reading from a screen doesn't embed knowledge into long-term memory (Armstrong, 2006); kids retain very little after the final exam is passed. When I asked my two graduated kids to help their brother with linear equations, which they had studied in an online class two years before, they couldn't remember any of it. What, then, was the point of them taking the class? To fill a checkbox?

As I am the parent, present inside and outside of traditional school hours, I become the default teacher of these online courses. I am the person providing the face-to-face explanation; I am the invisible help that makes such courses successful. When children take online courses and have no parental help, the dropout rate is around 50 percent. (ADLC, 2015) I provide the hands-on physical learning experiences that help them make sense of what is delivered onscreen. And I don't get paid.

More and more online courses are popping up to cash in on the free tutoring that parents provide to their children, subsidizing online and correspondence courses with this free invaluable support. Children who don't have adult support at home are most often unsuccessful at this type of delivery. Many times, a child doesn't want to wait a few days to get an emailed explanation or a phone call that still doesn't visually explain the concept, as a teacher in a classroom can do. When my son has a question at ten o'clock at night about using models to add fractions, I'm not going to tell him to wait until tomorrow to email his teacher. And most teachers won't accept phone calls. They insist on the student emailing them. They need work-life balance too. But many kids don't want to take the time to write out an email and wait for the response. Like any parent dealing with a child and his homework, I'm going to help him if I can. I'm not allowed to give the final assessment, but I do spend a lot of time "teaching" the course and I'm sure I'm not the only parent to do so.

The invisible teaching assistance provided by parents definitely frees up the teacher time; since they are not directly teaching, they can handle double the number of children in the "class" by being available only when kids need help. The school still gets the full "per student" funding. That's a pretty amazing cost savings over a face-to-face class! I'm convinced that the cost efficiency of having a single teacher provide delivery to so many students is what drives the government to expand its digital offerings. Again, it is an example of educational trends being fueled by economics, and not by what is the best learning environment for students. Cost savings? Yes. True learning? No.

My son does not occupy classroom space that requires maintenance and heating and he requires no bussing, so he generates no infrastructure costs. I pay for all his materials plus a tuition fee that covers the cost of marking. I pay for the postage to mail his marked assignment books. I pay for the supervision for his exams. I often wonder where I should send the bill for my invisible teaching and support services that make these "self-taught schools" profitable. More importantly, I question why we even stick to a government-controlled course. Why not go free and learn from any course offered over the internet—from London, Australia, or Malaysia?

Unschooling is different from homeschooling

Unschooling is similar to homeschooling, but instead of the parent controlling the program, it is the child who controls the planning, curriculum, delivery, and assessment. Alfie Kohn stated in a presentation, that "Homeschooling is taking the worst of school and bringing it home." (Kohn, 2009) I interpret that to mean that simply replicating a bad idea in different surroundings is not innovation. Deborah, an unschooling mom of two kids, says, "Strict, authoritarian homeschooling is not sustainable. I've known so many who burn out and think themselves failures, and the amount of curriculum on the market just underscores the belief that if they only bought the 'right' one, it would work. Unless you have a child that naturally gravitates toward that type of structure, it's going to be a poor fit."

The impact of government funding on self-directed education

In Canada, some provinces fund home education. In exchange, some of those provinces require adherence to a government-mandated curriculum; others do not. Some independent schools receive funding; some don't. Generally, the less-funded or non-funded schools have fewer requirements in reporting, following curriculum, hiring certified teachers, and giving assessments than schools that do receive government funding. (Van Pelt, 2017) The government is accountable to its citizens and all citizens have a vested interest in educating future citizens; thus, funding is usually tied to the level of public interest in education.

There are two main types of schools for self-directed learning. The first type is **government-funded**: because these schools receive government funding, they must follow the government program of studies, outcomes, and approved methods and resources.

When my daughter attended a self-directed school for the first two weeks of Grade 12, this passage was written in the welcome handbook: "Athletes, musicians, dancers, models, and others, require a flexible schedule to accommodate their off-campus obligations and pursuits." When she requested time away from campus to write her books in peace and quiet, "writing" was not deemed worthy of a flexible schedule. As well, the school allowed flexibility only in timing, not in content. Students had to take all the required government assignments even if they already had the knowledge, as was my daughter's case.

"Self-directed" schools are poorly named. When students have so little control over the course, they are anything but self-directed. My personal yardstick is the measure of motivation: if there is any hint of motivation problems in a self-directed school, it is truly not self-directed. It is government-imposed education.

These "self-directed" courses are often delivered online or with printed correspondence workbooks, but within a physical school that children are bused to. Children can attend such self-directed schools to undertake self-taught education via reading the online content and workbook modules, and then take the tests. These are also called "tutorial" schools because the students have to teach themselves the written content; teachers may be available for tutoring, answering questions, and providing general assistance. The teachers do not present or teach directly as they would in a traditional classroom. Students are "self-taught" a standard curriculum but they are certainly not "self-directed." They have no choice in what they study, how they study it, or how deep into the topic they can go. They cannot choose the materials, the assignment details, or the weighting of the marks. Only the *pace* is learner-controlled.

The school industry is financially motivated to maintain its own model of "self-directed" schools. There is money to be made in curriculum and material development (even in the self-directed learning model), teacher training, etc. Proponents of "new, progressive, inquiry-based, self-directed learning systems," charge big bucks to teach professional development in traditional schools and coach teachers on how to promote student autonomy and self-study. In many versions of this model, however, teachers are still little more than paid markers, when their true value is in establishing good mentorship relationships with students.

Many schools have also adopted an "inquiry-based learning" or a "discovery learning" model, which again is not true unschooling. Inquiry-based in some schools means "What area of bats do you wish to study?" True self-directed education is, "Are you interested at all in studying about bats?" The question is, "Whose agenda?" or "Who is controlling the inquiry?" In our buffet analogy, the child decides what goes on the plate, and perhaps the topic of bats is not on the menu this year. It might be—next year, or in five years—or it might never be. In "inquiry-based" government-funded schools, students are forced to "inquire" about subjects predetermined by administrators. Inquiry-based learning is still not voluntary, and that's why it doesn't fit into the self-directed model. Self-directed learning in a school must truly be "self-chosen" or it won't work. Motivation problems will continue.

The other type of self-directed school is a **"free"** or **"democratic"**: these schools are true unschooling environments. Approximately 280 free-schools operate worldwide. (Wilder, 2014) Mostly funded totally by parents or private donors, they may receive a token amount of government funding. But because they do not receive substantial government funding, they do not have to follow government curriculum or outcomes or even hire certified teachers. Free-schools are physical buildings in a location other than a home, stocked with resources students can use to explore their passions and interests, to play, and to interact with each other. The staff are adults, perhaps but not necessarily teachers, who facilitate students' access to resources, helping them find and access the resources they need to pursue their interests. They do not direct the child's inquiry. The learner truly leads. It's a great place for kids to go if both parents work, or if the child has no siblings and parents are concerned that the child doesn't get enough socialization at home. The Sudbury Valley School model in Framingham MA, founded in 1968, and Summerhill in the United Kingdom are the most well-known models of true unschooling schools.

What can schools learn from unschoolers?

Adults are more important than the curriculum or the syllabus. In most cases, even when homeschoolers don't finish a year, then start their child in the next grade the following September, their children do just as well academically. This again emphasizes that the single most important ingredient in education is the adult-child relationship. Not finishing the curriculum is less important. We are all humans. We procrastinate. We meander. We substitute the day's plans with whatever comes along that is more appealing or thought-provoking: Nice day outside? Let's go to the lake—the kids end up learning about sand and water tunnels. The news headlines a political attack? Let's look up where the countries are and learn a bit about their history. Company is coming? Let's find out what it is like where they are from! So what if we wander off the agenda? We are learning something that is more meaningful to everyone in the moment. Small adult-child ratio learning stimulates discussion, flexibility, and the ability to personalize education.

In 2014, Minister of Education for Alberta, Jeff Johnson, asked a symposium of education stakeholders the question: "If you had to choose between an excellent teacher or a smaller class, which would you choose?" He answered "excellent teacher." (Johnson, 2014) I would disagree. I would pick the smallest class possible, allowing for individual attention. Teachers can't be effective when they are expected to lead a class of 40 students, no matter how excellent they are. Flexibility and personalization are sacrificed. The logistics of taking those students out of the institutional box and into the world are not easy. Even Ms. Frizzle had only eight students on her spontaneous field trips in *The Magic School Bus*! Every school teacher should be so lucky.

What can homeschoolers learn from unschoolers?

Children are motivated to learn about what interests them. Topics must be freely chosen by the learner for them to entrench in long-term memory. One of the biggest mistakes people make is to equate learning and education with teaching. Teachers and homeschooling parents try very hard to cover those 1400 curriculum outcomes per grade. True learning is not accomplished by punishing children with detentions or withdrawing their privileges. True learning is not bribing them with frivolous pizza coupons or extra computer time to force information into their heads for just long enough for them to dump it into the final test, as they will never use it again.

True learning means receiving the intrinsic reward of finding the answers to questions—a reward that is long lasting and fulfilling. Teaching may include some learning, and learning may include some teaching, but the two are not inextricably linked. Learning is an internally motivated mechanism.

I was a skeptic myself. My kids wouldn't listen to me teach. How could they ever teach themselves? In school, my children were bored and unmotivated, losing their inborn love of learning. I pulled them out of school to learn at home and saw my five children teach themselves to read and write with no instruction from me other than answering their questions. I watched my son program his computer and build a website, with no enrollment in classes. I watched my other son show me how an engine works because he is so passionately into mechanics, and I'm not—I couldn't possibly have taught him about something I despise so much! Yet he is motivated to learn, without direction from me. My daughter writes a 27-page story for the fun of it. Another son works on algebraic equations because it helps him program. He has not learned from a textbook. Yet we are not anomalies. Countless children outside of the government school system learn this way.

If your children are resisting homeschooling, consider unschooling. Relationships become front-and-center and learning will happen—I promise!

Deschooling

If your child has been in school for a while and has lost the love of learning, you may want to begin **deschooling**. This means to take a break from "schooly" conventions such as textbooks, workbooks, lessons, classes, structure, and study and the worry about whether the child is learning or not. Learning will certainly continue, but in a different form—mostly through play. This practice of deschooling gets parents and children out of the mind frame of schooling and it can be hard on both. We are so used to thinking of "learning" as looking like school. But in a matter of weeks or months, in their own time frames, children will embrace further education and study in their own unique ways. They may watch movies and play video games nonstop for a few months, but they will eventually get curious and expand their activities to other learning pursuits. Then parents could offer a more structured program then, if the child wishes.

"Unschooling is like gardening. You are turning over soil, mixing in some rich compost, scattering in some interesting seeds, raking it over, watering carefully, and waiting. Planting and raking and re-planting won't work. Those seeds need time to germinate. You're not trying to make something grow, you're doing your best to provide the conditions under which stuff will grow." (Miranda H, 2001) Trust the process. It will happen.

Our story

Like many children of the '60s and '70s, we had few educational options. Parents signed up their children at the nearest walkable public school and never darkened the doorway again, unless the teacher requested a meeting at report card time. No routine parent-teacher interviews, no volunteering, no parent participation in concerts or field trips.

When I was 18, I graduated high school with a paltry 62% average; I had no expectation of going on to postsecondary studies although I had the matriculation subjects required for university. High school was a time of fun, followed by moving away from home, then working. I was going to be a stewardess, a social worker, or a hair dresser. Well, I tripped on the carpet at my stewardess interview; the social work faculty was overwhelmingly full; and I couldn't stand the smell of perm chemicals! I didn't know what kind of career to pursue.

After working at a retail store for two years, I followed my boyfriend to university to keep an eye on him. It was amazing that they even let me in with a low average! I partied. I was put on probation because I had no interest in studying. I married the boyfriend, separated two years later, lost all my money, and became ill. After a few more years of stagnating, I was broke and bored. I recognized that working an hourly retail job was not exactly a "career," so at 25, I decided to go back to university to take a general arts degree. Was I motivated to get that degree! With no money to party, I spent the time productively—studying.

I worked full time as a secretary during the day to pay my tuition. I attended classes full-time at night, with a four-course load. I graduated at 28, got divorced, and paid off debts. I married a wonderful man whom I met while volunteering on the city's distress crisis phone lines, had five kids, and loved parenting.

I found my passion and my calling: speaking, teaching and facilitating, on—what else? —parenting and child development. I had two sons, Mathew and Neil, a year apart. Then my daughter Sophie came along 20 months after my second son. We breathed a bit before having our fourth child, a son named Ryan, three years later. Finally, our "caboose," Anna came four years after Ryan. As my children grew nearer to school age, my interest moved on to education; not only for them, but as a career path for me.

If anyone had said to me back in high school that parenting could be a career, I would have laughed. It was simply not a typical career choice. But all my effort and sacrifice in getting my degree paid off when I was offered a position as a parent educator for our government health department—I would never have secured the position without the degree.

I had a good friend named Debbie whose children were older than mine. She unschooled them. New to the concept, I thought her approach to "teaching" was a wee bit batty, as I couldn't imagine why someone would deny children the right to an education. How could children possibly learn anything unless they were taught by someone? She was an attentive and patient parent, always responding when her children asked questions or put forth observations. One day, at McDonald's, her oldest son asked her how long a french fry was. She replied that it looked to be about 11 centimeters, but what did he think? He agreed. I thought, that's it? That was math for the day? In parenting, we have a saying, "Never Say Never!" Who knew that five years later I would be doing exactly the same thing with my children?!

My experience and training as an adult educator made me examine the assumptions present in educating children. It made me realize that adult educators are really facilitators, not teachers; adult students are usually willing, and are there by choice. I dug up books by Malcolm Knowles on facilitating and found that these concepts also apply to children. The only distinguishing characteristic between adult and child self-directed learners is that children do not have the same life experience as adults. But what they lack in life experience, they make up for in curiosity and exuberance.

Because we had four schools within walking distance and because my husband thought they looked very inviting compared to the British schools he grew up in, his insistence on the kids trying school was strong. My eldest son went to the neighborhood French immersion school for K – 1, and my second son followed. One son had a learning disability and French immersion was not helping him to read, so we moved both Mathew and Neil to an English school, where Mathew learned to read in Grade 2. At the time, many families were moving to the suburbs. Inner neighborhood schools including ours were not attracting new pupils, resulting in the consolidation of schools as enrollment slid. Schools were slated for closure; teachers and staff seemed demoralized. Sometimes the school would play classical music over the loudspeaker during lunch—that sufficed as musical education!

During their last year, I had to drag them out of the house in the morning; they clung to the door jambs, not wanting to go. We drove the two blocks to school where the principal would meet us on the front step for the combative handover. I would put my son in her arms and walk away, plugging my ears not to hear his crying; I would quickly slip into my car and cry myself before driving away. It broke my heart to see them so unhappy. School was supposed to be something children looked forward to. It was the norm. Yet, my boys hated it. What had I done wrong? My second son would walk home for lunch and refuse to go back for the afternoon. We had everything at home that the school had: blocks, computer, craft supplies, pets. My children loved being home. And I loved having them with me. I could not entertain the thought of another year like the one we had. We had to do something different.

In the spring of my eldest son's Grade 2 year, my husband asked for my consent to a project that would take him to Lima, Peru, for two years, working on rotation of 24 days in Peru, two days of travel, and 10 days at home. I agreed—if he would consent to schooling my way for the four kids aged one to eight. He agreed to homeschooling. The boys were so happy they were not going back to school!

That summer, we relaxed and had fun. Peter was working out of a Vancouver condo at Robson and Denman Streets, and we stayed with him. We felt so free as we explored Vancouver! We visited the aquarium, Stanley Park beaches, rode the SeaBus for fun, and made weekly visits to Science World. We explored the Skytrain and Lonsdale Quay. We met up with fellow homeschoolers. It felt so natural to be out in the world exploring, without dreading the return to school in September. The kids learned so much!

That fall, 1999, like most homeschoolers, I began by replicating school at home; I thought that was the only way to do it. Media images of homeschooling showed the mom in front of the blackboard mounted on the kitchen wall, the children at the kitchen table, surrounded by textbooks. Mom was smiling and children were listening attentively. What a crock! Later, I learned that people did do things differently—because the "attentive" children were anything but! However, for a while we did bring the traditional school classroom into the kitchen. I love structure, thanks to my Type A personality. My kids did not respond to that. One child liked structure and I would make to-do lists for her. But for the most part, they were not interested in my carefully planned lessons and colorfully decorated bulletin boards. In fact, they didn't want to be there at all. And, I quickly realized, neither did I! I hated teaching kids who didn't want to learn the lessons I had planned. Although I knew quite a lot about unschooling, like many homeschooling parents, I still didn't trust the concept and didn't know anything other than trying to teach from workbooks at the kitchen table. It was a disaster! Many times, both my children and I were in tears.

So, contrary to everything I had been taught, I terminated my career as a home school teacher and became an unschooling learning facilitator. I remembered our carefree, learning-packed summer in Vancouver, and I let go. I would show them things, present them with things to see what attracted interest from the kids. When something did, we would explore deeper. Otherwise, it was shelved. It reinforced the fact that I loved watching my kids learn, but hated trying to teach them something they had no interest in. I'm sure classroom school teachers feel the same way; the moment you try to open up their heads and pour information in is the moment the kids' eyes glaze over.

I leave items in their path. This is commonly called "strewing." If their interest is piqued, which is usually the case, they take the lead and let me know "how much" and "how long." It can be something as simple as a newspaper article, a new game, marbles, or fraction cubes. Sometimes the item is not picked up and that's okay. I might offer it again later on, or not. It's fun watching kids pick up something, grapple with it, and try it out in different ways. To me, that is satisfying their curiosity, and that is real learning, whereas memorizing facts and figures is short-term learning that is quickly forgotten. Even when our kids come home from university, I will rip an interesting article from the newspaper and leave it out for mealtime discussion. If no one wants to talk about it, that is okay, but it 99 percent of the time it spurs discussion.

When my daughter reached school age, she really wanted to try Kindergarten. She went for a whole year and even played the princess in the school play. The next year, for Grade 1, she came home to play with us because she could see how much fun we were having. Every year I would ask my children whether they wanted to go to school or homeschool. That is self-determination—the learner's choice.

When Sophie was technically in Grade 3 (homeschoolers do not define themselves by grade as the system does), she really wanted to try school. It was March of the year and no school wanted to take her as it was a provincial standardized exam year; she would have to write the tests and the results could affect the school's marketability! I protested the school's rejection of her application and insisted that they let her try while her interest was hot, not in September when she might no longer wish to try.

They let her in.

I would watch her get out of the car and happily skip off to the playground to greet her new-found friends, who absolutely engulfed her! She loved it. For three months. She was reading a Harry Potter book per week—in Grade 3. But the class was reading only Grade 3 level material, so she found much of the curriculum boring. Because she had wanted to go and I fought for her, I made it clear that she had to get herself up, get dressed, pack her lunch, and be ready to go, and I would drive her. She was motivated, so at age eight, she was organized and ready most mornings.

By September, the glow had faded and she decided that the school day was too long and the books too boring; although she liked her friends, homework didn't give her any time for herself after school. I never tried to talk her out of going to school. By letting her experience it on her own, *school* talked her out of school!

When Sophie reached Grade 9 level, she wanted to try school again. Since it is the last year of the three-year junior high school in our province, it was hard to break into well-formed social cliques, and she quit after two weeks. In Grade 10, Sophie went to an arts-centered high school for two months. She made lots of friends, was invited to many social events, and liked some parts of school, but she found the school days were long and left little time for her passion—writing novels. Her refusal to do homework also netted her zeros on homework assignments, while scoring in the 90s on in-class work. This resulted in a rather poor average, so she quit to do self-directed high school for Grades 10 and 11. She attended a "self-directed" high school for Grade 12 as well, but questioned why she should have to get up at eight in the morning to take an hour-and-a-half-long bus ride to a crowded school where there was no place to sit—when most of her work was on line! Most of her courses were self-taught, with scheduled tutorial help, and she had to check in every day with her supervisor. Again, she quit after two weeks and finished Grade 12 her way—by devoting time to courses she needed to learn and challenging the diploma courses on content she already knew. By doing it her way, she met the graduation requirements of 100 credits and scholarship marks under the supervision of a tiny homeschool program connected with a private school.

When Sophie was accepted into university, I worried that she would quit after two weeks, given her history! But she found university so different. Students were more mature, professors were more respectful, and she had control over when to eat lunch or go to the bathroom. She moved out of the house and lived in residence to be closer for her 8 a.m. classes, activities, and clubs.

My sons took different paths.

At Grade 11, Mathew entered a high school that had a great program for students with learning disabilities. He graduated with a high school diploma. As he disliked Math and Science, he finished with only the minimum requirements. A year after graduating, he decided on a career in healthcare rather than being a helicopter pilot, but he needed two sciences and pure math to apply for university in that field. Now he was motivated! He took two chemistry courses, a biology course, and three pure math courses at an adult high-school upgrading institution and finished with fabulous marks. "When the student is ready, the teacher appears." When kids need a course, they will enroll, study and do whatever it takes to pass it—again, providing they themselves perceive and understand the need. It took Mathew a year and a half to cover all his requirements for university—a small amount of time considering the fifty years of working life ahead of him!

Neil attended a regular high school for Grade 11. Although he had almost enough credits to graduate, the school would not allow him to take spares to work on his own private projects so he decided that school was not for him and he self-directed the rest of his high school. Neil's eleventh-grade Biology teacher said that he was ready then and mature enough for university. He taught himself Science and Math from textbooks, did some course work, and wrote the government exams. For English and Social Studies, he did a lot of independent reading and online courses to get his credits. At 99 out of 100, he was one credit short. He needed an option course. Even though he had done all three science streams (biology, chemistry and physics—for fun and interest!), he did not officially graduate from high school until the end of his second year of university, when he finally submitted course work to complete that credit.

Three of our five children had their first Math class in Grade 8. Two of them studied Grade 7 and Grade 9 math, skipping Grade 8. Their averaged Grade 12 exam mark was 81%. The boys' first English class was Grade 11, and my daughter has never had a formal course in English. She taught herself everything about fiction writing, reading books on plot development, character dialogs, and settings. She scored in the high '80s on government English exams. She studied Science and Social Studies starting in Grade 10; mostly self-taught from resources gleaned from Google and Kahn Academy.

My third son, Ryan, has never been to school except for one Grade 12 Biology course. He took his first formal Math class by correspondence in Grade 7, skipped Grades 8 and 9, and went online for the Grade 10 Math course. He self-taught most of the math and science content he needed to pass the final Grade 12 diploma exams. My last child, Anna, went to the first day of Kindergarten and refused to go the second day. She took a Grade 8 Math class online and proceeded to self-design some of her high school subjects and joined a homeschooling co-op for other subjects.

Two of my sons didn't learn to read until ages 9 and 10. Since then, they have both read the entire Warriors series of books; one of them even read all the Terry Pratchett Discworld novels. All five children are voracious readers, consuming everything from Jane Austin to Steven Hawking—because instead of the government telling them what they are allowed to read, they get to decide for themselves.

And the children played...

In summary, my five children received most of their education through play. After a brief blip of sporadic attendance in Kindergarten and Grades 1 and 2 schools for the oldest children, we decided that school was not a good fit for any of them. They spent most of their childhood, up to 15 years of age, playing. Their more formal studies, from ages 15 – 18, were mostly self-taught or acquired with resources outside the government system and led to passing the Grade 12 government diploma exams.

Each child had a minimum of eight solid years of unschooling (play), and some of the children were unschooled for the entire 12 years. Three of them underwent government-standardized testing in Grades 6 and 9 to help me gather evidence for this book. All the children scored Acceptable and some scored Excellence ratings on those exams.

Because we live in Alberta, they had to take the mandatory objective government diploma exams in Grade 12, which accounted for half the final course mark presented to the universities. Four of the children wrote 20 diploma exams, of which 12 were in maths and sciences and eight in English and social studies. Their average combined mark was 78%—equal to the average mark of the best private school in the city for the year 2012. So far, four kids received high school scholarships after graduation and went on to post-secondary education, where they earned still more scholarships.

Along the way, the kids were given the gift of an extra decade of childhood play, intellectual freedom, travel, and close family relationships. In addition, they escaped the confinement of preschools, the burden of homework, the stress of peer culture, the tediousness of after-school and summer-school enrichment classes, and the depersonalized programming of regular school classrooms. They escaped peer pressure, bullying, boredom, and coercive schooling where rankism runs rampant. We protected their curiosity, creativity, self-esteem, sibling relationships, and their love of learning. Even in high school, they deemed that two hours of self-study for high school subjects per day was enough for them to achieve balance and give them time to work, volunteer, pursue their interests in hobbies, music, and fitness, and of course—to play.

Today, our three oldest children have graduated from their respective universities. One child is still in university and the last one is enjoying self-directed high school her way and plans to attend university to study Humanities. Three of our children are in STEM careers.

4

Play is the Primary Learning Vehicle of Children

"We were homeschoolers that never really got around to homeschooling. We played!"

Play is learning

Jennie is sitting on the sofa reading a history book about Greece. Mark is sitting at the table reading a history book about Greece. They are two children in the same room, engaged in the same activity. Yet there is a fundamental difference in the way they approach their reading. Jennie is reading the history book to further her keen interest in Greek mythology. Jennie is playing. Mark is looking at the pages but not absorbing much information. He is not interested in Greek mythology but is studying it because it's in the Grade 6 learning outcomes. Mark is not playing. Mark is studying. What is the difference between Jennie, who is playing, and Mark, who is studying? Jennie is self-directed and intrinsically motivated to satisfy her curiosity, whereas Mark is complying with the school agenda and is extrinsically motivated by marks. One person's play is another person's work. In the long run, Jennie will retain most of the information because she is interested in it. Mark will forget it as soon as he passes the course test.

Unschooled children learn mostly through exploration and free play. Play is a child's right from birth to the adult age of 18, as expressed in the United Nations 1989 Convention on the Rights of the Child, Article 31.1: "The right of the child to rest and leisure, **to engage in play** and recreational activities appropriate to the age of the child and to participate freely in cultural life and the arts."

"Play to a child is foremost a fun activity. There is no planned purpose and definitely no competition with oneself or with other players. The pleasurable activity can be done alone by the child, with other children, or with one or more adults. If he does not derive enjoyment from the activity, the child will disengage from it. The activity stops and there will be no more play. The essential elements of play, therefore, are fun and enjoyment. A child who is hungry, lacks sleep, or is suffering from bodily or mental pain and anguish cannot really have fun and cannot actually play even if he is given a toy or is stimulated to do a fun activity. A child plays when he is healthy, physically and mentally ready to enjoy moments of fun," says Adelina Gotera, author of *I Will Play with You.*

When you look at what individual children do when they play, you can see early career paths or interests. One of my sons loved trains, Lego, Meccano, blocks, and any kind of building toy, computer games, pyrotechnics (more later about my older children's fascination with fire), and K'NEX. He, like the other kids, loved making things without pre-packaged instructions and some of his creations were amazing. He had a propensity for computer programming, machinery, and creating gadgets. He loved taking things apart to see how they worked. He is now an engineering graduate. My daughter loved reading and writing from an early age. Her brain was wired for it. An early reader at age four, she has always devoured books. Her bookshelf is full of the classics. My other son loved computers, K'NEX, Lego, and art. He showed early talent for composition and balance; he wrote comic books, and made lots of drawings, paintings, and sculpture. He still pursues art as a hobby and a life pleasure, choosing to not make a career of it so that he can keep it as play.

The definition of play is much more than people really think.

Play is defined as:

- An activity done for the pure enjoyment of it. Play is pleasurable. Play some-times includes frustrations, challenges, and fears; however, enjoyment is the key feature. It keeps us wanting to continue.

- Not compensated with money, rewards, or marks, nor is it forced with threats, punishment, or other forms of coercion. It is freely chosen and voluntary. How-ever, other players can be invited or prompted to play.

- Entirely self-motivated and self-directed. Play is its own reward to the player.

- An activity in which learning is the byproduct, not the goal.

- Entirely open-ended. It invites a diminished consciousness of self and time. A child is fully in the moment. He is not thinking about himself or concerned how he might appear to others. He is often unaware of observation.

Play is pretty much what we are doing when we don't have to be doing something else. Play is an undervalued and underutilized concept in most of the industrialized world. If it doesn't teach us a skill or make us money, it is useless, maybe even sinful. (Brown, 2010) Yet it is a component of human activity that has endured throughout human histo-ry. Animals play. Young children play. Even adults play when they can. It is as essential to survival as work, yet is often dismissed as a frivolous waste of time in our time-con-scious, efficient, goal-oriented society.

Everyone has heard the phrase, "Play is a child's work." But when does play cease to be a child's work? At what age is the child too old to play? The answer is that people are never too old to play. We all love to play, but adult responsibilities cut into the time we have for play; jobs, raising children, housework, family duties, and volunteer work all take precedence. If we have any time left over, we enjoy adult play in the form of reading, skating, or any activity that fulfills our soul. We feel guilty about play, but we live for it.

Play must be freely chosen by the child, undirected by adults, and should emphasize enjoyment of process

The "free" part matters. O. Fred Donaldson, PhD, states in his book, *Playing by Heart*: "Adults want to use play as training for adulthood. Games, activities and sports become increasingly used to pressure children to become adept at adult behaviors. Free play is essential to a child's development—not only to mental health, but to the acquisition of crucial abilities the child will need in life. To create more opportunities for your children to engage in free play, you ... need to convince other parents to do the same. The more kids out there on the block, available to play, the more appealing it becomes to go out and play."

For many children, play is only allowed if it builds skills and knowledge that will enhance their resumes. Violin lessons, Spanish preschool, organized soccer, art lessons and the like are not free play. They are scheduled, adult-led activities, much like school. Many hyper-parents today place pressure on kids, schools, teachers, and administrations to get their kids fast-tracked to higher education. We push, polish and protect our kids, but we don't let them live or feel the natural outcomes or consequences of their choices, especially in play.

Thirty years ago, children played freely in their streets and neighborhoods. They were turned out into the morning sunshine after breakfast and they knew to return for lunch and dinner. They were active, breathed fresh air, and learned much about life, their buddies, and themselves. True socialization occurred in the relaxed environment of discovery. Play has now changed. Play dates are scheduled by adults. Adults plan and time their children's activities down to the minute. Games and practices are organized and scheduled, and often mandatory. Extracurricular lessons are touted as "play" but are more often chosen by parents for the child's enrichment, rather than freely chosen by the child himself.

Free play is perceived as dangerous. Parents now are fearful of stranger abduction, school shootings, child injury, and bad school report cards. Free play is shunned in favor parent-controlled activities. Twenty years ago, we invited children over for play dates so that our kids would be occupied and we could get housework or projects done. Now, it is expected that the host parent will entertain the children. If the activities are academic or sports-oriented, it's perceived as being even better. It's no wonder the tweens and teens flock to that great sandbox called the internet, which adults can't control, supervise or organize.

The one point that experts seem to agree on is that free play does not include scheduled activities. It should be unstructured, undirected, and *fun*! Structured activities offer group belongingness and the ability to learn new skills, but restrict processing skills, reflection, and internal brain processing. Time, tools, and freedom are necessary for processing unstructured activities. (McDowell, 2006)

A 2007 report from the American Academy of Pediatrics said that unstructured play is healthy and "essential for helping children reach important social, and emotional, and cognitive developmental milestones as well as helping them manage stress and become resilient." (Ginsberg, 2007) A Scientific American article, "The Serious Need for Play" lauded the benefits of free play. (Wenner, 2009)

Learning and play are intrinsically one concept

When we ask parents what play means to them, they think of fun and games, and that is true. If play is not fun, why bother? Yet when you ask most people if school is fun and games, they think not. At least, they hope not. Although much research shows that kids and adults learn better when humor and fun are involved and when they are actively participating in the learning activity, many people don't equate learning with play. Play-based learning has a long and detailed research history dating back to the work of John Locke and Jean Jacques Rousseau in the 1700s. Research and evidence point to the role of play in children's development and learning across cultures. (Shipley, 2008) Many believe it is impossible to disentangle children's play, learning, and development.

What is the difference between play and learning? There is no difference, except that learning is often coerced and play is not. When children play, do they stop learning? No. Play and learning are inseparably intertwined. There are no subject areas that children can't learn through play.

Research shows that the more fun learning is, the more it sticks in the memory. (Klein, 2001) In teaching adult education, it is strongly recommended to incorporate play, games, and fun learning activities so that adults remember the concepts. Reading slides is boring and a waste of time—the audience can stay home and read their own notes. The best learning happens when the audience is interactive, participating, and engaging in play activities. Humans remember things linked to sights, smells, music, emotions, humor, and activities. For example, when teaching expectant parents how to handle baby's crying, I would have them stand in a circle and pass around a weighted infant doll. Then I would play a tape of infant wailing—the noise was constant, irritating, and loud! Each parent had to suggest one way of trying to calm and comfort baby before he could pass the doll to the next person. The exercise appealed to visual, kinesthetic, and especially to auditory learners. There were a lot of jokes and people had fun, but they also realized the importance of learning what to expect in the early months of parenting. This exercise would stick in long-term memory much better than viewing slides would have. For new learning to move to long-term memory, the brain needs time to process it. (Jensen, 1998)

In an education conference, the participants were asked to list "Ways I learn." The top three responses were "people, reading, and experiences." Other responses were self-discovery, reflection, listening, books, movies, classes, travel, play, experiences, media, arts, volunteering, mistakes, self-study, and culture. Then they were asked to list "Places I learn." The top response was community, followed by home and school. (Inspiring Education, 2009) I am sure the responses would differ if the same questions were asked of kids. Kids would probably pick school as the number one place they learn; yet as adults, we recognize that school is not the first nor the only place for learning.

Let us consider the conditions for optimum learning:

- The more learning is like play, the better the result.

- Real learning comes through trial and error and mistakes.

- Students will learn only what they have an interest in.

- Students will learn only when they are developmentally ready.

- Learning cannot take place outside of an appropriate context in which students can make links and connections.

- Real learning is used and applied on a continuous basis.

- Students must believe they can learn. How many people insist they are bad in math, just because they may have had initial bad experiences?

- Much learning takes place through cultural and life osmosis rather than formal instruction. (Klein, 2001)

Develop a "play ethic"

If we know that learning takes place when it is relevant, fun, and meaningful, then why don't we play more to learn? In society, we give lip service to playtime, but rarely admit we do it. It's a secret enjoyment that we can't divulge to our neighbors, relatives, or co-workers. When we meet someone we haven't seen for a long time, we often say "Been crazy busy!" and we don't mean very busy with play. We mean very busy with work. It's socially unacceptable to say that we spend a lot of time playing.

Adult play can take many forms: me-time, down-time, hobbies, leisure pursuits, date nights, and self-care. We aspire to a work ethic but in our goal to be crazy busy, we are losing our "play ethic." When we tell others that we are crazy busy, we are often using it as a way to say "No." We are really saying, "I'm so nutty busy that I can't add one more thing to my plate, so don't ask me to do whatever it is you want me to take on." We could just say "No," but we're not comfortable being that direct. And because our society values work over play, we elicit respect and admiration when we portray ourselves as wildly busy with work but feel we would exhibit sloth and laziness if we were to express our inner desire to play.

We need to unload the guilt and increase our play—without rules, targets, timelines or predetermined outcomes. We need to play with passion. We need to enjoy our children in play. And most of all, we need to allow our children the same joy.

To kids, play is not purposeful. It has no point, goal, or end product—those belong to the realm of work. As Bruno Bettelheim wrote in *A Good Enough Parent*, "From a child's play, we can gain understanding of how he sees and construes the world—what he would like it to be, what his concerns are, what problems are besetting him. Through his play, he expresses what he would be hard pressed to put into words. No child plays sponta-neously just to while away the time, although he and the adults observing him may think so. Even when he engages in play partly to fill empty moments, what he chooses to play at is motivated by inner processes, desires, curiosity, problems and anxieties. What is going on in a child's mind determines his play activities; play is his secret language, which we must respect, even if we do not understand it."

Barriers to free play

Unfortunately, despite all the evidence indicating that play is good for children's learning and development, the barriers to free play are still very hard to overcome. Let's look at some of them:

Poverty, lack of resources, and lack of family support

Some older children have to work to supplement the family income, and they lose their play time. In some families, both parents have full time jobs with long hours. Supervi-sion for younger children is necessary and organized activities after school provide a handy solution for keeping kids occupied and safe until they are old enough to hold part-time jobs.

Parents feel free time is better spent on structured, academic activ-ities

Play is often viewed as a break from learning, rather than a learning process in and of itself. Play is grossly undervalued as a learning vehicle. Parents don't trust play because its progress can't be measured. We treasure what we can measure. Parents value and prefer academic achievement and if play is woven into academics, so much the better. "Growing public concern about school readiness fuels a push in early academics in spite of research showing that this is not helpful. Research shows that it can hinder a child's confidence of himself as a learner. Most kids now spend their days in structured care and educational environments and even most play and leisure activities are structured and learning focused." (ECMap, 2011)

The promise of STEM learning is being used to market everything child-related, includ-ing toys, to tie learning in with play. Parents respond eagerly, buying everything from simple blocks to science kits, in order to give their child an academic edge. But parents who see such toys as a marketing angle are not taken in; know that every toy is educa-tional. A simple cardboard box teaches kids STEM knowledge.

Parents are also fearful of free time. The media and many parenting guides tell parents that kids who are bored and unfocused get into trouble by dabbling in vandalism or oth-er undesirable activities. The number of media articles that appear just before summer with headlines such as "How to keep your child busy this summer," implies that parents are neglectful if they don't have a minute-by-minute schedule of activities in place for summer holidays. Fear is also evidenced by the popularity of year-round schools. So, most kids in the school system are constantly entertained. This cycle feeds itself: kids who never learn to manage and occupy their time require constant entertainment. By the teen years, they don't know how to occupy themselves productively and they rely heavily on peers to keep them busy—and peer-led activities can get them into trouble if they include the wrong kind of fun. Even one so-called self-directed school holds that "kids get into trouble with too much free time."

Schools are more academic focused than play focused

Standardized testing has prompted the recent trend to focus on core subjects rather than the socialization of children in schools. There is pressure on teachers to deliver testable and measurable results on paper, rather than deeper learning in subject areas. Even in Kindergarten, and worse, in preschools, which are still voluntary in our country, there is a growing emphasis on paper-and-pencil learning, drills, and the push to learn to read, in order to pacify achievement-driven parents.

There is a rise in passive play, fueled by accessible technology and parents' perception of safety

Although today's world is statistically safer, it is perceived to be more dangerous for children. Outside of the home, fewer areas are recognized as safe for children to play. Concerned parents feel the need to have their children in structured, adult-supervised activities rather allowing them free play, alone or with peers, in parks and playgrounds.

Parents use technology to alleviate their anxiety and worry by insisting that their children carry mobile phones when away from their direct supervision. This does not build trust. If we outsource our trust to devices, we are not building our children's trust in other people. Children have the ability to ask other adults for help when they need it, but their self-confidence and their problem-solving skills take a nosedive if we don't let them find their own solutions to problems that come up in play.

Free play is messy; electronic play is clean

In electronic play, there is no paint to clean up, no sand left in the carpet, no play-dough to color the floors. There are no Legos to step on or craft bits to sweep up. No board game pieces to keep together. Parents hate mess, and screens keep everything tidy. But young children's brains thrive in a three-dimensional world of play—not two-dimensional—and they need to get their hands messy with paint and goop.

Fear of liability

In schools, children can no longer build anything more than five blocks high. They can no longer build forts or have snowball fights. They can't swing high. They can't play really fun games like dodgeball or Red Rover for administration's fear of kids' getting injured with a ball. And they certainly can't go on more than one field trip per grade, thanks to the administrative barriers of too much paperwork, supervision, transporta-tion, cost, and liability for the school. It's far safer to stay inside and not do anything fun.

The social, emotional and academic cost of not playing

Health care organizations know the value of free play to children's health from many research studies, yet that information is not getting out to parents, caregivers, and school administrators who stress academic achievement at all costs. (ECMap, 2011)

Look at the following statistics from a US study:

- Seventy percent of children drop out of organized activities by age 13, citing burnout, exhaustion, or dislike of a high-pressure or competitive atmosphere.

- Forty-one percent of 9 – 13-year-olds say they feel stressed all the time.

- The average 9-year-old today has one-ninth the free play time a child his age had in 1970.

- Sixty-six percent of 8 – 12-year-olds have never played outside on their own.

- Many see free play as dangerous or as a waste of time. (Harper, 2011)

Research conducted by Sergio Pellis on rats concluded that having no free play produced stressed rats with social incompetence and anxiety. "In the US and other developed nations, children's free play has sharply dropped in the past 50 years. Over the same period, anxiety, depression, suicide, helplessness, and narcissism has increased sharply in children, teens and young adults." (Gray, 2011)

"Overplaying the brain development-learning concept, runs the risk of pushing adults to manage or control play, both counter-productive to free play, which is supposed to be spontaneous, unpredictable and at times-seemingly pointless – something grown-ups should leave be as much as possible. Parents roles is to supervise to keep it safe, supply some of the requested materials and participate when we are asked. That's it. If it isn't fun, it isn't play." [sic] (Hoffman, 2005)

Is play a waste of time? No. Time is wasted in three ways: by doing something more slowly than necessary; by having nothing to do when activity is desired; and by doing something futile or unneeded. Play doesn't fall into any of these categories. Play is not a waste of time. It is a health necessity.

Benefits of free play

It's paradoxical that a little bit of "nonproductive" activity can make one enormously more productive and invigorated in other aspects of life. (Brown, 2010)

Play develops the academic mind in many ways:

- Play develops creativity, imagination, innovation, adaptability, and encourages exploration and risk-taking, which is the true essence of learning. "Children play to solve problems. They play out scenarios over and over and over again until they can put a resolution around it. We know that a child has resolved some issue when they move on to something new in play," (Dunbar, 2013). This is especially evident in unschooled children. They delve deeply into a topic and only move on to another when they are satisfied with their understanding of the first.

- Children learn new things about the world around them. As they satisfy their curiosity, play sparks even more questions for them to explore.

- Play expands children's attention span, building focusing skills through joyful activity.

- Play helps children think critically and develops reasoning capability by encouraging their problem-solving skills.

- In play, children plan, make decisions, and learn from consequences.

- Children learn logic, patterns, and arithmetic skills by manipulating and observing objects.

- Children learn language by listening, talking, reading, and writing.

- Play helps children develop their preferred learning style and multiple intelligences.

- Symbolic or role-play is often "pretend." It has a "what if?" quality. Play has meaning to the player that is often not evident to the observer.

Play develops the body by honing visual tracking and hand-eye coordination and by building gross and small motor skills. Play requires action and physical, verbal, or mental engagement with materials, people, ideas or environment. Children develop strength, agility, balance, and overall coordination. They learn to use tools safely and efficiently. They learn to listen, taste and touch.

Play develops social skills and communication. Children learn the basics of group dynamics. They listen to others and communicate through playing. They learn to make and follow rules. They learn to cooperate and resolve conflicts. They learn how and when to negotiate. They learn to lead and motivate others. They learn to take turns, share, include everyone, and organize people. Children learn executive function and self-control through group play when other children give them feedback on behavior. Play therapist Jean Dunbar says, "Play is also necessary for children to communicate and especially those that can't express themselves verbally. They play and act out experiences that happen to them. They actually put feelings to these experiences. In short, we talk, children play." (Dunbar, 2013) Group play teaches great life lessons.

Play promotes emotional development, allowing children to develop empathy for others. Play allows enjoyment, joy and happiness. Play heightens children's self-esteem by building their competencies. Play helps children enjoy solitude and independence by doing things on their own.

Play allows children to experience joy. It teaches them to take risks and assess the consequences. They learn to take initiative and develop a positive self-image. Play expands children's confidence because they play at what they are good at. Play helps children relieve stress, anxiety, worry, fear, and depression as they work through these emotions in their play enactment. When you watch little kids at play, they are not insecure or self-conscious. They express themselves freely.

"Play develops a sense of autonomy, healthy self-esteem, personal power, and choices. They get to make the decisions of what to do in play and how to do it. Pretending they are strong and capable helps children develop self confidence." [sic] (Dunbar, 2013)

Types of play

Play can include hands-on manipulation of objects, arts and crafts, music play, nature play, imaginary play, role-play, and physical play. (Hoffman, 2005)

Animals are mostly physical players. All young primates play. The complexity and types of play increase as primates grow and their brains develop more connections. Play improves their performance in nature, strengthens their immune systems, and increases their capacity to remember. Early games and interactions with other animals prepare them for adult life. Peter Gray, a psychologist at Boston College who recently published an essay entitled "The Decline of Play and the Rise of Psychopathology in Children and Adolescents," says, "Children, like many young animals, learn by playing. Children come into the world ready to play. It's part of human nature, which means that natural selection favors it. It has an important role in human survival." (Gray, 2011)

What kinds of toys?

Toys are important; even more important are the kinds of toys that will aid in their development:

- Children need toys that they can do things to or with, not toys that do it for them. Children need to apply the energy or they will quickly become bored with the toy.

- Children do not need expensive, complicated toys. Cardboard and tape can fuel the imagination!

- Children do not become smarter from toys that claim to be educational. Toys only exist. Children apply the creativity that gives toys meaning.

- Electronic toys do not develop a child's brain better than physical toys. Screens stimulate only two of the five senses. Physical toys stimulate all five senses: sight, hearing, touch, smell and taste.

- Children's brains are stimulated from interacting in the three-dimensional world around them, including all physical toys as tools. (Building Blocks, 2011)

Toys are becoming more prescriptive and structured. It's very hard to find basic toys such as blocks that encourage free play, creativity, and imagination. Unstructured toys are best for ages 0 – 13, as they allow freedom, creativity, and exploration in play.

Unstructured toys

Unstructured toys focus on process and experience and not the end result or goal. There is no right or wrong way to play with them. Consider the following:

- Children of all ages and varying abilities can use unstructured toys. Both an 18-month-old and a 10-year-old enjoy using blocks, for example, to build anything from a simple tower to elaborate structures and tunnels for a train set.

- Play with an unstructured toy is therapeutic. It helps children express their feelings and fears, and work through things that are going on in their lives at that moment.

- Materials can be combined in many different ways to stretch a child's imagination and draw on his creative abilities.

- Children get to make all the decisions in their play; building self-esteem and leadership skills.

- Unstructured play materials are the best value "toys," as they span a wide age range and are kid driven, not battery driven!

Try these unstructured toys for your child:

- *Blocks, markers or paints and paper (not coloring books), glue, scissors, sidewalk chalk, odds and ends of craft materials*
- *Cardboard boxes, tape, wood, nails and other building materials*
- *Pots, pans, spoons, plastic containers, food and dishes, play kitchen, cash register*
- *Goop, play-dough or clay*
- *Bikes, balls, pails, sand, water and containers*
- *Lego, K'NEX, Meccano*
- *Dolls, stuffed animals, puppets, dress-up clothes*
- *Musical instruments*
- *People, cars, houses*

Structured toys

Structured toys can only be played with in a certain way; they have a "beginning" and an "end." Examples are puzzles, shape sorters, kits, coloring books, board games, remote-control cars, and electronics which kids watch and push buttons on, rather than apply energy to.

- Structured toys often come with instructions and batteries; children lose interest once they have mastered the toy.

- Children don't add much energy to the toy; it does everything for them. Children just watch it.

- Children can become frustrated with the toy if it's too difficult for their developmental level, or bored if it is too easy or infantile. Structured toys appeal to a narrower age range and are better saved for tweens and teens.

Creativity

Creativity is not a trait. It can be developed in anyone willing and able to think outside the box and take risks to act on their ideas. Creativity is closely linked to healthy self-esteem. If kids feel confident enough to take risks to create, and be okay with imperfection, they will be amazingly creative. If they experience mistakes and failures, without penalty, they will learn to enjoy the creative process. School penalizes mistakes. Play doesn't.

A creative child has an immense gift that enables him to brainstorm solutions to any problem; this skill will take them far in life. Unschooling allows a parent to do so much to nurture creativity that is not allowed in schools:

Oral expression: Let your children tell you their stories, fantasies, fears, explanations, and ideas. Listen for as long as they are talking.

Initiative: Avoid squelching their ideas, even if they seem far-fetched. Encourage negotiation and problem solving. If they wish to set up a lemonade stand in the middle of winter, help them. Let them make their own mistakes.

Encouragement: Supply them with what they need, add encouragement, and let them go with a project. Encourage them even if you think it won't work. Say, "That's a great idea...what do you need to start that project?" The worst thing a parent can say is "Hmm... I don't think it will work. Let's do something else instead."

Curiosity: Parents can model curiosity and follow through. For example, trying a new baking recipe; refinishing a piece of furniture; or writing a book. Encourage questions. Ask out loud. What if? How? What do you think would happen? Answer their questions with another question to help them uncover another level of curiosity.

Parents can best unleash their children's creativity by allowing them to explore with materials and surroundings. Allow painting, sculpture, craftwork, access to the sewing machine, supervised access to the workshop or kitchen; give them their own garden space. Yes, creativity involves mess! Show them how to clean up, but don't ban an activity just because it might be messy, costly, or inconvenient. You might designate a special room for a particular activity, but often, children want to be in the company of parents and prefer to work on the kitchen table. Take them shopping for the materials they need and chalk up the cost to the price of their education.

Don't expect a perfect project in the end. It's the process of creating that spurs innovation, not the goal of ending up with a perfect product.

Don't ban screen time. Often, children apply their video and computer experiences to their creations. For example, after playing video games, my kids sewed little Nintendo characters, made wood replicas, and wrote storybooks, with Kirby, Mario, Yoshi, and Princess Zelda as the main characters. They used their viewing experience to make things. They added creative energy to their screen-time experience.

Nurturing creativity in young children ages 0 – 5

Children this age love to play with anything and everything. They may reconfigure and recombine toys to suit their play, using and enjoying them differently than the manufacturer intended. Parents must allow this combination, even though they might prefer to keep toys organized and sorted. My kids would mash the play-dough in the sandbox to make "breaded patties." Yes, it ruined the play-dough, but they learned about the adherence properties of sand to gooey materials. They would tape math pattern blocks together to make spaceships, although the blocks were intended to demonstrate fractions. And, oh, what they could do with a roll of tape! They would make gondola cars out of Lego blocks, sticking roll after roll of tape across the kitchen counters.

Use open-ended unstructured play materials. Such toys have no one right way of being played with and they offer excellent play value. They spur the imagination and inspire creativity. Take the example of a coloring book versus markers and plain paper. The coloring book dictates how the color is to be drawn, what color should be used, and so on. Plain paper does not impose any preconceived ideas on the child. It's the same difference between Lego kits and a bucket of Lego pieces; the kit can only be built a certain way to build a preconceived project; the bucket of pieces can be made into anything the child imagines. See the blog at judyarnall.com for lots of creative play ideas.

Nurturing creativity in older children ages 6 – 12

Older children carry on imaginative play through playing house, theater, puppets, pirates, aliens, and action figures. They play with household items and construction materials. Unfortunately, parents often pack up or give away creative materials such as dress-up trunks and arts and crafts because they assume that children have such things, or better substitutes, in school, which is not always the case. Parents often prefer the neatness of screens and controllers to paint on their rug, and who can blame them? But it is important to keep a range of creative play items accessible to their children and keep adding to them until about age 13, when they start leaving behind their physical toys.

In one of our best summers ever, we dug up the roots of two huge spruce trees that we had cut down in our backyard. The whole backyard was one giant mud puddle. Pails, shovels, toy cars, and a garden hose provided 20 neighborhood children with days and weeks of building fun. Their parents weren't too impressed when I sent them home to use their own bathrooms, but the children had a blast! Mud, dirt, water, sand, props, and imagination. What more could they ask for?

Parents also need to let go. Give your child the chance to be bored. Then give them access to materials and they will use them to make their own fun. Don't feel you have to fill their time.

And never give in to the urge to "fix" your child's creation! Let it go. I see so many parents at the home improvement store's Kids Building Days who totally take over their child's project and build it themselves to get a perfect result. They even "touch up" the child's very creative paint job! Kids notice, and it matters.

Our local mall has a children's Halloween pumpkin-carving contest every October. It's interesting to note that the elaborate, parent-carved pumpkins are not the ones that win! One year, we were too late in purchasing pumpkins for the contest. The kids really wanted to be included, so I asked them what we could do to solve the problem. They suggested we go to the store and purchase another kind of squash. We ended up with mini watermelons. Although we didn't win the contest, people marveled at the creative melon faces and our kids learned that mistakes can bring out the creativity in people. Now that's not only creativity in action, but problem solving as well!

Nurturing creativity in teens

Hold off on allowing screens as long as possible, but don't be afraid of them either. I lamented when my teenage daughter quit writing, doing art projects, and drawing story books as she had in her younger years. I worried as she spent more time online and finally asked her why she didn't do projects anymore. She replied, "Mom, I do lots of projects, I'm just taking my creativity online." Sophie showed me what she did on her computer that was creative: she wrote fiction, poetry, short stories, and novels. Indeed, she was still very creative but in a different medium, somewhat like paint artists are different from sculpture artists.

Many computer games are based on creative play: The Sims, Garry's Mod, Minecraft, and Spore all have creative elements embedded in the game. Because we never banned screen time, Sophie, Anna, and their brothers would modify computer games to customize characters, settings, and other content. Oblivion allows the creation of whole new sections of the game; World of Warcraft permits making new mods to customize the interface. Teens can write coherent essays and opinion postings in gaming forums, especially when they are arguing with another gamer on a debatable topic. There are online galleries where teens can post their artwork and photography and get feedback. They can post images from a tablet made especially for capturing charcoal-like drawings. My son designed and created websites, wrote code to run electronic robots from the computer, and designed comics. Many teens create blogs, vlogs, PowerPoint presentations, music compositions, funny memes, and videos. In fact, much of teens' use of the internet is to generate content, not simply to view it—and much of what they create is brilliant! Kids are spurred to use technology for creativity, because they can so easily *share* what they create; and if it's funny, it becomes even more fun.

Can play always replace curriculum?

Yes. During the school-age years, free play is self-directed education and can certainly replace mandatory government school studies. As children grow into teens, they may desire a more paper-based education, but play is welcomed at any age.

Play-based learning is already in the classroom

Montessori, Reggio Emilia, and Waldorf philosophies are all based on the concept of children's interest-based learning, but the curriculums and teachers' roles differ.

Montessori education encourages self-directed learning from the child and observation from the teacher. The child's environment is adapted to his development. Montessori has a definite prescribed curriculum and the teacher's role is to guide the child through it.

The Reggio Emilia Philosophy of education was created in 1945 by Loris Malaguzzi in Reggio Emilia, Italy. Again, the child is directed by his interests. However, the teacher does not guide the child, rather he plays alongside as a learning companion. There is not a prescribed curriculum. Reggio is more hands-off than Montessori, but both programs value creativity.

Waldorf education is very unstructured and is based on the educational philosophy of Rudolf Steiner, founder of anthroposopy. Its pedagogy emphasizes the role of imagination in learning, striving to holistically integrate the intellectual, practical, and artistic development of its pupils. (Wikipedia, 2018)

Many schools practice these philosophies and are in high demand. They all have a play component and are evidence that children learn through play.

Unschooling is different from these in that the adult is very much hands-off and the learner is in control of his educational buffet plate.

5

Unschooling at School

"To me, science is just formalized curiosity." — Chris Hadfield, Astronaut

My kids loved watching *The Magic School Bus* videos. Then they played the computer games and read the books. They eagerly awaited each new episode to see what kind of science design was on Ms. Frizzle's dress, and from that they tried to guess the science concept of the day. They especially loved the part where Ms. Frizzle would say, "It's time for a field trip," and Arnold, her student, would groan, "Not again!" As an aside, my kids learned everything they needed to know about science concepts in Grades 1 to 8 from watching this brilliant show!

Unschooling can be done in a school. Ms. Frizzle of the Magic School Bus had only one-fourth of the number of kids in a normal class. She was a classic example of a teacher who spontaneously followed her students' interests and turned everything into a field trip. If learners could choose the content and teachers could facilitate, with a major reduction in class size, student engagement would soar.

Andragogy versus Pedagogy: facilitation versus teaching

I first came across self-directed learning when I was studying theory of adult education, which promotes facilitation over direct teaching. Adults hate being preached to and children even more so, because of their inability to sit still very long. Adults, though, will sit and *appear* to listen in order to be polite, even if they are bored out of their minds. Children, not so much. They will put their heads down, talk to one another, and misbehave if they are not getting much out of the lecture.

Malcolm Knowles is an acknowledged expert in facilitation and he outlines the differences between the self-directed learning of Andragogy and the teacher-directed learning of Pedagogy. Agogus means "leader of" and aner means "adult," while Pedagogy is from the Greek words meaning "paid" and "child." (Knowles, 1975) Knowles came to the conclusion that educational philosophies should not be divided along age lines, but rather according to the nature of the learner-teacher relationship and the educational goals.

The following framework moves from a dependent learner to an increasingly independent learner. Learners acquire knowledge both informally, from many sources, and formally, through classes and teachers.

Concept	Teacher-Directed Pedagogy	Self-Directed Andragogy
Learning theory	Dependent learner	Independent learner
Role of learners' experience	To build knowledge and skills	To build knowledge and skills
Readiness to learn	Varies with level of age; learns by way of coercive tools	Curiosity is spurred by life's problems
Orientation to learning	Subject compartmentalized	Problem or task oriented
Motivation	External rewards and punishments	Internal curiosity and desire
Learning climate	Authoritative, hierarchical, and competitive; formal and judgmental	Informal, mutually respectful, consensual, collaborative and supportive
Planning and Goal Setting	Teacher plans	Learner plans
Diagnosis of needs	Teacher diagnoses	Learner diagnoses
Designing a learning education plan	Content in linear sequenced units, lessons, chapters	Projects and content not sequenced; may be used out of order as needed or not at all; sequenced in terms of learner readiness or perceived usefulness
Learning activities	Assigned readings and one-way transmittal techniques that engage learners' five senses in early years but only two senses (reading and hearing) from Grade 3 on; content is applied, absorbed, expressed and assessed	Experiential learning through five senses all through life; play, travel, projects, independent study, and experimental techniques, volunteering, internships, jobs, and experiences are dominant learning devices; learning and application may not be expressed, although it is absorbed and applied
Assessment	Teacher grades expression; learning that is invisible is not assessed	Self-assessment on perceived learning value inspires change

Comparison of learning concepts between teacher-directed and self-directed education

(Chart adapted from Knowles, 1975 and Barer-Stein, 1993)

Adult Learning Theory: does it apply to children?

As an adult educator, I see fundamental differences in the way adults and children learn, but only inside an institutional framework. In a home or community setting, there is not much difference. Both adult and child are problem driven to learn and will not stop until they find a solution. The only difference is that the child plays more than the adult does.

The following seven common principles prevail in adult learning and can be applied to children:

1. Adults participate in planning and implementing their learning experiences; if children are not subjected to a standard curriculum, they become active participants in planning their play, and hence, in their learning.

2. Adult learning takes place in a climate that encourages and supports learning. If children are not graded, judged, or penalized in their learning environment, they are encouraged to take risks within a supportive climate.

3. Adult learners are self-directed. All learners are self-directed. If they breathe, they learn.

4. Adult learners draw from experience as a resource for learning. This is a hard one for children; their experience as a resource is limited simply because they have not lived as long. That being said, learning for anyone is the process of deriving new meaning by drawing on previous knowledge, so children do in fact draw on recent previous experiences, however limited, to learn—especially teenagers.

5. Adult learners are problem oriented in their learning. Learning must be relevant to their present situation. Similarly, new information can be presented to children as it relates to their world and experience. To learn the times table, for example, the information must apply to their world and their lives and must be useful to them. Learning math from a book has no relevance to a child; using math as a tool to solve a problem while operating a lemonade stand does.

6. Adults must be actively involved in their learning process—the more immersed, the better; it's the same with children.

7. Adult learning fosters a spirit of collaboration. This applies to children as well, when adults become facilitators rather than direct teachers.

Myths of childhood education:

Learners need teachers

No. Learners need resources. Teachers are appropriate resources when children can't learn by discovery and self-teaching. In subjects such as high school calculus, signing up for a teacher-directed course may make sense. Still, it should be the child's choice. Even then, they might not need a class. I've witnessed my own children teach themselves high school calculus, biology, physics, chemistry, and critical writing using free resources from the internet.

Children need adults to organize their time

No. Children who are not used to having their time programmed by an institution are perfectly capable of filling their day. Learning time management requires practice long before learners enter university.

There are "educational" resources and "junk" resources

No. All resources "teach" something. Even video games! All are equally valued on the education buffet table.

Learning and socialization can only occur in school

No. All learning and the development of people skills occurs everywhere, from people, places and things. Diverse relationships are found outside a homogenous school.

Play is frivolous and wastes time, and learning doesn't occur if play is happening

No. Research on early childhood education proves that play for all ages is educational.

Early education and more of it is better than late education and less of it

No. Research shows us that kids can do well on less education. (Moore, 1975) When my daughter was halfway through her final year of university, she told me that she was burned out and was "so done with school." I told her that is probably why kids often want a gap year or two of freedom when they graduate from Grade 12 after 16 years of school. They are indeed burned out. More school in the form of university right after high school may not be appealing for some.

Mainstream schools are already moving toward unschooling

In our province of Alberta, the school industry is already moving toward changes based on the unschooling model. It is promoted under the terms of "personalized learning" rather than the term "unschooling." In the past ten years, two major initiatives have been undertaken that have gathered opinions from more than 30,000 people. The governing School Act has not been reviewed since 1988, and the world has changed tremendously since then.

The provincial government started their "Inspiring Education" initiative in 2009, and re-started it in 2011, renaming it "Our Children, Our Future." The project was designed to gather input on the desired direction of education in the future. How would a student's 950 – 1000 hours in the school building each year be spent? (McClure, 2012) The input was to come from teachers, parents, business persons, industry leaders, principals, administrators, and lobby groups, as well as education-related organizations such as teachers' unions, universities' faculties of education, parent council associations, and other sources. The big question was: What do children need to learn in order to be gainfully employed in the next 50 years? What are we educating them for? How and what should we focus on? The government recognizes that people have academic content at their fingertips: on the internet, on mobile devices. With that in mind, what are we supposed to teach kids in the schools?

In the past, simple content taught as history, facts, and theories sufficed. Today, it is assumed that children can access such content, and critical thinking should be emphasized to "connect the content dots" and foster innovation and advances. It is interesting that formal education is getting away from teaching the basic three Rs of reading, 'riting and 'rithmetic and moving closer to the realm of parenting by teaching social responsibility, cultural awareness, and communication. When a parent is not available, teachers are needed for providing children with the seven critical Cs. (See Chapter 2)

The core objective of the report is to move the school industry from teaching content to teaching competencies. From assembly-line, fill-up-their-heads instruction to teaching how to sift through information to learn. The goal is to turn "what you know" into "what you can do with what you know." Yesterday's schools worked in an era of lesser knowledge, the theory goes. Nearly everything kids learned was supplied by teachers working from textbooks. Today, though, knowledge is everywhere. The teacher's job is less about supplying knowledge than showing kids how to find it, evaluate it, and work with it.

One hundred and fifty years ago, a teacher would have gone to Normal school to study content and teaching techniques and was probably the smartest and most educated person in the village. Now, we have technologically advanced children helping teachers in the classroom, troubleshooting their Smartboards, PowerPoint projectors, and graphing calculators. One day my son was taking a class in a school with a few homeschooling friends. During a free and unsupervised period, they were practicing their coding skills and "accidentally" broke into the school's internet system. The school administrators cranked up the security after these few 13-year-olds found its holes! The entire school industry today struggles to catch up to kids who are smarter than the system.

Today, teachers are needed and relevant in our educational system, but their role has changed drastically. They are more like "parents in place," fulfilling jobs that parents have outsourced; they are definitely the facilitators of learning rather than just teachers. Both parents and teachers work hard to ensure the best outcomes for children. Both are overworked, underpaid and undervalued. Dave Hancock, Education Minister in 2009, said, "Teachers must give up being the sage on the stage to become the guide on the side. From teaching to facilitating." (Zwaagstra, 2009)

As a participant in both government stakeholder initiatives, I was convinced both times that they had a giant paper shredder outside the back door! Other than showing up in glossy brochures and on the government website, I doubt that any of the recommendations made by the participants will ever make it into the frontline—the classrooms. While the report espoused personalized learning, for example, theory has not been put into practice. When my daughter was in Grade 12, she wrote a 92,000-word novel for fun in one month for NaNoWriMo (National Novel Writing Month). Could she use that for some of her course work for a Grade 12 English course? Surely, that counted as personal learning? She read library books on writing style, character development, and plot sequence. Her quest to learn how to write well was fueled by her own motivation. No. She couldn't use the novel for course credits. The School Act had no provision for that kind of initiative!

The second initiative in 2011, "Our Children, Our Future: Getting it Right," adapted many of the Inspiring Education philosophies. This time, to their credit, they also included students' opinions. About five percent of the stakeholders in the large conference hall were children aged 14 years and up. It's too bad that younger children were not also given a voice, as there are few studies on how younger children experience school. No one asks them. Given Alberta's high school completion rate of 70 percent, I would have preferred to see input from children who had already given up on the school system; not the bright-eyed children who were probably chosen from the cream of the class or had won essay competitions in order to participate.

The school system is a huge administrative entity with many policies and rules. People ask why I left the system instead of trying to change it from inside. In my view, the only way to effect change is by making a dent where the administration takes notice: economics. When enough people force change by walking with their feet, and their funding, to better options, hopefully the system will change and become more child- and family-friendly. As worldwide numbers of home educators climb every year, the pressure is building.

The surprising proposed recommendation of the two projects is that the current pre-scribed 1400 outcomes per grade be condensed to a mere 10 broad outcomes. The subject areas would include Literacy (language content) and Numeracy (math content) within the framework of the following 10 competencies:

1. Know how to learn
2. Think critically
3. Solve problems
4. Manage information
5. Innovate and apply
6. Create opportunities
7. Apply literacies of reading, writing, math, technology, languages, media and finance—the "academics"
8. Communicate and work cooperatively
9. Demonstrate global and cultural understanding
10. Apply career and life skills

Can children learn all 10 competencies through their self-directed play? Yes! The public education system is definitely becoming more broad-based in their outcomes and more similar to the unschooling model.

I think these 10 competencies are exactly what we need in order to educate our citizens for the next 100 years. Both government initiatives got it right on that account. We all agree on the future direction of education: it must be meaningful and personalized; prac-ticed anytime, anywhere, and any way. Not rote memorization, but meaningful contex-tual application to real-life problems. And if this model of education can become global rather than local, all kids will benefit.

What the government didn't get right is that the system itself does not exercise the very competencies they expect and demand of our children: creativity, innovation, and prob-lem solving. While trying to expand the think-outside-the-box model, they won't go so far as to toss out the box and take a serious look at entirely new and innovative models to modernize the system. It is still focused on the building or the virtual model of school as a hierarchical bricks-and-mortar control center where students are the last consider-ation, lagging behind budgets, buses, infrastructure, employment, and other economic concerns. Parents must still answer to the minister of education for their children's edu-cational outcomes; that is not something the administration will give up easily.

The government serves the people, not the other way around. Or should. As homeschooling grows worldwide, governments scramble to regulate, to maintain control, and to retain jobs. This does not always serve the child's best interests, and that is what should be front and center in every education-related decision. The $10 billion (Fletcher, 2018) Alberta provincial education industry comprises a lot of jobs and accounts for almost 80 percent of the education budget. The school industry has a vested interest in not letting parents know that their children can learn the 10 competencies by playing video games all day!

The Finland-Alberta Comparison Project

The Programme for International Student Assessment (PISA) is a worldwide competition in which over 80 countries send 500 randomly selected 15-year-old students to write standardized exams in three subjects. Canada consistently ranks in the top ten countries for Reading, Math and Science scores, but Finland consistently trumps Canada. What does Finland do that Canada doesn't?

It is not a matter of funding; increased education budgets do not necessarily equate to better test results. According to USC Rossier Online, the US spends $7743 per child, per year; Canada spends $5749 and Finland spends $5653. (USC, 2011) The PISA results, however, show Finland near the top, Canada next, and the US further down the list. Clearly, more funding alone does not produce better results.

Finland's system is closer to unschooling than Canada's in the following ways:

- Children begin school at age seven; earlier is not better.

- School is only 3 – 4 hours a day; children spend the rest of the day playing and socializing.

- High school students have less than half an hour of homework and there is no homework in elementary or junior high schools.

- There are no standardized exams until high school.

- Gifted and struggling students are taught in the same room. Children are given as much help as they need.

- There is emphasis on hands-on experience; class numbers are kept below 16 so everyone gets attention.

- Recess is 75 minutes. Schools in other countries schedule one-third of that.

- The national standard curriculum is very broad to allow for individual needs based on student composition.

- Teachers are given full autonomy over lesson plans, curriculum, and resources. Most teachers hold master's degrees and are well respected in the community.

- There is an emphasis on cooperation, not competition. (Moore, 2015)

Shanghai, Hong Kong and Singapore, which base their learning models on rote memory and have classes of 60 kids, are also near the top of the list for the 2012 PISA standings. (Klassen, 2012) However, as some of the exams measure problem-solving abilities, exam results in some countries do not demonstrate those same excellent outcomes on questions that require theoretical or critical thinking-based responses. Rote learning does not lend itself to outside-the-box thinking, which is a necessary competency for the future.

How unschooling would work in the regular school system

We know that unschooling works in the free-learning Sudbury and Summerhill schools, but what about the regular school system?

In the interests of maintaining high learning levels, improving creativity, and keeping kids motivated, schools need to take a more unschooling approach. They need more adults present—teachers as facilitators—and less administration and curriculum, emphasizing competencies rather than content. Here is my idea of a self-directed government-funded school:

The ideal self-directed school model incorporates the three elements required for unschooling: free time, rich resources, and a facilitator or mentor. The facilitator (teacher)-student ratio is one adult to five children. The teacher is responsible for only the five children in his or her "pod." That would mean hiring six teachers for a class of 30 children. With this low teacher-student ratio, teachers could facilitate interests rather than teach.

Groups would be divided into subject and interest areas in which the teacher is passionate about the topic, and the children assigned to that group, equally passionate. The group would constitute a learning pod. The groups would be fluid. As children's interests changed over the months, they would move in and out of the pods as their interest waxed or waned.

With such small groups to supervise, teachers could easily organize field trips every day, and help with hands-on activities. I've found that five children with varied interests are easy to keep on track. The teacher's administrative work would be kept to a minimum so they could dedicate their time to learning activities. With no lesson plans to prepare, teachers could work a shorter day. With reduced workload in curriculum development, fewer textbooks, and fewer administrators, the government could fund more teacher-facilitators instead of administrative employees.

I realize that accountability is still relevant and stakeholders want a measure of assessment. Children could write English and Math exams every three years to show progress in these important areas. Progress in Science, Arts, and Social Studies would not be measured, as they are subject- and interest-specific. For this very reason, The Canadian Test of Basic Skills measures only English and Math.

Children would not be age-graded and would benefit from mentoring within the group at different development levels. The pod participants would delve only as deeply into a topic as they themselves dictated. The groups would also be open to homeschoolers who have an interest in a certain subject and wished to drop in for that topic. For example, my sons had a keen interest in welding, but I couldn't find a safe outlet or a teacher that would show them outside of the rigidity of a high-school welding class. Now, 10 years later, we have maker spaces—community drop-in centers with communal tools available for anyone to work on their own projects. Kids have access to tools they would not have had the means to rent, and they don't have to take a class to use a lab. They can work on their own projects and not be subjected to a prescribed curriculum. People share their learning at these places, as multi-age groups form naturally, based on shared interests.

In homeschooling, it is common for shared-interest groups to pop up—they will typically include a facilitator or mentor, kids of different ages, and a single passion—such groups really work, even though they are fluid and informal. My kids went to a computer club, a girls' writing club, a youth environmental group, a daytime homeschooling Cubs group, a Beakerhead project group, a First Lego League group and a Minecraft Club. When some of the kids reached high school age, we formed a teaching co-op, where the adults would take turns teaching one outcome in a course. All groups had at least one mentor and kids of different ages and abilities. The bond? A common interest. These groups are like families; they develop natural leaders and followers. They have conflicts, but just like families, they work things out. The most important factor is that they have fun. They joke around, cooperate, and help each other learn. My son said that the computer club of peers he was in from the ages of 12 - 16 really helped him surpass expectations in his first-year computer science course at university—he had already learned everything in the course outline!

In my model, pods would operate similarly to these informal homeschooling groups, with a teacher facilitating interpersonal social skills and conflict resolution within the pods.

The children would not age-graded, but rather interest-sorted. A vehicle would be available for the teacher to take children out in the community every day to visit museums, libraries, parks, and zoos. A teacher could be facilitating a pod of children keenly interested in computer programming; children would be allowed to stay in that learning pod for as long as they wished. When they felt they had learned about the topic to their satisfaction, they would transfer to another pod, based on another interest. Within those interests, children would pick up numeracy, literacy, science, and social study skills. What's more, teachers could also transfer among pods according to their own interests. They may get tired of teaching computer programming and want to share their love of gardening.

There would be no homework. No curriculum, no forced learning plan. Learning would happen joyously and spontaneously. If one child in the pod wanted to learn Java, then that would be the plan for the day. If the next day another child wanted to learn C++ programming, then the pod would learn about that. The teacher and the group would totally follow the interests of the learning pod. Advanced kids would teach the others. With only five kids, each one would work on a single aspect of the topic or interest.

Student participation in the school pods would be voluntary; they would not have to attend or participate. But in this model, parents would have a place to drop off their children in the morning so they could go to paid work, and their children would love to go to school, excited for what the day would bring. And what child hates field trip day?!

High school might be the first introduction to more structured classes with a set agenda, lectures, exams, and deadlines—more like school as it is today. But only for those who want a more structured high school experience; children would have the option of remaining in the pod system. Minimum age for high school would be 15, based on a child's brain development and his ability to process abstract thinking. Or children could do one or two structured courses in junior high school, between the ages of 12 – 15, to prepare for a more heavily structured high school experience. Again, not mandatory. Many unschoolers go right into structured postsecondary institutions without ever taking a structured high school class, and with great success.

"The workplace is much like this model. People no longer stay in their jobs for 30-plus years. They consider their jobs to be shorter-term, interest-based endeavors which they may decide to change in two to five years and head in a new direction." (Pauli, 2012)

Summer day camps are a good model for how the pod concept would work inside a school. Day camps are usually one week long and geared to an interest such as space, science, arts, or sports. Kids can explore an interest without making a long-term commitment. They try different activities every summer, as their interests change. This could work similarly with school. If the child's interest were sustained, he could stay in the group and deepen his level of knowledge through self-directed activities facilitated by the teacher; if not, he could move on to another group.

Much like unschooling, this model would give teachers increased autonomy. They could use their professional judgment in facilitating the children's learning. Like homeschoolers, they would not be chained to curriculum guides dictating what to teach or the time and resources they must use. Of course, there would be common sense limits. *Game of Thrones* might not be appropriate material for a Grade 2 class! There could still be a large range of approved age-appropriate resources to offer the children.

Teachers would be given guidance on how to assess learning by observation, as there would be no grades assigned. Children would not be compared to each other. They would be self- or facilitator-assessed every three years in Math or English, comparing individual progress from one report to the next. And they would progress. Guaranteed. Every child would progress in some way in the course of a year.

We know that by the age of 18, most children will reach, and may exceed, standards comparable to those of their forced-curriculum school counterparts, as evidenced by the many unschoolers who score well on standardized diploma exams at the end of "schooling." Teachers need freedom, autonomy, and trust from their administrators, as well as confidence that their abilities to engage students and direct their interests into deep and meaningful learning will provide rich and creative education in the classroom.

Like homeschoolers, teachers could draw up a yearly education plan for each child—as opposed to lesson plans for the whole class. Such a plan would be voluntary and would be liberally applied, allowing freedom to deviate. An unexpected snowfall might cancel a planned outing to the space center; the group might use it instead as an opportunity to learn about the scientific properties of snow. An annual educational plan would allow for a lot of meandering and seizing interesting teachable moments.

Shouldn't every child have such an opportunity? This type of school encompasses the best of everything: a place for children to go while their parents work; the same benefits of low adult-child ratio as homeschoolers; and the freedom to explore the world of interests that unschoolers enjoy. Of course, there are hurdles to overcome, such as how to fund a teacher-student ratio of 1:5 when teachers' salaries already comprise 80 percent of the education budget. Perhaps savings on administrative jobs and curriculum could offset the cost. Partnerships with libraries and community centers would also reduce costs, by offering free play for half the day. Teachers could facilitate learning in the pods for the other half a day.

In many countries including the United States, the federal government controls education and the departments have a set of targets for children to reach. The country has a common core standard over which individual states have very little control but must meet through standardized testing. (Common Core, 2010)

In contrast, Canada has no federal jurisdiction over education; it is regulated by the individual provinces. Standards outline what students must know, the attitudes they must develop, and the skills they must acquire; but they do not dictate how children must reach those standards. That is up to the parents, the learner, and the teacher. At the very least, schools could offer two tracks: one a self-directed, interest-based free-school such as the one I have described, and one the government-directed, curriculum-mandated model we presently have, for those families who are comfortable with the current system.

But parents must know that school is only one option for educating their children. Homeschooling and unschooling are viable paths. All strive for a common outcome: educated children.

PART 2:
WHY UNSCHOOLING?
THE DIGITAL GENERATION NEEDS ADULTS AND SELF-DIRECTION MORE THAN PEERS AND CURRICULUM

6

A Brief History of Education

"Eternal vigilance is the price of liberty." — Wendell Phillips, Activist

Homeschooling was the norm until the 19th century

"It is the responsibility of the parent to educate his child in all areas of life. Parents, you need to make sure that your kids get an education whether their school does its job or not. Why? It is *your* kid. The uneducated 35 year old working for minimum wage and struggling to pay his bills won't end up the responsibility of the school system. That 'kid' won't be coming back to the principal asking for help making his mortgage payment or to move into the spare classroom because he got evicted from his apartment. That 'kid,' your kid, will be coming back to *you*. Is that what you want?" [*sic*] (Winget, 2010)

Parents taking control of their children's education is not some new, untested fad. Since the beginning of time, home education and apprenticeships have allowed children to play and work alongside their parents. Many wealthy Europeans were schooled at home by tutors and governesses of varying expertise. Famous homeschoolers were Leonardo Da Vinci, Leo Tolstoy, Amadeus Mozart, Albert Einstein, Benjamin Franklin. Even Taylor Swift and Elon Musk's kids homeschooled.

The industrial revolution of the 1800s was a major agent of change. The invention of engines gave rise to the building of factories for mass production. Factories needed workers, so parents moved from working in the fields or in apprenticeships at home to working in the factories, creating the problem of what to do with the children while the parents worked. The most educated person in the village was hired to watch the children. In the UK, the British government viewed education as a way of lining up cultural identification with Protestantism, customs, and the English language. If every child underwent a formal induction to appropriate values, standards of behavior, and thought processes, many societal problems such as crime, poverty, and loitering would be eliminated. (Canadian Encyclopedia, 2014)

The original school system was based on a plan from Prussia and was mostly concerned with churning out obedient factory workers who would not think critically. The fear of the rural population's force, as demonstrated by the French revolution, created a school system that rewarded obedience and discouraged dissent and uprisings.

Public mass schooling for 100 years

In the US, most students were taught in one-room schoolhouses. In 1837, well-traveled educator Horace Mann introduced public school curricula. He innovated the age-grading of students in 1848 and by 1852 compulsory attendance laws were being passed. (Education News, 2013) The first intelligence tests were developed in 1905 by Binet and served to sort children even further. The Elementary and Secondary Education Act was formed in 1965. (Armstrong, 2006)

In Canada, the first schools were operated in New France (Canada) by the Catholic church missionaries from French settlers. In the early nineteenth century, the Protestant government set up Protestant schools. Later, Catholics and Protestants could not agree on how children should be taught, so both religious school systems were enshrined in the BNA act of 1867. (Wikipedia) By 1871, compulsory attendance and public funding were signed into law. By 1883, one-room schools were well on their way to becoming the system we know today. Teacher training, classroom age/grade sorting, and mandatory textbook curriculum were embedded in the system.

For the next 150 years, the education system was based on the industrial factory-and-assembly-line model. Children were viewed as buckets to be filled with knowledge. Tod Maffin, CBC's national technology correspondent, makes the analogy that students are processed like rocks in a tumbler—tossed in for 12 years and tossed out according to government outcomes. (Maffin, 2008) They are told what curriculum to learn and when to learn it. Kids that learn differently or don't conform are labeled failures.

Religion and language became points of contention. Except for Quebec, which is predominantly Catholic and French, the Canadian education system was Protestant and English. Schools had morning prayers, Bible studies, and Christian values. (Byfield, 1998)

In 1882, Rev. James Turner started the first school in Alberta in the basement of his home, in what is now known as Edmonton. In the early days of the one-room schoolhouses, girls were taught homemaking and boys were taught trades and factory production skills. The system valued conformity because good students turned into good workers and good consumers, which in turn made money for factories and retail trades. School boards were formed in 1938. Young female teachers were hired to provide the nurturing role model to young children; they were supervised by male administrators who saw themselves as the real educators. Even today, teachers are unequally gender-balanced within the system, with females comprising most of the elementary school and preschool teachers, and males making up the lion's share of supervisory positions. Education became the $10 billion industry we have in Alberta today. (Byfield, 1998)

In the late 1700s, Jean Jacques Rousseau promoted children's natural curiosity, and in 1899 John Dewey began pushing for a model of progressive education that seemed to have a lot of child direction and experiential learning. Their intentions were good, but their philosophies got lost in the mire of ever-increasing government involvement in education. With school boards came standardized, mandatory curriculum, and the wishes of parents became sidelined.

74

School boards also allowed the teachers to establish their vocation as a profession. That was a good thing, because until then, teachers labored under very poor working conditions. Established in 1935, the teachers' union today is a powerful lobby and a political force, with 43,000 members and millions in annual dues. (Wikipedia, 2018)

After the war, the baby boom created a huge demographic that required schools. It seemed that every neighborhood built a school in the 1950s and '60s as demand exploded. Modular classrooms were created to handle the overflow. Then, as more women moved into the workforce in the 1970s, families became smaller and less classroom space was needed. In the 1990s, schools became underutilized and some rented their excess space to alternative programs and private schools. Although private school attendance is only about five percent of the school population, it meets a need for diversity in types of education. Charter schools also filled a need for parents wanting alternatives in education. Both private and charter schools must teach the government program. Only homeschoolers are exempt.

Home education catches on again in the 1970s

In the 100 years of public school from the 1870s to the 1970s, curriculum, teaching methods, and even buildings were experiments, born out of scant evidence that innovations in teaching systems would actually work. Let's talk about school buildings. In the 1970s, many schools were built without windows on the presumption that they would distract children from their studies. "Someone might look outside and take their mind off their concentration." said, John Gibson, Director of new school projects at Alberta Infrastructure. Today, our new schools have plenty of windows because studies show that natural light boosts performance. Given that, why can't we go even further and let children actually play outside on playgrounds and in parks, or go on hikes and camping trips? As Frank Coppinger, superintendent of facilities for the Calgary public board, states, "That's the key mantra nowadays, incorporate as much flexibility into the design as possible. You're not quite sure how classroom education will evolve in the future, so you need that flexibility." (Gibson, 2012)

Public school systems continually experiment on teachers and children. When whole language was introduced in the 1970s to replace phonics, there was great disgruntlement among parents and teachers used to rote learning. The system swung back to teaching phonics. Eventually the pedagogy compromised, teaching phonics and whole language together. Meanwhile, if the kids caught in the middle of the experiment couldn't read—too bad for them! More recently, the government imposed the "discovery math" method on curriculum over the past five years with no significant research to prove it would work. In fact, unschoolers know it works very well in a family setting—but not in a hierarchical institution like school. Another experiment had two or three teachers team-teaching open classrooms of 60-plus children; that yielded only noisy classrooms full of distracted children and resulted in a quick return to individual classrooms.

When parents have had enough of the experimentation and are tired of their concerns being ignored by administration, they walk with their feet and their wallets—and bring their children home. The current group of homeschoolers has chosen this path primarily for two reasons: Pedagogy, the delivery of education, and Ideology, the content of education.

Children of the "hippie generation" of the 1960s and the "me generation" of the 1970s were pulled out of mainstream schools because the pedagogy—the delivery of the education—did not suit parents who preferred a more natural, organic brand of education; their desire to return to the land and to nature did not mesh with the rigid military-like feel of the schools. Child-centeredness was the goal and allowing children to learn naturally resonated with many families.

John Holt, the guru of this type of home education, started a magazine in 1970 called *Growing Without Schooling*. Holt believed in the ability of children to learn what they needed, when they needed it, and was an early promoter of unschooling with the publication of his 1989 book *Learning all the Time*. But many earlier practitioners of this type of home education were investigated for perceived evidence of child abuse or neglect—anything that authorities could use to force their children back into school. Original homeschoolers in the 1960s and '70s were eclectic and practiced a mix of structured and unstructured homeschooling: they were unschoolers.

The 1980s saw the beginnings of a progressive division between church and school, and most public schools were made secular. God, prayer, and any reference to Christianity, including Christmas, were eliminated in deference to political correctness with the increasing enrollment of non-religious families and those who practiced other religions. Schools that wished to maintain traditional religious references had to become private schools. As an alternative, parents turned to homeschooling.

Fundamental Christians were the biggest proponents of homeschooling, based on ideology. Parents wanted to teach their children about creationism, did not want to teach evolution, and wanted a God-centered curriculum. Seeing a niche market developing, many curriculum companies stepped up to the plate and produced packages that parents could use to easily teach their children at home. Saxon, Bob Jones, Alpha Omega, and Lifepac all produced complete grade and subject curricula and many with a religious framework. Linda Dobson and Mary Pride were leading authorities on this type of homeschooling, mostly in the school-replicated-at-home format, and represented what most people think of as homeschooling today, portrayed in the media with a mom at the kitchen blackboard and children studying around the table.

At the turn of the millennium, the internet was in full bloom. Online classes became popular and were provided by school boards across the nations. When the Kahn Academy organization began posting free video instruction in math and sciences that learners could access anytime and watch over and over, teacher instruction became free for anyone willing to learn. And nowadays, anyone can learn anything on the internet, from haircutting to calculus. Mathew called me once from university to ask how he should iron a shirt. I started explaining and he said, "Never mind... I'll look it up on YouTube!"

Education is becoming globalized and borderless; it has even incited turf wars because a student can access teaching anywhere. A course accessed from a Canadian school may not be any better or more valuable than one accessed from a school in Japan. With education that is now free and universal, schools and universities now sell accreditation as much as they do education. Their testing and certification generate revenue to compensate for declining enrollment in their physical classes.

In Canada, seven million students aged 5 - 18 attend school. (Hildebrandt, 2014) Five percent of those students go to private schools and two percent home educate. The home education statistics include only parent-controlled homeschooling, not online kids studying at home, which is called distance education. Because it is impossible to distinguish between students who take all courses online and students who take one course online, they are not counted in homeschooling statistics. I would guess that most students take an online course from home at some point in their 12 years, artificially inflating the statistics for distance education. Of the two percent that homeschool, approximately 10 percent self-identify as unschoolers and are educated entirely through self-direction. Homeschooling in Canada is growing at the rate of seven percent per year and reached 29 percent over the past five years. (Roslin, 2010) (Boesveld, 2011) (Van Pelt, 2015)

There are 56 million students in the United States and over two million, or 3 to 4 percent of these homeschool, of which 10 percent unschool. Homeschooling in the US has grown at annual rates of seven to 15 percent for over a decade, according to the president of the National Home Education Research Institute. (Martin, 2012) Worldwide, homeschooling numbers are growing every year in every country except those where it is still banned. Even there, parents either home educate off the grid or opt to move to a homeschooling-friendly country. The movement is growing because no parent wants to hold back their child.

When the assembly line model of education was at its peak in the 1950s and before computers were invented, amassed knowledge would double every fifty years. Today, in the midst of the digital revolution, knowledge doubles every two years. No one can wait 10 - 15 years for the school system to design new curriculum when content is needed right away. As children acquire smartphones, often by age six, they have incredible knowledge in their tiny little hands. The teacher is no longer the most educated person in the village. Education is constantly changing and it's anyone's guess what we can expect to need for the next 50 years.

Unschooling is legal

Homeschooling and unschooling are totally legal in most parts of the world because a child's parents are his first and lifelong teachers. Section 3, Article 26 of the Universal Declaration of Human Rights states, **"Parents have a prior right to choose the kind of education that shall be given to their children."** Parents control philosophy, curriculum, resources, delivery method, and assessment. Education begins in the home when a baby is brought over the threshold and ends in the home when a child moves out permanently. Parents know their children best and are the master teachers in their home, whereas in schools, teachers are masters over their classrooms.

Even in government schools in Canada, parents' rights supersede all others. Alberta's Bill 44 ensures that parents can veto the content their child is exposed to in school. Yet homeschooling parents and even school parents are still viewed by the system as outsiders in decisions about their children's education. Most school industry organizations disagreed with Bill 44, introduced and passed by the government, which established parents' right to pull their children out of any classroom teaching that disagreed with the family's values or religion. It clearly states that parents are the supreme controllers of their child's education, including if and how they use curriculum; and this makes unschooling legal. If parents want to hand off the direction of their child's education to the child himself, they have every legal right to do so. Parents are the legal controllers of a child's education until he is 16 years old.

Most provinces' education model is outcome based. Outcomes are the goals that teachers and parents aim for, by using methods and resources they choose. This leaves the educator a lot of discretion.

Homeschooling is still viewed skeptically by many schools. There is such an us-against-them pervasiveness between home education and school. There could be so much more collaboration and sharing of resources and materials. After all, home education parents are taxpayers too, and pay for the resources in schools that they are barred from using. Some parents would like to home educate part-time but are not allowed to homeschool just one or two courses; schools protest the concept with the refrain, "We educate the 'whole child' in our institution." What they mean is "We don't get funded if we only teach one course or teach partial grades." So, for most families, teaching one or two courses at home and sending the child off to the neighborhood school for the rest is not an option in Canada. Except for online courses, attending classrooms has to be all or nothing. This does not serve the child's best interests. Home and school should encourage resource sharing.

Parents are excellent teachers. Although parents may lack subject matter expertise in some areas, they do know their child best. Research shows that the education level of the parent doesn't matter. It's the one-on-one attention the adult provides that makes home education successful. (Van Pelt, 2015) Parents who homeschool can easily provide a customized education for each child. Many parents did not go to university and most do not have a teaching degree. They may not know about learning theory or classroom management. But for thousands of years, parents have been teaching their young without studying the art of teaching; even non-human mammals do it, by instinct. At the very least, parents know how to shop for the expertise their child needs.

With this knowledge, most homeschooling parents are well equipped to teach the academics until at least Grade 8; at some point, they may wish to hire teachers or tutors to directly instruct their children, if they no longer feel confident enough in their own knowledge or expertise. Or their children might take on self-teaching, using resources from the internet. Many of today's parents have the subject matter expertise to help their children all the way through high school. My husband is an engineer; although he wasn't a teacher, he could help the kids with science. Today, with the internet, parents and children can find lessons, texts, and videos that can help teach anything. I've had four children teach themselves most of high school, some with minor tutorial help, and pass the government exams. It was great practice for postsecondary learning.

Even teachers need help. Some might find it difficult to teach art, for example, when they have no background in it, but often, when there is no funding for an art teacher, they must take it on. Outside of school, a yoga teacher cannot teach Zumba—she must be licensed. Yet an art teacher can be required to teach math.

A common remark I hear is "Why don't you just volunteer more in the classroom if you want to be involved in your child's education?" One of education's biggest problems is the efficiency of their resources, not lack of them. There are reams of research in the education field showing that the more involved parents are in their child's education, the better the student's outcomes; yet there are many barriers to parents being involved. Administration prefers to ban parents from the classroom. When they are allowed in, they are assigned menial jobs such as cutting snowflakes for bulletin boards or photo-copying worksheets. Teachers' unions make sure that parents are not taking on any part of a teacher's or an aide's job, and this keeps parents on the sidelines. Yet government cuts the funding for "official" aides, leaving children without the benefit of more caring adults to help them read or discuss topics. I know that many grandparents would love to read to children in schools, and that adult volunteers would like to assist with cutting, drawing, or math calculations. But the logistics of organizing, scheduling, and training volunteers is another job that should not be the teacher's responsibility; someone must be hired to do it. So, volunteers in the classroom would be nice—but difficult to organize.

7

Academic Benefits of Unschooling

"Creativity can't exist in a culture of fear. To be creative, one needs to take risks."

Unschooling is one-on-one learning with an adult

Studies show that the more access children have to an adult, the better they absorb content. Many parents are willing to pay for the private school ratio of one teacher to 16 children. But what about families who don't have access or can't afford private school?

Typical school class sizes are increasing. In Canada's public school system, the ratio in the lower grades from Kindergarten to Grade 3, when "learning to read" is the primary goal, as opposed to "reading to learn" from Grades 4 onward, is about one teacher to 23 children. From Grade 4 through junior high, the ratio is approximately one teacher to 30 students, and in high school, it can be as high as one teacher to 40 kids.

Children need adults more than ever, but teachers' administrative load eats into the time they have available for helping students. "Twenty teachers at our local city schools logged their hours in May 2011. They were teaching only 19 hours per week but spent 25 hours on marking and administrative tasks. Another 10 hours were spent on supervision, clerical activities, and mandatory professional development. Teachers spend more time working outside the classroom than they do in front of students." (Teghtmeyer, 2012)

In unschooling, the ratio can be one adult to one child. This is arguably the biggest academic advantage of homeschooled children: unlimited access to adult help. Many homeschoolers do so much better academically than even private school students (Basham, 2007) because even in large families, the ratio of adults to children is still far lower than the 1:16 ratio maintained by private schools.

Children's vocabulary expands with time around adults

Another benefit is access to hearing language. Children that hear adults and converse with them on a continual basis increase their vocabulary exponentially. (ECMap, 2014) This has been proven in young children under the age of five, and there is no reason to believe that it would not continue as they grow. Studies show that children who spend more time with adults hear more words as well as a more sophisticated vocabulary, and can more easily interact in a "serve and return" response. (Leman, 2009) Screens cannot provide that customized human "return."

The $7-a-day daycare plan instituted in Quebec several years ago is another wide-scale example of how institutionalized children fare less well than children who stay at home with at least one adult. It theorized that the daycare children would be academically more advanced than their at-home peers, and that was not the case. Conversely, being with peers in a classroom disadvantaged the children. (Maclean's, 2014) A room full of noisy, chattering peers does not provide the best learning environment. A home environment that is quieter, less stressful, with richer adult language is much better for children.

Children in school are not allowed to talk to adults. They are told to sit down and be quiet in order to stay on task, and to not disturb other children. They are not allowed to speak to or converse with one another. When my children were at home, they chattered with each other constantly, even while playing computer games, as they were connected in the same room. They would laugh and describe plays and characters and joke about the other gamers and what they would do. Hence, they heard and used language continuously. And contrary to the opinion that homeschooling does not offer socialization, unrestrained opportunity to chat with siblings is a huge facet of socializing.

It is interesting that many people note that homeschooled children are more likely to make eye contact with adults when speaking with them, a result of many years of practice engaging in conversations with adults.

Graham Clyne, a children's advocate and researcher, states that the best way to have good emotional, social, and educational outcomes for school-age children is for parents to play games and read with them, turn off the screens, and be involved in their homework and sports. He was referring to school children, but the same applies to homeschooled children. (Clyne, 2008) Adults matter because they return child's serve for attention and communication.

Unschooling prepares children for the future, not the past

Schools teach history, which is about yesterday; they teach the knowledge and skills needed today. They do not teach for tomorrow. Children need to learn about history, but they also need competencies to equip them now and for the next 60 years of their working lives.

The system curriculum is reviewed and overhauled every 15 years. That time frame is not long enough to print textbooks and provide teacher training. In Alberta, the Science, Math and Social Studies curriculum overhaul took place from 2007 to 2011. English Language Arts has not been reviewed in the past 20 years. Core subjects will not be revised again until 2024. The optional subjects are even worse. The subject of Parenting, for example, has exciting new research in the area of brain development—yet the course materials in use date back to 2005! The Social Studies textbook was published in 2007, when we could not have imagined the globalizing effect of smartphones. The system does not have the budget to update textbooks every two years. However, with our knowledge base doubling every two years, the current time frames for updating are too long. We are teaching our kids outdated facts.

Some schools still teach handwriting skills. Nice to have, but is it needed? Today, teaching every child HTML coding (hypertext markup language) will prepare them for the future—this is far more useful to them than penmanship! —yet it is not even taught in some schools in Canada. Mastering HTML allows the average child to do be extremely creative on the internet, designing web pages, formatting a blog, resizing and naming photographs and much, much more. These are skills every child needs today and will continue to use in the future. Handwriting? Not so much. By 2020, 26 billion devices—machines, smart consumer goods, medical equipment—things we cannot even imagine today will be linked to the internet. In Estonia, all students enrolled in Grades 1 to 12 by 2012 learn how to program and create web and mobile applications. (Mac, 2016) Coding is useful. If children, especially girls, in developing countries were to learn coding, their employment prospects and consequently their life prospects would change tremendously.

In unschooling, children learn what interests them. It could be new technology, such as apps and coding; and perhaps older skills such as penmanship or calligraphy also appeal to them. Some children are keen to learn code, which can take them far into territory yet unknown. Others may not be so keen, and that's okay—they can go equally far in other directions. Unschoolers can seek out the newest ideas, cutting-edge technologies, and content, because they don't have to follow an outdated curriculum. And they have plenty of free time to tinker and learn, something kids in school don't have.

Unschooling is a personalized education

Personalized learning is decreasing in schools. Each child is unique and deserves a customized education. Most schools do profess lip service to personalized learning, but in reality, bureaucratic logistics make it impossible to provide a personal, customized learning experience for each student in a large institution.

Public education is delivered in economies of scale. Textbooks are bought in bulk because the unit price is far lower when purchasing 40 units than one. Thus, all students in a grade must learn the same content. If a child is keenly interested in learning about Japan but Brazil is on the curriculum for the grade, she is forced to learn about Brazil. If she is not interested, she will tune out during class and read up on Japan after school. What a waste of time and energy! If she could only study Japan in class, she would be satisfied and engaged.

Classrooms are built for group learning. Desks might be configured in rows or circles, but the topic is standardized. A child can spend most of his days in one room, in the same seat, with the same peers, for years. Bulletin boards, teachers, and decor may change, but it's the same room. This blandness and unrelenting sameness makes sense when the school system is educating hundreds of students. It does not make sense when educating one child.

The rationale for not providing personal learning is that schools and boards do not wish to be perceived as giving special attention to one student. "It wouldn't be fair for the other students," is a common litany when accommodation is requested for a child's special needs. Even online courses that could easily accommodate more personal learning have standardized content. Again, each course will enroll 60 - 100 children but hire only one teacher for marking—and they couldn't possibly provide assessment for 60 different learning projects! The only personalization built into online courses is allowing students to set their own due dates, within reason.

Many people ask whether the new inquiry-based curriculum isn't more personalized. The answer is no. In this model, the school asks the students to ask the questions that the school wants him to answer—not real questions born of the students' genuine inquisitiveness. In a roundabout way, it's the school that is "inquiring," and not the students. "Students may have choices in how they learn the content, but not in choosing the content itself." (CCSDL, 2012) They are forced to ask questions whose answers they may not care about.

Unschooling allows customization not only for the family as a unit, but for each child in the family. When unschoolers say they do what works for their family, they mean they have also taken into consideration what works for each individual child. I have my preference as to what would work for me as a mom and teacher. I'm a workbook nut. I would love to do school-replicated-at-home, and I have one child who works that way. But the other four are totally different. Each year finds us investigating education options based on what each child needs for their age, gender, and desired knowledge. One year, my daughter took an online math and science course. Another year, she wanted a complete break and we left math and science—in fact all academics—aside. She knitted, read, did art projects, and played 10 hours of World of Warcraft daily. That's what she needed. Her brothers had different needs that year. So, the key is finding the balance between what works for the whole family, what works for each child, and also what is workable and tolerable for parent.

Every child is entitled to a personalized learning experience like unschooling, unique to his learning style, personality, interests, and intelligences.

Learning is intrinsic

Compulsory education means that someone else is deciding what a student needs to learn. Yet from the beginning of time, most humans know exactly what, when, and how much they need to know in order to solve their problems. This is called *intrinsic* learning; the impetus comes from within. Extrinsic learning occurs when something or someone external to the learner bribes, forces, or punishes a student into learning a particular idea in a specific fashion.

Public school is, by definition, *extrinsic* learning.

When I started homeschooling, I thought I could just unzip the children's heads, pour in the content, and zip them up again—that what was poured in would stay in; check it off the list as "done." The teacher just keeps pouring in more and more until the children have a broad range of knowledge! I was very surprised, when I questioned my kids about two years after teaching them a unit about boats, floats, and sinkers, to find that they remembered nothing! Like many parents, I thought that everything I taught them was stored in the brain and that they could simply retrieve the knowledge when they needed it; that they would just keep amassing knowledge. Of course, the kids hadn't used the boats-floats-sinkers information on a daily basis. It was only later, when I learned about short- and long-term memory, that I realized that much of what I taught them would not stick.

From what we know about brain development, experiences stimulate neurotransmitters that help to build and strengthen the pathways between neurons. Repeated knowledge and experiences strengthen pathways, and the brain prunes away the pathways that are not often used. If children are going to retain what they learn, they must be continually and repeatedly exposed to a particular knowledge or experience for the brain to strengthen the pathway wiring and move the learning into long-term memory. When kids are taught something only once, it disappears. Young children often want to hear the same bedtime story or watch the same movie over and over. They learn through repetition. Information needs to be presented and used continually. If we had covered the boats-floats-sinkers every week for six years, they would certainly have remembered it!

On the other hand, I am amazed at how they remembered the names, music, and content of all the video games they played. But no wonder, because they played them often. Ten years later, many of the computer and Nintendo 64 games we owned have been rendered obsolete by changing operating systems and consoles. But the kids can find the games online and still remember how to play them, and they laugh about the way they loved the music and the characters. They could still recite the PokeRap song! Video games indeed reached their long-term memories.

What shuts down intrinsic learning in children?

- Parents or teachers pushing skill mastery or content too fast or too hard.
- Factual information being taught without context—usually by rote memory.
- The learner having no buy-in on the topic.

When my daughter was seven, she absolutely loved to tinker on the piano. She would make up songs and play and practice for hours a day. Noticing this, I enrolled her in lessons. Her interest gradually decreased; she would go to lessons but stopped playing and practicing for years. Her intrinsic motivation was gone.

Unschooling allows a child to engage his interests and embed his learning in long-term memory because he chooses the content. If he wants to learn more about a subject, he can seek out increased knowledge in any form he chooses—including formal instruction. If he does not wish to learn more, he wastes no one's time; not his teacher's, his classmates', nor his own. With huge amounts of free time, children can truly pursue their passions.

Unschooling accommodates all learning styles

School can undermine children's confidence in learning when the content is not delivered in their learning style. Children are often labeled as having learning disabilities, when in fact there is a Content Delivery System Disability in play. Teachers will usually teach in their own learning style; as an adult educator, I know how difficult it is to change that and teach to the student's learning style. If the teacher is a visual learner like me, for example, she will use a lot of visual learning techniques such as Power-Point.

In the early years, from babyhood to age five, children learn through all five senses: touch—that is why they have to touch everything; taste—why everything goes into their mouths; hearing; sight; and smell. Health organizations encourage parents to promote this type of learning. As children edge past the age of five, they exchange the oral exploration of tasting for talking. They enjoy discussion and conversation, building their language skills. They continue experiential learning through free play.

Kindergarten is the most experiential learning grade in public school and often has play centers. But experiential learning goes downhill from there, with Grade 1 seeing the introduction of seatwork. Six-year-old children have a hard time adjusting to a full day of seatwork when their bodies still need to move. Energy best burned off in play must be diverted into sitting still and concentrating.

As children progress through the grades, teaching delivery moves from the five senses of touch, taste, sight, hearing, and smell to only two: sight and hearing. Once kids are able to read—which they are expected to do by the end of Grade 1—delivery becomes largely text based, whether from page or screen. Not because it is a premium delivery method, but because it is a cost-effective, if one-way, form of transmitting information or techniques to a large group. When teachers admonish children to "sit down and be quiet!" they have just taken away two important forms of learning: kinesthetic and discussion. And who can blame teachers, when the noise from 35 chattering students can reach a pretty high decibel level!

PASSIVE LEARNING ACTIVITIES: Average learning retention rates (%) after two weeks	
Reading	10
Hearing (lecture or speech)	20
Seeing Images	30
Watching a demonstration or video; seeing an exhibit	50
ACTIVE LEARNING ACTIVITES: Average learning retention rates (%) after two weeks	
Participating in a discussion, giving a talk, seeing something done on location	70
Participating in role play, dramatic presentation, or simulation	90
Doing the real thing	100

Dale, 1969, Cone of Experience

As shown in the chart above, we learn through all five senses; this is true not only in childhood or Grade 1, but even into adulthood. Experiential learning encompasses all the senses, embedding learning into the brain. Online and textbook learning, while economically efficient delivery methods, are not optimum for retention because they only involve the two senses of sight and hearing. Online courses provide "discussion by requiring students to post and respond to a post." A one-line written post in response to another learner's one-line written post is not a discussion. It is not a real in-person back-and-forth conversation.

Most adult education is even worse, with conference presenters or university lecturers reading bullet points from slides. Online learning, university lectures, and conference PowerPoints all deliver to only two senses. Again, I emphasize that we need to have all five senses tickled to make learning stick! Advances made in adult education require that educators teach to all learning styles and intelligences. Delivery methods that work best encompass all the senses by using humor, music, emotional tie-ins, and a host of other sensory devices.

Dale's Cone of Experience demonstrates that the unschooling method of allowing, in fact encouraging, students to "do the real thing" nets a near-perfect retention rate. Unschooling builds confidence in learning because all forms of learning are acceptable at all times.

Unschooling learning sticks, whereas forced learning fades

French immersion is an example of how learning is lost when it is no longer consistently applied. Data from Statistics Canada shows that kids who stayed in French immersion schools for all 12 grades lose some of it after graduation. In the 1996 census, 16.3 percent of 15 – 19-year-old French immersion graduates said they were bilingual; in the 2011 census, only 9.6 percent of that cohort still considered themselves bilingual. (Friesen, 2013) The same happens when people do not continue reading Shakespeare, speaking Latin, or using polynomials on a regular basis.

In school, the child learns the content and passes the test, but the knowledge only ever enters the short-term memory and quickly exits the brain. Although teachers try hard to make mandated curriculum interesting, it will never be as engaging as topics children themselves choose according to their inborn developmental needs and processes. Inattention and disengagement will always be a problem as long as neither content nor delivery choices are determined by the learner.

Unschoolers tempt children with tasteful educational delights. If it sticks, great—the interest will flourish and lead to a desire for greater depth and breadth of knowledge. If there is no interest, there is no point in wasting time, resources, and the efforts of both child and parent, because the child will reject the learning. Kids retain learning in topics they are interested in, as evidenced when Nintendo moved their video games into the school market! I can't count the number of times I asked my older children in their teens, "Do you remember when you were seven and we learned to do addition on paper?" They responded with blank stares. I would joke and say, "You mean I could have parked you in front of the TV and lounged around and eaten bonbons all day and you would wouldn't be the worse for wear?" They laughed. My children may not remember details of their play, but the experiential learning gained from participating in child-directed activities strengthened pathways in their brains and laid the foundation for applying their learning to paper. When a high school textbook described the physics of an arrow shot straight up in the air, and at what point it would start to fall based on its velocity, they had intuitive knowledge of it from having really shot arrows at the archery range when they were seven.

I asked my university kids what they remembered when I dragged them off to classes and homeschool field trips when they were young. Their answers were surprising. Not one child remembered the content taught in the class. However, they did remember things like the candy dispenser in the lobby, the long car ride, and fighting over who would sit in the front seat. They did remember the fun classes, such as clay modeling, karate, and Lego. My son remembered playing with chocolate pudding in the bathtub, but not the lesson on boats and buoyancy. All the kids remembered having a fascination with fire; we experimented with fire outside under my supervision (because I was afraid they would do it anyway when I wasn't around!). They all remembered their favorite movies. I asked my son, who went to high school for a year, what he remembered from the experience. He replied that he did learn a bit in the courses, but the overwhelming lessons he learned were "how to obey authority" and "how to fit in socially." Those were his survival concerns in that environment. I want to tell my homeschooling friends who do school-replicated-at-home and my friends who public school not to worry if your child is not "getting it." They won't remember it anyway! Yes, education trains the brain and fires those neurons, but there are many enjoyable ways to do that—such as reading what they want to read, and not what the system tells them to read. Unschooling moves learning from short-term to long-term memory by cementing the concepts children learn when they are engaged.

No summer-slide learning loss, because education is year round

Summer learning loss occurs only when kids are forced to absorb the system's agenda and curriculum. Research shows that students regress and lose about one month of school instruction during a long summer holiday, and a study from Ohio State University found that test scores were no different for students on a year-round calendar. Year-round schools have only four weeks of summer vacation, and longer breaks during the fall, Christmas, and spring holidays. (Cuthbertson, 2012) Reading comprehension and math skills take the biggest hit. The research tells us that children lose progress in content retention, but it does not test whether they were engaged or bored with the content. Children retain knowledge in areas they are keenly interested in; my children could recite all 150 Pokemon over the summer, but not the math times tables. Summer learning loss occurs only in the areas that children are forced to learn; however, they may learn many new things that are of interest to them.

In terms of brain development, this makes sense. Brains cement the pathways between neurons in areas that are well used, and prune unused pathways. The brain is always "filing" information into useful short- or long-term storage, based on need. If a child doesn't need multiplication facts over the summer, it gets dumped in favor of useful information—such as the Pokemon stats for card game playing sessions!

Much of what children learn is invisible to us. How much knowledge they absorb and retain is directly related to their level of interest in a topic. When left to their own devices, children learn the new information and skills needed to accomplish a particular task or goal. And summer is for play. Children learn through play.

If you want your children to develop initiative, cooperation, and a passion for learning, you cannot foster that development by shoving worksheets at them. Instead, encourage their interests; listen to their questions and help them look for the answers. That's what unschoolers do.

"The brain does not have 'open' and 'closed' hours. It takes in information, sorts it, draws correlations, makes connections and stores 24 hours a day and 365 days per year." (Tracy R, 2002)

We found that summer learning far exceeded winter-month learning. I didn't have to work in the summer and had much more time to facilitate their interests. All the most-desired books and videos were available in the library because schools had checked them back in. We spent many long, unstructured hours reading because most homeschooling classes, activities, and programs were closed for the summer. Summer was the most unstructured time of the year, and the most productive. My children's reading progress flourished.

Indeed, unschooling in the summer produces abundant learning. When learning is continuous, there is no summer-slide learning loss.

Unschooling integrates learning with context

Compartmentalized subject learning is disconnected learning. Classroom time is tight. So many subject outcomes are packed into the curriculum that learning must be carefully divided into scope and sequence. Many learning outcomes are repeated across various subjects. Critical thinking is an outcome in English, Social Studies, Math, and Science—learning it once checks off all those boxes. Working with a team is another learning outcome in all those subjects. But a child doesn't need to learn teamwork in every subject. Once is enough. The outcomes are duplicated because the social studies curriculum developers work in a silo, away from the math curriculum developers. When a child learns at home, there is no duplication. Teamwork is teamwork.

Unschooling doesn't compartmentalize subject areas. All core subjects are related to everything else. In unschooling, a child can delve into a topic as deeply he wishes. Subjects overlap each other so that Math, English, Social Studies and Science, Art, and Phys-Ed might all be covered in a single topic of interest. For example, World of Warcraft teaches art through the beautiful graphics in its landscapes; math through percentages; language arts through writing and reading the instructions in game; interpersonal skills through problem-solving issues among members of the guild; science through movement and the physics involved in movement; social studies through navigating the politics of the various members.

A trip to the local farmers market is another example. School children might go on a trip to the market with a teacher who has an outcome-laden curriculum guide, leading children to learn about certain areas of the market. In comparison, unschooled children might go on a field trip to the same market and individually discover objects and ideas unique to their own perception, soaking up information naturally geared to their stage of development. Children learn subject matter without a particular sequence or plan. Yet they compile a storehouse of information that adds meaning and depth to knowledge they already have. Every experience adds to their learning; information need not be categorized or presented in order. It is "subjects divided by the bell" that is an artificial construct and not real learning.

Every child in school lives by the clock, buzzers dividing learning—or at least instruction—into categories by subject and time. Real learning is stopped short by the ringing of a bell when a class is over, when it's time for recess, or when it's time to go home. A child may be engaged and want to keep learning, but he is forced to quit—then forced to begin again the next day, whether he wishes to or not.

When people move as a group, every small task takes longer. When our family of seven goes on vacation, we move only as quickly as the slowest child and there is an incredible amount of waiting time. In school, though, the schedule is all-important. Meandering for learning's sake is not allowed—time is too tight; deviating from the schedule means not being able to fit in all the prescribed outcomes. This is probably why my children hate travel tours to this day: they can't meander and the schedule is not their own.

Unschooling puts all types of learning and resources on an equal footing; experiences considered "educational" and "junk" carry equal weight. As children age, they make surprisingly healthy choices: in their bedtimes, diets, their occupation of time, gaming limits, and educational attainment. Research supports this notion, for example, in food choice. We know that when we serve dessert and dinner on the same plate, when we don't elevate one choice as preferable to another, children will eat all the parts of their meal. (Satter, 2000) By the same token, if we don't give workbooks more importance than video games, children won't perceive our subtle judgment and will choose what is relevant to them at the time.

Children learn from curiosity, not standardized testing

Standardized testing is one way for schools to show accountability to taxpayers, government, and other stakeholders. Unschoolers and homeschoolers do not need testing—they are accountable to no one; responsible to no one except themselves. Because the learning in unschooling is often invisible, scattered, and not age- or time-graded, it is impossible to test for specific content at a specific point in time. The Concordia University study by Chang, 2011, may have had different results had they chosen to measure children at 18 instead of 10 years of age.

To unschoolers, it doesn't matter if the child studies Japanese warfare in Grade 3 or Grade 8. In school, children are tested on it in Grade 8, but what if the child is not interested in the topic until Grade 10? He would do better on the exam if he were very interested in the subject matter—or mature enough to intuit that studying the material for the test would result in the desired mark, even if he wasn't thrilled about the subject matter.

The school child will learn the material for a test, then instantly forget it when it is no longer needed, as described in a previous section about summer learning loss. If the information is so disposable, why should children be forced to learn it in the first place? If the child really needs to know about Japanese warfare for a job, or university course, or because he wishes to travel to Japan, he can study it then, when he actually needs it. Our children did not write government exams in Social Studies and Science in their earlier years because the tests include specific topics that they may have chosen not to learn about yet. They did write those exams in Grade 12, however; by then, the accumulation of knowledge over 18 years, and not just a single year, gave them the learning they needed to do well in the exam.

The individual learner recognizes the scope of information he needs, and when he needs it.

Unschooling invites intense concentration

Interruptions are constant in school. Learning stops suddenly when the bell signals a change of rooms, teachers, or subjects. Visitors come to class; the teacher is called out; intercom messages constantly interrupt the flow. Children who are keen to learn are annoyed by the interruptions of others who don't care to learn. Students must learn how to focus and concentrate.

Unschooling provides time and space for intense, unbroken concentration.

Critical thinking is encouraged

Large bureaucracies do not handle questioning well. They operate, by their very nature, on the contingent of obedience, unquestioningly toeing the party line. If there are too many disrupters, they get bogged down and lose time and efficiency.

Critical thinkers are disruptive because they interrupt the prescribed flow of content delivery. Classroom dissenters are often dealt with by being sent to detention or shamed into silence. They are punished for questioning.

All children should be critical thinkers. They should respectfully question everything they don't understand, from content to rules and regulations. Critical thinking is about gathering information, exposing embedded values and assumptions, breaking down data, and analyzing arguments.

Unschooling promotes questions without punishment.

Problem solving is encouraged

When schools have problems, teachers, principals, and support staff are expected to solve them. Children are rarely consulted. Yet problem solving is the most valued among the top ten skills the Financial Post looks for in their hiring process. (Financial Post,

2007) Most problem solving in the education system ignores the central stakeholder—the learner. Problems involving students are "solved" by using punishments and bribery, not by consulting and collaborating. Children are not asked to brainstorm solutions; they are rarely asked at all about their opinions on major decisions in which they are the affected stakeholders. Yet success in life is attained by solving problems. When win-win is always the goal, life becomes easier and healthier, with far less stress. Outside of the institution of school, with an adult's help, children are free to practice problem solving on a wide range of issues.

Initiative and grit is encouraged

School is an institution; it must have rules, routines, policies, procedures, and permissions. To run efficiently, it must adhere to those elements above all other considerations, including personalized learning. A student who wishes to do something outside of the norm is often shut down because of "liability issues," or "safety concerns," or just plain "policy." The beauty of unschooling rests in its very lack of these constraints. If your son wants to make a potato gun, let him! As long as it is safe, it can be done! Unschooling allows for yeses, instead of "No, you can't do that. It's against our policy."

Encouraging student initiative should be easy. I say "Yes!" to almost any learning opportunity. I want to reward inquisitiveness, not stifle it. We have only two rules: the endeavor must be safe, and they have to clean up their messes. Any activity that involves a measure of risk must be supervised by an adult. The kids are excited. They love to try. They learn best by experimenting and experiencing the results and consequences—good or bad!

Unschooling is multi-aged and interest-sorted

Children in schools are graded by age, not by interests or abilities. Thus, they are often corraled into the wrong group for their actual level. Some could go up a grade but are held back because of age policies. Some kids should repeat a year but are promoted because of system's belief that failure affects the child's self-esteem. Failing a child and having him repeat a year used to be commonplace in schools. This no longer happens. Children are assigned to grades based on age alone. They move ahead even if they have not mastered the year's curriculum, on the premise that peer culture can be cruel and being held back could subject them to bullying. Children in the same grade are not assessed on their progress; rather, they compared to each other and evaluated according to the class progress. This system itself invites bullying.

As well, children advanced in a particular subject area are not allowed to take a course that is more than one year beyond their age level. This is very unfair. If a child excels at math, she shouldn't be held back because of her age. If her interest and abilities demand a more complex challenge, she should have access to a course that matches her level of understanding. On the other hand, if a child needs help, she should be presented with customized learning materials to aid her, without making her feel inferior.

True personalized learning cannot be offered in same-grade classes. Learning must be as multi-age friendly as unschooling is.

No streaming or tracking

School children are sorted and ranked according to the government system's judgment and placement criteria at around age 15, or Grade 10, in North America; sooner in Europe. In some countries, children are streamed as early as age 10. This is wrong. Research consistently shows that children's brains do not develop their pre-frontal cortex and children do not develop their abstract thinking abilities until age 13 or 14. Thus, children are sorted even before they have demonstrated their capabilities.

Teachers make recommendations to parents on which courses their children should take to follow a certain track. Among tracks are the "work and employability" track, the "arts and humanities postsecondary" track and the "STEM postsecondary track." In Canada, children can move between the tracks quite easily by taking an extra course or two, but parents are often unaware that they have the final say on which stream their child enters. My son struggled with math. His teacher slotted him into the Work Math for Grade 10. I knew he could take the Arts Math and pushed for it; he did well. He then decided to go into STEM Math. With a lot of hard work, he succeeded, qualifying him to apply for a university program in Science. When children unschool, they are not streamed until they apply and write the entrance exams for postsecondary courses. They always have an equal chance to demonstrate their abilities and decide which course is right for them. Learners should always be able to stream themselves. No one else should. They know best what is right for them.

Unschoolers can delve deep into a topic

In schools, topics are broad and diluted. Schools teach wide and shallow in order to give bits of everything to their students. The goal is maximum exposure; time constraints do not allow for deep, involved learning. Children become masters of tidbits and experts on nothing. Deeper learning must be done on their own time. Schools pick and choose among topics. A child cannot possibly study every country within 12 years, so the system picks a few: Japan, Brazil, Peru, Greece. Why should the system choose? Why can the learner not choose?

Clearly, customization is the adult model. People are *not* masters of all topics. We specialize. The idea that children should need to know "a little bit about everything" is outdated.

Most children don't know what they want to do in life when they finish high school. Many blindly enter college or university without having had time to pursue their passions and narrow down their true areas of interest. They are urged to enter postsecondary to obtain a profession and make good money. But an engineer might have preferred to be a baker; a psychologist might have been happier as an artist; a teacher might have had a passion for medicine.

When children need to know something, they can consult their mobile devices; information is readily available. What they need more is to focus on their true passions, gaining a deep understanding of things that are important to them. Some parents augment school curriculum by focusing on kids' interests at night, as I initially did. This is called "afterschooling," but eventually you wonder why you are sending them to school for the best parts of the day, where they seem to learn nothing. You "afterschool," trying to help them learn what they really want to learn. But by that time, they are tired, cranky; they may not muster much enthusiasm even for a subject they are passionate about.

World War I and World War II are enormous subjects. When the world recently celebrated the contributions of World War I soldiers, my husband and I discussed the history of that war. I voiced my concern that although my oldest son had studied Canada's involvement in WWI when he was in Grade 11, the curriculum had since changed and the younger siblings would not learn about it at all. My husband Peter said that even in England not much was taught about either of the world wars. That surprised me, but he explained that because of the sheer quantity of history in Europe, schools can only cover so much and must pick and choose what to teach. Their history lessons mostly covered medieval England, and very little about the last century or two.

Schools everywhere pick and choose a few topics from many. In unschooling, students choose. They can go as deep as they wish, for as long as they want.

Unschooling gives them the time.

Unschoolers learn entrepreneurial skills

Schools can't teach how to run a business until university. Hence, many children may have art or products to sell, but not the business skills needed to do so. Success in business requires critical thinking, risk-taking, creative problem solving, listening skills, and initiative. Great communication and interpersonal communication skills are essential. Organization and record keeping require long hours, discipline, and responsibility. Success requires persistence—not taking a thousand noes to heart and pushing forward for the yeses. Success requires unwavering faith in a product or service in the face of naysayers. Success requires making mistakes and learning from them; rejigging a model, idea, or product until it's perfect.

A bureaucracy such as school does not teach how to operate a business or how to succeed in a competitive environment. Schools barely touch on the topic of financial literacy—indispensable knowledge in today's world, regardless of a person's choice of career or profession.

Many young unschoolers start businesses. They learn math, English, science, and social skills through the execution of the business.

Unschoolers have flexibility; they are encouraged to engage in entrepreneurial activity.

Unschooling grows creativity

Prescribed curriculum kills creativity. Play promotes creativity. One day, my daughter's Kindergarten class was doing an art project. The children cut pieces of fruit in half and dipped them in paint to make imprints on paper. As the parent volunteer, I was assigned a group of five children to supervise. I showed them the "template" to make the fruit art.

I watched as four children dipped the fruit into the paint. Most matched the colors—the lemon halves got dipped into yellow paint, the orange halves into orange paint, and so on. One little boy decided to dip his lemon half into blue paint. I watched in fascination as he swooshed his fruit in beautiful swirls all over his paper. He continued to do that with other fruits and other paint colors. Swooshes, not prints. Different colors. I thought, this kid is going to go far! Here is a real out-of-the-box thinker! The other children warned him that he was "doing it wrong." Apparently, indoctrination begins early! I told him that I loved his interpretation. We parent volunteers collected our groups' artworks and laid them on the table to dry. Twenty minutes later, I saw the teacher quietly look over the pieces while the children were engaged in another activity. She held out the swirled painting and asked the parent volunteers whose group it was from. I was instantly transported back to my own school days. Filled with fear, I raised my hand and managed to stammer out, "He's in my group. Isn't it beautiful?" She asked me to sit down with the child and show him how to redo the painting. "The paintings are to be displayed on the bulletin board outside the classroom and this one doesn't match the rest." When I protested that I would not be asking the creative child to redo his artwork, she asked another parent volunteer to do it. I never volunteered in that classroom again.

What do kids bring to Kindergarten? Creativity, curiosity, initiative, and lots of self-confidence. When their ideas get shut down enough times in the interest of adhering to the established curriculum, children give up. They acquiesce. Most of those lovely, spontaneous qualities are stifled out of them by Grade 3. They get quiet. It's easier for them to follow the norm than be forced into a do-over.

We need to consistently provide supportive environments that allow kids to come up with new ideas; we need to throw out the old model of force-feeding and regurgitation. Children should be encouraged to invent new outcomes, not conform to outdated ones. Templates are a crutch; kids are so much more creative without them. We need to teach kids to love learning for the joy of discovery—not to score an A on a test by giving the "right" answers. No one in the field of education denies that creativity is important; yet the reality is that creativity is often shut down in subtle but very clear ways: a child challenges the teacher's knowledge and gets a detention; a student reaches the correct answer on a test in a non-conformist way and it gets marked wrong. It happens frequently in math—a correct answer attained through an "incorrect" method.

Never has there been a more critical need for innovation as the primary rationale for education; the world's problems today demand it. Creativity—innovation—involves experimentation, risk-taking, failures. Failure is essential to the creative process, in forcing both trial after trial to perfect the end result, and the perseverance necessary to do so.

Our society badly needs innovators, engineers, architects, designers, researchers, inventors, thought-leaders, and scientists. Many will fail a thousand times before they come up with something useful. In the TED Talk entitled *Schools Kill Creativity*, Sir Ken Robinson defines creativity very simply as "original ideas with value." He says that creativity is even more important than critical thinking, because creativity invents new solutions to both old and new problems; solving problems critically *requires* creativity. When I asked Sir Ken what his thoughts were about unschooling, he replied, "Love it." (Robinson, 2013)

One of my favorite scenes in the movie *Apollo 13* is the one in which they tried to brainstorm how to fit a round hose onto a square fitting and ripped the cover off the flight plan to use it in the modified component. Protocol was thrown out the window in favor of creativity and the problem was solved. When my son was attending university, he had no car. He and a friend had purchased a sofa from a place about a mile from their house. They decided to carry it home! After a few hundred feet, they were tired. They resolved their dilemma by flagging down a pick-up truck and offering the driver $20 to carry them and the sofa the rest of the way. Creative problem solving works!

Howard Gardner, proponent of the theory of multiple intelligences, states that creativity is not an intelligence, but that there is creativity within each of his eight proclaimed intelligences: logical, linguistic, musical, bodily-kinesthetic, interpersonal, intrapersonal, natural, and spatial. Logical, linguistic, and spatial intelligences are measured in traditional IQ tests. The other intelligences are not as valued in school, as evidenced by the lack of standardized testing in those areas. (Gardner, 1983)

Poet Sheri-D Wilson says, "Everyone has a talent for something. It's just a matter of finding it. Creativity is about desire and curiosity and sometimes you just have to play around and see what happens." (Loney, 2012)

Everyone is creative. As we age, our ability and desire to be creative is often squelched. We are too tired to fail. We have too much at stake. When you ask little kids if they are creative, they will all say yes. Ask 10-year-olds and about half will answer yes. Ask adults and they may well say no.

Creative people take bits of information or materials around them and recombine them in new ways. Both right-brained and left-brained people are creative. MRIs carried out on subjects while engaged in creative tasks show that both sides of the brain are active. In "Brain Studies," published in *Social Cognitive and Affective Neuroscience*, author Lisa Aziz-Zadeh, assistant professor of neuroscience at the University of Southern California, states that MRIs can even pick up the "aha" moment. When people completed a puzzle, the emotional parts of their brains lit up, demonstrating the dopamine flood released by the pleasure of success.

My husband's engineering firm had many music-loving employees who got together once a year and put on a concert. They practiced during their lunch hours. Many of their songs were original. This same group later produced a visual arts show, combining their efforts in a completely different, but equally creative endeavor.

What is it about unschooling that especially nurtures children's creativity?

1. No plan, template, model, image or expectation is preconceived

Templates lead children down the tried and true path meant to result in a preconceived outcome. In unschooling, kids are encouraged to come up with original ideas.

2. **Resources and supplies**

Unconventional ideas sometimes benefit from resources and supplies not obtainable through the school supply systems. Unschoolers are in the enviable position of being able to purchase interesting materials for their projects, or even rummage through attics or scavenge through sewing rooms or garages to find things to complete their projects or fuel their creativity.

3. **Time**

Everyone knows that the brain needs water, nutritious food, and adequate sleep to function well. Exercise is also important. But to be creative, the brain also needs downtime. Children spend six hours a day in school, three hours being transported, and another three hours doing homework. They often have very little time to process their thinking and just "be." Yet this is critical. Freedom from the distractions of mobile phones, people, and screens is important in order for the brain to postulate, formulate, imagine, and percolate new ideas. People today do not have enough time to "veg out." Brains need to be able to relax and de-focus. To wander wherever their thoughts take them. Creative blocks happen; when they do, allowing the brain to relax is helpful. Often a resolution comes unexpectedly when we are not under pressure to force it.

I find that the six-hour road trip from Calgary to Saskatoon is a great time for me to think of new ideas, and I dictate them to a hands-free voice recorder. Many people do their creative thinking on the treadmill, or while in the shower, meditating, or lying awake in bed. An idea might wake them during the night. Some people feel more creative in the early morning, waking up refreshed after a good night's sleep; others late at night, with their brain in a relaxed and unfocused state. Curiously, those who routinely exercise their creativity are more likely to be extreme "morning" or "night" people.

4. **Mistakes are celebrated**

We have all seen little children try to hold a heavy project together with a little piece of tape or a spot of glue. It takes a lot of messing around to figure out what will work. I remember building a sugar cube castle with $27 worth of sugar cubes and some liquid glue. It was the wrong glue and melted the sugar into one gloppy mess. "Kids in school today don't learn such things because projects, materials, instruction, and outcomes are pre-planned and prescribed. Kids don't get a chance to be wrong." (Stephanie J, 2000)

When people are afraid of making mistakes, they refuse to let themselves entertain creative ideas. They overthink them and discard them. Ideas flow when they are not weighted in evaluation. That's why brainstorming with other people is helpful in coming up with creative solutions. The more ideas that are generated, the more likely it is that at least one of them will work.

In our family, when someone makes a mistake, we ask, "What did you learn from this?" Instead of developing a climate of blame and punishment, we forgive mistakes and encourage learning. Our society would be better if everyone did their best to support others' ideas and promote the ones that work.

I dream of a day when kids will win scholarships based not on academic averages, but on how many mistakes they have made, taken responsibility for, and creatively fixed!

5. Self-esteem is healthy

The overwhelming punitive peer environment in school can be heavily damaging to an individual's child self-esteem. Even the most popular kids are always on guard, afraid of making mistakes. Yet the ability to make mistakes and learn from them is an essential component of creativity and risk-taking. Kids with healthy self-esteem will take risks and not be afraid of failing. We need kids to be able to say, "Oh well. That didn't work. Let's try this..." The ability to pick themselves up and try again is critical to attaining success in their careers and in their lives.

For our family, the phrase, "I wonder if..." has been the best idea stimulator. No one is criticized for any idea, whether it is feasible or not. We all have enough self-esteem to let things go if they aren't working, and the freedom to recombine elements in a different way to try something a second time. The day my kids combined the elements of play-dough, sand, and water, my visiting friends were horrified because "it's just not done,"—yet my kids did it, had fun, and discovered the properties of breaded play-dough.

Unschooling allows children to play and explore during the school years, fostering creativity that a prescribed curriculum cannot. This is one of the most crucial reasons for re-examining our school system.

Unschooling eliminates cheating

The school system is the worst for drilling into kids the idea that mistakes are a bad thing. The entire system is based on grading to motivate kids, but in doing so, low grades punish them. On a test or project, they are not rewarded with marks for the time they spent or the effort they put in, nor is the quality of their learning assessed. They are marked negatively, on the basis of the mistakes they made. Ideally, all students should be marked and then given the chance to fix every marked item before the final assessment. That way, learning actually takes place and poor marks are not permanent. But that would be too time consuming.

More people learn from their mistakes than from their successes; mistakes, therefore, are critical to the learning process. Mistakes allow people to recombine or reconfigure elements. People must make bad decisions to learn that they are bad—and why. The consequence of marking by punishing mistakes is that kids will cover up their mistakes.

Covering up mistakes has unforeseen consequences that, at worst, can endanger lives—I don't want my child's brain surgeon to have cheated on her exams. At best, it shuts down creativity. Most commonly, it encourages the culture of cheating. Cheating is rampant in our schools. According to a survey of Canadian university and college students, 73 percent had cheated on written work in high school; 58 percent had cheated on a test. (CBC, 2016) A survey of 23,000 US high school students showed 51 percent had cheated on a test. (Huffington Post, 2012) When the majority of students cheat, something is wrong with the system.

There is no cheating in unschooling because there is no fierce competition for marks.

Parents, teachers, and caregivers learn too

We must continue our learning and our enthusiasm for learning throughout our lives. When we set an example for our children by following our own pursuits, by being curious, or by taking adult education courses, we stoke their enthusiasm for learning.

In unschooling, learning is caught, not taught.

Children have more time to read

School children are made to read one novel in English per grade. That's it. My informal poll of home education parents of various ages revealed amazing reading habits. Homeschooled children read from 10 to 40 novels in a year. Why? Because they had free time. Reading enhances ideas, discussions, world knowledge and provides pleasure. Reading is never bad, and with so many hours of free time, unschooling children tend to be voracious readers. Even boys read a lot. And not just graphic novels. Boys in school typically dropped reading in teen years due to the lack of really interesting adventure stories, although that genre has definitely grown. I've witnessed my teen boys read at least 15 books a year, both fiction and non-fiction. As young adults now finished with school, they continue to be avid readers.

Sleep grows children's brains

Time for sufficient sleep is a physical benefit of unschooling, but it also contributes hugely to academic performance. The natural sleep rhythms of young children in elementary school are early-to-bed, early-to-rise, which works well for an early morning start to school. However, when children get older, their circadian rhythm shifts to later-to-sleep, later-to-wake. Adolescents are sleep deprived because of early-hour starts, a critical factor affecting their performance in junior high and high school. Teens should be allowed to sleep longer in the morning; our society should adapt to their needs. My 16-year-old goes to bed at 1 a.m. after reading for an hour in bed every night. He sleeps until noon every day. I am certain it gives him an incredible advantage over children his age who have to get up at 7 a.m. to get to their classes on time. University kids have somewhat more flexibility in scheduling their classes around their need for sleep.

Reut Gruber of Montreal's McGill University and The Douglas Hospital Research Center led a study on children's sleep. She found that cutting back on children's sleep increases their loss of temper and makes them more likely to cry and become frustrated, all of which are barriers to learning. The study of 7 – 11-year-olds showed that more sleep led to better behavior. (Seaman, 2012) And we all might guess how it would affect pre-teens and teenagers!

We are at risk of high blood pressure, stroke, diabetes, heart disease, compromised immune systems and the propensity to gain weight when we don't get enough sleep. Dr. Stanley Coren, professor of psychology at the University of British Columbia (UBC) claims that we temporarily lose one point of IQ for every hour of sleep lost the night before. A report in the *Occupational and Environmental Medicine Journal* states that a person suffering from sleep deprivation can experience mental impairment similar to the effects of drinking a glass of wine. (Rainey, 2012) Yet most high-stakes exams for 18-year-old teens at the end of Grade 12 are held in the morning to facilitate scheduling, even though research shows that teens might do better if the exams were scheduled in the afternoon. Another example of the child's best interests not being the system's first consideration.

Kids eventually do have to prepare themselves for 8 a.m. workday starts, but not until they reach adulthood, when seven hours sleep a night is sufficient. When the time comes to adjust to a new schedule, they will.

Children who unschool can sleep in until noon or later. A full night's sleep benefits their developing brain cells.

8

Social Benefits of Unschooling

"Forced association is not socialization." — Anonymous

Bullying is minimized

Only two institutions in the world are exactly similar to school, with forced attendance and a definite hierarchy: prisons and mental institutions.

- All are compulsory. Members may not escape and they are forced to be there for a fixed number of years.

- All are hierarchical with a strata of rights, perks, control.

- In all cases, the hierarchy controls the lowest members of the strata by a system of rewards and punishments, both of which are forms of behavior control.

All impose on one's time.

School, jail, or mental hospital? (Paris, May 10, 2014)

A social order emerges from the stress they induce. Administration is at the top level and the student is at the bottom. Rankism creates stress for all levels involved. Bullying is a byproduct of rankism and is rampant in all schools and in all grades. Bullying causes stress and stress causes more bullying. Studies show that even rats under stress tend to bite other rats!

Bullying.org estimates that Canadian high schools experience 282,000 incidents of bullying per month. Some more serious incidents have led to teen suicides, the second leading cause of death among teens. (Press, 2012)

There are very few bullies in unschooling. Most parents do not bully their children. There is no top-down hierarchy, no social class system in this form of learning. Because the learner is free to choose his own path, the single biggest factor that impulses bullying—control—is eliminated.

Homeschooling communities include children that might be bullied in school because of physical, learning, behavioral, or emotional differences. Bullying occurs to some degree wherever there are groups of children. Bullying is never eliminated; it can occur in homeschooling as well but it is on a much smaller scale, and is more easily contained and dealt with, thanks to the involvement of caring adults. Homeschooling children are more closely coached on the respectful way to treat others with physical or mental differences.

When an instance of bullying does occur in the homeschool environment, parents are around to support both the child victim and the child perpetrator, as well as the hench-men and bystanders. They are generally able to avoid damage and turn the situation into a teaching moment.

In school, a single lunchtime supervisor is not enough to monitor and manage up to 200 children on the playground at the same time; bullying happens under the supervisor's radar. It occurs in the playground, in washrooms, on buses, on the walk home, and in the locker room. And aside from physical bullying that might be noticed and dealt with by an adult, these days, bullying is particularly pervasive in social media, and much harder to detect if the victim is not forthcoming. This kind of bullying at the very least eats away at a child's self-esteem and can have far more serious consequences.

Homeschooling parents don't have to wait until 4 p.m. or bedtime to hear about an instance of bullying from their child. And many homeschooled children, especially young ones, do not have mobile phones; it is so much easier for a parent to monitor any bullying experienced, or indeed instigated, by their child, and coach them accordingly in a loving and supportive way. Clearly, instances of bullying in a homeschooling environment are infrequent in comparison to those that occur in schools.

Carrie is the ultimate school bullying movie. Interestingly, there is very little difference in school relationships between the first movie in 1976 and the new release in 2014, except for the means of the bullying—technology and cyber bullying were featured in the second release. These new vehicles give opportunity for 24/7 bullying—incredibly stressful for young victims.

We used to think that bullies had low self-esteem. We now know that is not necessarily so. Bullies possess an uncanny sense of entitlement that makes them feel powerful when they put someone down. Education about bullying and prevention tactics such as posters and caring cards are not effective. Schools have always had bullying issues and will continue to have them unless and until they become truly voluntary, consensual, non-punitive, and non-hierarchical. The system must change fundamentally, instead of ignoring the cause of the problem while hanging up "We care" posters.

True self-esteem comes from real achievement, not from peers building each other up one moment, shooting each other down the next. Self-esteem is built through respectful relationships, first between parents and children, then between children, parents, teachers, and administrators. We must all commit to eradicate bullying and hurtful intention.

Many people think that homeschooling children shelters them from the real world. I believe that homeschooled children *are* exposed to the real world—under the sheltering guidance of adults acting in their children's best interests. In my unschooling presentations, I show two photos. The first shows a tree that is strong and tall and has beautiful branches; I comment that now that the tree is grown, it is strong enough to withstand the strongest winds and fiercest storms. The second is a picture of a gnarled, twisted tree, with its trunk split and bent to a 90-degree angle by the forces of nature. I make the analogy that children are like trees. Their self-esteem, dignity, wonder, and love of learning must be protected—by homeschooling parents—until they have grown strong and straight enough to resist the negative influences and effects of peer pressure, bullying, overpowering teachers, and other forces do not have their best interests at heart. Sheltering and staking the tree is necessary for a child to grow strong. As parents, our job is to safeguard our child's mind, body, and spirit until he is ready to do it on his own. Bullying is not something that children can handle on their own.

That being said, bullying certainly also occurs between adults in a hierarchical system. As the author of *Dropout: How schools are failing our kids (and what we can do about it)*, Leslie Gavel says that bullying occurs between teachers and parents and principals and students and government in a system that is laden with rankism. In my personal experience, bullying occurs in homeschooling as well, because it still involves the system—not so much among children, but among adults. Parents are still under the control of the supervisor, who is under the principal, who is under the area supervisor, the school board, the government. I have had school board principals ask me to sign documents without giving me a copy. I have had verbal pressure, resistance, and the silent treatment (a month to respond to my emails) from administrators and government in response to my insistent demand to exercise my rights and those of my children. Schools can refuse to register certain children. Government can pull schools' funding and accreditation or worse, force a time-consuming and stressful audit. In a hierarchical system, this kind of bullying is the means of control.

I repeat what I said in an earlier chapter: know your rights and insist on them! Go all the way up the food chain if you have to. The order of appeal is teacher first, then principal, area director, government, ombudsman, and media. Get everything in writing. Study the government regulations, because often, the school or home education supervisor acts to protect the institution and its funding, while parents act to protect the best interests of their child. Do not take anything at face value. Look it up. Then go to bat for your child—in either system.

I know that there are many schools, teachers, and administrators that are warm, nurturing and caring with the children we place in their hands, but I also know that there are many that are not.

There are few, if any, bullies in unschooling.

Parents have less administration and more interaction time with children

We have already discussed that teachers' workloads are increasingly complicated by taking on a parenting role. Being a teacher in North America's schools today is a tough job. Teachers are constantly pushed and pulled between parents, children, principals, and curriculum demands; they must be competent, professional, and respectful to all. They must have a huge capacity for patience, tact, self-control and knowledge.

Many teacher friends state that teachers are being burdened with too many duties that have little to do with the classroom. This is bad for children. The more time that teachers spend on administrative tasks, the less time they are able to spend teaching children. Students with special needs were integrated into the classroom along with teacher's aides to assist them. Then funding cuts eliminated the aides. The special needs students are still in the classroom; teachers are now on their own, with very little assistance in such a great responsibility. I cannot think of a profession that expects so much of an adult, other than nursing and parenting.

Class sizes vary, but there can be up to 30 students in upper elementary classes and up to 40 students in high school, all with diverse learning needs. Teachers have to cope with as many different temperaments, personalities, learning styles, physical needs, and IQ levels as there are students. They have to plan lessons and prepare the materials to implement interactive learning. They have to give assignments, mark, and record them. Teachers have to cope with demands for benchmarking ESL (English as a Second Language), technology infusion, curriculum renewal, alternative assessment, project planning, group work, inclusion, and differentiated instruction for many learner profiles. They have to complete paperwork for IPP's (Individual Program Plans), lesson planning, report cards; return parents' phone calls and emails, and conduct interviews. Teachers are expected to supervise lunchtimes and coach sports or run clubs and extracurricular activities. The average teacher's work week can reach 56 hours with instruction, marking, planning, and supervision duties. (Calgary Herald, 2012) That is just the academics. Then they have to spend time coaching and listening to students' emotional and social concerns, in addition to their academic concerns. No wonder they burn out.

In unschooling, the teacher or parent doesn't have to plan, deliver, or mark. The adult observes the learning that takes place organically. It's enjoyable and exciting. What parent or teacher doesn't love it when a child gets that "Aha!" moment?

Unschooling provides much more time for family and interests

School has a huge impact in a children's lives. Other than sleeping, no other activity occupies such a large proportion of their days. School consumes time that might be used for exploring interests or spending time with family. The average child spends 180 days per year in school—12,000 hours of his life! That is six hours a day, not including bussing time. Schools are assigning heavier homework loads at a younger age. A child sees more of his teacher than his own mother and father. Peers interact more than siblings do. Yet research shows that nothing is more critical to a child's health and well-being than family, which should be front and center in a child's life, even in the teen years. (Neufeld, 2004)

The assumption that children and adolescents cannot decide on their own what to read or what to learn or what to do with their time is imbedded in schools' philosophies; that they need constant supervision to stay on task; that when left to their own devices, they will get into trouble or waste their time on mindless pastimes. They insist that children need the system to control and fill their time. So, children's presumed incompetence becomes a self-fulfilling prophesy—they become convinced they can't learn without a teacher. They become passive machines: "Fill me up with knowledge; tell me what to do; give me something to occupy my time; entertain me!" Children lose their autonomy and the personal responsibility for organizing their time.

Time: it is the holy grail for families. We need time to nurture relationships among siblings, parents, grandparents, friends, and extended family. Our local high school newsletter admonished in the August 2006 issue, "Please understand that our school schedule is important and please respect it by scheduling extracurricular activities and family time accordingly." In other words, school is of supreme importance and all other activities, including family time, should take second place.

The traditional school system tends to shut parents out. If parents are happy fundraising or photocopying worksheets, then the school welcomes them. But parent volunteers actually looking for effective participation in the classroom are problematic. Teachers must provide something for the parents to do and supervise them, often adding to their workload. And the volunteering parent cannot bring their child's siblings into the class-room; among other reasons, liability is an issue and insurance coverage could be voided. To be involved in your child's school, you can join the PTA (Parent Teachers Associa-tion) or Parent Council, but you are rarely permitted into the classroom.

Often kids will earn a spare or two by working ahead or taking a summer course. But school policies do not allow the student to use the "spare" time as "spare time!" They may not be permitted to spend that spare at home with family or in school working on personal interests. My son actually had to take a formal course to fill a spare because the school's policy dictated that Grade 11 students could not have more than one spare, and Grade 12s no more than two. The rationale was that kids with "so much" free time are aimless and can get into trouble. So much for personalized learning and family time.

Unschooling supports family involvement in the entire learning process. Babies, toddlers, and preschool-age siblings participate in family learning activity. No one is left out. Every child learns at his own pace and level of understanding.

Even when they are not actively learning together, families have time to do other things—go for walks, run errands, read, watch videos, and definitely have a family dinner together—*every* night. Research shows that the children in families who eat meals together have fewer behavioral problems in later years. Children of families who dine together perform better academically and have a lower risk of developing depression, substance abuse, and obesity or eating disorders. (Warren, 2017) Yet in many homes, eating even one meal a week together is difficult because family members are going in too many different directions during the supper hour.

Many homeschooling activities are scheduled during the day because parents prefer to keep evenings for the family instead of crazily running around to venues and activities where only one sibling participates.

Unschooling maximizes family time.

Peer culture is minimized

"Yes, my kids are socialized. I lock them in the bathroom every other day, beat them up and steal their lunch money," says a homeschooling mom.

In school, peer culture rules. School is most efficient when delivered by a few teachers to a lot of kids. This is economy of scale, not best learning practices. Kids are age-graded into peer groups. From the ages of 5 - 18, kids are ruled by peer culture and develop strategies to cope with the mandatory togetherness. They cling to peers even when they don't particularly like them—they feel it's better to face the unknown with another person than to go it alone.

Children should freely choose whom they wish to associate with, not be pressured into convenient relationships. This becomes ever more important as they grow. Peers, like inmates, can provide buffers against institutional life and make it more palatable by joking, supporting, and commiserating, but they can also be a source of stress. Peer pressure compels kids to fit in by wearing the right clothes, owning the right phone, and conforming to a behavior.

Even children who want to resist peer pressure often cannot. Children socialized in warm, structured homes can still be pushed into doing things they really don't want to do. Peer pressure can lead them to risk taking part in binge drinking, drugs, sex, shop-lifting, vandalism, pranks, and crime. Kids don't often think past the instant gratification of peer approval. They don't think about safety, consequences, or future ramifications. The immediate impact on the pleasure centers of their brains overrides their sense of caution. (McMahon, 2015) Group behavior studies show that when peer groups discuss risk, the voices of reason can easily be drowned out by the louder voices that clamor for validation and acceptance. Group mentality inhibits the instinct to help someone in need. One study looked at bystander behavior when a person was injured. A single by-stander would call for help 70 percent of the time, but only 40 percent of the time while in a group. Group mentality tends to make people think that someone else will take care of it, a phenomenon known as the "bystander effect." (Beilski, 2015)

Because children spend so many of their waking hours at school, their peers are the major influence on them there, although parents remain the primary influences on the home front. Peers, by their very nature, are not nurturing, not like parents and adults are. A child's close friend can be nurturing, but the peer group on the whole is not. I grant that peers can have positive as well as negative effects, but there is no denying that the sheer amount of time peers spend together in close contact is enormous. (Neufeld, 2004)

In unschooling, family is the front and center "peer group" in the formative years and provides a far healthier environment for raising children.

Children are encouraged to stand out rather than fit in

Schools house a huge number of children. Because they are emotionally too young to understand that it is okay, even preferable, to be an individual, they cling together and bond through conformity. The pressure to fit in is wielded through the school norms of dress code, such as uniforms or certain types or styles of clothing; speech patterns such as prefixing everything with the word "like"; similarity in the look of school work, making all projects look or sound alike; and tastes in music, hair styles, jewelry, colors, bikes, and many other attributes and possessions.

Children who do not fit in are socially ostracized, if not bullied. This social isolation adds to a child's stress and should not be considered a necessary rite of passage. Children who grow up feeling accepted are socially and emotionally healthy.

In unschooling, a group of children at an organized activity might include a child in a wheelchair, a boy wearing purple hair and pink glasses, a girl transitioning to become a boy, or a child with Asperger syndrome. The diversity in homeschooling and unschooling groups of children is amazing; children are encouraged by both peers and adults to express their individualism. The principal of my school board once asked my 14-year-old son, "What do you want to be when you grow up?" He replied, "I'm already being it."

Unschooling provides optimal diversity in socialization

"Every single one of my daughter's report cards said, 'She spends too much time socializing in class.' Now that we homeschool, that won't be a problem anymore. She can socialize all day!" says a mom in a homeschooling group.

It may be argued that peers provide a good source of socialization. However, socialization in the real world involves more than daily association with an artificially formed same-age group. Children need to learn how to socialize in their own neighborhoods, communities, or cities, and thanks to internet, in the global community. Basic socialization skills are required to chat with a neighbor over a backyard fence—or emailing with someone from China.

Kids need a sense of belonging and engagement. They can find that full-time in family and community. They can learn and work with others in social institutions such as clubs and groups, or by volunteering. They do not need a full-time quasi-social institution such as school to socialize and to feel a sense of belonging. In fact, without caring adults to ensure all kids are included in school social groups, school can make someone feel very much an outsider.

Concrete walls and wire fences isolate school children from real life, family interactions, community involvement, workplace interactions, and diverse populations. As an adult, I have many different kinds of friends. Children also need to be exposed to people of different cultures, ages, religions, identities, genders, nationalities, sexual orientations, and disabilities; they cannot do this when they are in school, removed from the real world.

Unschooling children interact more with the community by doing errands with their parents, going on field trips, and volunteering. They truly experience the community's rich diversity.

Socialization is better learned in home and community, rather than in an institution

Children are socialized by four agents in society: parents, school, communities, and media, but most people think that school is the only socialization agent. Yet when pressed, most people would admit that a large children's playground with minimal supervision is not the ideal way to teach children to get along with and enjoy others. Kids in school are free to socialize during recess, on the busses, and at lunch time. Anyone who has ever been a bus monitor or lunchroom supervisor will know that the "socialization" consists mostly of teasing, bragging, one-upmanship and bullying. Not much conversation, listening, or caring comments go on in a room full of school-age children with few or no adults. Let's look at where social tools *are* learned:

Manners are first learned at home as toddlers.

Sharing allows others the use of one's possessions, space, and resources; it is taught at home from a very young age and continues throughout childhood.

Teamwork—negotiating within a group, taking turns, and working toward a common goal can be taught within the family through activities, homeschool groups, projects, and video gaming.

Kindness is shown by empathizing with friends, offering help, volunteering—in fact, through almost every activity in which we interact with others. "Everyday philanthropy" doesn't make newspaper headlines, but it is the bread and butter of what makes our cities, communities, and societies good places to live and teaches our kids to be ethical citizens. Unschooling allows children plenty of time to shovel their neighbors' walks, mow their lawns, walk their dogs, run errands, and volunteer at places such as food banks and homeless shelters.

Conversation and discussion are skills best practiced out-and-about in public. Play dates and entertaining visitors are great opportunities for children to hear and learn the conventions of adult conversation. Let's not forget the dinner table—it's a living classroom for learning about listening and conversing!

Good sportsmanship is about learning how to win without gloating and how to lose graciously, remaining optimistic and upbeat. It's a difficult skill to learn, and an invaluable one to possess. Any kind of competitive activity teaches this skill.

Cooperation and collaboration, helping out or hanging out with a group or team is a staple in many school curriculums and can also be learned at home through sports, field trips, home chores and activities, video gaming, volunteering, and traveling. Simply living in a big family demands cooperation on a daily basis. Joining a common-interest group such as a writing club or Minecraft entails and hones cooperative and collaborative social skills.

Problem solving employs empathy, conflict resolution, the fine art of negotiation, and finding solutions; it is best learned through relationships built with family, friends, work, and community or organizational groups.

A study by a Canadian homeschooling group found that 67 percent of homeschooled adult respondents said they are "very happy," as opposed to the general population's 43 percent. (Cummings, 2013)

Personally, I think the peer culture of school is the worst type of socialization. The person best able to teach a 15-year-old boy how to be a man is not another 15-year-old boy. It is an adult man.

Unschooled children are just as socialized as other children. Perhaps more so.

Unschooling promotes close friendships

Parents of homeschooling families are commonly asked, "What about socialization?" We hear it so often, we want to gag. Curiously, many people are fine with the academic achievement of homeschoolers but worry that children who do not interact daily with same-age peers will lack the necessary social skills to grow into a well-rounded citizen.

When people ask, "What about socialization?" they don't mean, "How will my child learn to be a decent, compassionate, communicative adult with healthy relationships?" What they do mean is, "How will my child find friends?"

This is a valid concern. But first, friends do not always come from school. Children thrown together in age-specific groups do not necessarily get along with each other; they have different temperaments, cultures, and gender role expectations. Friends may be found everywhere in a child's life, not just at school. Clubs, sports teams, churches, interest-based classes, and neighborhoods are great places to meet a variety of diverse friends.

Second, children are more in need of adults than they are of peers. One friend is all a child really needs; they don't need a whole classroom full of friends.

Third, there is a myth, unsupported by research, that children exposed to negative socialization behaviors, such as bullying, sarcastic comments, teasing, etc., learn how to deal with such negativity better as they grow older. Research proves the opposite: a child who has been exposed to minimal bullying and teasing grows into adulthood with long-term self-esteem and self-confidence, while early exposure to nasty socialization leaves lifelong scars. The solution is to have a lot of adults around to monitor negative socialization and gently correct it, as well as to model assertiveness, positive confrontation skills, conflict resolution skills, kindness, manners, and empathy.

Whether a child is educated at home or in a physical or online school, the following checklist may help to determine whether their social skills are up to par. In fact, many adults could use a brush-up on these basics!

Social skills checklist

A person with good social skills...

- Greets people with a "Hello," and a handshake; asks them how they are and listens to the response.

- Can start a conversation by noticing a detail.

- Maintains eye contact.

- Smiles and nods while listening.

- Respects other people's personal space. In North America, it's a periphery of about 18 inches.

- Asks questions, listens, and responds after listening.

- Gives opinions that are generally positive and upbeat.

- Never criticizes other people.

- Gives his own ideas, opinions, and personal anecdotes rather than those of other people.

- Talks for 15 seconds, then listens while the other person talks for about the same length of time.

- Doesn't talk too much about himself but does share enough that the other person has something to ask him about; visibly shows interest in the other person.

- Is not distracted from a conversation by electronic devices or other people.

- Doesn't interrupt conversations and waits for the proper moment to interject.

- Can interpret visual and auditory clues, such as expressions, voice tone, and gestures, to gauge people's moods; exceptionally skilled listeners empathize with others and encourage them to share.

- Encourages others when they talk about their woes.

- Exits a conversation by saying "Thank you, it was nice speaking with you," and "Good-bye."

- Uses "Please," "May I," and "Thank you," as well as "I'm very sorry."

- Asks permission to use others' belongings.

- Asks for advice when unsure of how to handle a situation.

- Knows what constitutes unacceptable public behavior, such as swearing, picking noses, and passing gas.

- Knows when it is appropriate to not speak.

- Politely and respectfully uses "I" statements, beginning with "I think," "I feel," "I would like," or "I am disappointed," to express opinions and assert needs.

- Initiates cooperation to find win-win solutions when there is a difference of opinion or plans.

- Knows his own limitations and is comfortable saying "No, thank you," to requests.

- Shares, takes turns, and offers help to people in need.

- Asks consent before touching or giving a hug.

- Knows the different levels of conversation and which is appropriate for particular audiences and situations. For example, level one is making small talk for strangers, level two is sharing facts with acquaintances, level three is sharing beliefs and opinions with friends and finally, level four is sharing feelings with family and intimate friends.

- Does not feel lonely in solitude; knows when he wants to be alone and when he wants to be with other people.

- Queues in public lineups and does not let friends join his space in line.

- Can find common ground for conversation with people of different ages, cultures, religions, genders, and social status.

It's important to remember that most of these skills are learned in the school-age, teen, and emerging adult years. It takes a lot of practice and comes with time. Children don't need a whole plethora of friends to learn socialization; at least one good friend and at least one supportive adult are enough to help them master socialization skills.

My adult children have completed their university years and all three are still close with the home-educated friends they grew up with, even though they have followed different paths. Their friendships were cemented based on real liking and true understanding of each other, not on being thrown together in a classroom.

Respectful questioning is encouraged

"Always question everything. Learn something! Never stop!" said Euripides. Most top CEOs have the uncanny ability to always question things. How does that work? What makes that run? Why is that so? As a parent, I often get tired of questions. I'm sure teachers do too. We are human. Sometimes we just want to say, "Do it because I said so." or "Because it just is." "Never mind." We, as adults, welcome questions when we have the time to explore a subject. However, teachers are overburdened.

Kids should be rewarded for respectful disagreement, dissent, and questioning meant to satisfy their curiosity. Many times, they are not purposefully being disagreeable—they just want to know! Especially when it comes to rules for the sake of having a rule and not for a true purpose. Asking questions is not heckling. It is truly seeking answers.

Unschooling encourages asking questions.

Unschooling is collaborative, not hierarchical

There are clear divisions between the weak (students) and the powerful (the system). School is the first place outside the home where a stranger exercises power over children. Children are often denied their basic desires: to answer a question, to go to the bathroom, or get food or drink; to ask a question the teacher doesn't have time for, to express a thought, to chat with a friend. No one asks a child's consent—the child is told what to do. But the child is always asking other people's consent when her needs are not being met.

Children rarely complain about school. Children learn quickly that rewards come to those who follow the rules and toe the line. Children obey teachers more than they obey homeschooling parents for two reasons: they are more intimate with their parents, and they are with parents for the long term. Teachers are unknown quantities and they are only with the child for a year. Parents are familiar and share a family history with children.

But don't children have to learn to respect authority? Of course, they do. There are many hierarchical institutions in society that kids must learn to respect, but the responsibility for teaching children respect is in the realm of good parenting, not in that of academic education. Many workplace cultures are now based on collaboration, team-building, and consensus rather than blatant hierarchy. Again, in collaborative workplaces, authority comes from experience, knowledge, and sharing rather than from the power of rank.

When unschooling groups form, the supervising adult is not the boss of the group but the facilitator, and helps the group to function smoothly. She helps the group to move forward with their projects and acquires resources for them. Children in the group are encouraged to learn from each other. In my daughter's writing group, they would read samples of their writing out loud and offer each other support and valuable feedback. Some of the girls would happily tutor or work alongside those who could use help. Of course, there were kids who were not on task and chose to spend the whole time laughing and gossiping, but for them, perhaps it was the right thing to do at that time.

Unschooling is democratic, respectful, and collaborative.

Unschooling promotes self-improvement over competition

The school system is full of contradictions. Children are grouped in large classes with strangers, even possible enemies, yet they are expected to relate harmoniously. They are expected to cooperate and help each other but then are placed in competition for marks on a Bell Curve. Schools promote conformity and submission—yet it is individualism that is valued in our society. (Gray, 1994)

In unschooling, the focus is on community rather than the individual, and unschoolers learn to cooperate, share, and help. Children are afforded the same respect and dignity as adults, even though they have less experience and knowledge. Community is emphasized in learning and in practice. Conflict is normal, even in unschooling, but the adults model the help and behavior the children need as examples.

In unschooling, there are no marks; there is only learning for learning's sake. There is neither competition nor reward for a "being an 'A' student"; Bell Curve grading is unnecessary. Traditional grading in school breeds contention, not collaboration—yet in the real world, the ability to work as a team is the highly valued skill. Only a certain number of students in schools get scholarships and awards. Not only does this breed cheating, but also a win-at-all-costs mentality. The world needs collaborative leadership, not competition. "The world needs to hand out more kindness awards instead of economic or achievement awards," says Sandra, an unschooling mom of three.

Unschooling promotes leadership over obedience

School teaches kids to be good, obedient followers. Not all children can be leaders. But teaching good work habits is as important as teaching content, and in our school model, that means the child obeying his first "boss"—the teacher.

Although the terms are negative, our society acknowledges that forced obedience and the oppressive use of power are sometimes needed, or rather, perceived as needed, in large institutions such as the military, schools, offices, hospitals, airports, and many others. It's distasteful, so we don't talk about it. Schools have two curriculums: the academic one and the hierarchical one I have already referred to earlier as hidden curriculum. It is often used to refer to schools teaching not so much content, but how to be obedient and compliant citizens.

A "good" student is one that pays attention and follows the teacher's direction. Although schools promote student leadership outside the classroom in projects or volunteering endeavors, it is not encouraged within the classroom because it is seen to challenge the teacher's authority. The teacher is the leader in the classroom and there is no room for another. A class clown is a leader in a way, but one that is at odds with the teacher. A good student pays attention in class, does his homework even if he has mastered the material, raises his hand in class discussions, and does not disrupt the class by asking too many questions. A good student may not be smart but tries hard. Schools, like prisons or mental institutions, reward obedient behavior.

A child's initiative and strategic thinking are not welcome in the classroom. My son's Grade 12 Biology course included 20 assignments that were worth only eight percent of the final mark. After evaluating the workload from those 20 assignments, he chose not do them because he was already getting great marks on tests and exams. However, his teacher insisted that he do them anyway because she had spent the time and effort to create them—and how dare he question her teaching methods! She felt that he was challenging her authority and gave him a lower mark on the course because of it. Thank goodness for the diploma exams that he aced; because they were worth an objective 50 percent, he pulled up his final mark.

In parenting classes, I often had parents that were there by court order. It was forced learning. Their bodies were there, but not their minds. They would come in and sit down, text or surf the internet on their phones, sleep, or tune out. We are forbidden to give marks in adult education. We can only report attendance. Perhaps schools should do that.

Children must learn to respectfully question their instructors, regardless of the authority they hold. Curiosity demands unrestrained questioning.

Children need and should press for explanations within a safe environment such as unschooling, where a questioning attitude is encouraged, not stifled.

Unschooling grows a healthy work ethic

"If kids don't have to go to school if they don't want to, where will they learn a good work ethic?" This is a common question asked of unschoolers. Like the "Where will they find friends?" question, it assumes that the only place to learn a good work ethic is in an institution. Children learn discipline by participating in life. When they sign up for lessons, volunteer work, and other activities, they are informed about the requirements and asked whether they are ready to commit to it for at least the first three sessions, to give it an honest try. They might commit to joining Girl Guides, soccer teams, and video gaming guilds. Many times, my kids didn't feel like going to an activity they had committed to; as a good parent, I encouraged them to go, and invariably they were happy they had gone. Our family philosophy was to always "default to going" because otherwise we would never know what we missed; our children accepted this.

All of the Team of Thirty had jobs. They all made it to early university classes. When my kids got their first jobs, they did not struggle with getting up early, even after all those years of sleeping in. They were fine getting up at 5 a.m. to be at work by 6 a.m. or getting up at 6 a.m. to make an 8 a.m. university class. They never called in sick when they weren't. Kids will meet the requirements that their commitments dictate. We don't have to spend years "preparing" them for the workplace.

Unschoolers learn good habits by example and through their own experience. When they need to show up, they will.

Unschooling discourages consumerism

"Our schools teach our children early to chase after money as their main goal in life. We breed addictions of substances and gambling and shopping by promoting lifestyles of consumerism, distraction, and obsession with external sources of satisfaction, rather than encouraging each other to simplicity and attentiveness to our genuine deeper needs." says Alfie Kohn, educational futurist at a conference. (Kohn, 2009) He believes that our traditional school system is primarily concerned with grooming skilled workers that are unquestioning, that follow the status quo, and that work hard to keep corporate North America's profits high. Get great marks, go to university, get a high-paying job, and buy, buy, buy. The goal is job preparation, which is good, but education should also be a preparation for the enjoyment of all that life has to offer—travel, art, poetry, music, and so much more.

Schools promote consumerism in various ways: through fundraising efforts such as pizza days, for example, and selling chocolate bars, gifts, plants, and other items to fund educational basics. This pressures kids to sell—or at least, get their moms or dads to sell—an ever-increasing number of such items in their workplaces so the child can earn a prize for the most sales!

Schools have also considered accepting corporate sponsorship—funding in exchange for putting a company logo on materials, classroom naming rights, etc., but the concept is distasteful to a public that thinks corporations will abuse the relationship by indoctrinating students and interfering with the "unbiased" curriculum. This is a reasonable concern, given that children younger than eight years cannot differentiate between advertising and unbiased information. But companies often get in anyway by providing free branded teaching guides, classroom supplies, and sports and music equipment—many useful teaching items are branded, providing low-key advertising for the sponsor. "Petro Pete" is a book character that has flooded Oklahoma classrooms with teaching guides, subtly influencing children toward a pro-oil bias. (Zou, 2017) At annual teachers' conferences, companies hand out bagfuls of goodies, logos perfectly visible, to be used in classrooms. Commercialism violates the trust between student and teacher.

The very nature of peer groups promotes consumerism. Dress "codes" and phone models encourage kids to want what their peers have. I believe that children younger than 13 do not need a mobile phone; they do need one when they begin to travel alone on public transit. Yet peer pressure demands they have one. Packed lunches must meet a certain standard. If the whole class is patronizing a ski resort, your child doesn't want to be the only one who can't afford to go. Even graduation costs about $100 a plate! We could not afford to take our entire family of seven to one child's graduation at that price.

Yet we stuck out like a sore thumb when we chose to attend only the ceremony and not the expensive hotel dinner. Needless to say, we opted out of the limousine, flowers, tux, and many other unnecessary "necessities." Education is about learning, not about buying stuff.

Back-to-school sale ads depict relieved parents giddy over the thought of their children once again spending most of their days in school and away from them. How sad. We need to shield children from insipid consumerism and protect family values. We have the most control over that within a family setting, not in a school. At home, children are not judged on what they wear or whether they have the latest gadget. They can wear flood pants or holey shirts, and it's all okay. Homeschooled peers are quite an accepting bunch.

Unschoolers can opt out of consumerism because we want to raise children to value relationships rather than stuff.

Learning is valued over status-seeking

When I spoke to friends in Europe about unschooling, I discovered a peculiarity: in Europe it's not the learning that matters, but the reputation of a particular school! Listing the name of a recognized, high-status school on a resume is very important in landing that first job. If "taught by Mummy" is listed on the resume, the child will go nowhere! Connecting with peers who have influential or powerful parents is endorsed and encouraged, as part of the allure of private school is the formation of the strategic relationships necessary for entering and advancing in the professional world. This status-conscious state has been around a long time and will not go away in the foreseeable future; however, with the undeniable and unstoppable growth of online learning and virtual schools, the status chasing may lessen over time, as online relationships are more difficult to initiate and maintain.

In unschooling, relationships are formed based on the healthy goal of friendship and shared interests, not career-climbing.

Siblings grow up close and remain close through adulthood

We will end this chapter with homeschooling's biggest social benefit of all—close family and sibling relationships. All members of the Team of Thirty mentioned that their sibling relationships were closer than those of their school-educated friends, and that sibling bonds continued in their adult years. Children who do not grow up in an age-segregated us-versus-them learning environment do not think of siblings as unsuitable playmates. In school, grade sixes only mix with grade sixes. At home, children mix with all ages, including siblings. They are not conditioned to think it is uncool to do so. So, children babysit and play with their younger siblings. They tag along with their older siblings. They hang out with adults. They play with babies. My 24-year-old son will build a computer together with his 13-year-old sibling. The other siblings play computer games over the internet as a team, even though they live in different cities. They tutored each other while attending universities miles apart. These relationships continue throughout their lives.

Of course, all children encounter conflict at some point in a relationship. I remember one of my children being angry with a sibling; for a week, he played computer games next to his sister—but with his back to her instead of side by side! Some days, when the fighting got really bad, we thought we might want to give them to the school so there would be less to squabble over. However, when kids get to school, they become distanced from their siblings. They won't take the bus together, hang out at lunch together, or do homework together. It is not cool to hang out or even say "Hi" to a younger sibling in the hallway.

What are the long-term benefits of close sibling relationships? You get young children playing board games and Lego, making a puppet theater, building a fort, and many other activities as they grow together. I have five children in an age span of 11 years. They all play with each other when they are home, or game together when one is away at university.

Here are some activities that our children did:

- Play video, computer, and board games together; even living in different cities, they connect on Discord to chat and play.

- Accompany the family to airports and bus stations to welcome home or say good-bye to an out-of-town sibling.

- Go to the theater or binge-watch a Netflix series together.

- Go camping or travel together, whether close by or overseas.

- Share in family dinner around the table every night. When they are away studying, we Skype them in on a laptop and they bring their cooked meal to their screen and "sit" at the table and chat with us. They participate in family debates over current issues.

- Drive each other to work and appointments. Meet for lunch at the university.

- Go to restaurants together with parents and their friends. Go to lunch and each other's clubs together with friends.

- Attend teen and adult parties at home.

- Help with renovations and other family projects.

- Edit and give helpful suggestions on each other's university essays that they circulate via email. One son even proofread my last book, and his sister proofread his Atlas Shrugged scholarship contest essay.

- Help the younger high school siblings with online work and sometimes help teach the course.

- Play League of Legends, Heroes of the Storm, Roblox, Overwatch, World of Warcraft, Planetside, Starcraft 2, Mafia, and Minecraft together as a team. Two of my sons play a long-term game called Lacuna Expanse with their dad. Play board games such as Dungeons and Dragons (and dress the part!), Settlers of Catan, Poker, Life, and Scrabble.

- Cook and bake together.

- Go to the park and toss a football, baseball, or frisbee; work out together at the gym.

- Teach a younger sibling a new language for the fun of it.

- Go to church with the family and attend friends' or family members' funerals.

- Vote together, volunteer together, and give blood together.

- Drive each other to school or university when they are running late. Once, my daughter missed the bus and woke up my son to have him drive her to the train. Instead, he drove her all the way to her destination, because he cares about her.

- Embark on projects together: build gaming computers, make candles, laser cut art pieces, make furniture, build electronics projects, decorate a Christmas tree, work on a Beakerhead project.

When my husband and I went to Peru for our 25th wedding anniversary, one of our sons who was away studying surprised his four siblings by coming home to spend a week-end with them. The three eldest cooked and went to the pub together. They all played cards and games together. One son drove the other back to his out-of-town university.

These kinds of interactions usually come much later in life for school children, after grown-up siblings have forgiven each other for school-age meanness. Such interaction is rare in teen and young adult years, but it does happen with unschooled children because it has always been their norm. Family is still the best social structure for raising kids, although in some families, it is getting squeezed out in favor of academic progress. We must protect and nurture our family relationships over the long term. Pat Farenga, author of *Teach Your Own*, said, "Don't sacrifice family closeness on the altar of education."

Unschooling promotes lifelong sibling relationships.

9

Emotional Benefits of Unschooling

"An education ministry has 700,000 students, a school board has 150,000 students, a principal has 600 students, a teacher has 40 students and your child has you...and you know what is best for your child."

Children need an emotional sanctuary

Many workplaces have a room for people to just think and reflect. No electronics. Visual delights such as aquariums and nature scenes allow people listen to their real, inner voice. When I went to school in the 1970s, we had smoking rooms. School is stressful and children need a respite from stress. Recess and lunch time give respite from academic stress, but not from social stress. This is hardest on introverts who feel they must wear a brave, extroverted smile and project an extroverted manner for six hours a day, until they can come home and be their true selves.

Introverts draw their energy from inside; they need time alone to recharge and reenergize. Extroverts draw their energy from interacting with other people.

Some home-based education families never stay home—they are constantly on the go to events and activities. This works for them, providing that an introverted family member can choose to stay at home in pajamas!

Unschooling works for introverts by allowing them time to be social but also giving them time alone to reenergize themselves. It works for extroverts by allowing them to be as social as they wish.

Children don't burn out by high school age

Thirteen years of structured compulsory institutional school for most kids, on top of three years of preschool and followed by four to seven years of postsecondary education—a total of 20 to 25 years of schooling! —is a long time. Most all of their childhood is spent in an institution. No wonder only 40 percent of high school grads pursue a postsecondary education. They start their education way too early and they burn out.

In Canada, Grade 12 is the only school year in which marks really count, as acceptance into postsecondary education hinges on Grade 12 marks. Children at age 16 and 17 should be striving for success in Grade 12; instead, after more than 12 years in school, they are simply looking forward to escaping! They are sick of exams, assignments, and structure. Even most prison sentences are shorter than the average number of school years a child is sentenced to! To compensate, many students party or become involved in undesirable activity. In the US, student burnout is worse. Mandatory frequent testing leads to kids beginning to burn out by Grade 4 and to really hate school by junior high. (Abeles, 2009)

In contrast, unschooled children who begin formal education in the high school years are eager and engaged. They are gearing up at a time when other kids are burning out. This is one of the most important academic reasons to unschool.

Burnout is caused by subjecting kids to excessively structured formal classes too early. For many children, academic pressure causes incredible stress. I've seen daycare "schools" that introduce worksheets, all-day lesson plans, and even uniforms for 1-year-old toddlers! Such an early start to an academic-style environment appeals to ambitious, well-intentioned parents, but they are doing their children more harm than good.

The other cause of burnout is little or no downtime. "Pushy parents risk damaging rather than enhancing their children's prospects." says Mike Grenier, a housemaster at Eton and a proponent of the slow education movement. "Downtime is not a bad thing. If children are overly controlled, they can become demotivated. Our entire education system is hopelessly out of sync with children's real needs. Curriculum, with its emphasis on prescribed goals, and rigorous testing is not doing kids any good. A system that marches cohorts through examinations based on the date of their birth dehumanizes each of them." (Grenier, 2012)

School, on its own, might be okay. If children just went to school, had no homework, and had all their extracurricular activities scheduled during school hours, they would have much more downtime after school and would be healthier emotionally. But they don't. Our culture celebrates busyness and idle time is frowned upon.

If some enrichment activities are good for kids, are more even better? Do you feel the pressure to enroll your children in something, or in many things? One year, I didn't sign up my 10- and 14-year-old kids for any structured activities. We made time each day for opportunities to unfold. We ended up always being busy; we were never bored, nor were we stressed. Parents must realize that children cannot be involved in everything! When you say yes to one activity, you say no to another. Children desire and value time with you. Where two decades ago the latchkey kid was the neglected one, he is now the overscheduled one. Parents say that their child thrives on staying busy with many activities—but we need to ask the child whether that is really the case. Often, problems emerge later. Even Sundays, traditionally a day of downtime and family activity, are no longer immune from scheduled activities. What has to go? Family dinners, get-togethers with relatives, family game nights, weekend trips, family vacations, lunch dates, and evening time together are sacrificed for sports competitions and practices, lessons, homework, camps, and activities. Two parents working long hours may be able to provide their children with clothes, luxury cars, boats, and motorhomes, a big renovated house, fancy vacations, pools, and restaurant meals, but these things may come at the price of solid family relationships that create whole, well-rounded, emotionally healthy children.

Some parents are actually afraid of being alone and being un-busy with their children. The intimacy of spending unprogrammed time with their children scares them; scheduling activities with outsiders is easier. Parents must ask themselves why they use tools, toys, and diversions to avoid connecting closely with their children.

How can you tell if your child is burning out? Stress is manifested in physical symptoms: headaches, sleepiness, neck and back pain, stomach aches, shortness of breath, heart palpitations, and sleep disturbances. Stress can cause behavioral change. Teens might experiment with drugs, alcohol, sex, gaming, or gambling. They might develop eating disorders. They may experience anxiety, social withdrawal, or tantrums. They may become hostile or violent. Their grades may drop. They may be unable to play or entertain themselves. (Abeles, 2009)

How bad is the lack of free time? Baby boomers had 250 percent more free time than our kids do today. (Smith, 2005) Involvement in too many activities brings out the worst in children. They don't need more tutoring, hockey camps, dance lessons, or sleepovers. They need more time with parents, siblings, and especially, themselves. They need you. Quite simply, your children want more of you.

Seven years ago, we took four of our children, aged 9 – 20, to Ireland for a four-week holiday. No phones or computers. We got by with a deck of playing cards, Uno cards, and paper and markers. The kids entertained themselves continuously. They became creative by using the materials available in their immediate environment. It was a welcome break from routine that spurred a lot of conversation and discussion.

Unschooling brings a lot of relaxing downtime.

Unschooling is uncrowded and serene

Schools are noisy, crowded places that are hard to concentrate in. Buses, movie theaters, churches, and lecture halls are crowded too, but people rarely stay in them for six hours a day, five days a week. Some say that kids, whether introverts or extroverts, have to learn to live in a crowd. Studies with rats have shown them to become stressed in crowded environments; how much more does that apply to human beings! But in the real world, people can choose how and where to work. Some choose to be entrepreneurs, some choose to work in smaller family-style companies, and some choose to work for large conglomerates. Children in school don't have the choice of a more intimate setting. Even the best private school classroom has a ratio of 12 students to one teacher, but the entire school is still a crowd.

In unschooling, children are able to choose the best setting for them, based on their personalities and individual learning styles. For many children, that setting is a calm, serene, soul-enriching space.

Unschooling is unstressful

Grades, peers, social navigation, bullying, weapons, sexual pressure, sleeplessness, exams, corporal punishment, clothes, relationship woes, teachers' personalities, schedules, homework, activities, parent expectations, boring curriculum, peer pressure, and unrelenting emphasis on getting good grades—in other words, school! Take school away from a child and you have just removed 95 percent of his stress factors!

A survey polled 103,000 Grade 7 to 12 students of the Toronto District School Board, one of the largest in the country. (Hammer, 2013) Results from the same poll showed that three out of four high school students worry about their future. They can't sleep at night and they often feel like crying.

Everyone is subject to stress, even unschoolers. Stress is not all bad. There are three kinds of stress: positive, tolerable, and toxic.

Positive stress is motivational and builds resiliency. It is precipitated by events, people, and circumstances that kids worry about: birthdays, traveling, exams, class presentations, new playmates. Positive stress motivates kids and enhances their sense of accomplishment when they meet a challenge or overcome a fear.

Tolerable stress is nasty and unpleasant but subsides when the child is supported by caring parents. It is not ongoing. Tolerable stress can be caused by bullying, peer pressure, overwhelming workload, too many exams, mean teachers, and any number of negative forces. For the most part, children can tolerate the stress of school because it is buffered by caring parents.

Toxic stress results when children consistently endure tolerable stress but are not supported by caring adults and the stress is ongoing. Many children do not have support systems at home to help them cope with school's tolerable stresses, and tolerable becomes toxic. Even worse, for some kids, home life is yet another a source of stress, only adding to their distress. They may be living with ACES (Adverse Childhood Experiences). This affects the growth of the child's brain by releasing too much of the steroid hormone cortisol and the "fight or flight" hormone, adrenalin. Toxic stress can alter brain architecture and cause a host of health problems later in life. (Palix, 2017)

Some would argue that life is stressful and the earlier a child learns to manage stress, the better. However, children's brains are very changeable during those first 13 years. The later they are forced into managing tolerable and toxic stress, the better. In unschooling, most of the stress is positive: driver's tests, swimming lessons, volunteering, and meeting new people. Children are not immune to stress simply by having a different education delivery, but an unschooled child is not hammered with tolerable or toxic stress on a daily, unrelenting basis. A school child might have a friend or a teacher support his stress, but parents can't be at school every day and teachers are busy. School friends may be the source of stress rather than a buffer. Less stress in the early years prepares a healthy brain to withstand normal adult stress in later years.

An unschooled child's stress is temporary, and most always supported by caring parents.

Unschooling doesn't require punishment or bribes

I am a firm believer in not punishing human beings—ever. Physical and emotional punishments do not motivate people. Problem solving does. Yet punishing kids to force them to learn is the most common "solution" to disengagement, both in schools and in homeschooling. We beg. We bribe. We punish. We coax. We spank. We take away electronics or privileges. We sometimes succeed, but only until the next test of wills. There is nothing worse than trying to teach a person something when they don't want to learn. I feel for teachers with a class of 30 grade niners, only two of whom really want to learn about polynomials, and the rest just want to check their friends' Facebook updates. I feel for homeschoolers who are trying to get their children's attention at the kitchen table so they can drill them on addition while the children are giggling at the dog's antics, in spite of the threat of a spanking if they don't pay attention. I empathize with the frustrations of the teacher and the homeschooling parent. The simple solution is to let go of the agenda and have some fun!

School is a constant evaluative setting and this affects learning. It's not just what a child does that counts, but others' evaluation of his efforts. Teachers evaluate with marks and peers "evaluate" with social status. Learning is not enjoyed because it is constantly measured. It must have a purpose. But real learning happens for the simple joy of it. In unschooling, a parent never has to do battle with a child to get the work done. Here are three more positive differences in unschooling:

1. Unschooling values inner motivation rather than outer control

Children do not require rewards to learn. They should choose to read because they love to read, not because they are bribed to read.

Children do not learn by being punished. I've seen schools mete out strappings—yes, many schools still support physical punishment—and order detentions, writing lines, and extra chores; or give low grades for work not completed. I've seen homeschooling parents spank, give time-outs and take away play dates, computer games, video time, and outings for work not completed. Unschoolers do none of these things. They allow their children to learn what they want.

There is much research in the parenting field that shows how punishments impair relationships and communication. In schools, group punishments are often used to get to the bottom of a problem. They are unfair and teach the children to bully each other and cover up wrong-doing to avoid punishment of the whole group. Cooperation and encouragement are discouraged. Tattling is encouraged.

2. Unschooling has no grades

When work is not graded, it is undertaken for its learning value. Grading was invented by the Prussians to control people. Grades are dangled in front of children to get them to read, study, or digest unpleasant, irrelevant information so that schools can prove they delivered the content. That's why adults are generally not graded in adult education. They are there because they want to be.

Grading changes motivation. Children ask, "Will this be on the test?" or "If this is not graded, why should I do it?" Indeed, if it's not to be graded, why would children learn the material? Grading encourages children learn to budget their time to cover only the learning that will be judged by others, not what interests them.

And when we don't have grades to bribe children, we tend to package school-related things to "sell" children on learning. Parents and society sell school to kids by reading books about starting school and bribing them with new clothes and school supplies, or perhaps a new mobile phone or computer. Kids love learning; it's school that has to be sold to them. There are so many picture books on starting school that make it look like a wonderfully positive experience. Do you see any books on going to prison that would make incarceration more palatable to adults? Workbooks, textbooks, and educational computer games are produced in beautiful colors to look more attractive to children.

I confess. I once was a parent who tried to control my children with bribes. I realized the futility of it one day when my son, who was paid an allowance for doing chores, opted to buy his way out of them. Company was coming and when I asked him to do his chores, he retorted with "I don't need money this week, so no thanks, I won't be doing them." That was not acceptable! I needed his help. Since that day, I refused to pay my children for helping in the home. I refused to use candy to get my children to toilet-train. I refused to give them an allowance for doing chores. I refused to allow treats as a reward for finishing school assignments. I refused to pay for good marks or volunteer work. I hid every balloon, pencil, sticker, and pizza coupon they were given by others for doing what they should be doing anyway—behaving like the awesome kids they were and learning for the joy of it.

If children are never, ever graded, will they even get off the couch? Of course! But grades inherently communicate to children what type of learning society values and what type it does not. My son Neil, at 13, would bring a high school-level physics textbook to the beach to read. He was not being graded, nor forced in any way to study physics. He did so because he wanted to learn about physics and he enjoyed the learning. In our family, this happened frequently with all our kids, with many subjects and activities: learning piano, guitar, Latin, Japanese, German, and philosophy; learning about making beer, baking bread, gardening, sewing, making candles, and computer coding. These and many other things were learned during and after their school-age years, for no credit or reward other than the pleasure of increasing their knowledge.

When I would ask the kids to do something and they replied, "What do we get for it?" I would always tell them, "My Undying Love And Appreciation!" (MULAA) Now, as young adults, when they ask me to do something and I say, "What do I get for it?" guess what they say? We thought we might start a family crypto-currency, like Bitcoin, and call it a MULAA coin!

Parents say that children must learn that hard work is rewarded in the real world, and that they are preparing their children for that by paying them for studying or for doing chores. Yes, it's true that hard work is rewarded in life—or should be—but it seems to me that we should teach our children that hard work often needs to be done for its own sake, without recognition, reward, or personal gain. It's a harder lesson to teach, and parents don't know to start teaching it when their children are used to asking, "What's it worth?"

When they begin homeschooling, parents soon learn that they can't successfully replicate the authority of the teacher at school. Homeschooling as "school-at-home" may work in authoritarian homes where the strict rules and routine are followed unquestioningly, but not in families with other parenting styles. Kids refuse to do the workbooks because they can: at school, they are a tiny bit scared of the teacher but at home, mom and dad are a known quantity. There is no fear in the relationship and they know from experience exactly how much resistance their parents will tolerate. When children refuse to work in the homeschool environment, many homeschoolers modify their expectations and make the work more fun—in fact, more like play—or they give up homeschooling in favor of unschooling or put their kids back into the school system.

In our house, we have never bribed or punished to foster learning. The kids could play video games or go on outings even if they didn't learn anything new. My husband and I have modeled love of lifelong learning, reading, and service work through our visible enjoyment of those activities. Our children all read for pleasure at least three hours a day, even the teen boys, and write for the sheer joy of creative expression. They learn math because it gives them the tools to solve problems. They learn science and social studies because it teaches them about their world and gives them the confidence to share their knowledge. They experience the thrills of mastering a skill and acquiring knowledge.

Grading is a handy way to evaluate the quality of work. But it is problematic because the evaluation is outside of the learner's control. It is clouded by the evaluator's biases. Why can't students grade their own efforts and the quality of their work? Self-evaluation is the best teacher and the fairest. Watch a child as he evaluates himself in play—he makes adjustments until he is satisfied with the results.

Self-evaluation is one of the best motivation methods, yet it is judged as suspect. Research shows that the results of self-evaluation frequently equal or exceed those of a teacher; children are often harder on themselves than a teacher would be. "The odd child will abuse the privilege and rate himself higher, but for the most part, children benefit from the trust and empowerment that self-evaluation implies." (Kohn, 2009)

The moment that play is graded, it becomes work. My son Mathew loved to create art but would not consider it as a career choice. He could draw and paint beautiful scenes from World of Warcraft, but he felt the joy of creating would instantly vanish if his work were judged by a boss or paid for by a client with certain expectations. He would no longer own his creation.

3. Unschooling is uncontrolling and builds relationship influence

Control and influence are mutually exclusive. The more you try to control people, the less influence you have on them. Influence is powerful because it's ongoing. It's compelling. It never wanes in a mutually respectful relationship. An adult's influence stays with a child even when he is not present.

I do not advocate punishments or rewards in parenting (as indicated in my book, *Discipline Without Distress*), and I certainly do not advocate it in education. Many unschooling parents and teachers model lifelong learning; their influence is reflected in their great relationships with children, and the children's emulation of their actions and values.

With influence, there are expectations, although not usually rules. No enforcement is necessary. Of their own will, children rise to high expectations. They want to know what is expected, but they don't want to be forced to conform to that expectation; they want to choose it. The same, of course, applies to adults.

Nagging, shaming, ultimatums, bribing, yelling, and punishing will not motivate kids. Desire to improve must come within, and unschooling unleashes it.

Unschooling celebrates failure

In school, failure is bad. Children handle failure in school by cheating or dropping out. Unschooling provides a built-in mechanism for using failure as an important part of learning. Failure is never punished. Failure is not to be feared. Failure is a tool that lets the learner know it's time for change. People more often learn from failure than from success, and we must celebrate its usefulness.

Most top CEOs (Chief Executive Officers) list failure as a contributing factor to their success. All children need to learn how to handle adversity. Children who get knocked down and get right back up to take action, make changes, and try again will go far in life. They show initiative, tenacity, and persistence. Some people call it "grit." When schools protect children from low marks they are acting as "snowplow" schools, just as parents can be snowplow parents by shoving adversity out of the child's path so they can have a happy life. In one school in our province, a teacher was fired when he refused to give nothing but zeros when kids didn't hand in their work. (Chan, 2014) Coddling children by protecting them from failure does not benefit them, either in the short-term or the long-term. Parents and schools that allow their children to experience failure in driver's tests, swimming badges, musical competitions, and other tests and competitions help their children to develop stamina and the confidence to know they can be knocked down and get back up fighting. It builds self-esteem and reassures them of their capability to move forward after a fall, having learned a life lesson that will stand them in good stead.

Failure builds grit and determination. One of my sons spent four falls trying to get into a particular program. The fourth time, he succeeded. His victory was satisfying and taught him persistence and perseverance. Struggle made him stronger. Later, it also made him a better employee.

Unschooling teaches many useful life lessons that are not taught in school.

Children develop excellent communication skills

Kids are not supposed to talk in school. Socializing in school is controlled and artificial. Teachers control the flow of conversation in the classroom, if and when it happens. Schools need quiet so kids can concentrate and teachers can focus, but it is an artificially quiet environment. Noisy classrooms are not viewed as hubs of activity and learning, but as wild chaos. When kids are finished their work in school, they are assigned busywork to keep them quiet. They should be able to converse and socialize everywhere, just as adults do. Everything they say should be listened to and they need to be spoken with often.

Online learning is even worse. It is silent and quiet. Writing is not the same as speaking. A one-line sentence is not a discussion.

In unschooling, children can talk and chatter and listen as much as they like. They develop conversation skills and storytelling skills, vocabulary, and interpersonal communication skills with other children and adults.

Children crave human touch

In school, one person is not allowed to touch another. Yet children need the constant, non-sexual human touch that caring adults, siblings, and friends can provide. They need hugs, pats on the back, high-fives, and handholding.

Numerous studies have shown that affectionate touch such as cuddling can decrease stress, enhance language acquisition, improve memory, and increase IQ. (Hatfield, 2009) Unfortunately, regulations no longer permit teachers to touch children in school. Taking turns curling up in the teacher's lap at circle time is no longer allowed, and yet it is one of the most cherished memories of my childhood.

In our cold, digital world, a hug can still penetrate where technology cannot go. In unschooling, children and adults can cuddle to their hearts' content, as long as whoever says "No" is respected.

More time for family dinners

Psychotherapist Dr. Michael Haggstrom says that eating together as a family is not a waste of time. Parents think they are showing their kids love by transporting them to endless after-school "enrichment" activities, and then wonder why kids think their parents don't care about them. Haagstrom states that "it's better to have fewer activities and more sit-down meals together." (Bodner, 2009) Spending 20 minutes a day over a shared meal, without technology, swapping stories and opinions and having conversations makes a child feel like part of the family. No topic should be off limits. Tackling a difficult topic tells children that they can talk about anything. And it doesn't have to be formal sit-down meal. Humans have been sharing food and conversation around the campfire since stone-age days; campfire or dining table, sharing a meal remains an important bonding and educational experience today. Children who are practiced in discussions with adults do better later on and are more comfortable addressing their professors and other adults. Also, getting the kids to help with meal preparation and clean-up teaches more skills and promotes healthy eating choices.

More facilities have recognized the demand for extracurricular activity and lessons during daytime hours and now frequently offer them during low-use times of day. Unschooling families can program most of their community activities and lessons during the day and have family dinners and evenings together every night.

Emotional intelligence is enhanced

Students from schools overseas achieve amazing academic grades in their home countries in math and sciences that require rote learning, but they come to Canada to learn the soft skills that can't be memorized or taught by rote: leadership, optimism, creativity, gratitude, confidence, communication, and teamwork.

Unschooling allows the whole child to develop—not just into smart learners, but into good people. Their social, emotional and spiritual development is just as important as their cognitive development. Children can laugh, cry, and express the entire range of their feelings in the comfort of their home. They can worship and pray without feeling isolated. They have time to participate in the community as part of their education, not in addition to it.

Unschooling facilitates emotional expression and character development.

Self-esteem and self-confidence is protected

Formal classes undermine our confidence in self-teaching. If we are constantly told that we can't learn without a teacher, classroom, and workbook, we will never trust in our ability to learn on our own.

There are companies now that will teach children how to ride a bike; that used to be a cherished rite of childhood—with memories made and treasured by parents and children alike. Parents now outsource teaching their kids about cooking, safety, driving, manners, problem solving ("Little Engineer"), Lego, home-alone guidelines, and babysitting classes. Learning fun activities also gets outsourced: skating, soccer, and many activities that parents used to teach their children are now entrusted to expensive instructors outside of the home. Parents have lost confidence in themselves to teach their children.

I was just as bad as the next parent, thinking I didn't have the skills to teach my child. I signed up my first child for all kinds of lessons, and as he got bored in the classes and the structure, rules, and waiting took all the spontaneous fun out of mastering a skill himself, I quit trying to talk him into signing up. The next three kids kind of dropped off from any formal lessons they tried. When my fifth begged me to never sign her up, I finally got the message! The last three children all learned to skate, ski, ride a bike, drive a car, and cook on their own. "Parents are hiring experts to lead kids by the hand through the most basic of childhood events." (Lakritz, 2012) We saved a lot of money and the kids are confident that they can teach themselves most anything.

In unschooling, children who have learning or behavioral difficulties are raised in an environment that bolsters their self-confidence by tailoring the learning methods to suit them. Unless a child chooses, there are no grades, homework, or testing that might indicate to a child that he is a poorer learner than the next child.

Unschooling builds self-esteem by building a child's self-worth. Children grow up believing that they are just as valuable as the next person. A child is encouraged and celebrated when he is successful at something. The child's self-esteem also grows when he engages with the wider community, interacting with diverse people. He will value his place in society as a contributing member.

10

Physical Benefits of Unschooling

"Seventy-five percent of teen angst is caused by lack of adequate night time sleep."

Home is a healthier learning environment

As a child of the 1970s, I remember smelling the freshly mimeographed half-wet worksheets that were handed out to us students. We loved the smell and breathed it in deeply as soon as we got our copy. The ink was fresh and left purple stains on our young fingers. I often wonder how bad that was for our health! There were other toxins, including the cleaners that were used to sanitize desks and left a thin film of grit that we used to swipe off, and then eat our lunch on the desk without washing our hands. Even today there are environmental toxins in schools: in the smells from dry-erase markers and photocopy machines; in the fluorescent lighting that can produce headaches and behavioral issues for kids living with sensitivities; and even in chalk, which is toxic when breathed in. There is still a lot of asbestos behind the walls and ceilings in older schools. Backpacks are dangerously heavy and kids are carrying more than 10 percent of their body weight in books—a surefire recipe for future back problems. And the idling buses and their gas fumes! I had to hold my breath when I crossed the lawn to pick up my kids from school so that I wouldn't throw up. And kids stand in those fumes for 30 minutes every day as they line up for their buses. Children should have fresh outdoor air in natural environments for most of their waking time.

The jury is still out on the effects of wireless technology on children's health. Although Wi-Fi transmitters such as mobile phones are deemed safe by Health Canada, the technology is still too young to have had any long-term, broad-based studies to inform school policy on the safety of such technology.

Younger kids are vulnerable to the effects of environmental pollutants because their skin is thinner and their brains and nervous systems are still developing.

Unschooling in a home environment allows families to control and minimize exposure to toxins.

Meals are homemade and healthier

In schools, nutrition means packaged food. Children who unschool can enjoy a hot, unprocessed lunch and breakfast every day. Families often schedule extracurricular activities during the day, so most members are home for family dinner every night.

There is more time to cook from scratch, which is healthier. Eating less processed take-out food eaten on the run means better nutrition.

It's not as if unschoolers don't eat junk food, but they eat far less of it than the average family with kids in school and parents at work.

Children get more sleep

I have already discussed this at length in previous chapters. School-age children need nine to twelve hours a night. Teenagers need eight to ten hours a night. (CPS, 2016)

Unschooling allows kids to sleep in so each individual gets as much sleep he needs.

Children get more physical activity

Freed from a school schedule, children and parents have more time to take a walk, or to run their errands by bicycle. When the crowds go back to school in September, unschoolers take back the parks, beaches, playgrounds, zoos, tennis courts, and other recreational areas during the daytimes when they are not crowded.

Recess is dwindling in schools for two reasons. Some schools eliminate recess as a punishment and many other schools do it in order to cram in more academics. Both are wrong.

Kids benefit from recess. In fact, it may be the second most important part of school after teacher relationships. Kids' brains get a break because their attention span extends only to 40 or 50 minutes. (Arnall, 2014) During recess, they get exercise from running, jumping, and climbing on the playground equipment. They build social skills such as negotiation, sharing, and teamwork. They are able to concentrate better and be more productive and less disruptive when they are back on task in class. In Japan, children get a ten-minute break every hour. In Finland, recess is even longer.

Unschoolers can take a break from play or activities whenever they wish. They get all the benefits of recess in unrestricted blocks of time.

Unschooling is safe

Children do not bring weapons to school. They are less likely to be kidnapped while walking to school, less likely to be hit by a car, and less likely to be attacked by a shark!

Freedom from the school schedule reduces stress

Ask any parents of school-age children to schedule a playdate see how it complicates their lives! Everything they do centers around the school schedule. Children must go to bed early on school nights so they can get up early the next day. They can't stay up late to watch a major astronomical event like an eclipse. Weekends are planned for errands and birthday parties, so families can't spontaneously play games or just be together. Weekday dinners are rushed. Unschooling reduces stress.

11

Benefits to Society

"I'll never let schooling get in the way of my education." — *Mark Twain, Author*

The best interests of the child are always the first consideration

Funding shapes more decisions in education than any other factor and it reigns supreme, even over what is in the best interests of the children. In many cases, research informs us on new and successful practices, but we keep funding the old practices because they save money, and education is a business that keeps the economy humming. Consider the following educational initiatives that persist because they are more feasible economically, despite research that shows little results or advances in children's achievement:

Diploma exam scheduling

Research shows that the teen brain needs to sleep later in the morning to accommodate its circadian rhythms. Yet it would cost too much money to move diploma exams from the morning to the afternoon, when teens' brains work more efficiently.

High school start times

Teens are sleep deprived. Starting school at 8:30 or even later would result in significant improvement in achievement, not only on first morning classes but throughout the morning. (Macmillan, 2017)

All-day Kindergarten

Junior Kindergarten, for children of ages two to five, and full-day Kindergarten for five-year-olds are initiatives that began in Ontario, based on very little research. One report shows that after two years in Kindergarten, there are only slight benefits gained by already disadvantaged children, and no gain at all for average children. (Maclean's, 2014) Those children would be just as advantaged, or more so, staying home with an attentive parent and a cardboard box to play with.

Digital textbooks and class delivery

Another educational trend to minimize the expense of textbooks and teachers is the adoption of online learning inside schools. There is little research that proves retention of basic content taught in this way; in fact, very recent research now indicates that retention rate actually declines. (Retrieve, 2017) Certainly, kinesthetic learners miss out.

No spares

Mandatory fill-in of high school option classes persists, even though studies show that kids are stressed and need more downtime. Schools' funding is based on the number of courses students take at the high school level, which results in elimination of spares that would help them focus on their core subjects, particularly when they already have enough credits to graduate. Schools argue that taking more options will widen students' opportunities. Couldn't students work on options—of their own choosing, in their own way—outside of school?

Non-core course cuts

Most funding cuts in schools are made first on programs that kids love—physical education, music, arts, sports, bands, and home economics; and on science supplies and hands-on equipment. When money is tight, it is only funneled to the core subjects of Math, Science, Social Studies, and English.

Disallowing voucher funding

Vouchers allow parents to fund their individual educational choices, whether directed toward school or to purchasing learning resources for the home. Parents should have equitably funded choices for their children's education. The government should not force parents to choose an inappropriate program for their child just because they don't have to pay for it.

Education systems that don't fund choices equally, don't value children equally. Every child deserves a personalized education. The $15,000 per year, per child that the school receives to "educate" students who don't want to be there could provide a parent with the means to stay at home, if they chose to, and facilitate their own child's learning. The same per-child funding for home-educating multiple children could finance hands-on learning materials, tutors, toys, crafts, games, field trips, and travel.

Unschoolers are educationally accountable only to themselves

There are great checks and balances for financial accountability in our education system. Public taxpayer money is accounted for, as it should be. However, accountability in educational results is never tied to financial accountability in the system and should not be in the home either.

The Universal Declaration that parents have a prior right to choose the form of education for their children assumes that parents know best which educational philosophy works for their child. Every child has a right to a funded education for the good of society.

Unschooling parents should always receive funding because they are providing an education.

Should funding bring more scrutiny? Yes, for financial accountability. Parents must show that they actually bought piano lessons by producing a receipt. That is fair. But absolutely not for educational accountability. Parents should not need to show children's test results to prove that funding is well spent, any more than public schools should. Curiously, when standardized testing shows poor results, schools often receive more funding!

Some home educators do not want any funding. However, just because a few families can afford to home educate without funding does not mean that all families can. Some worry that increased funding will bring increased scrutiny of educational accountability. The evidence does not bear this out; in fact, the opposite has occurred. The history of home education in Alberta clearly proves that as financial allotments to parents were reduced over the past 40 years, the number of home education regulations were increased.

Educational accountability is a gaping hole in the system. Because of the power of unions, very few education staff have ever been fired for job incompetence. But it does exist. And who can parents turn to when they encounter incompetence in the system? They are passed around from one supervisor to another until they give up in frustration. I was trying to track down my son's Grade 9 government achievement tests and was endlessly and futilely passed from government to school to teachers, principals, markers, superintendents, and on and on. No one ever found his records, and I gave up after months of fruitless searching.

The system is never held accountable. The government gives school boards $300 million per year to reduce student-teacher ratio but has no systems in place to measure the rate of return on their investment. (Ferguson, 2018) Governments change with each election, and their ultimate goal is to get re-elected and hold on to power. Civil servants remain, but they have no interest in change and exist only to maintain their department's funding and protect their own jobs at all costs. All departments cover for other departments. Answers are vague or non-existent. The best interests of each individual child are never the first goal of any government educational policy or decision.

As for financial accountability, school systems are bloated and waste is rampant. Our local school board has a whopping 700 administrators for 200,000 students. We have one of the top-heaviest school systems in terms of overhead and school support costs. (Labby, 2017) Each department operates like an island. Departments could be downsized and made to share resources in order to get the best educational value for the dollar—the taxpayer's dollar. (Beiber, 2017)

When unschoolers have control over how to spend funding, they are guided only by the best interests of their child. They are some of the most prudent spenders around and are best able to make financial purchasing decisions directed to the needs of each individual, unique learner.

Unschooling saves public money

Unschooling my five children for the 13 years of their education saved taxpayers half a million dollars. We received a stipend of about $800 per child per year but saved the government the spending allocation of $15,000 per child per year on teacher salaries, resources, buses, buildings, and infrastructure.

Unschoolers subsidize the cost of public education two ways.

First, they pay education taxes to the government. In our case, we paid $5000 per year in property tax, $2500 of which went to the public school board. Second, educating our kids outside the system left $14,200 per child per year in the system's coffers for the benefit of kids in school. In 2012, homeschoolers and unschoolers in Canada saved the public education system almost $300 million in that single year. (Van Pelt, 2015) It is very clear that parents and children can do just as good a job of education at home, with far less taxpayer money. But this option should not just be for those that can afford to subsidize the system in such a way.

True choice in education is a funded choice

No matter how much funding goes to the education board, schools will always declare that they are underfunded. When school boards want more funding, they appeal to the public by saying, "This money can then be redirected to the classroom." Many unions, public interest groups, and government officials want home education choices shut down so that money will be directed only to a single target—the classroom. Former Education Minister Jim Johnson defended funded choice when he stated, "It's parents who get to choose where their kids go... and why we provide many different opportunities for children to succeed. We recognize that not every child can fit into the same box. We want to invest in their success, not just invest in a school and not just invest in a system." (Alberta Views, 2013)

When government and society truly value personal learning and the focus on children's best interests, they will fund all education choices equally. Home-educating children has a cost, and if there is little or no resource funding, it becomes a choice only for those who can afford it.

Parents direct their children's education because of love, not because of money. But again, I emphasize, that is not to say that there are no costs to home education. Most of the expense is invisible, though. Parents pay for what their child needs, and those costs are rarely tallied on paper. The government sets home-education funding limits without ever studying the actual costs. So, parents make do. They cannot borrow resources from the neighborhood school because schools in the system do not want the administrative burden of monitoring their resources; home-education parents purchase their own or share resources among neighbors. As each of my children prepared to go to university, we followed the government curriculum plan for Grade 12. It cost $2245 for each child's books, and more for the resources and tutoring required for projects. All this was out of pocket, as we only received $850 of funding.

As well, we must acknowledge the cost of losing a full-time income for the stay-at-home parent. Many parents are okay with giving up this income, and it is reasonable to assume that parents should not be paid for teaching duties because they are not professional teachers. But no child should go without the materials, lessons, tutoring, and resources he needs.

The bare-bones annual hard cost for home-educating a child in Grades 1 to 9 is around $1200, which covers only a library card and an internet connection. Children with special needs and children in high school grades need much more to cover specialized tutoring costs. However, the resource chapter in the next section lists some of the materials recommended for a rich unschooling environment. Hands-on, kinesthetic learning aids, manipulatives, software, technology, sports, and music lessons are not cheap. A math workbook only costs $20, but a three-dimensional math manipulative set costs $129.

In addition, schools can purchase supplies in bulk. They enjoy economies of scale by purchasing 50 textbooks at $80 each, while a parent pays $160 to purchase only one.

Unschooling saves society money, but that cost savings should not be at the expense of the child, or a family that cannot afford to pay for needed resources. Families should receive at least the same financial allotment for resources that school children enjoy, and the parents should receive a hefty tax deduction for not drawing on the government's educational budget for teachers' salaries. To offset the cost of a lost income, home-educating families should also be allowed to income-split to reduce their tax bill.

Another factor is optics. Governments fund what they value, and funding SDE (Self-directed Education) resources would validate their understanding of alternative education methods. It would encourage SDE and could spur researchers to study it further. Self-directed education would become more mainstream if it were funded, because more families could afford to at least try it.

Costs for unschooling at a free-school

For unschooling to work in a school, teachers' salaries would be the biggest expense. Instead of hiring one teacher for 30 kids, the ratio would be one teacher to a pod of five children. That would mean five more teacher salaries for the same 30 children; plus a vehicle, fuel, and maintenance costs; plus resources. Savings to cover these additional expenses would come from the money saved by the system on curriculum development, administration, testing, licenses, and curriculum supplies. Capital costs would continue, as schools would still have to be built and maintained as a base and a social hub for children. Buses would still have to run. Since students rarely read books anymore, favoring digital options, perhaps libraries could reinvent themselves and partner with schools, sharing space to serve the community in an all-ages learning environment.

Unschooling benefits all stakeholders in education

Following are the benefits to the unschooled child:

- A one-to-one adult-child ratio enhances personal attention and relationships.

- A child learns concepts when he is ready for them, rather than when the school wants to present them; this builds confidence in learning.

- There is far less school-related tolerable and toxic stress.

- The relaxing environment encourages the child to be creative and take risks in learning.

- Learning is inextricable to children's current interests; they remain engaged and retain learning.

- The child's self-esteem is protected if she is a late reader or has a learning disability.

- The child learns at his own speed, breezing through concepts he understands and taking more time to master those he finds difficult.

- Children have friends of all ages, genders, social standing, and ethnic backgrounds—it is a real-world mix.

- Efficient use of time provides a balance between play, downtime, activities, and learning.

- Children control the time they spend on their activities. They own their time.

- The child has active time, snacks, breaks, and quiet, when she needs them.

- A child with a learning disability can modify his environment to meet his needs.

- Teens can sleep in and follow a sleep cycle more in tune with their circadian rhythms, aiding their brain development.

- There is almost no bullying or peer pressure.

The facilitator, whether parent or teacher, realizes the following benefits:

- No fights with a child over getting her to produce work. Ever.

- Technology makes it easy to acquire resources from anywhere to enhance learning: videos, internet, hired tutors, unit studies, email, and others.

- Watching children learn is the joy and privilege of parents and teachers. It is as exciting as watching a child take his first step. Watching him start to read or seeing the light-bulb go on as he finally "gets it" is a truly rewarding experience.

- There are no lunches to pack, notices to read, checks to write, baking to provide, shopping for the teacher, school council meetings or parent-teacher conferences to attend, fundraising to do, newsletters or notices to read, nor volunteering to sign up for. All the time that parents would gain would be funneled into quality, fun, "together" time.

- There is no getting children out the door on cold winter mornings or driving them to school while wearing your housecoat!

- There is no coaxing, bribing, or threatening children to get off the playground to come home from school.

- There is no need to buy backpacks, lunch containers, replacement mitts and hats, inside shoes, snow pants, or the coolest electronic device the child absolutely must have, only to have it lost by November.

- There is no bussing, driving, or walking the child to and from school four times a day.

- There is no more teaching children who don't want to learn!

The entire family benefits:

- There is less pressure on parents from their children to provide them with mobile phones or buy the right clothes.

- There are fewer time pressures and far less school-related stress. There is a less rigid schedule. No more "Hurry, hurry, hurry, we are going to be late!" Rather, the cry is, "Please take your time. You can do it!"

- The more efficient use of time provides a balance between play, sports, learning, projects, and work.

- Life is much more relaxed, allowing time for deepening relationships. More time is enjoyed with family and siblings of all ages.

- Parents can apply concepts to daily activities in and out of home so all the children, regardless of age, can make connections. They have first-hand knowledge of the child's interests.

- Education and parenting merge. Parents spend more focused time with their children on unschooling activities, so a child can busy herself on her own at other times, leaving the parent free to get her own work done.

- Learning becomes part of life and loved for its own sake. Learning is not confined to Monday to Friday from 9 a.m. to 3 p.m. Learning occurs any time of the day or night.

- Children learn to work cooperatively with siblings and friends rather than competitively with classmates—a valued skill in the workforce.

- Families can avoid weekend and after-school crowds at malls, parks, theaters, zoos, playgrounds, restaurants, and sports complexes.

- If one parent works out of town, he or she can spend days off with the children on any day of the week.

- No homework. Ever!

- Families can travel off-season to save money and avoid crowds.

- There are no more preschool costs, tutors, or summer school levies.

The community benefits as well:

- Children get out into the real world, exploring on field trips any day or time they desire, in activities that correspond with their interests. They actually see how people in the community work, play, and live, and learn about their place in the community.

- Learning continues forever. Curious children grow into curious adults. Communities benefit from a curious and educated population.

- Community organizations benefit by being able to offer home education programming during traditionally daytime quiet hours when school-age kids are typically in school.

- More charities get family volunteers during the day.

Even business benefits:

- Unschooled children develop more creativity and initiative, as well as problem-solving, critical, and analytical thinking, information management, healthy lifestyles, and social and communication skills. Well-rounded individuals with these soft skills, combined with technical skills, make great leaders, managers, employees, and entrepreneurs.

- When kids don't want to be in a school, teachers are forced to give "corpse-in-seat" marks for showing up, which undermines the teaching of responsibility and accountability—two personal values that are essential to successful businesses.

- Kids learn work ethic and commitment through adult-guided jobs and volunteer work.

- Retailers get more customers during off-peak hours.

- Unschooled children are highly educated and learn how to apply their skills.

Postsecondary institutions also benefit:

- Unschooled children are more educated. Acceptable level of understanding material in schools is estimated at 50 percent. Intrinsically motivated learning can result in up to 100 percent acceptable levels of understanding.

- Unschooled children are well practiced in independent learning and time management. They don't need to be spoon-fed information or constantly reminded to turn in work. They work very well independently.

- Unschooled students are well read, having had time to read from so many sources on many different subjects.

- Unschooled children are already well socialized and comfortable with the population diversity in a postsecondary environment. They have grown up with people of differing ages, religions, cultures, races, and abilities, and have had practice conversing with them and learning from them.

- Unschooled students are more mature and are ready to settle into serious learning for the career they have chosen.

- Serious, engaged students appreciate professors' time and attention, set class morale, and help to establish a fertile learning environment. They are there because they want to learn, not there someone else's agenda has placed them there. They ask thoughtful questions and stimulate productive discussion.

PART 3:
HOW TO UNSCHOOL —
3 CRITICAL COMPONENTS OF A PERSONALIZED EDUCATION

12

Adult / Facilitator

"Teachers are education professionals in the classroom. Parents are education professionals in the home."

The 3-legged stool

When my daughter was two, she would cling and cling. Every time I put her down to attend to her brothers, she would say, "Up, up!" She was very persistent, and I would comply and pick her up every time. Onlookers would chide me for being so accommodating, but I continued. When the same girl turned 22, after graduating from university, she decided to go to Italy. Her travel friends backed out and she asked if I wanted to go, since I didn't have a full-time job. I jumped at the chance. It was so much fun to have free time, a friend who was also my daughter, and a wonderful country to visit. All those times I picked my daughter up and gave her what she needed paid off. As well as a close family relationship, we have a lifelong friendship as a result of non-punitive parenting and educational upbringing.

Unschooling must comprise three simple components:

1. **Adult**: This can be a parent or teacher (acting as a facilitator), grandparent, mentor, older sibling, aunt, uncle, neighbor, friend, or caregiver.

2. **Resources**: These can be as basic as a library card and an internet connection.

3. **Time**: Abundant, unstructured, and truly free.

That is it. Like a stool that cannot stand with only two legs, all three components must be present. Let's look at these in depth. This chapter focuses on the role of the adult, which is the most important of the three components.

In an unschooling home, the adult is the parent; in a free-school, the adult can be a teacher, coach, or another caring adult—any person who will help the child access what he needs or desires. The parent takes care of a child's physical, emotional, and social development from birth to school age. Traditionally, parents outsourced their child's cognitive development to a school and a teacher, but as parents become subject matter experts in many areas, they are able to take on the facilitation of cognitive development at home. The adult is far more indispensable than curriculum. In a digital world where much contact is remote, more adult contact in the physical world is critical. "Students, especially the most marginalized and most difficult, need to feel that they have a place at school, to feel connected to the adults in the building, to feel someone is on their side." (Gavel, 2014)

What does the adult actually do? The adult does not directly teach, unless the learner really, really wants her to. Rather, the adult facilitates. The adult shops with the child for supplies, accompanies her to the library and on field trips, reads and writes for her when she can't, and answers questions. The adult contributes enthusiasm, knowledge, and the ability to seek out more resources if the child desires. In the early years, from ages 0 - 12, the adult also provides supervision. As children move into the teen years and are generally capable of accessing resources on their own, the facilitator takes on more of a mentor role.

Under home education regulations, the adult takes responsibility for providing the child's education, but doesn't necessarily have to teach it—only to ensure that it happens.

Is the adult supervised?

In some provinces, the law requires that a certified teacher supervise the adult and child. This supervisor can be called a facilitator, a learning leader, a home education manager, or a coordinator. I prefer the term "reporter," because their basic role is to report the child's progress to the government. I may have needed their help and support during our first years of home-educating, but with experience, I became confident in our process and in my mind, their role was relegated to reporter.

Other unschooling parents provide peer assistance via Facebook groups and support blogs. In Canada, teachers receive no formal, mandatory training that fosters their understanding of home education, yet the law puts them in a position to supervise homeschooling families. Teachers with no training or experience cannot presume to evaluate home educators or learners. There is absolutely no need for teachers or the government to oversee home education.

Sample unschooling education or learning plan

In jurisdictions that require a plan for educating the child, the sample below might help unschooling parents. These outcomes reflect the fundamental guidelines of the Alberta government for a basic, adequate home education program, and could serve as a model for other governments. We are not required to follow the school system's grade-by-grade outcomes.

These are the government home education targets, and the plan is completed when the child turns 20 years old.

Sample Self-Directed Home Education Plan

Name: Unschooling Child

Year: 20____, Grade 11, age 17

Outcome (Subject)	Resources **Bolded** items are to be purchased and submitted for funding reimbursement	**Means of Assessment** Observation, discussion, quizzes, tests, writing samples, oral reading, oral questions, portfolio review, demonstrations, presentations, product, instruction receipt, time logs, photographs, video
(a) read for information, understanding and enjoyment (English)	Library books, home library and internet, **ebooks, Kindle, Laptop or Desktop Computer**	List and library receipt of books read
(b) write and speak clearly, accurately, and appropriately for the context (English)	As required	One writing sample and discussion
(c) use mathematics to solve problems in business, science, and daily life (Math)	Purchase **textbook** and child will self-teach using problems generated by our basement renovation project	Observation and photographs
(d) understand the physical world, ecology, and the diversity of life (Science)	Nature walks, discussion, **Unlimited museum, zoo, park**, and **science center visits in various cities**	Observation and photographs
(e) understand the scientific method, the nature of science and technology, and their application to daily life (Science)	Computer, Raspberry Pi, electric motors and garden supplies; **observe an electricity monitor**	Observation and photographs
(f) know the history and geography of Canada and have a general understanding of world history and geography (History and Geography)	Videos, and discussions, **museum visits** and **places of historic interest.**	Observation and discussion
(g) understand Canada's political, social, and economic systems within a global context (Social Studies)	Discussions on current news topics; **possible visits to political venues such as the legislature; travel to other countries. Magazine subscriptions to Maclean's, Time, and The Economist;** watch **videos**	Observation and discussion
(h) respect the cultural and religious diversity and the common values of Canada (Social Studies)	Attend the Gay Pride Parade, volunteer at the food bank, and help out neighbors	List of events attended

(i) demonstrate desirable personal characteristics such as respect, responsibility, fairness, honesty, caring, loyalty, and commitment to democratic ideals. (Teamwork and Life Skills)	Siblings and family life; video gaming	Observation and discussion
(j) recognize the importance of personal well-being and appreciate how family, friends, and community contribute to that well-being (Health)	Shower, soap, fridge, microwave, stove, groceries	Observation
(k) know the basic elements of an active, healthful lifestyle (Health)	**Treadmill**, lake access for canoeing and swimming; **skating; ski passes; horseback riding lessons; kitchen supplies** to learn how to cook healthy homemade meals; **CPR course**	Observation
(l) understand and appreciate literature, the arts, and the creative process (Arts and Humanities)	**Art supplies, theater tickets, concert tickets; fabrics and supplies** for making costumes and learning how to sew	Photographs of art, ticket stubs to productions
(m) research an issue thoroughly and evaluate the credibility and reliability of information sources (cross-curricular)	**Computer and internet access.** Discussion.	Observation
(n) demonstrate critical and creative thinking skills in problem solving and decision making (cross-curricular)	**Video games, board games, online computer games;** clock	Certification of levels achieved
(o) demonstrate competence in using information technologies (cross-curricular)	Computer and software programs	Demonstration
(p) know how to work independently and as part of a team (Life Skills)	Siblings join in guilds and as a team for League of Legends and Overwatch; games from Steam	Discussion
(q) manage time and resources needed to complete a task (Life Skills)	Clock, computer games, chores, volunteering	Demonstration
(r) demonstrate initiative, leadership, flexibility, and persistence (Life Skills)	Family life, volunteering, chores, jobs	Observation
(s) evaluate endeavors and continually strive for improvement (Life Skills)	Life, self-reflection	Discussion
(t) have the desire and realize the need for lifelong learning (Life Skills)	Internet and classes provided by online schools	Class certificates

Adapted from the (SOLO) Schedule of Learning Outcomes for Students Receiving Home Education Programs That Do Not Follow the Alberta Programs of Study, (Alberta Education, 2010)

Adults facilitate rather than teach

The word "facilitate" comes from the word "to draw from," meaning to ask questions in a way that prompts learners to seek the answers. A facilitator asks "thinking" questions. This invites children to empower their own learning. (Nichols, 2000)

This illustrates why home education children do not need parents as teachers. In fact, the Fraser report showed that parents do a great job home educating their children all the way through high school, even when lacking a high school education themselves. (Van Pelt, 2015) Because they do not teach, they do not need to have all the subject matter expertise. They just need to know how to guide the child to adequate desired resources.

Teachers are the best thing about school, and most children do not get enough teacher time. However, teachers must give direct instruction, whether kids want it or not. Many kids are happy to figure things out for themselves and only need teachers to be facilitators that will support learning when the student is ready.

The system of "school" is imposed on teachers, too

I believe that teaching and parenting are the noblest of professions. Both teachers and parents go into their jobs with a sincere love of children and a desire to make a difference. So much of their work is unpaid and unrewarded and especially, unvalued, yet is invaluable to the individual child and to society as a whole. What parent or teacher doesn't love that moment when a child "gets it"—it's such a joyful moment!

I have such great respect for teachers, particularly as they are working in a system that must keep parents, kids, principals, administrators, and government happy. I could not juggle all that and am constantly amazed by the teachers who can. Successfully keeping 30 kids on task for six hours a day, 200 days a year, is a task worthy of sainthood.

Much of a teacher's day is spent on assessment and administrative tasks rather than on the children. We must free teachers of these administrative burdens to allow them to become facilitators.

When the government mandates new curriculum or teaching methods, I've sometimes heard from teachers that they simply close their classroom doors and do what they have always done. It makes sense in that it is hard to make huge changes in curriculum every few years that may not be evidence based. Teachers are human. Why mess with what works?

It must be incredibly hard for teachers to deal with children who don't want to learn. Disengaged students may experience barriers to learning, from learning disabilities to a difficult home life. Through no fault of their own, they may find it hard to engage with the mandated government program. Finding ways to motivate such students is a real challenge for teachers.

The role of facilitator is one that influences rather than controls; motivation follows. Teachers influence and impact when they don't try to control the play or the agenda.

When children—or adults, for that matter—sense they are being controlled, they are more apt to rebel and not engage.

In school, teaching directly to the middle of the class does not work. Only the 50 percent in the middle benefit. The kids who catch on quickly become bored and disruptive, and the kids who take more time to grasp concepts lose out because they get the message that they are somehow defective for not "getting it" quickly. If teachers could help each child at their own level in their own time, everyone would benefit.

When my kids wouldn't take instruction from me nor from the schools, I took a break. When my fourth and fifth children were born, I had so much on my plate that I didn't attempt lessons at the kitchen table anymore. The fifth one was very spirited and high maintenance. Juggling a fussy baby in a sling, a gentle toddler, a curious Kindergartener and two homeschooling boys was too much for me. That went on for two years, during which I noticed, observed, and noted how much learning still went on—even without me as the "teacher." Firmly planted in my role as facilitator, the kids were self-determining their learning and absorbing so much knowledge on their own.

Learners need teachers to guide their questions—or do they?

Many theorize that inquiry-based, experiential, or discovery learning doesn't work. Kirschner, Sweller and Clark, in their piece, *Why Minimal Guidance During Instruction Does Not Work*, argue that discovery learning only occurs once learners have sufficient background knowledge to be able to problem solve. (Kirshner, 2006) I disagree.

First, the authors have not accessed enough studies on pure free-learning unschoolers, simply because not enough research exists; and second, the current version of school-based inquiry learning is not anything like unschooling. Unschooling means a learner is truly free to ask and find answers to his own questions. In school, learners undergoing an inquiry-based approach are told what subject they must inquire about. Their questioning is not initiated by them and consequently, they may not be truly motivated to seek the answer. Whose inquiry is it? Not the students'.

Educational theories are not based on unschooling populations and certainly the above-named authors were not basing their studies on non-institutionalized learners. It's very much like studying animals in captivity in the zoo versus studying animals in the wild. There are many differences. Studying children in school that are forced to "ask powerful questions" of someone else's choosing is very different from studying children in a home environment who ask powerful questions arising from their own curiosity. In the former, the student doesn't care about the answers; in the latter, you can't stop them in their drive to find answers.

And that is why our country's math scores are dropping. All math in school is inquiry-based. Students in schools are forced to solve problems in five different ways to come to the same conclusion. How confusing! The problems are not their own. They are not interested in knowing the answers because the math problems are contrived. No kid wants to know why Dick brings 30 bottles of water to a picnic. As my 13-year-old son said, "No kid ever brings water to a picnic!" When kids come to you and want to know if $80 from their savings will buy a video game worth $55 and three extra skins at $15 each, they are motivated to find at least one reliable way of solving that math problem. One method, one answer. For a real-life scenario, they will find it.

I believe that direct teaching is necessary for many learners in the higher grades of math, but keep in mind that some children self-teach all the way through Grade 12. When they self-teach, they do need good step-by-step textbooks that teach at least one reliable method of solving math problems. When my children were first learning math concepts by playing, I observed them learning fractions through baking, decimals through shopping, and percentages through video gaming. They had all the mental math they needed right through the first seven grades. In Grade 8, they needed instruction to learn how to add equivalent fractions on paper, but they had an intuitive feel for the concept because they had learned to add fractions mentally.

In these later grades, I found the opposite of what Kirschner, Sweller and Clark hypothesized. Grade 8 is a good level to begin formal math skills on paper, especially if your child is leaning toward a STEM career. Around 13 years of age, when abstract math concepts were introduced, my kids did require more concrete, direct instruction, either from a teacher or a text. They had the background experiential knowledge, but the new math "inquiry-based" textbooks did not teach. The textbook posed problems and the learners had to solve them on their own. This was frustrating. When kids do want to learn concrete steps, they deserve a book that gives them those solid instructions. Even my husband, who is an engineer, tossed the textbooks aside and asked "Where do they teach how to do quadratic equations? There is nothing in here that shows a step-by-step example." Canada's PISA scores from testing 15-year-olds illustrate this problem. (Angel, 2018)

A common question is, "What about parents who just let their kids do nothing?"

I have to say that there were times when I was *not* interested in facilitating my child's desire to learn something (like the Second World War) and it was *not* my decision to further his education or not—he would pester me for resources, eventually finding them on his own when I wasn't forthcoming—great practice for future university research! We seem to think we are the gatekeepers to knowledge, but we are not. We are facilitators when we choose to be—but on occasions we choose not to be, our children will find out what they want to know anyway, despite any obstacles in their path. It is arrogant of us to think that we can stop a person from learning. We can't.

What does the adult actually do?

Answer questions. When a child asks a question, we should give a factual answer; if we don't know the answer, we must look things up together or suggest other resources—a book, movie, computer game, or expert. Sometimes those questions come at inconvenient times. Run with it. One mom told me, "I unschooled last week. It was the most exhausting week of homeschooling I ever had. I dug up stuff and went to places, and it took much longer than the one hour a day we normally spend on seatwork!"

Ask questions. Take a curious interest in the world and share your observations and discoveries. Sometimes you will stimulate the child's interest. Other times it will fall flat, and that is okay. Let it go.

Listen. Listen attentively when your child shares something with you: an insight, a story, an experience.

Find mentors. We can connect our children with friends we know that work in an occupation that interests the child. They may suggest a workshop, or perhaps job shadowing.

Help with projects. Kids don't know where we keep everything, so we need to help them dig for things in our house. If we don't have something, we have the financial and logistical means to help them get it.

Find and hire tutors for older children whose knowledge is more advanced than parents'.

Purchase supplies. Adults have money. Kids don't. Adults can drive. Kids can't. When my young teen son wanted old appliances to take apart, I grabbed the car keys and said, "Let's go." We would head out to the recycle drop-off regularly or purchase cheap appliances from Goodwill. I would put the call out for donations on my social media groups. As a facilitator, I could help him get the resources he needed.

Administer the "program." The adult takes care of government home education administrative requirements. She or he may need to provide an educational plan and assessment to comply with government regulations.

Expose things. Also called "strewing," this is the practice of leaving interesting items out on tables, carpets, or in the car that children might find fun to explore, read, or play with. Introduce games, puzzles, books, toys, kits, and lab experiments. The kids never take down the box of pattern blocks from the shelf to play, but when I take down the box and spread the blocks on the table, they saunter into the room to pick up something else and instantly start manipulating them. If the children are not interested, they will leave it alone, and that is okay too.

Take them on field trips. Explore your city, go to theaters, galleries, museums, zoos, science centers, sporting events, restaurants, and shows and meet a variety of people.

Travel. Always a great learning experience.

Talk to strangers. People in line-ups, on the bus, and everywhere are very interesting. Children who see their parents talk to strangers find out that the world is full of fascinating people with amazing stories, and that most people are open and trustworthy.

Get back to nature. Get outside with your kids. Most kids hate going outside until an adult offers to go out and play with them. Then they have so much fun that you can't get them back inside! Organize duties. Engage children in daily adult life around the home: chores, cooking, gardening, composting, renovating.

Be patient. You won't see results right away. Changes in your child will happen over time, as he realizes that learning is fun and can be done all the time in lots of ways. You may feel frustrated that your kids don't want to study, or read, or write papers. Let them play music instead, or play pretend games, or read comic books, or play outside. Whatever they want to do, let them do it.

Trust. This is hard, but it is the key to successful facilitation. You must trust the power of self-directed learning.

Adults are not perfect

We homeschooling parents are anything but perfect. And that's okay! People often say, "You must be a brave soul. I would never have the patience to homeschool." To which I would like to respond, "I yell at my kids as much as the next parent!"

We are not elitist, either. In the news, you regularly hear of homeschoolers getting into Harvard or winning spelling bees. Yes and no. Most of us are pretty average people. A homeschooling group I attended included a child who was a festival violin winner at age seven, and another child who read Lord of the Rings at age nine. My two children were in the corner with their action figures saying "Die, die, die!" In fact, depending on the day, if the kids were being kind, helpful, and decent to each other, I would tell the store clerks, "Yes, we homeschool." If they were being little hellions, I would say that it was a school PD (Professional Development) day!

At several of the Inspiring Education input sessions, participants were asked the following question:

What was your worst learning/teaching experience?

They answered: Teachers are inappropriate, short-tempered, boring, lack knowledge, have no sense of humor, are not at same level of understanding, have no passion, no energy, are condescending, play favorites, teach because they have to, have big egos, and they threaten and punish. Made me feel embarrassed to be in front of the class.

What is your best learning/teaching experience?

They answered: Teachers are inspiring, humble, funny, believe in you, care if you understand or not, take time to help you learn, have sense of humor, are genuine, flexible, enjoy what they are doing, are non-judgmental, connect with learners, trust that the group knows, ask questions, let us make mistakes in order to learn, are knowledgeable, engaging, and giving. (Friesen, 2009)

Children will always, always need adults—whether parents or teachers—to facilitate their learning. Try to emulate the positive characteristics above and learners will love learning. But don't kick yourself over the bad days!

Strewing

Human beings learn from each other. That's how have always adapted to our environment. Ergo, adults are hard-wired to teach. The entire job of parenting is teaching.

Children copy. Watch a grandfather teach a girl to fish, or a grandmother teach a boy to knit. They are patient, use age-appropriate language, and answer questions. We are natural teachers.

A common question is "What about exposure?" Unschoolers are not "unexposed." Strewing is leaving objects lying around to see if they might attract interest. If so, the child will ask questions and use the object—perhaps as it was meant to be used; perhaps in an entirely innovative way. If not, the object will sit there to be cleaned up the next time the room is tidied. Parents introduce symphonies or theater by inviting a child along. There are many things we don't want our children exposed to, but eventually they will stumble upon them anyway. Underexposure is never a problem with internet so accessible.

Can the unschooling parent work outside the home?

Yes, of course. In fact, many parents feel that having a part-time job or an at-home business—or a new baby, for that matter—helps take the focus off of controlling the child's learning by channeling energy into another part of their lives.

I worked part-time while unschooling my children and it really helped me. I am a very judging (the "J" in Myers-Briggs Personality Preference Tool), controlling personality, and to be more relaxed about my children's learning, I had to channel that part of me into something else. So, in my paid job teaching child development to adults, I am organized, structured, and very methodical. This allows me to be more flexible and meandering with my children.

The only drawback to working part-time was finding childcare for my school-age children. Children under the age of 12, depending on the maturity and problem-solving ability of the child, still require adult supervision. I was in a babysitting co-op, which helped, but the children didn't want just to go and play with the sitters' preschoolers all the time. The sitters didn't know how to entertain school-age children other than with television, and they weren't comfortable letting the children entertain themselves. We cobbled together childcare as best we could by hiring homeschooling teens to supervise in our home in addition to using the babysitting co-op. The kids entertained themselves for the most part and continued to learn on their own. There were a few messes to cleaned up at the end of the day, but they were worth it.

I found full-time work was a harder and I could not do that and still provide facilitation for the children. The odd time, when I had to attend a course for five full days straight, it was a huge challenge to organize meals, do laundry, and clean up messes. I can see why parents who work outside the home full-time send their children to school. They have peace of mind knowing that their children are not setting the house on fire or running out onto the road.

I did depend a lot on the older children to babysit the younger ones, and that was a paid job for them. No other chores were paid, but childcare yes, because I really needed them do the job diligently and with a high standard of care. But we added a twist: we paid both the caregiver sibling and the younger sibling, to encourage cooperation between the two. It worked, in that it didn't give more power to one over the over. They were a team! We also found homeschooling babysitting co-ops helpful.

As the kids got older and started more formal learning in self-taught or online courses, I could easily walk out of the house and depend on them to meet the obligations of their courses because they were used to independent learning.

At what age should parents cease to be facilitators?

I don't want to be a helicopter parent, doing things for my children that they should be doing for themselves. But we should let go gradually, as children's capabilities grow. In Part 4 of this book, there is a section on age and development as well as capabilities. In the teen years from ages 13 – 18, kids should start doing some of their own administrative tasks. This is the final third of parenting—start handing it over! For example, at age 15, children should be able to make their own doctor's appointments. Parents might ask themselves why they are still doing that. Is it to feel needed? Letting go of responsibilities doesn't mean that we love our children less, but that we are putting their growth before our own desire to feel needed.

When children become young adults and leave home for college, they will need organizational skills to handle banking, doctors, dentists, prescriptions, lab tests, student loan officers, course registrations, professors, dorm supervisors, office staff, and much more. They must be able to advocate for themselves, especially in light of today's privacy laws that prohibit institutions from dealing with the parents of an adult child.

How proactive should parents be, in anticipating what you think your kids might need? I simply waited. If they needed something, they asked. In any case, with five kids, I couldn't anticipate that well anyway—they had to be pretty vocal to get my attention! I really wanted to encourage them to seek out what they need, especially as they moved out of town. For the most part, they have proved to be resourceful and self-sufficient.

Why children don't always listen to homeschooling parents

Authoritarian education works in a school environment, but not in the home. Teachers are told not to crack a smile in the classroom until after Christmas, so that students learn who is boss and the teacher establishes his authority. But this does not work in the home environment.

In a historic decision on January 30, 2004, the Supreme Court of Canada voted to uphold Section 43 of the Criminal Code, which continued to allow physical punishment in the home, but removed it from the schools. It emphatically stated that the teacher-child relationship in schools is fundamentally different from the parent-child relationship in the home. The parent-child relationship is unique, and this is demonstrated in every home education family. The statement adequately reflects the sentiments expressed by thousands of home educating parents who have participated in my support groups and workshops. When a child leaves the school system to be home-educated, he comes home to a safe, "known" environment. He is free to express his feelings, likes, dislikes, and interests with people he loves and who love him.

When parents try to replicate the authoritarianism of the school by insisting their child complete a certain curriculum, they end up in power struggles, battles, confrontations, and tears. I had my share of all of those in the first year that I tried to do "structured school-replicated-in-the-home type of homeschooling." It's very difficult to wear the two distinct hats of parent and teacher. Kid's don't separate the roles; families shouldn't either.

The main difference in home education is the lack of fear in the relationship. Both child and parent feel safe. Your child can scream at you, "I hate science!" and know that you will still love him tomorrow. Your child doesn't worry that you will humiliate her in front of her peers by asking her to do a complex math problem on the blackboard. So, your "teacher authority" will not work in the home.

On one particularly trying day, I was trying to teach long division to my two older sons. They were giddy-gaddying as 10- and 11-year-old brothers will do. Their eight-year-old sister was teasing the four-year-old brother, who began crying. The baby was howling to be picked up and nursed. I became very frustrated and like most homeschooling parents that have lost it from time to time, I threatened to put the kids into school. At least then I could be the after-school milk-and-cookies loving mom, letting the school teacher be the baddy who had to teach them long division! Surely, teachers in school got more respect than this! The boys started crying. The next day, I noticed "Math sux" scribbled on their math workbook. I felt terrible! I know that I am not alone. On online homeschooling forums, many parents echo the same sentiment. The child is not ready or is disinterested in the material and he balks; the parent is pulling her hair out in frustration and anger, under pressure to meet government outcomes.

As we slid into unschooling, we relaxed. I no longer had to fight with the kids to do work or produce output for fear of getting into trouble with the supervisor or the government.

Unschooling made our home so much more loving, fun, and relaxed.

Teaching styles and parenting styles

I came to the conclusion that home-education teaching styles are very much tied to parenting styles in the home, and very different than the teacher-student dynamics in school. In parent education programs, we teach parents that in a collaborative parenting style, there are four areas over which they have little control: eating, sleeping, toilet training, and learning. A parent's job is to facilitate the conditions that make those actions happen, but they can't force them to happen. The collaborative parenting style has been researched and proven (Gordon, 2000) to have better outcomes for children in their emotional, physical, and cognitive development, more so then the authoritarian or permissive parenting styles. The collaborative style of parenting meets the needs of both parent and child, whereas the authoritarian style only meets the needs of the parents.

An essay might get written, but at what cost to the parent-child relationship? Mark Anielski, a presenter at Inspiring Education, stated, "Success is not economic but enduring happiness and well-being. How is that truly reflected in our children's education system?" (Anielski, 2009) In study after study, relationships are what we value most in our society. Family is what we value most. Are we teaching what we truly value?

Unschooling is not unparenting

Radical whole life unschooling is taking the child-led approach to education into the parenting arena. Many radical unschoolers dislike rules and structure of any kind and although they profess that their families don't have rules, in reality, everyone has them, whether they are defined or not.

Unschooling by definition means that the parent or caring adult is most always present and attentive. Neglectful parenting is a situation in which the parent leaves the child alone to fend for himself. An unschooling adult is never uninvolved. In fact, the one-on-one parent-child ratio provides far superior attention than any school could give.

Sometimes, unschooling is criticized in the media as an indulgent, almost abusive parenting style. Media chooses to frame unschooling stories by showing children running wild or fighting each other with sticks, giving the viewer the impression that the children have no guidance, limits, or structure. This is not true. Media always frames a story with a slant, and most stories on unschooling have unfairly been negatively portrayed. In Part 1, I described two distinct types of unschoolers: educational unschoolers and radical whole life unschoolers. Examples of families practicing radical unschooling are portrayed under an "extreme" lens. In reality, unschooling families have a wide range of parenting styles. Some are more structured on the parenting side and looser on the education side, as is the case in our family, or loose on the parenting side and stricter on the educational side. There are many shades of parenting; no two families are exactly alike.

Not only are families different, but children are as well. Temperament is inborn; some children are very determined in choosing what they want to learn and how, others are easygoing and accept whatever is plopped on their educational plates.

There must be a good fit between the child's and the parent's temperaments. A very structured parent who wants to direct teach a very spirited child who has his own ideas is going to have power struggles. Laid-back, easygoing parents with laid-back easygoing children must agree on some structure to maintain order in the home.

My spirited children craved some structure and began imposing it on themselves at about age eight. They created a plan for the day that included reading time, going for walks, visiting time, and quiet time. As a parent who is also on the spirited side, I craved a plan for the day as well. I made my own plan, which had some structure but was looser to accommodate my easygoing children who needed more downtime.

Radical or educational, unschooling can work for all families. The key is getting the right fit between the parent's temperament and personality and the child's. As long as it works for all family members and no one is crying, all is well!

The Parenting Style Axis

A parenting style is defined as the way a parent consistently behaves the majority of the time, or about 70 percent, toward his or her children. Parents waver from their preferred parenting style about 30 percent of the time, when they are sick, under stress, absent, or on vacation. They also waver when their children are sick or on holidays, or during other unusual circumstances. Parenting styles are a continuum of two elements necessary for healthy child rearing: nurturing and structure.

I describe various parenting styles below. Research from many sources shows that practicing the Authoritative or Collaborative style most of the time results in optimal outcomes for children. The Authoritarian, Indulgent, and Neglectful Styles are associated with poorer outcomes. The less punitive the style, the better for the child. (NLSCY, 2004) (Arnall, 2013, 2014) (Baumrind, 1971)

The Authoritarian parenting style: "It's my way or the highway"

Parents make most decisions and set goals for the child, who has almost no input. Parents' needs are supreme.

The Authoritative parenting style: "You can have input, but I will still decide"

Parents make most of the decisions and set goals and rules but consider the child's input. Parents' and child's needs are equally important and they strive to satisfy both, although parent's needs will triumph in the face of true conflict.

The Collaborative parenting style: "Let's find a win-win solution together"

Collaborative parenting strives to involve the child's opinions, feelings, and age-appropriate decisions. Parents don't hand the power of parenting over to the child—they don't give the child the whole rope but do give him longer and longer pieces of the rope as the child grows, under their watchful presence and guidance. Parents' and child's needs are equally important. The parents set few rules and give their child as much freedom as possible except in physically dangerous or unsafe situations. Enforcement of rules involves solving the problem rather than meting out arbitrary consequences or punishments. This parenting style was predominant in the families of many of today's leading CEOs. (Alter, 2016)

The Indulgent (Permissive) parenting style: "He can't help it"

Children are given too many material items and parents take over many of the tasks that children should be doing. Parents try to shield their children as much as possible from difficult or unpleasant experiences and from the natural and logical consequences of their actions. This is also called "helicopter" or "snowplow" parenting. Parents require no age-appropriate contributions from the child in the form of chores, financial help, educational attainment, or employment.

The Uninvolved parenting style: "It's not my problem"

This style does not require any respect or contribution from the child. Parents are often absent and are as removed as possible from their children's lives; when they are present, they indulge the child and make few demands. Children receive almost no supervision or direction from their parents.

Personally, I think that nurturing is even more important than structure. The outside world provides plenty of structure in the form of laws rules in society, workplaces, and schools, from teachers, coaches, extended families, and friends. But only family and close friends can steadily provide nurturing, listening, comfort, and responsiveness— in essence, unconditional love. Nurturing provided from even one attentive adult can prevent most toxic stress and provide resiliency when adverse childhood experiences occur.

Ideally, parents should strive for the Authoritative and Collaborative parenting style (upper right quadrant in the figure below) most of the time. This zone incorporates a high level of structure and nurturing. It is impossible to be in this zone all the time, but if parents aim to be there 70 percent of the time, they are consistently doing well. (Arnall, 2014)

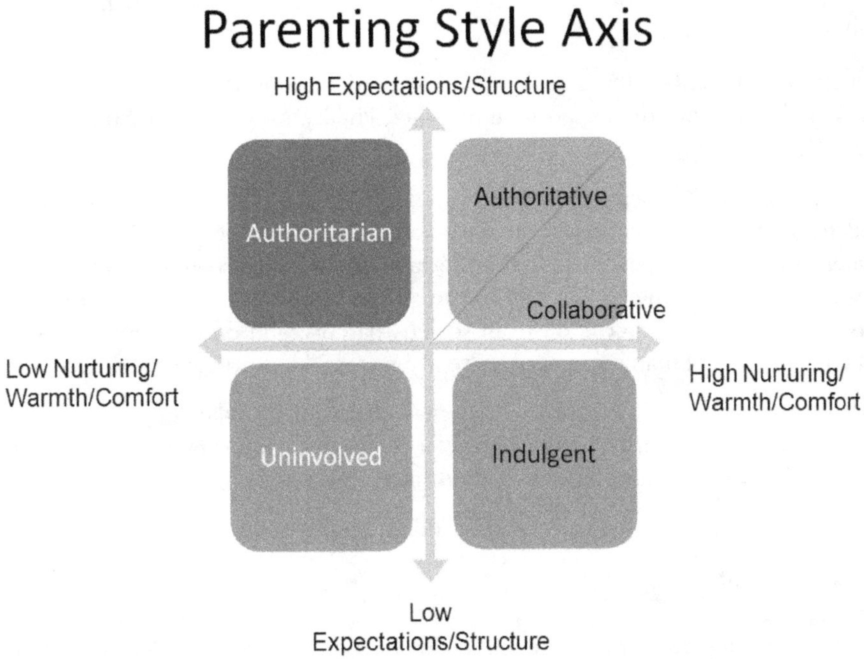

Parenting Style Axis

High Expectations/Structure

Authoritarian

Authoritative

Collaborative

Low Nurturing/
Warmth/Comfort

High Nurturing/
Warmth/Comfort

Uninvolved

Indulgent

Low
Expectations/Structure

The Parenting Style Axis (Arnall, 2014)

Nurturing, warmth, comfort

If structure is like putting a bandage on a child's scraped knee, then nurturing is the kiss to make it better! Studies begun in the 1950s, most notably the one conducted by John Bowlby and Mary Ainsworth, have consistently proven the validity of attachment, warmth, nurturing, and comfort in the parent-child relationship, beginning at birth and never ending. (Bowlby, 1988) Some ways that parents can demonstrate nurturing behavior are:

- Expressing unconditional love through kind and encouraging words, comfort, care, and attention.

- Listening and giving emotional validation.

- Providing non-sexual touch such as hugs, pats, cuddles, kisses, and stroking.

- Solving parenting problems without any form of emotional or physical punishment.

Expectations and structure

Everyone has expectations, spoken or unspoken, of others in the family. An example of an expectation in our house is that the teens will turn off the lights when they retire to bed, long after we do.

Unschooling parents value education and learning but not necessarily schools and systems, and most have the expectation that their children will seek out knowledge when they need it.

Expectations must be age-appropriate and geared to the child's temperament, gender, and personality. It helps if parents have some knowledge of child development and understand what to expect of their child socially, emotionally, cognitively, and physically. My 17-year-old daughter once said to me, "I never knew that not going to university was an option. The expectation from society, parents, and others were always there." Of course, she had many options, but we live in a world of preconceived expectations.

Structure includes the presence of parental scaffolding (guidance), advice, direction, mentoring, supervision, and monitoring of a child's behavior, even in the teen years. All of the following are examples of structural support:

- Providing for physical, social, academic, and emotional needs.

- Providing or facilitating an education.

- Allowing age-appropriate and child-appropriate decisions and the natural evolution of consequences, when safe.

- Guiding, facilitating, mentoring, coaching, and teaching to navigate life situations.

- Using the collaborative problem-solving method for all conflicts and disciplinary problems.

- Setting family rules and limits together.

- Establishing routines, rituals, and celebrations.

- Providing supervision and monitoring, even through the teen years.

- Setting reasonable, age-appropriate behavior expectations.

- Addressing bad behavior without using punishment, rather than ignoring or tolerating it.

- Modeling responsible citizenship and relationship skills.

- Expecting the child to live up to his or her potential.

An authoritarian approach that might work in a classroom is not effective in a home setting, except in the cases of a very few authoritarian parents who practice this parenting style in their homeschooling. Forcing a child to follow the government curriculum is relatively easy when a parent is authoritarian. However, forcing a child to learn specific subject matter outcomes that he is not interested in or ready for is stressful, unproductive, and detrimental to the parent-child relationship. The child's self esteem is affected and he could develop fears and mental blocks to learning when the material is forced on him before he is ready. "My son's school saw him as a problem to be solved and they taught to his weaknesses, to the exclusion of his strengths. He began to see himself as they did and this created much pressure to succeed on their terms," says a parent on a homeschooling list.

Parents practicing collaborative parenting choose a home education style that meshes with their parenting philosophy and builds bonds between parent and child. Unschooling is one educational philosophy that fits well with the collaborative parenting style. See the book *Parenting with Patience* for more information on parenting styles.

Performance pressure

A common concern is that the government will coerce parents into forcing learning outcomes, subject matter, and methods on their children and force them to do seatwork against their will. In public school, teachers encourage but try not to push children through subject matter they can't handle. The government cannot hold homeschoolers to a higher standard than that required of their public school counterparts. Just as no supervising school should tell a parent which parenting style to use, no supervising school should pressure a parent or child to study things the child is not interested in or adopt a home education approach that does not work for the child. If parents have to push hard for the child to remember content, the child is simply not developmentally ready to learn it. The government must respect the autonomy of parents; they know their child best.

A mom in an unschooling forum once said, "In the first eight months that I was home-schooling, I used every method of discipline I could think of to make my child pay attention while I was lecturing, with negligible success... I've since stopped lecturing and started exploring, with my children, the areas that interest them. I've realized that curriculum is only one of many tools for learning. The difference in the amount of learning taking place is phenomenal—but it's nothing compared to the improvement in our relationship. It does take a real effort to learn to look at your children not so much as your creations that you must constantly strive to improve, but as your fellow travelers on life's path."

8 parenting and education myths that are not evidence-based

There are some common parenting and education myths that have frequently popped up as questions in my parenting classes over the last 20 years. I am constantly amazed at how widespread they are across the globe. There is very little research to support these myths, but they tend to persist as advice gets passed down through the generations.

1. Bad habits last a lifetime

I'm sure you have heard at least one relative or friend say, "You don't want to bring your baby into bed with you, because then you are starting a bad habit and he will never leave!" Should we then not start our babies off in diapers for fear that they will get too cozy in them and never learn to use the toilet? I often ask parents, "Should I start hitting my child over the head with a fry pan now so he gets used to the pain when he begins having childhood headaches later? No!"

It's the same with other lessons in life. Preparation is good, but it doesn't take years. It takes days. Children change and learn new things when they need to learn them. It takes a child three days to break a bad habit; it takes an adult 21 days (we are a little more set in our ways as we age!). So, do what works now. When it no longer works for the adult or the child or both, then make the change. This applies to everything in parenting from sleep hygiene, to bribing kids to use the toilet, to instilling good study habits.

2. Children should have impulse control by age 3 and should therefore "listen" to the adults

No, they don't have impulse control by age three. Young children are egocentric, meaning that their needs matter more to them than yours do. As they should—this is normal development. As they grow into the school-age years, they become aware of and begin to care about others' needs. They begin to have better executive function—self-control, listening, paying attention—by age five or six; that is why school is not mandatory until that age. Even through the school years, they don't have maximum executive function. They develop a good dose of it in puberty and an even higher level around age 17.

3. You must correct mistakes or misbehavior in the moment or young children will immediately forget

Again, there is no research that supports this. Yes, children may forget the place in time when events occur, but they do remember something from earlier in the day. If you are angry, take your ten-minute time-out to calm down and then come back to address the situation calmly and wisely. Or address it at bedtime when everyone is feeling good and the teaching might stick. Young children will still remember! Lots of repetition will help them develop routine good choices.

4. Children remember things forever, so pack in lots of learning, activities, lessons, experiences, and travel while they are young and before they resist as teenagers

I wish! For all the worldwide traveling we did, carting five children around the globe, they remember nothing before age 12. For all those lessons we stuffed into their heads, they remember nothing now. Well, maybe one or two memories stick out, like three-wheeled cars in England and sinking boats in the bathtub as a science experiment, or the one cool snack someone brought to the soccer game when they were six, but nothing else brought back memories when I showed them photographs from when they were young. Surely those experiences built their brains unconsciously, but they don't even remember their childhood best friends. On the flip side, when I asked my university-age kids if they remember how much yelling I did when they were young, they replied, "None!" Good thing, too!

5. Young children need harsh discipline to nip bad deeds in the bud, or the deeds will snowball and they will turn into raging, rebellious teenagers at 16

Children develop and grow their brain in stages. Parents and caregivers should learn about physical, emotional, brain, and social development and what to expect at each stage. A child at 13 is a different child than he was at age three. His more developed brain understands his needs and allows him to adjust his behavior. He has much more self-control—he can use words instead of physical aggression.

Don't project ahead. You have many childhood years to teach and explain to your child and learning appropriate behavior will stick when they "get it." Parents feel they have to teach the most important lessons, hard, at a time when young children's brains are least equipped to understand them. That doesn't mean you just let little Nathan hit his friends. Address the behavior with teaching words—over and over again. "No, we don't hit our friends. Here, stomp your feet when you are mad!" By 13, Nathan will have the self-control to do it on his own. Aggression is like water coming out of a tap—none in the baby stage, full gush at age two, flow at age four, trickle at age six, dribble at age eight and the occasional drip at age 10. By age 12, most children use their words instead of their hands, simply because of brain development and self-control and not as a result of harsh discipline.

6. If I don't enforce consequences on my child, how will she learn how the world works? She needs to be punished to learn

All the other parent figures in your child's world, including teachers, friends' parents, and coaches, will be all too happy to enforce consequences on your child that might include timed, punitive time-outs, withdrawal of privileges, and a host of other punishments. Let them.

You, on the other hand, have a vested interest in teaching your child a real-life, valuable skill called problem solving. It takes time but it pays off in increased communication, mutual respect, and love. When you problem solve with your child, aiming for a win-win solution, you are teaching her a life skill that is of far greater value and will last a lifetime. There is no research to support that punishment enhances parent-child respect, communication, or close relationships; on the contrary, there are plenty of studies that show how detrimental it is.

7. Children want limits to feel secure

No, they don't! In fact, children want their way—just like adults do. We hate it when we really want something and someone says "No" to us, and children feel the same way. What makes both children and adults feel secure is the ability to maintain their autonomy while being informed of expectations. For example, if we are attending a ball, we want to have some idea of what to wear. We don't want to be dictated to or forced to wear a certain item of clothing. We want the choice, but we also want to know what is expected so we can make an informed and appropriate choice. Children are the same way. They want information and the ability to choose. Offering them choices along with a little background information helps them to make a decision and empowers them.

8. Teens don't want to hang around with parents

Wrong. Most studies done on teens who rebel, act out, and engage in delinquent behavior indicate that they do not have warm, caring parents or structure in the home. Teens want privacy, but they want involved parents who respect them, care about where they are, worry about them, and help them navigate the world. Teens don't want or need parents that punish, belittle, or dismiss them. Be close to your children but let them set the pace. If you are their trusted coach, non-judgmental information source, and problem-solving mentor as well as a fun person they can beat in video gaming, they will love you forever!

Tips from veteran unschoolers:

Relax and enjoy your children

Celebrate the time you have together as a family. As your children enjoy a stress break from the pressures of school, they will start getting along better with siblings.

Stop trying to do formal-school-at-home and discover the secret of successful unschooling; see how much children learn on their own

Life in the community offers a full curriculum, so get out there and explore it. Children learn as much from parent-child discussions, people-watching, computers, volunteer work, siblings, and videos as they do from textbooks. Embrace the hands-on, or kinesthetic, style of learning. Go on field trips around the city. Many lesser-known community services offer great educational opportunities. Organize a visit to a recycling depot, newspaper plant, fire station, or chocolate shop. Volunteer at a homeless shelter. At home, you can teach your children cooking, baking, sewing, knitting, and woodworking—or a thousand other things that might tweak their interest. Play word and math board games. Provide the props for a play. Put together an art supply bucket. Put on some music and dance with your children. Snuggle on the sofa and read to your children. Have them read to you. Watch historical movies and videos together. Go for walks in our many great parks.

Let your kids experience boredom

Offering bribes is not the best way to motivate your child to learn. The best way is a great little concept called boredom! Believe me. If homeschoolers had to entertain their children all day, we'd burn out pretty quickly. The less responsibility a parent takes for filling a child's time, the more the child has to take on the job himself.

When children become bored, they learn to take responsibility and find creative, fun, and challenging learning projects on their own. Your job is to supervise and help them find materials. How long it takes for a child to switch to inner-motivated learning projects from outer-motivated ones will probably depend on how long they've been in an institution where they have always been told what to do. Observe how much your child will learn if he follows his own interests.

But first, he has to discover them. Children with a lot of free time discover the joys of learning—not because it's on a test, but because it brings them pleasure and satisfaction. The focus is on the process, not the end result.

Don't force learning

The only thing this will do is create a power struggle in your relationship and teach your child that learning is disagreeable. If the learner is not intrinsically motivated to learn the subject matter, it is unlikely any real learning will occur. No number of bribes or punishments will change that. Learning is not always an outcome of teaching. Learning happens when the learner merges new information with previously held information. It involves the important brain functions of memory, perception, and concept formation. These tasks are all under the learner's control, not the teacher's. Children are natural-born learners. Have fun!

13

Resources

"Play is the key to university."

Experiential learning is better than book learning

> I tried to teach my child with words,
>
> They often passed him by unheard.
>
> I tried to teach my child with books,
>
> He only gave me puzzled looks.
>
> Despairingly I turned aside,
>
> How can I teach this child, I cried?
>
> Into my hand, he placed the key,
>
> "Come," he said,
>
> "And play with me!"
>
> — Anonymous

"School-replicated-at-home is not sustainable for many homeschoolers. I've known so many who burn out and think themselves failures, and the amount of curriculum on the market just underscores the belief that if they only bought the 'right' one, it would work. Unless you have a child that naturally gravitates toward a seatwork and workbook type of structure, it's going to be a poor fit." (Deborah S, 2004)

Experiential learning is so much easier to do outside of the system. It's so much more meaningful to study an actual frog in a pond than to read about a frog in a textbook. Remember that for children of all ages, there is no distinction between play and learning, or between toys and educational resources. All of it is educational. A child learning to tie his shoes, or take photos with a camera, or push a round block into a square hole is trying to manipulate his environment. Call it play or call it learning—it is about a child trying to reach a goal.

Once a child has mastered reading, fiction books are great. Non-fiction books, textbooks, and workbooks have their place when the child desires and is ready for them but they are overused in today's schools. As a society, we need to move beyond our dependence on books for teaching. Teaching from a book and having kids write out responses is easy. Setting up experiential learning activities in a school takes much more preparation and more class time to do the activity and does not produce easily marked output; because of the additional work, experiential learning is not the preferred teaching method in schools. As an adult educator, I know how much easier it is to "tell" a learner rather than let her "discover" by participating in an activity. But the discovery method is so much more memorable because the learning sticks.

In our culture, video is the new "book"—through YouTube, Netflix and many other video channels on the internet. I'm not sure why we still force our children to read Shakespeare when they can experience a live play or watch a movie that that makes it a rich learning experience in a way that a book cannot. But if a book is the only resource available, add a costume trunk to the activity to allow children to re-enact a Shakespearean play. Resources for learning in the unschooling method are endless.

Schools have to use books; unschoolers do not.

Minimum resources for unschooling families

A library card and internet access are the bare minimum resources for unschoolers. Textbook and workbook curriculum is not necessary unless it is desired by the learner. I extend my apologies to textbook manufacturers.

Our library allows lending of up to 100 resources per person! I went crazy trying to manage seven library cards and books with many different due dates. Books got lost and it cost time and money. But I discovered a few tips that worked!

- Set a regular day each week as your library day. Check online to renew the books you wish to extend, then go to the library in person to return oldies and get new books. Every Monday is library day in our house.

- Have library lending cards only in the parents' names. You may need cards in the children's names to register at the library, but only use them for that purpose. Check out all books under the parent's name—you will have less checking to do!

- Make it a family rule to never, ever shelve a library book. That just gets them lost faster.

- Have a designated library book basket in the living room or family room to deposit oldies to be returned on your next library day. Get the kids involved by having them check online due dates, write out the list of books to be returned, and search the floors, couches, cars, and bathrooms to gather the wayward books.

Resources that are nice but not critical

We had many resources in our home, to be used however the children wanted. Because of the minimal financial support from the government, we had to be creative in acquiring our resources. Mostly, we purchased materials at garage sales, previously enjoyed children's toy stores, and book and curriculum sales. Many of these books and resources were from the 2000s decade so some are now obsolete, but it gives you an idea of what a rich learning environment looks like. We also had an extensive collection of books and reference guides.

Posters, timelines and maps were hung in hallways and bathrooms and changed monthly. It gave the kids something to look at while they were brushing their teeth!

Although we had a lot of resources, many of them went unused, if the children were simply not interested. I had to overcome my compelling obsession to use every resource in the house. A helpful thought came from a friend who said, "If you were meant to use it, you would have. Now is probably not the time, or place. Maybe it will never be used. That's okay. Sell it, give it away, or toss it. Let go of the guilt."

Sometimes I get the same feeling when I go to curriculum fairs at homeschooling conferences. I walk out feeling inadequate for not even looking at all the subject areas my child won't get to explore because I didn't provide the resources. What a bad mother! On the other hand, I feel good walking into homeschooling used curriculum sales and seeing all the resources that had just one page written in them before the child put his foot down and refused to fill in the rest of the book! Yes, I feel vindicated! I saved myself money and I avoided stress in our parent-child relationship. There are many workbooks at used curriculum sales that didn't work for the seller's child—that's why they are selling them. Consider carefully whether they will work for your child.

I found one neat little curriculum package in a tiny blue box that worked for all my kids. It was called a Nintendo GameCube. They learned English by reading the Nintendo Power magazine for cheat codes and game help. They learned math by budgeting for more games. They learned social studies by following Link all around Hyrule, and they learned science by observing the force times mass of Mario swinging Bowser around in a circle.

The video games could be listed under every subject area as they all require and develop reading, writing, problem solving, delayed gratification, critical thinking, and creativity skills. Many of the games develop specific subject areas, such as reading skills in Legend of Zelda, and commerce, economy, and team building in World of Warcraft. To avoid repetition, the video games are all listed at the beginning, but they are recommended for all subject areas. Computer and video games marketed specifically as "educational" are listed under each subject area. Adults are urged to follow the ERSB (Entertainment Software Rating Board) ratings on age recommendations so that the game level matches the player's development in understanding and ability. There is no division between educational and off-the-shelf video games because no video game is uneducational.

Cross-curricular video/computer games

Here are some of the games the Team of Thirty played that contributed to their knowledge base: Myst, Fable, World of Warcraft (teamwork), Age of Empires (history), Riven, Civilization (history), Dune, Diablo, Starcraft, Legend of Zelda (fishing), Mario and Luigi, Oblivion, Skyrim (politics), Half-Life (theoretical physics), Graal (math),

Transformice (cooperation and teamwork), Terraria, Spore (biology), Spiro Nights (teamwork), Sonic (cooperation), Yoshi (cooperation), Minecraft (logic and math), Roblox, Club Penguin, Battlefield Vietnam, The Sims Series (health), Call of Duty, Halo, Overwatch, (problem solving) and League of Legends (teamwork).

Language Arts			
Books	**Computer games and audio/video**	**Toys**	**Board Games**
Library card Home collection of hundreds of fiction and non-fiction books, various reading levels and genres	Reader Rabbit, Jumpstart, and various learn-to-read computer games Word processing and keyboarding skills software Online encyclopedia English, sign, and foreign language instruction and translation software Desktop publishing software such as InDesign, Website creation and blogging software Dictation software: Dragonspeak Digital voice recorder and video recorder PowerPoint, Prezi, and Photoshop software Microphone E-reader, audiobooks, CD, DVD, and MP3 player Genealogy software such as Legacy Family Tree	Word Wall of word cards made from reading lists Sentence builder tent cards Phonics flash cards Pens, pencils, markers, pencil crayons, crayons, paper, tracing paper, journals, diaries, card sets Magnetic letters and words Typewriter or laptop Alphabet shapes and letter blocks Telephone Calligraphy kit Crossword puzzles, anagrams, search-a-word puzzles, decoding puzzles, Sudoku Laminated posters of assorted topics Post Office Center: stamps, stamp pads, old junk mail envelopes, stickers, paper pads, stationary, and cardboard boxes for post boxes	Monopoly Scrabble Risk Quiddler Blurt Boggle Outburst Mastermind Mad Gab Clue Password Scattergories Trivial Pursuit Upwords Balderdash Things in a Box Sudoku Taboo Hear-me-out Any game in which a child needs to communicate (write) with others in game or outside of game

Mathematics

Computer games and audio/video	Toys	Board Games
Kahn Academy, Math TV, and YouTube videos	Math-U-See manipulatives and fraction overlays	Poker
		Fraction Pizza
Math-U-See, Bill Nye, Multiplication Rap videos	3D shapes with net inserts	Solitaire
	Algebra tiles and Cuisenaire rods	Blackjack
Cluefinders, Mathblaster, Minecraft, Sonic Schoolhouse,		Rummy
Freddie Fish, Logical Journey of	Dry erase board grid	Uno
the Zoombinis, Math Munchers,	Place value stamps	Keeno
Reader Rabbit Math, Math Rock, Logic Quest, Chessmaster, Brain	Math-U-See fraction overlays	Backgammon
Teasers, Suduko	Pattern blocks and numbered multi-sided dice	Battleship
		Bingo
Database management software such as Excel	Measuring tape, cups, and kitchen weigh scale	Dominoes
		Candyland
Financial management software such as Quickbooks	Multiplication and division flash cards	Tetris
		Chess
Computer programming/coding software such as Codeacademy	Decimal, fraction and percent stacking cubes	Checkers
		Chinese checkers
	Balance weigh scale and weights	Clue
	Abacus and calculator	Connect 4
	Laminated posters of assorted topics	Guess Who
		Mastermind
	Brain teasers card packs	Othello
	Clocks: 24-hour, digital, Roman numeral, and traditional	Payday
		Parcheesi
	Coin sorting machine and rolling papers	Quarto
		Bracko
	Store center: cash register and play/real money, items to buy such as toys or real food, wallets, purses, play or real money, and old credit cards	Blokus
		Sequence
		Triominos
		Where in the USA is Carmen Sandiago?
	Garage/Workshop center: wood pieces, hammer, nails, screws, tools, saw	Yahtzee
		Cribbage
		Monopoly
		Skipbo

Science

Books	Computer games and audio/video	Toys	Board Games
National Geographic magazines Make magazine Science experiment books The Magic School Bus Science reference books	Bill Nye Science videos Magic School Bus computer games Computer-aided construction kits such as Lego Mindstorms Sim Ant, Sim Safari, Sim Tower series	Rocks, minerals, shells, or metal collection kits Rock tumbler Ant farm Terrarium of carnivorous plants Chemistry set with graduated cylinders and plastic flasks Spoons, mixing bowls Acid litmus paper Microscope Laminated posters of assorted topics Annual pass to the city's science center and zoo Science kits in chemistry, electronics, electricity, making gum, soap etc. Rain gauge, bird feeder, frog pond Play-dough and spoons, plastic knives, beaded necklaces, rings, potato ricer or pasta maker, cups, muffin tins, rolling pins Compost and vermiculture bucket Miniature toy animals and plants Hiking and camping equipment Home planetarium, sky globe and constellation projector Night vision and spy glasses, binoculars, magnifying glass and prisms of different shapes K'NEX, Meccano, Lego, erector, Lincoln Logs, Gears, and blocks Models of the body, brain, heart, skeletons, muscles, of humans and animals Indoor/outdoor garden center: good quality shovels, ploughs, potting soil, containers, seeds, apron, recycled clear plastic vegetable containers with lids, and plot of land Electronics center: motors and wires, batteries, led lights, circuit closers, mini-motors, electronic assembly kits, etc. Nature center: nests, pet cages, pets, sticks, pebbles, feathers, grass growing kits Kitchen center: play kitchen, real ingredients, real and play tools and utensils Sand center: shovels, buckets, water, mud, sandbox	Mousetrap Bees Bugs and Slugs Jumanji National Geographic

Social Studies, Geography, and History

Books	Computer games and audio/video	Toys	Board Games
World atlas and wall maps National Geographic, Maclean's, The Economist and Time magazines World history timelines Encyclopedia Various country reference books	Google Earth Collection of videos such as Schindler's List, Mississippi Burning or a Netflix subscription Computer games such as Age of Empires, Age of Mythology, Age of Mythology Titans, Where in the World is Carmen Sandiego?, Zoog Genius, Sim City, Escape from Monkey Island, Civilization, Dune, The Sims	Globe Country and world map puzzles Laminated posters of assorted topics Annual pass to museums and visits to local festivals	Risk, Where in the World is Carmen Sandiego? Family Feud, Ouija, Careers, The Game of Life, Settlers of Catan series.

Health and Wellness

Books	Computer games and audio/video	Toys	Board Games
7 Habits of Highly Effective Teens (life skills) Effectiveness Training by Gordon Training (communication skills) What Color is My Parachute? (career choices) 7 Kinds of Smarts (multiple intelligences) Learning style tests Temperament tests Personality tests such as Myers-Briggs	Career search software	Laminated posters of various topics Health and Beauty center: brushes, hats, wigs, curling irons and rollers, nail polish, tooth floss, make-up, nail tools Playhouse center: dolls, blankets, baby equipment Medical center: masks, lab coat, doctor's kit, stethoscope	Scruples Careers The Game of Life Risk Judge-n-Jury Therapy True Colors The Ungame

Visual Art

Computer games and audio/video	Toys	Board Games
Electronic drawing tablet	Various topics laminated posters	Pictionary
Pinterest	Jigsaw puzzles, 2- and 3-dimensional puzzles	Cranium
Graphic image processing software such as Adobe	K'NEX, Lego, Meccano, blocks and building sets	Tic-Tac-Toe
Home and garden design software	Art sets and kits, and portfolio case	Pin the Tail on the Donkey
	Canvas, cards, paper	
Graphic image libraries such as Clipart, Getty Images	Pens, pencils, and drawing instruments	Battleship
	Coloring materials: markers, crayons, pencil crayons, oil pastel crayons, charcoal, chalk and chalkboard	Myst
Computer design software such as AutoCAD	Video camera, camera	Stratego
	Knitting, weaving and fibrecraft machines and tools	Lego
PowerPoint and Prezi	Acrylic, tempera, oil, watercolor, face, finger, fabric, wall, and ceramic paint	3D Blokus
Scanner	Craft glue, glue guns, tape, glue sticks, Velcro, magnetic strips, glitter glue, wood glue, grout, and epoxy	Mousetrap
Computer aided construction kits such as Lego Mindstorms	Assorted brushes, Q-tips, marbles, toothpicks, toothbrushes and sponges and popsicle sticks	
Photo and video processing software	Varnish and matt finish and plastic containers	
Draw and paint software	Craft supplies such as sequins, jewels, glitter, beads, popsicle sticks, flowers, ribbons, fabric odds and ends, wool, string, cotton balls, wire, thread, pipe cleaners, embroidery thread, feathers, googly eyes, pompoms, felt, glass bits and sand	
Fashion software		
	Calligraphy set	
	Model airplane and car kits	
	Stamps, pads, and bingo dabbers	
	Gift wrap, greeting cards, bows	
	Plasticine, clay, play-dough, Sculpy, goop	
	Origami paper, tracing paper, newsprint paper, crepe paper, colored construction paper, white paper, card stock, roll paper	
	Different cutting-edge scissors, hole punches	
	Shape templates, 3D human figure	
	View-Master projectors, LED projectors, Etch-A-Sketch	
	Mask making and face painting materials	
	Woodworking center: tools and equipment such as a scroll saw, handsaw, hammer, nails, screws, file, sandpaper, wood, band saw, lathe, router, screwdrivers	
	Sewing center: hand sewing bucket, sewing machine and table, threads, patterns, bucket of scrap fabrics, bag of batting	

Physical Education, Gym, and Sports:

Computer games and audio/video	Toys	Board Games
Physical fitness software High-action simulation software such as Flight Simulator Action Play and Arcade Games: Star Wars, Star Trek, Military, detective, police and auto racing Video games: Mario golf, Mario racing, Wii fit, Wii sport, Dance Dance Revolution Human anatomy and health reference guides	Sports equipment, purchased or rented: roller blades, skates, skis, skateboard, snowboards, tennis rackets, squash rackets, yoga mats, golf clubs, etc. Bicycle and helmet, Frisbee, badminton, baseball, football, soccer balls, basketball hoop and balls Air hockey or pool table, trampoline, pool Kites, jump rope, hula hoop, scooter Big appliance size cardboard boxes to make a house, rocket ship, etc. Old sofa cushions, sheets and paint poles or floor mop poles to build forts Yearly passes to play places, bowling alleys, and indoor play gyms Laminated posters of assorted topics	Jacks Tiddlywinks Pick-up Sticks Jenga Ker-Plunk Twister

Music, Drama, and Performing Arts:

Computer games and audio/video	Toys	Board Games
Musical recording and mixing software Musical instrument instruction, theory and notation software Tone recognition, singing, and melody memory software Sim Tunes, Guitar Hero, Rock Band, Dance Dance Revolution Video camera and MP3 player YouTube and Vimeo Digital sheet music	Puppet theater, stuffed animals, blankets and puppets Magic kits Season passes to theaters, opera, ballet, and concerts Laminated posters of assorted topics Musical instruments: homemade (drums, rattles, shakers, pots and pans), rented, or purchased (violins, pianos, keyboards, drums, guitars) Recorder, karaoke machine, radio, stereo Music center: recording devices, and instruments Fashion center: belts, shoes, pieces of interesting fabric, fishnet, textures, hats, jewelry, gloves, vests	Encore Notability Song Burst Simon Henry Charades Cranium

14

Unstructured Time

"We need to trust in children's curiosity; then all we have to do is feed it."

How does an unschooler change a light bulb?

This scenario gives you a picture of what a typical unschooling day looks like and how much informal learning can be easily slotted into outcomes:

Mom gets up to get a coffee and complains about the family room being dark. She asks a child who is already up playing computer games to go get a new light bulb from the garage. The child is fascinated by the squiggly LED bulb and wonders how it works; he returns to the computer to look up light and electricity (science). The child makes a model of the light bulb from play-dough and reads a biography of Thomas Edison (social studies).

He talks his sisters and brothers into performing a skit about Edison's life (drama). The siblings now become interested in different sources of light and beg Mom to buy some supplies to make candles (science) after driving to morning daytime homeschool piano lessons (music). Mom outlines the cost of the supplies while driving home for the children to figure out whether they have enough homeschooling funding left to pay for the candles (math). Once home, Mom shows the children how to write a letter to their government representative to ask for more funding for unschooling projects (English language arts). This leads to a discussion about the government structure and who is actually responsible for education decisions (social studies). Now the children want to hold a debate (English language arts) among themselves over computer rights in the family (social studies). The children can't decide, so they hire their siblings as lawyers to re-enact a courtroom complaint (social studies), complete with stuffed animals acting as judge and jury.

They get hungry and decide to stop for lunch. Mom calls out from her office that it must be a nutritious one (health). After lunch, the courtroom scene loses the children's interest and they turn it into a restaurant, where they decide to mix ingredients from the kitchen (science) and offer potions for sale to the rest of the family (math). The children make signs, brochures, and menus (English language arts and visual art) and set up a cash register (math). One by one, the children again lose interest, and leave the kitchen in a mess. Mom reminds them to clean up (work experience) and the siblings argue over who is doing more work. Mom coaches them in emotional intelligence and conflict resolution skills (health).

After the kitchen is tidied, the children are herded outside to continue their squabbling (socialization). Three hours later, Mom checks outside to find the children happily and cooperatively engrossed in making mud cities, condos, and shopping centers for the worms and insects that live in the huge dirt hole in the back yard that was created when we removed the giant spruce tree (science and social studies). The neighborhood children joined them in the building project after they came home from school. Ten muddy children ring the back doorbell, wanting snacks and the bathroom. Much to the neighbor's annoyance, Mom sends the children to their own respective houses to hose off the mud. Dad comes home and the family sits down to family dinner (socialization and English language arts).

The neighborhood children who aren't being ferried to activities during rush hour come back after supper to haul out chairs, pillows, sheets, stuffed animals, and play dishes, and set up camp in the front yard, where they huddle under the makeshift tents and tell stories, jokes and anecdotes (English language arts). They set up a lemonade stand (math, art, English language arts) by the campsite and earn over $50, thanks to generous neighbors who wish to reward and encourage entrepreneurism. This leads into a conversation about division and fairness, and musings over what to spend their money on (math). They meander down to the school playground where they play grounders, tag, and hide-and-seek until dark (physical education).

The neighborhood school children have to go home for baths and bed, so all our children come home too. They grab their favorite books and head for the family room to snuggle, read (English language arts), watch DVD's (social studies) or play family board games (math). They notice how dim the family room has become, so Dad asks a child to get a new light bulb from the garage...

School children get one hour of individual attention each week

If a teacher has 30 students and there are 30 hours of teaching time in a week, each student gets one hour per week of individual time with the teacher. A homeschooling parent gives 30 hours of individual attention during the same period.

Ever wonder how kids spend time in school? Are they engaged and actively learning six hours a day? Not a chance. Research shows that kids are on task about 10 percent of the time. That would be 36 minutes per day—about the same time it takes a homeschool child to do seatwork, at least during the elementary years. Children in school have to spend their day lining up, waiting for everyone to be quiet, taking seats, waiting for class photo money to be collected, waiting for field trip permission slips to be handed out, sharpening pencils, waiting for everyone to be quiet, putting on coats, lining up, sitting down, listening to announcements on the intercom, waiting for everyone to be quiet, passing in papers, waiting for everyone to find page 76 in their math book, waiting for the teacher to help six students find page 76, waiting for everyone to be quiet... (Stephanie J, 2000)

6 things most useful for children to do throughout childhood

What do kids do all day when they don't go to school or homeschool? "We get up, check email, play games, eat breakfast, go outside, play Lego, go on errands or field trips, work on a project, make things, grow things, make messes, and find the answers to our questions. We play, we learn, and we live," says Linda C., unschooling mom of two. In addition to daily living, we squeeze in more:

1. **Access information**: From computers, books, speakers, telephones. Children must be given time and space to read every day.

2. **Travel if possible**. The best way to learn Social Studies, Science, and people skills is to travel. It also makes one appreciate one's country all the more.

3. **Volunteer work**: This should be done on a regular basis in order to develop a strong work ethic not motivated by extrinsic rewards such as pay, marks, or promotions. There are many different kinds of volunteer work: job shadowing, apprenticing, or doing group work with many different agencies. Festivals, concerts and plays need volunteers. Our children over age 12 volunteered every week at the food bank. The younger children could shovel a neighbor's walk, bake cookies for a sick friend or relative, or make a craft for someone who is sad.

4. **Socialize with people in many different settings**: Playgroups, sleepovers, dates, community activity outings, dinner parties. These are wonderful ways to learn interpersonal communication skills such as starting and ending a conversation, problem solving, emotional intelligence, assertiveness, empathic listening, and conflict resolution.

5. **Get outdoors**: Being outside in nature leads to improved well-being through physical activity and exploration. Camping, picnics, walks, and sports.

6. **Embrace projects**: Conceptualize, research, design, implement, and evaluate projects—everything from a lemonade stand to a 3D (three dimensional) printing project.

Is learning from unschooling really that much different from traditional school?

No. They are amazingly similar. When children can choose what they want to study, they pick common childhood interests.

Most children's interests naturally follow the government outcomes, at least in the elementary years when their cognitive development is in the concrete operational stage. That means that they can process additional information as long the concepts are familiar to them in their daily life and relate to tangible things they can see and touch. In fact, government curriculum developers choose the school outcomes to align with the familiar in children's lives, such as insects, gardens, floats and sinkers, magnets, seasons, community and family, colors, counting blocks, planets, airplanes, cars, and books. They choose to do so because most every child will develop an interest in at least half these topics entirely on their own, without any parent introduction or school direction.

The difference is that although every child is interested in boats and buoyancy at some point in their childhood, it may not always be at the Grade 2 level, which is when this topic is presented in school. Show me a child that doesn't love to play with magnets. Or a child that is not inquisitive about caterpillars and their needs. However, in school, they are only allowed to study those interests at specific points in time.

10 most common concerns of new unschoolers

When considering unschooling for a child who has reached school age or when the decision is made pull a child out of school, parents unschooling for the first time have a lot of questions, worries, and fears. The following concerns are common to almost all new unschoolers:

1. **Can I balance home and learning? I am worried that my parenting duties will suffer with all the time I would spend spending facilitating**

You probably already blend parenting and facilitating, and there is not that much distinction between the two. You have been a facilitator since your child was born and that loving style won't change. Let your passions loose and share them with your child. Let your children share their passions with you. Many parents find the roles of teacher and student reverse because the parents learn too. Think of teaching your child not as having to fill a little person's brain with facts, but as a journey in which you and your child will travel and explore together.

2. **I'm worried that his education will not be recognized by a good postsecondary institution; I want him to have the same opportunities as traditionally schooled kids**

By high school age, many motivated unschooled kids actively seek out courses to help them pass leaving-school exams and move toward their goals. Worry about postsecondary admissions when the time comes.

3. **My kids didn't listen to me when I nagged them about homework last year. How will it be when their entire education is in my hands? What if they don't listen to me when I make a suggestion?**

Even the school-replicated-at-home type of homeschooling takes much less time than school. As previously mentioned, in many cases it is even less time than what school children spend doing homework.

Kids are born to learn and will seek out knowledge. It's natural that humans, from infants to seniors, want to know about their world and how it works. However, at times, your kids just might have a different learning agenda than what you have planned for them. If you have a dreadful day, just go with the flow, have some fun, and enjoy building your relationship.

4. I'm worried that I will burn out trying to entertain my kids all day

Don't even try to occupy your kids all day! I'm not sure where the notion came from that parents must be constant entertainers, but it's a habit you don't want to start. Leave things out for them—a board game today, craft supplies tomorrow, and a costume trunk the next day—they will learn to occupy themselves. You will be amazed at their creativity once you stop trying to direct them. Don't say "No" to their ideas. Get into the habit of saying "Yes," and then outline the parameters: "Okay, but you have to clean up!" If you don't get into the habit of entertaining them, they will not get into the habit of looking to you to fill their day, and you will have free time for yourself. Many homeschoolers use this time to run a home business, write, or work part-time. The bonus is that children will develop their creativity, decision-making, and problem-solving skills. Be sure to insist that they clean up messes, though.

5. I'm only homeschooling one sibling. How will the children get along?

Kids readily accept that their siblings may have different education situations. That's okay. They may want to homeschool or unschool as well, and they may not. If you give each child the choice every year, it takes the power struggles out of the inevitable complaints resulting from their choices.

You will have bad days when the kids are fighting nonstop and you wonder if they wouldn't be better off in school. But they would have those days even if they were in school. Most unschoolers report that older siblings enjoy much better relationships because they learned to get along with each other in the early years.

6. How can I teach them things I don't know very much about, like fractions?

Your kids are going to learn fractions whether you teach them or not. Math concepts are learned from everyday life: baking, shopping, sharing. Language is learned from avid reading. As kids get to junior and senior high school age, online teachers and tutors can teach your kids what they need and want to learn that you can't teach. Trust that when the student is ready, the teacher will appear! And developmentally, by that time they are mature enough to listen to an outside teacher, even if they won't listen to you!

7. What if I made the wrong choices this year? Programs? Curriculum? Classes?

It's only a year! Nothing is written in stone. Your education plan—the worksheet you submit to your supervisor with your year's plan—is a work in progress that you can amend at any time. Dump activities if they don't work for you. You are in control! Most seatwork homeschoolers don't finish their goals for the year. We are human, and humans procrastinate. Sometimes life just gets in the way of our best intentions—we may have a holiday opportunity, or visitors come, or a new project comes up and other things slide. And even though many homeschoolers don't finish a grade, the kids still move on to the next grade and do just fine! Enjoy the time you have with your children.

8. **I worry about what my kids will miss out on by not attending school: school portraits, holiday parties, riding the school bus, Christmas pageants, field trips**

The homeschooling community will provide all those experiences too. In school, the complex logistics involved in organizing field trips for large groups only allow for one or two field trips per grade per year. As a family, can go anywhere, anytime! Join a support group that organizes a lot of outings and you could find yourselves on field trips every day. The artists, writers, presenters, and special guests that present programs in schools will also present to a group of homeschoolers. All it requires is organization. In our earlier years, the homeschooling community provided school photos, year-end talent concerts in which anyone could perform—regardless of talent, weekly field trips, parent-organized holiday parties, music lessons, and group discounts to plays and attractions. The possibilities are endless.

Some parents love to organize. If you are one of them, pick something your child would like to do, pick a date, and advertise it—you will have a group together in no time.

The only thing missing is the school bus experience, and perhaps children will get that by joining other groups! My daughter got a taste of it when she rode on a school bus to Girl Guide camp.

9. **When I tell relatives what we are going to do, I am met with skepticism, silence, and negative comments. How do I handle being judged? It is undermining my confidence**

Unfortunately, until homeschooling and unschooling becomes more widely understood, you will continue to be judged! Most people hold stereotypical notions of the "social" and "academic" aspects of homeschooling and are misinformed by ignorant and negative portrayals of it in the media. Many families just smile and say, "It's the best choice for our family." Grow a thick skin and let negative comments bounce off.

10. My child is so social. How will she develop friendships?

Friends are found everywhere, not just at school. Some kids love being with other kids. Some kids love being home without a lot of people around. You can provide both in homeschooling, where you set the pace for social activities. Most cities have homeschooling clubs, events, classes, and outings; there are organized activities and groups for everyone—outdoor enthusiasts, the sports crowd, writing groups, and even the Friday afternoon Minecraft Club at my house! Not to mention the usual community organizations, such as Boy Scouts, church groups, community classes, and many more.

Relax, seek out a mentor for the bad days, and most of all, enjoy your children and the learning. It really is a great ride that you and your children will never regret!

Restoring relaxed and connected family time

Today, family time is in short supply. All children need their parents to be available, not just a few designated moments during the day or week, but all the time. A loss of family connectedness can lead to health problems, such as asthma, ulcers, heart disease, anxiety, depression, suicide, drug abuse, irritable bowel syndrome, and others. We need close family connections to buffer the day-to-day stresses of both parents and children.

Eat together—every day. Insist on gathering at the table, even if someone is not hungry. At least enjoy each other's company.

Protect family day—similar to a date night with your spouse, family day should be sacred—the one day of the week that you all spend together, without friends tagging along to dilute the family social interaction.

Refuse homework if your kids are in school.

Resist encroachment of activities and practices on special holidays, birthdays, and family get-togethers.

Recognize and celebrate the rights of passage—birthdays, special occasions, high school graduations, achievements like getting driver's license, and university children coming home for holidays.

Reconsider the value of individual activities outside the home. They take away valuable family conversation time, sharing fun, and learning together. Is it worth giving up? You only have your child for 18 years.

Boredom is the key to fostering creativity

Boredom is good. Empty time allows a child to build introspection, reflection, and solitude skills. Children who are constantly entertained do not learn how to occupy themselves, nor do they get those creative flashes that occur when their brain is relaxed and not engaged or focused. They don't learn drive, initiative, or stick-to-itiveness if someone else constantly manages their time. This is probably why so many unschoolers succeed in entrepreneurial endeavors. Their creativity was born out of boredom, and they have disciplined themselves to turn that creativity into productivity.

What will kids do all day if not directed by adults?

Children miss so many opportunities and discoveries when they are in school. They would get the chance to explore more things in life if their time were not constantly directed by adults.

Unstructured time worries people. They are uncomfortable without evidence of structure, especially externally imposed structure. But consider the following two ideas.

First, children who need structure impose it upon themselves as their executive function grows. My 15-year-old daughter disciplined herself to go for a walk every day. My 17-year-old son hopped on the treadmill every day at 5 p.m. We have breakfast, lunch, and dinner at regular times. The children read in the evenings, not during the day; daytime just doesn't work for them. We take our vitamins and read the newspaper every day. Except for the teens, we go to bed most nights at midnight and get up at 9 a.m. Yet most people consider our day unstructured because we don't homeschool or school. Just because the government doesn't impose structure in the form of established school-day hours doesn't mean that people don't impose their own internal structure on their time. Ask any retired person and they will tell you that they are busy and that their days and weeks have structure, rhythm, and purpose.

Second, an unstructured day doesn't mean that children will be up to no good. Children who are used to filling their time with projects and meaningful activities will not spend time loitering around malls, vandalizing, shoplifting, taking drugs, or having sex when adults are not around. The adults in their lives trust them to fill their time productively, and they have had lots of practice doing just that.

"We like to unschool because we actually get some time to do something else. If you go to school, you have to get up at 7 a.m. and then stay at school for 10 hours doing lots of math that you already know. Like, if you learned Division or Multiplication then you'll have to answer a million more questions. Then you come home, do your math book, go to sleep, and then it starts all over again. While if you unschool, then you can learn math from other things. For example, I found an online computer game called Graal where my brother and I learned spelling, math and grammar. You also get plenty of time to play. Thank you for the wonderful opportunity to homeschool." [sic] wrote a 10-year-old unschooler, in a letter to the government.

One mom said, "We do things in four ways—I do things with her that she needs and wants to do (play and projects). She does things with me that I need and want to do (work), then we do things together (chores and errands) and we do things separately (I practice piano while she plays)." (Stephanie J, 2004)

My son Neil went to a high school for eleventh grade. He had more than enough credits to take two spares in school instead of the one spare that the school allotted to Grade 11 students. When he was caught up on homework, he would go to the library during his spares to sit and reflect. The adults were unhinged by this behavior. Why wasn't he doing an activity instead of just staring into space! No wonder he came home to finish high school his way the following year.

Here are some activities my kids did entirely on their own *because* they were bored! This list might look very daunting. But there were also many, many days that my kids played video games nonstop! We eventually expressed our need for them to vary their activities, and they agreed to turn off the screens and look for something else to do. (See more on video games in Chapter 18.) I've also indicated the subjects that each activity can teach, to show the reader how simple activities are educational without even trying to be.

What do they do all day?			
5 – 11-year-old children			
Legend:			
M–Math E–English SC–Science SS–Social Studies A–Art D–Drama PE–Physical Education			
Cook and bake	M	Play restaurant, factory, garage, etc.	M, E, SC, A
Play board games	M, E, SS	Do household and neighborhood chores and projects	M, E, SC, SS, PE
Make board games	E, A	Play postal person and deliver mail to members of the house	E
Paint, sculpt, arts and crafts	E, A	Make potions and set up a shop	SC
Make craft kits	A	Build carpentry kits from home improvement stores	M, SC, A,
Sew, knit, or crochet dolls, puppets, stuffies, and blankets	A	Do projects and badges from Girl Guides, Scouts, 4H, Jr. Achievement, Jr. Forest Wardens, Cadets	M, E, SC, SS, A, D, PE
Do puzzles	E, SS, A	Play casino	M
Build workshop projects	M, SC, A	Visit friends and have sleepovers	E
Play Barbies, Polly Pockets, Pokemon	E	Garden	SC
Build snowmen and snow sculptures	SC, A	Gave a demonstration or speech at a homeschool fair	E
Make sand sculptures	SC, A SC	Watch videos: Pokemon, Magic School Bus, Bill Nye the Science Guy	SC, SS
Play Stock Pot Inn (paper dolls)	A	Make movies	E, A
Make circuits	SC	Video record a homemade movie	E, A, D
Read stories, comics, and reference books	E	Create a theater, mime, or puppet show and make tickets, signs, scripts, puppets; sing, dance, perform skits	M, E, A, D

Make a dictionary, diorama, cookbook, list, map, mobile, mural, photo album, puzzle, tape recording, time line, poster, animated movie, movie, etching, picture, TV program, dinner, trial, survey	E, A	Create a dance, filmstrip, model, musical instrument, newspaper, cartoon, radio program, recipe, slide show, slogan and ad, board game, bumper sticker, petition, piece of art, questionnaire, experiment, new product, costume, display	M, E, SC, SS, A, D, PE
Write stories and illustrate picture books	E, A	Play at the park alone or with buddies or in groups	PE
Scribe and illustrate books (before reading age)	E, A	Play badminton, catch, roll-erblade, swim, ski and many other sports	PE
Illustrate a story, diary, calendar, chart, collage, mosaic or collection	E, A	Host a lemonade stand	M
Research items of interest on the internet and in stores	M, E	Go on field trips to city ameni-ties, zoos, and manufacturing plants	SC, SS
Make trains, castles, and cities from cardboard boxes	M, E, SC, SS	Collect cans and bottles for recycling	M, SC
Make bumper stickers	E	Shop	M
Collect items, research and organize them, and display the collection	E, A	Plan a journey	M, E, SC, SS
Write a book, computer program, letter, letter to the editor, new law, news report, poem, song, story, essay, article, play	E, SS, A	Travel	M, E, SC, SS, A, D, PE
Volunteer	M, E, SC, SS, A, D, PE		

What do they do all day?			
12 – 15-year-old children			
Cook and bake	M	Do household, neighborhood, community chores and projects	M, E, SC, SS, A, D, PE
Play board games	M, E, SS	Clean rooms, help with home maintenance	M, SC, A, PE
Make board games	E, A	Fix cars	SC
Paint, sculpt, draw cartoons, make arts and crafts	E, A	Learn to maintain appliances	SC
Make kites	SC, A	Build projects in workshops	M, SC, A
Build snow sculptures	SC, A	Work on a lathe	M, SC, A
Sew, knit, or crochet dolls, puppets, stuffies, and blankets	A	Run errands with parents to learn about consumer relations	E
Do puzzles, sudoku, crosswords	E, SS, A	Visit friends and have sleepovers	E
Go camping	SC, PE	Garden	SC
Work out at the gym individually or in group classes	PE	Give a speech, demonstration, or evaluation at Toastmasters Youth Leadership	E
Go for bike rides, walks; go rollerblading, skiing, skating	PE	Participate in interest-driven homeschool groups	M, E, SC, SS, A, PE, MU
Play computer and video games	M, E, SC, SS, A, D, PE	Go on field trips E	M, E, SC, SS, A, D, PE, MU
Program computers, design apps and websites	M, E, A	Host a debate	E
Participate in social networks	E	Plan a training session	E
Read books, newspapers, websites, blogs, and forums such as Reddit	E	Participate in a mock interview	E, D
Write in a journal or learn a language	E	Play music	MU

Write stories, novels, comics, blogs	E	Play musical instruments: guitar, piano, drums; play in a band	MU
Research items of interest on the internet and in stores	M, E	Write music	MU
Self-study with textbooks and workbooks; work out the problems and review the solutions in the workbooks	M, E, SC, SS	Participate in interest-based clubs such as First Lego League, NaNoWriMo, Computer Programming, Writing, Parkour, Beakerhead, Sports, Karate, etc.	E, A, SS, SC, M, D, PE, MU
Collect items, research and organize them, and display the collection	E, A	Work at a job outside the home	M, E
Travel	M, E, SC, SS, A, D, PE, MU	Volunteer	M, E, SC, SS, A, D, PE, MU

What do they do all day?			
16 – 20-year-old children			
Cook, bake, make beer and jam	M, SC	Do household, neighborhood, community chores and projects	M, E, SC, SS, A, D, PE
Paint and sculpt	A	Participate in home renovations	M, E, SC, SS, A, PE
Work on projects that will strengthen knowledge and appreciation of the arts, environmental stewardship, community engagement	M, E, SC, SS, A, D, MU	Work on bicycles, motorcycles, cars	SC
Play sports, work out, ski, skate, toboggan, ride bike, go camping	PE	Fix and maintain appliances	SC
Attend formal online or physical classes of academic subjects or personal interests	M, E, SC, SS, A, D, PE, MU	Go to maker studios to work on projects of many kinds	SC, A
Fix computer viruses and reformat hard drives	SC	Build a 3D printer	SC
Program computers, scripts, java, video games; design apps and websites	M, E, SC, A	Run errands for parents: dry cleaner, bottle depot, craft store, supermarket, bank, etc.	M, E
Read novels (both genders read about 3 hours a day, every day)	E	Visit and host friends for parties, gaming sessions, and events	E
Read books, newspapers, websites, blogs, and forums such as Reddit	E	Give a speech, demonstration, or evaluation at Toastmasters Youth Leadership	E
Keep a journal, or learn a language	E	Participate in interest-driven homeschool groups	M, E, SC, SS, A, PE, MU
Write novels and short stories	E	Go to concerts, festivals, and day trips to local amenities	M, E, SC, SS, A, D, PE, MU
Spend time at the library	M, E, SC, SS, A	Mentor young or inexperienced person in an interest, such as coding, Latin, French	E

Self-study with textbooks and workbooks; work out the problems and review the solutions in the workbooks	M, E, SC, SS	Take drivers' education and learn to drive	M
Visit relatives in distant countries, alone or with family	M, E, SC, SS, A, PE	Teach themselves to play a musical instrument	MU
When traveling with family or friends, visit the local cities' museums, zoos, science centers, and cultural centers	E, SC, SS, A, PE, MU	Participate in interest-based clubs such as First Lego League, NaNoWriMo, Computer Programming, Writing, Parkour, Beakerhead, Sports, Karate, etc.	E, A, SS, SC, M, D, PE, MU
Work in temporary office, retail, or warehouse jobs	M, E, SC, SS, A, PE	Volunteer	M, E, SC, SS, A, D, PE, MU

This is the back-to-school schedule when you unschool:

1. Early August: Schedule the "Not Going Back to School" picnic for the first day the neighborhood school kids go back, so you and all your unschooling friends get the park all to yourself:

1. Relax

2. Relax

3. Middle of August: Schedule in plans to visit the parks, pools, museums, zoos in the month of September while the weather is still nice and the schools don't yet have field trips scheduled

4. Relax

5. Relax

6. Late August: Go shopping during back-to-school sales and buy nothing but Lego kits

7. Relax

8. Relax

Sticking to the school schedule adds incredible stress to the life of both parent and child. Who wouldn't want to get off the rat-race track? One of the biggest benefits of unschooling family life is relaxed, happy time to just be together and learn.

15

Assessment

"Not everything that counts can be counted, and not everything that can be counted counts." — Albert Einstein, Scientist

Learning objectives and assessment

People often ask me, "How do you know they are learning?" My response is, "How do you know they are not learning?"

American singer and actress Eartha Kitt once said, "I am learning all the time. My tombstone will be my diploma."

It can sometimes be hard for unschooling parents to trust that learning that is taking place, in that their children do not produce many of traditional schools' physical trappings—they don't have a binder full of completed worksheets to hand to the government, or a wall full of artwork, or a workroom full of projects, or a collection of essays.

Governments require schools to assess what is taught because they are accountable to the public and must demonstrate that schools are doing their job. "Assessment is how we know if learning has or is taking place." (CBElearn, 2013) In the education field, there are three types of assessments; all are necessary in a classroom setting. (McTighe, 2005) (AB Assessment Consortium, 2013) The assessments are used not to measure whether a child is learning, but whether the child is learning a particular set of government-prescribed outcomes. In contrast, none of these types of assessment are necessary in homeschooling for the reasons described below.

1. Assessment *for* learning (or Formative Evaluation)

We use this type of assessment in adult education to discover what the learner already knows and what he needs to know next. We call this a "needs assessment." Similarly, at the beginning of a school year, a teacher has 30 students who are unknown quantities—she does not know each individual child's capabilities; clearly, this is not the case in a homeschool environment. In school, a teacher needs to assess not only what each child already knows, but how he learns. In homeschooling, you are already familiar with both his knowledge level and his learning patterns, his temperament and personality, his intelligence strengths and weaknesses, and his likes and dislikes. And your child has many ways of telling you what he wants to learn about.

Spending every minute of every day in close contact with the child allows the unschooling parent to assess the child's learning without any form of testing.

2. Assessment *as* learning (or learning provided by evaluation)

In school, teachers give ongoing feedback as the children produce. It goes something like this: the child writes an essay and the teacher gives him feedback; the child incorporates the feedback and rewrites the essay; the teacher returns it, with more ideas and feedback. In unschooling, the learner gets feedback mostly from self-evaluation. The learner decides what is and what isn't working in pursuit of this particular knowledge goal. This is also called problem solving. Because this happens internally in the learner, neither the parent nor an external supervisor needs to assess the child's work. This continuous self-evaluation in unschooling occurs naturally and is most effective, because the learner determines his own outcomes and his self-assessment finishes when he has learned a subject or mastered a concept to his satisfaction.

3. Assessment *of* learning (or Summative Evaluation)

This is the traditional type of assessment, meant to prove to the government that the learning of a prescribe outcome has indeed occurred. The vehicles for this kind of assessment are quizzes; exams; essays; discussions; presentations; and evidence of work product, which is often the final mark. This assessment is necessary in schools as they are accountable to the system for producing results; the assessments are meant to evidence those results.

In home education, parents are accountable to no one. The kids are accountable to themselves. As they have no need to prove learning to themselves, no assessment is required.

Who is testing really for?

In homeschooling and unschooling, parents already know their child's capabilities, having observed and spent time with the child since birth. Primarily for this reason, unschoolers do not believe in or nor submit to testing, although doing so could produce valuable research to showcase unschooling as efficient, effective, and ultimately, highly successful in preparing our children for the future.

In the school system, assessments serve multiple purposes. Teachers need them to prove to their principals that they are teaching the outcomes effectively. Principals need them to prove to the school board that their schools are implementing the prescribed curriculum in order for the outcomes to occur. School boards need them to prove to the government that they are administering the school system according to the government's mandate. The government needs them to prove to taxpayers that their education tax dollars are being spent wisely and that education is being duly delivered for the betterment of society. Everyone has a vested interested in knowing that the educational system is validated and working well to educate our future citizens. Assessment, testing, and evaluation provides the proof.

Unschoolers and homeschoolers do not need proof. They know learning is constant.

Unschooling planning and assessment is the reverse of school planning and assessment

If you re-read the section, "How unschoolers change a light bulb," in Chapter 14, you can see how the learning path meanders. There was no plan for the day except to start it with a good cup of coffee! Yet at day's end, we saw that much was learned. This is the time of day when parents might record learning; hopefully, they have captured the campsite, courtroom, lemonade stand, skit, candle making, and mud condo construction on camera to demonstrate to the authorities that learning has taken place. I did, and years later the children and I enjoy watching what they got up to. I hope to post some of the photos on the unschoolingtouniversity.com blog.

School assessment works like this:

Government-Outcomes-Course Designer-Teacher-Student-Assessment

In school, assessments must be specific, measurable, and reasonable. The plan begins at the top with the government and ends at the bottom with the learner. The government establishes the ultimate goal and the learning outcomes to meet the goal. The course designers then write the course content. The teacher studies the content and decides how to teach, present, or deliver the material contained in the syllabus or course outline in order to meet the outcomes; then decides what materials to use—this is called curriculum. The curriculum is delivered to the student via direct teaching, inquiry questions, readings, text on a screen, or many other ways. The student does the corresponding assignments (output) and the teacher marks them and provides feedback; the student might redo an assignment if the teacher allows it. Sometimes, the student only accesses the teacher if he needs help (tutorial learning). The teacher uses a rubric, quiz, or exam to objectively assess how many of the outcomes have been met. In the form of marks, she delivers her assessment of the learning outcomes the student has met, not met, or is developing. This assessment is delivered to the student, the parent, the principal, and ultimately, back to the government.

Specific assessment is problematic with unschooling because there are no pre-planned objectives or outcomes; nor are the delivery methods or curriculum preset.

Here is a comparison:

Unschooling assessment works like this:

Student-Parent-Supervisor-Outcomes-Government

The plan begins with the learner and ends with the government. The child plays. The parent observes closely and records what the child has done or seen. Perhaps she takes photos. The parent reviews activity with the supervisor, who decides which learning outcomes are complete and records the assessment. The supervisor returns the learning outcomes assessment back to the parent (as if it were news!) and reports it to the government.

Most unschoolers do not set out to follow government-prescribed outcomes, although their child's spontaneous learning could easily be slotted into them. We are not focused on grades or subjects. Each child is different. A child may be reading at a Grade 11 level but learning math at a Grade 2 level. That's okay because he is not being compared with other 30 kids.

Unschooling celebrates the uniqueness of each child and respects developmental schedules.

Educators who are entrenched in the school's assessment system adamantly insist that research supports the validity of school assessment. "Research tells us (see *Understanding by Design* by Wiggins and McTighe and/or *A Framework for Student Assessment* second ed. by Alberta Assessment Consortium) that when planning is done with the objective in mind first, and then activities are planned to support that objective, there is a deeper learning experience and a greater opportunity for the brain to learn. Finding a fun activity first and then trying to slot it into some kind of purpose or objective leaves us with little correlation to understanding." (CBE Learn Website, 2013)

The problem with that particular research is that there are no credible wide-reaching studies on unschooling children who learn primarily on their own self-directed timetable, and their accumulated knowledge at age 18. Unschooled children plan their activities, not their parents. The research by Wiggins and McTighe was done only in an institutional school setting. It was not done on children who are free to learn outside of an institutional environment and its prescribed objectives. Consider the difference in studying whales in their ocean home and studying them at SeaWorld. The environment plays an integral role in any study and if not taken into consideration, will substantively skew the results of any study.

Unschooled children already have an objective in mind. They wish to solve a problem. Perhaps they want to know how birds fly. They themselves plan an activity that to learn about that. They crack open a book or look it up on the internet—they choose the method that will work for them in that moment, not one preset by another person or by an institution. You can see how it works just by observing your child. It's amazing how much they learn and enjoy learning on their own agenda. If you record the changes in your child every month or so, you will notice that, amazingly, they pretty much cover all seven years of primary school outcomes simply through their own initiative and curiosity. This was our experience. We even documented the way their inner motivation lined up with government outcomes in spite of their discovery learning process. (see Recordkeeping)

Young children learn without any preconceived agenda. They learn to walk, to talk (they come pre-wired to learn any of 4000 languages!), to eat; they learn colors, numbers, and some even learn to read before Kindergarten. They don't plan these activities with learning outcomes in mind! Why should they start to need them at age six?

15 problems with testing unschoolers

Testing is the most common form of assessment in schools. Yet it is problematic in unschooling because of the unique content and delivery method of the education.

1. Unschooling learning is neither compartmentalized nor linear—the very forms in which tests are designed to measure; exams test the wrong outcomes

The Concordia University (Chang, 2011) study measured not what the 12 unschooled children learned, rather what they didn't learn that the government thought they should be learning. We could say the test was measuring different objectives.

Unschoolers don't follow subjects or a school year. There are too many areas in science and social studies, history, geography, languages, and art to test children. Unschoolers who choose an area to learn about don't go looking for a test in that area to measure their learning achievement. There is no point. As well, it would be unfair to subject unschoolers to grade-level exams as they may not have chosen to learn about any of the topics tested on the exam. Learning is constant, across all disciplines. Only school chops learning into subject areas, periods, and school years.

Mothers worry if their children are taking enough vitamins for health; governments are concerned about whether the children are learning. Mothers don't measure the vitamin A in their child's body every week to see whether it has been absorbed, nor should teachers have to give tests every month to test learning. Parents know that over the period of a month, their child will eat a variety of good foods that with give him the nutrients his body needs. Similarly, parents know their child learns. The trajectory of educational progress is often more like that of a butterfly, rather than that of a bullet. It is neither straight nor linear. It has plateaus and hills and valleys that depend on the child's development, age, interests, and personality.

Many times, learning is invisible. Learning takes place even when there is no output or measurable proof; when children do not write exams, make a product, or write an essay, there is no output to prove the learning. But it does not mean learning has not taken place. That is why recorded parental observation should be considered a valid, and valuable, assessment tool, as it is often the only one parents have outside of the learner's self-assessment.

2. Assessment changes the learning

When assessments enter the picture, the nature of play changes. As soon as outcomes are targeted, the play becomes directed and is no longer free or spontaneous. If children know they will be tested, they will focus on the material they will be tested on instead of enjoying the learning for its own sake. They learn to allocate their time and energy. They don't "waste time" learning what will not be on the test. Nothing kills the enjoyment of reading a good novel faster than knowing you will have to write a book report on it!

Children cannot explore new subjects or delve deep into subjects because measurable outcomes must usually be met under significant time constraints. When my daughter was advised in university to take some easy courses to raise her GPA (Grade Point Average) before applying for a master's program, it became even more clear to me that education has lost its emphasis on learning and placed it—or misplaced it—on marks. Marks do have their place, but should they determine curriculum, or should curriculum determine the marks? Many teachers complain that "teaching to the test" takes a lot of time and places unnecessary constraints on true learning, in that it curbs meandering and discourages natural curiosity. I agree.

Even option courses have grades. Why? The purpose of options is to stimulate a child's interest in an area. It's a low-stakes way to try out something new. If a child knew he wouldn't be marked, he might take more risks in learning and strive to meet new challenges.

Unschooling promotes true learning that is free of the bondage of marks.

3. Testing takes a lot of time and is stressful

Testing in schools is expensive and time-consuming. It takes time away from actual teaching, which is the main function of schools.

4. Testing becomes the content and may not be the best way to learn

How do teachers know that they've nailed it? They read children's faces. When they don't have that feedback, in online learning, for example, they give a lot of assignments to provide the necessary assessment component. My son took a Grade 10 Physical Education class online. It consisted of 50 hours of writing assignments and only 7.5 hours of recorded physical activity! Clearly, the school did not trust the children to do the physical activity and they needed a way of evaluating them, so they assigned them 10 quizzes, three essays, two projects, and mandatory marked written discussion. The writing component of the online class was far more difficult than it would have been in a physical class. This does not make sense. Teachers and parents know that kids are learning when they are engaged and enthusiastic.

5. Tests assess teaching ability at the learner's expense

Teaching and learning is like throwing and catching a ball. Teachers know when a child catches it by the excitement on their faces. But it is hard for teachers when they throw a ball and a child does not even try to catch it. In school, the responsibility for learning must be on both: the teacher ball-thrower and the student ball-catcher.

In unschooling, it is only the learner's responsibility.

6. Tests often don't tell where areas of weakness are

A single number or letter mark does not tell a story when a teacher assesses a student; many biases can positively or negatively influence a test score, such as misunderstanding the meaning of a question.

Most institutions or programs will not allow a student to review their marked tests to see where they need to improve to move on to the next level of learning. This is wrong. All test-takers should be allowed to view their mistakes and at the very least, be shown the correct answers to show them where they went wrong. A grade of 80% is great—but it doesn't tell them how to correct the 20 percent of the questions they got wrong.

There is great value, however, in using tests for self-assessment. If a child wants to start a math program and needs to determine his level, a test is a great tool. The resulting mark is insignificant; it's importance is as an indicator of the optimal starting level for the student.

7.   Tests are often geared to future students, not current ones

Standardized achievement tests allow schools to plan improved delivery and content for the next year's crop of students, rather than current students. Consequently, the test results may not correctly evaluate learning.

8.   Tests often measure the ability to take tests, instead of measuring the learning

When my children began taking tests at 12 years of age, they needed instruction on how to mark the bubbles and not get lost on the bubble sheet. They needed guidance on how to gauge and budget the time allotted for the test and how to reduce pre-test anxiety. Often, test questions are formulated so poorly that the learner cannot decipher what is being asked. The problem is the test, not the learner's knowledge.

Unschooled children are not used to tests and may do poorly even when they know the content, simply because they are not schooled in the testing procedure. One of my sons had a bad experience that illustrates this. Going into an exam, he was not told to reset his calculator before the teacher cleared it, essentially sabotaging his configurations. His math test answers were incorrect because his graphing calculator was in radon mode instead of degree mode. Obviously, the test results did not accurately reflect his knowledge.

9.   Testing must cover a beginning and an end

Learning doesn't end or begin. It doesn't start in September and end in June. It goes "off track" naturally. My children learned the most during the summer months, when they had access to a broader range of books and videos from the library. During the "school year" we were busy running to outside activities, groups, and play dates, and we often didn't have much time to read a book in a hammock. So, if the kids had been tested in September, they would have shown a great increase in knowledge since June. By the same token, June testing would show less progress. As well, there are dry spells when kids don't appear to learn much academically, and that is okay—after a dry spell comes a tsunami of provable academic learning! Testing cannot possibly capture the ebbs and flows of meandering learning.

As well, testing has time limits. Very few events in real life are timed. The stress of a timed event can impact the learner and prevent her from successfully outputting her knowledge, resulting in an artificially low mark.

10. Academic testing only measures the learning during a particular chunk of time immediately prior to testing

Testing does not measure knowledge retention a few years after testing—that is to say, it is not an indicator of true, intrinsic learning. If leaving-school achievement tests were given to adults two years out of school, they would almost certainly fail them, unless they were actively working in the field!

11. Tests teach values

Test questions are very school-biased and give a child the impression that school is "normal" and homeschooling is, therefore, "abnormal." His learning experience and that of his homeschooled peers is not reflected in the questions. My daughter took a Grade 3 Math exam and figured out, at age eight, that over 70 percent of the questions featured "boy" scenarios. What does that tell her about math and girls? Because parents rarely see the test that are given to their children, these biased embedded values are rarely caught.

12. Testing measures subject matter content only

Testing does not measure the fundamental soft skills essential for success in life: initiative, honesty, creativity, problem-solving, or interpersonal communication skills. Children may be highly gifted in intelligence areas such as music, art, dance, drama, sports, movement, and other personal skills that cannot be measured by testing. Heavy emphasis on test results in core subjects tells children who excel in art, humanities, and sports that their intelligences are inferior.

13. High-stakes testing promotes cheating

When my kids went to university, their exams were weighted at anywhere from 50 to 90 percent of the final course mark. When I asked why so high, the explanation was that cheating in course assignments was rampant, and that it in an exam environment, it was easier for administration to control cheating.

14. Grades can damage self-worth and self-confidence

Grading compares a child to others, rather than evaluating her own progress. Grades hurt self-esteem, especially in children with special needs and learning disabilities that have many alternative aptitudes, intelligences, and abilities. As Thomas Armstrong and Howard Gardner note, there are at least eight ways to be intelligent. School tests only measure two: linguistic (English) and logical (Math) abilities.

15. Learning can be assessed through many forms other than testing

Assessment of portfolios, projects, photographs, physical evidence, observations, and self-reflection are valid to prove learning. However, this form of evaluation can make it difficult to compare one student to another—a required element in our environment of mass delivery, standardized curriculum, and conveyor-belt education. Bias is embedded.

One teacher may reward an essay with an A—another might evaluate it quite differently. The best assessment, always, is the learner's self-assessment.

Do we test for social, emotional and physical health?

There are four dimensions to a child's development: social, emotional, physical, and cognitive. As a society, we do not regularly or mandatorily test a child's physical, emotional, or social health to ensure that taxpayers are getting a reasonable return on the funding of parenting programs, health care delivery, or even child benefit payments. We leave it up to the parents to monitor child's health in those three dimensions and ensure satisfactory progress from six to 18 years of age. To demand that parents subject their children to a "well-child" check-up every year in exchange for continuing to receive their child tax benefit would be considered undue interference in the private realm of parenting. We have to trust that parents are not giving their children ACES. So why are we so concerned with testing a child's cognitive health every year? Are they learning? Are they keeping up with their cohorts? And why is it important that they keep up with their cohorts in learning? What is wrong with personalized learning that allows comparison only in relation to a child's own progress?

As in healthcare, government regulation and interference in unschooling should be non-existent.

Trust parents

In 99.9 percent of homeschooling families, parents have their children's best interests at heart and their well-being firmly entrenched as their first priority. We have to trust that parents know their child best in all four areas of development and give them the ultimate say over their child's education and cognitive development, in the same way we trust them with their child's emotional, social, and physical development.

No marks until high school or beyond

Test-taking is a life skill and we all need to learn it. We take tests for driver's licenses, yoga teaching qualifications, swimming and karate levels, and postsecondary admittance. But do we need to start when kids are six years old? No. At that age, they don't need to endure the stress that testing causes; they will learn test-taking skills when they need to. The first tests some of my children wrote were the non-mandatory Grade 6 government achievement tests in Math and English. Some of them did not write a test until Grades 9, 10, or even 12, in some subjects. They caught on quickly when they needed to. High school is plenty of time to learn and polish their test-taking skills.

Grades were also unknown to our children until high school. Believing that self-evaluation was the best form of assessment, we asked our children from time to time, "What was interesting about that? What did you learn from...?" We did not record their responses. We asked questions to start them down another line of thought. Our record keeping consisted of keeping track of the resources we offered to the children, not what they produced with them. Much of the time, they didn't produce anything that looked "schooly." How do you write, in educational jargon, that the kids put on a puppet play over their bunkbeds? When they produced something interesting, we took lots of photos and videos. Those are things I still treasure today, and always will.

3 forms of unschooling assessment

The province of Alberta offers three forms of formal assessment for homeschooling learning; some other provinces and states have a similar regime. Only the yearly portfolio assessment is mandatory, and Alberta is the most regulated province in Canada.

1. Mandatory yearly portfolio assessment by a certified teacher-supervisor

Homeschoolers and unschoolers who choose a traditional, parent-directed home education program are required by law to have only two annual visits from a certified teacher-supervisor. In the first visit in fall, the parent and teacher review the education plan, including 20 outcomes, that has been prepared by the parent. (see Chapter 12) Parents are in charge; their plan must be accepted. All the outcomes are to be reached by age 20, and they are flexible enough that they can be satisfied by many kinds of learning activities.

The second visit occurs later in the year, when the certified teacher-supervisor is convinced that the learner has achieved some progress in the education plan's outcomes and signs off. She or he comes to visit the child and the parent over a cup of tea and listens attentively as the eager child shows off the portfolio of all the exciting things he has been up to. The parent reviews the child's accomplishments with the supervisor, who transcribes the details in a written report. Appropriately, parents are not required to fill out any reports, as they are not paid to teach or engage in administrative work. Also, the teacher knows best how to translate "fighting with siblings" into a positive educational phrase such as "demonstrates conflict resolution skills."

The teacher completes the final one-page report with the following statement: "In my professional opinion, as a Certified Alberta Education teacher, I declare that [student's name] meets the 20 outcomes of the Schedule of Learning Outcomes for Home Education. Signed, The Teacher." The parent receives a copy of the report.

This fairly minimal level of interference, namely the two visits, can be seen as good or bad. Some parents feel it is too invasive. They don't want the government to encroach on their family life at all, let alone twice a year.

However, one benefit of having a such a report, however superficial, is that it exempts the family from the criticisms such as "the child is not learning," or "the family is hurting the child's future by not teaching them anything," or "the parents are not providing the minimal educational program." This legal document, showing that a child is learning and progressing, can help prevent ex-spouses from claiming in court that unschooling is not a valid educational choice; nosy neighbors from lodging complaints with Child Protection Services; or vicious relatives from trying to gain custody of a child.

This type of assessment is also favorable in that children's progress is only compared to their own individual previous reports. My son was not yet reading in Grade 3, but by Grade 4, he was reading novel series. He was not subjected to classroom segregation, embarrassment, or teasing from peers. He was assessed only in comparison to his previous year's reading level, and his progress was cause for joyous celebration. Every child learns from year to year and progresses in some areas. Thus, every child is successful. No child ever unlearns, or does not learn something over the course of a year, even by watching TV; this type of assessment takes that into consideration. It holds the naysayers at bay and validates self-directed education.

2. Non-mandatory standardized testing

Standardized tests are given to all school children every three or so grades, depending on the jurisdiction. To acquire an "Acceptable" level of understanding of a subject, they must get 50 percent of the test answers correct. Most unschooling children can master at least 50 percent of the topics covered in elementary grades by self-learning.

In the interest of furthering my research for this book, I asked my unschooled children to write the standardized exams. Three of my children wrote some Grade 9 tests in Math and Science, and some wrote Grade 3 and 6 tests in Math and English Language Arts. They all scored at least in the "Acceptable" category (50 – 80 percent of answers correct) and some in the "Excellence" category (80 – 100 percent of answers correct).

These tests are given in the core subjects of ELA (English Language Arts), Math, Science, and Social Studies. They are not mandatory for any child, even children in school; however, they are given in schools on certain days when attendance is mandatory. In Science and Social Studies, the tests are grade- and topic-specific and are not meant for home education or unschooling children who choose their own topics and learn at their own pace. For the same reason, even basic skills in Math and English can sometimes be problematic for unschoolers. As home educators do not have to follow the government curriculum outcomes, their learning may or may not be in sync with their public school counterparts or the material on the tests.

In the US, mandatory testing is required for the Common Core.

3. Government Grade 12 diploma exams, SATs, ACTs, or equivalents

This is where the rubber meets the road. If a child is knowledgeable in a subject, he can prove that knowledge by writing the government exams, regardless of whether he acquired that knowledge in school, in homeschooling, or through self-directed unschooling. Although the exams do not specifically prove an accumulation of knowledge as they are course-specific, successfully writing the SAT (Scholastic Aptitude Test), ACT (American College Test), or the Grade 12 exams proves that the child has a competent enough understanding of the subject matter to further their education at a postsecondary institution.

It's too bad that not all provinces have this standardization. A high school program in Manitoba may not be as rigorous as a high school program in Ontario, so postsecondary institutions now give their own entrance exams regardless of which province a student is coming from.

The beauty of these "end of schooling" exams is that they are the most objective measure of a child's progress. They are marked by at least three government-hired teachers who do not know the child.

In places that do not have end-of-school exams, unschoolers who write the SATs or the ACTs can confidently apply to postsecondary institutions worldwide. See Chapter 20 for more on final exams.

Falling behind

No one in unschooling falls behind, because every child is compared only to himself. He is unique. Some parents worry that if they want to place their child back in school one day, might he be hopelessly behind the rest of the class and be teased mercilessly for it? I do not know of a single unschooled child who returned to school and was singled out in this way. Usually, no one knows the newcomer was homeschooled unless the child himself speaks up. Most children fit into their assigned grade perfectly well. "My doctor knows a lot more about sickness than I do, but I don't have to take my kids to see her every day to know whether they are well or not. I am with my children every day. I see how they are doing. I know what they know and if they want to know more, I can help them." (Diana S, 1993)

Outcomes versus curriculum

In Canada, our education system is outcome based. The outcomes are more important than the method used to meet them. There are regional differences among provinces, but each grade is relatively similar. In Alberta, each grade and subject has the same 1400 outcomes, regardless of whether the school is private, public, charter, or virtual. The only exception is home education, which has 20 outcomes per childhood.

Think of outcomes and curriculum as archery. The learning outcomes are the targets. Curriculum is the means to meet the targets—the arrows. Curriculum comes in many forms, only one of which is workbooks and textbooks. Some regions may have a list of resources recommended for homeschoolers and mandatory for teachers, such as high school English novels, but even these are flexible. Each school board has its preferred curriculum and parents are free to use it or not. The curriculum industry in North America is dominated by several major manufacturers: Pearson, McGraw Hill Ryerson, and Houghton Mifflin. However, use of these products is not obligatory in either print or digital form.

We could even go so far as to say that adults are "curriculum" too. As education moves from content to competencies, students will need human assistance for developing those competencies—and that comes from adults, not textbooks.

The methods of delivering the curriculum vary as well. In the self-directed unschooling method, students can choose to learn by participating in co-ops, discussions, presentations, direct teaching, role-play, reading and responding, or application.

If homeschoolers don't meet the government outcomes, should they be forced to quit?

Absolutely not! If public school children fail the standardized achievement tests, should they be forced to homeschool or unschool? Again, absolutely not! It would be arrogant for proponents of any system to assume that theirs is the only model of education. Government systems, while the most prolific, are not the default gold standard. In unschooling, the child randomly chooses both the target and the arrow, according to his interests at a given time. In school, if the learner does not accept the instruction or meet the outcomes, the teacher is absolutely not to blame. In home education, the parent is not to blame either.

Learning is entirely in the control of the learner. The most that parents can do is offer a stimulating educational environment, attend to their child's curiosity, and facilitate meeting their intellectual needs. As in toilet training, eating, and sleeping, parents can facilitate the learning process but cannot force or control the outcome. Nor can teachers. All the detentions in the world cannot make a student read. And a scolding from a parent is not going to make a child enjoy fractions.

All a parent is legally obligated to do is facilitate a child's education. Simply providing a rich learning environment already fulfills the legal requirements. A child can choose to accept or refuse what is offered. In school, teachers can threaten bad marks, take away recess, or promise pizza coupons, but they only have that child for one year. Unlike the parents, they are not building a lifelong relationship with the child. They are merely hoping to get through the school year with at least minimal tolerance of each other.

Parents should never be forced to put their children back into school because they haven't met government outcomes. Governments cannot hold parents to a higher level of accountability than they do school teachers.

Recordkeeping

It is imperative that parents keep good records of the intellectual stimulation offered to their children in unschooling. Although it's not right, parents are often judged on how well they have documented their methods in presenting a certain subject area, rather than what the child actually learned; this is especially true in cases where there is very little tangible output from the child. The two mandatory supervisor visits in Alberta force us to do this. In the parts of Canada where there are no supervisor visits or other types of government interference, unschooling families enjoy not having to comply with recordkeeping requirements. Lucky them!

In Alberta, the supervisors will seldom directly question children on what they know; rather, they will base their evaluation on information the parents provide. And although the parents' documentation may not be a perfectly accurate measurement of the child's learning, so far it is the only method, besides non-mandatory testing, that the government has of measuring a child's progress in home education.

Let's say you put on a video about electromagnetism and the children watched 10 minutes of it before declaring it was boring and left the room. You still document that you presented the video. You have done your part as facilitator. You cannot force a child to learn. Ever.

Documentation can take the form of recording the field trips your child attended, places they traveled to, their program and class outlines, the library books they checked out, the videos they watched, the projects they made, the photographs and videos of their projects. Some parents blog or compile photos on social media, which makes a nice timeline for them and their children to enjoy later. Other parents make a learning journal and jot down conversations that take place. There is no need to write down everything, just a representative sample.

If you live in a country, province, or state that requires recordkeeping, the following is a sample.

Grade 1 Science: Color

- Played with play-dough and saw how different colors mixed
- Painted with combined colors
- Examined a color wheel
- Watched a video called "Colors"

Grade 1 Math:

- Number Theory, counted and sorted Lego pieces according to color
- Counted coins to purchase item

Grade 3 English: Reading

- Son read the Archie comics and Captain Underpants series this year. He really loved reading Stuart Little, Willy Wonka and is starting on Harry Potter books

Grade 3 English: Writing

- Son wrote a letter to Santa this year. (That's it. He wasn't interested in writing so that was the only thing he did. Not going to push it! Maybe next year. Maybe not. When he sees a need to learn to write, he will learn then.)

Grade 6 Social Studies: Greece

- Played computer game "Age of Mythology"
- Read library book "Encyclopedia of The Ancient World"
- Read Usbourne book on Greek myths
- Visited Greek restaurant Mykonos and had a Greek dinner
- Watched video called "Ancient Greece"

Grade 6 Math: Number Theory

- Absolutely no interest in math this year. (Not going to push it.)

Translating life into "educationalese"

See the activities in Chapter 14 and how they have been slotted into subject matter categories. Many other daily activities can be considered educational as well. Think:

Library trip – research, resource identification

Shopping – consumer education, geography, health

Family outing – resource field trip

Chores – home economics, manual arts, trade skills

Gardening and weeding – botany

Dentist, Doctor – health, career research

Reading the newspaper – social studies, current events, civics

Join a home education support group and protect your rights

As school moves further and further into the home via online learning, we must be vigilant in protecting our right to keep traditional home education viable, ensuring that the parent maintains control and has the ultimate say in their child's self-directed education. All parents must know their rights. Online and correspondence courses are school; parents have no say in that. But in traditional home education and unschooling, parents have the ultimate say.

You most certainly do not need to purchase defense insurance from a homeschool legal group. Homeschooling is legal. Period. Although there will always be nosy—albeit well-meaning—strangers or acquaintances who do not share your educational philosophy, no one is going to come to your door and take your children away just because you homeschool. Don't let the fear of that stop you from going out during the day. Although many community professionals still don't understand homeschooling or unschooling, legally they must accept it.

Since the Fraser report was in the news on numerous occasions since 2007, homeschooling has become so common and mainstream that in the last ten years my school-age kids are rarely asked by store clerks "why aren't you in school today?" I don't think our poor social workers, with their inhumane caseloads, are going to act on a single complaint by a neighbor—to warrant action, there must be repeated complaints from various parties, such as clubs, neighbors, and relatives, against a single perceived offender. If you need evidence, check with child protection services in your state or province and ask how many cases of homeschoolers have they investigated in the last twenty years on the basis of homeschooling alone? Know your rights and keep advocating for them. We are well connected to each other thanks to the internet.

Government regulation violates boundaries

It's always interesting to me that society, school administrators, and the government feel the need to provide educational oversight and regulation in home education. They insist that parents must provide an education "equal to the education children would get in school"—as if school were the ultimate educational model. Many homeschooling parents provide an education that is indeed not equal—rather, it is far superior to the education children might receive in school.

The school industry is disrupted. In the story *The Emperor's New Clothes*, by Hans Christian Andersen, everyone sees that the emperor has no clothes and they keep up the pretense until one child calls everyone out. Everyone participates in the farce. Similarly, although we know that children can learn everything they need to know from the internet, their homes, and their communities, few challenge the industry's self-serving lobbying for job protection that demands mandatory school attendance or home education regulations, or mandatory online instructional hours in lieu of school attendance. Let's examine the problematic concerns embedded in regulation.

The home is private

Every country, province, and state has different rules for homeschooling. Systems must interfere and regulate less, not more, in homeschooling. Schools must be regulated for the common good of society and for the protection of children, and because they are institutions accountable to the taxpayer. However, the home is sacrosanct.

Mandatory school attendance was instituted in the early 1900s to ensure that children got an education instead of working in factories or on the farm. This is no longer an issue, as government labor laws prohibit employment of young children. Consequently, government no longer enforces school attendance punitively. Why not get rid of regulation? Parents who want to send their children to a school can. Parents who don't, do not have to. Children will still learn.

The price of educational freedom is constant vigilance of government rules. We must hold back the encroachment of government regulation on the freedom to homeschool and unschool. Governments can regulate schools, but their boundary ends at the school-yard fence. Parents are only teaching only their own children, not other people's. The school system may not infringe upon the sanctity and privacy of the home. All families are encouraged to know and understand their rights and to speak out when those rights are subjugated.

Government and schools should not be in the business of telling families how to live, what to value, or what beliefs and attitudes to hold. Schools exist to teach children academic knowledge, nothing more. In a secular public school, curriculum is regularly reviewed to cull biases and ensure political correctness. I am pleased that most of the social studies programs in our schools are somewhat neutral, but often subtle values are slipped in. My daughter's high school biology textbook referred to the Athabasca hydrocarbon resources as "oilsands." Her social studies textbook called them "tarsands." Which term is the more emotionally value laden? There *is* bias in schools. Parents must be in control of the values their children are taught, not schools. The school's job is to teach critical thinking; how to think, not what to think.

Teachers should not assume the role of parents but they are increasingly called upon to do so. Again, we encounter the "hidden curriculum," in which school curriculum is designed to compensate for what might be lacking in the home, by teaching manners, caring behavior, interpersonal skills, socialization, and leadership, and providing emotional support. This was not school's original intent, but it is sometimes necessary for the small percentage of children who have little family support in these areas. But they are not the majority. If teachers had to choose between teaching math content or developing caring relationships with their students in class, I would vote for the mentoring relationship. Children can access math and science online but they cannot access caring adults online. In developing a relationship with a student, it is true that a teacher might impart her own values and biases, but that is a reflection of the real world! Kids are going to run up against conflicting viewpoints all of their lives. It is good to be exposed to a variety of opinions and views. However, teachers can have bias and values, but the curriculum must remain neutral.

Parents have the right to teach their values

A common regulatory concern is that parents may choose to teach their child values different from those held by the government, and by extension, the community.

Values are the reason many parents choose to homeschool in the first place. Teachers are great at modeling character, honesty, virtues, manners, and ethical citizenship. But there are other values hanging around the school yard. Parents don't want their children to learn consumerism, peer pressure, sarcasm, attitude, class hierarchy, bullying, authoritarian dictatorships, and unquestioning obedience as byproducts of their school attendance. My son told me that when he went to high school for a year, he learned very little academically, but he did learn a lot about hierarchy and bullying!

Meeting regulations is time-consuming

Parents have better things to do than meet government demands for program planning, proof of learning, and test results. Time spent on administrative tasks that the parent is not paid for, is time that could be diverted to learning activities.

Parents are in the best position to decide if the education provided is adequate

Even when the government provides funding to defray the costs of homeschooling, they have no right to demand academic outcomes of individual students, any more than they would for a child registered in a school. Much funding and grants go to programs for parents of ages 0 - 5 with no accounting for the return on investment. Even school grants are not tied to performance in Canada. In addition, governments have no right to dictate curriculum, program, or outcomes because parents know what is best for their child. If governments cannot dictate curriculum or program, they certainly cannot dictate testing either, as testing by definition is dependent on a standardized curriculum. If parents are not allowed to teach what they want, what is the point of homeschooling?

Many times, I attend education conferences and people ask, "How do we know the kids are getting the basics if there is no regulation?" The assumption is that homeschooled children are being shortchanged. Many parents homeschool because they know they can do *better* than the average public school. If academic performance was rewarded with bonuses, home education parents would be rich!

Covering government educational mandates takes valuable time away from subjects that parents and children deem important. Currently, school children in Canada receive no education at all on robotics or HTML coding. Dominating skills in these areas is critically important to our children's future; parents should be able to focus on subjects such as these, rather than following an outdated government program.

School personnel are inappropriate supervisors in home education

In light of this, it is important to remember that schools, school boards, and governments serve families—not the other way around. As Thomas Armstrong states in his book *The Best Schools*, "Educators are the experts in teaching and learning, not politicians, government officials, accountants or standardized test companies." Parents are experts on their children. They know what is best for them and what homeschooling or unschooling methods work in their home; teachers know what is best for their students and what works in their school classrooms. One should never oversee the other. Teachers in Canada with a degree in education have no mandatory training in the unique philosophies of home education or unschooling. Nor do education accountants and social workers get professional development in home education. Mandating that teachers oversee home education as supervisors violates parental rights and oversteps the boundaries of school's authority.

There is no regulation in parenting

Scientists tell us that the most crucial period for brain development is from zero to six years of age. Children need 3D experiential learning to develop brain cell connections for healthy growth. Does the government intervene in parenting in order to provide children with the optimal conditions for development in those years? No. There is no interference, monitoring, or assessment for recipients of government taxpayer-funded programs. Why, then, for the school-age years? If there is no government oversight in parenting, there should be no government oversight in home education either. Parents do not suddenly require surveillance the year their child turns six!

Parents know their child's academic abilities best

Should parents be subjected to home visits from certified teachers? Absolutely not! Parents know their child's temperament, learning style, and quirks, and have proven strategies to deal with them. They know their child's strengths and weaknesses in each of his many intelligences, and his progression on a daily basis. They know the stresses their child faces and how he deals with them. They know his likes and dislikes. They know what resources their child is drawn to. They know how he best socializes and they know how to coach him in interpersonal skills. They are there to support their child, not abandon him to a playground of 200 peers with a single adult to teach them "social" skills. They know their child's friends, the friends' parents, and the community members. They know all this by observation and involvement, not by an outsider's evaluation. Parents do not need a teacher to pop in twice a year to assess how their child is doing in the homeschool; and a visiting teacher cannot possibly see in a one-hour visit what parents have learned by living with their child all day, every day. Such visits are a farce and only serve to undermine parents' confidence in their ability to teach their child.

Hard cases make bad laws

The other reason society wants to regulate home education is the perception that homeschooling children may be maltreated, and that such maltreatment could be avoided if children were under the daily oversight of teachers, coaches, bus drivers, and school nurses. The media broadcasts stories of horrific child abuse, and when the family in question homeschools, reports it even more spectacularly. Proportionately, the number of abuse cases of children registered in public schools is far higher, yet the homeschooling family makes the news. There is no research-based evidence that homeschooled children are at a greater risk than others of being abused or neglected. (Ray, 2018) This is because homeschooling is growing and those who have a vested interest in maintaining the public school system want stricter laws and regulations—which create jobs—to discourage parents from homeschooling. Ninety-nine percent of homeschooling parents do a fantastic job. They must be trusted. For the few children that are at risk in a homeschool environment, everyone has a duty to report maltreatment, not just teachers.

We don't make laws based on minuscule percentages of abuse incidence. About 26 percent of the adult population in the US grew up with at least three ACES (Adverse Childhood Experiences. (Palix, 2017) Those toxic experiences affected the children's developing brain architecture as they were growing up. I'm certain that the schools rarely knew about these children's home situations, and even more rarely did anything to help them. The lifelong health problems and resulting medical bills of these individuals are the burden that the health system, and ultimately the taxpayer, must now bear. Unschooling is not an ACE.

Studies show that the vast number of abused children are toddlers and preschoolers, not school-age children. Shaken baby syndrome is highest in ages one to four. Yet no one intrudes on the sacred realm of parenting under the guise of "checking up on parents just in case they might be abusive."

Funding needs oversight to ensure appropriateness

Yes. This one needs regulation. Funding for home education comes from the pockets of taxpayers, and they want to be assured that the money is being spent on education and not the parents' trip to Hawaii—although it might be argued that Hawaii is very educational! There is a need for guidelines and monitoring of receipts and reimbursements. If parents do not want the funding, they can refuse it.

Pushback on regulations

When parents take on homeschooling, it is extremely important that they get to know the regulations and the rights and responsibilities of everyone involved. Many parents do not know their rights, and schools can overstep their boundaries without parents even realizing it. When I notified the school that my children would be leaving, I was not obligated to give them any explanation. But they asked many questions they had no right to ask, including where the children were going; they questioned whether I was fit to take on the "enormous" job of teaching my children. Their questions undermined my confidence—as they were meant to.

As a parent, I have the highest vested interest in helping my children attain their education. Their development is my number one concern, motivation, and focus. From the day they were born, I would not outsource their development or their education. If the system fails my child, it's my basement he will be living in when he is 30 years old, and unemployed. He will not be in the teacher's, principal's or education minister's basement. So yes, I will confidently take on his education, because I can and I will do it better.

On the other hand, the system is concerned about, motivated by, and focused on a multitude of other aspects of education: building maintenance, policy, teacher-student ratios, teacher certification, class sizes, budgets, accountability, and School Act regulations. Because public education is an institution, most of the time children's best interests are not its number one concern. The number one concern is financial sustainability for the industry.

Investigate the sponsor behind any research. Think critically. Know your rights. Get involved in activism and advocacy.

Just as for parenting, government oversight should not be required for homeschooling.

PART 4:
UNSCHOOLING AND CHILD DEVELOPMENT STAGES

16

Brain Basics

"Your gifts are the things you do well without remembering how you learned them." — David Irvine, Speaker

Child development research is based on institutionalized children

"Human development research should inform educational practice." (Armstrong, 2006) In this part of the book, we will look at the "normal" development of children. It's best to keep in mind that studies on the normal development of school-age children have always been carried out on those who spend most of their time in an institution with peers and hierarchical authority, rather than in a family environment. Child development research has only been around for the past 70 years and school was well entrenched by then. We know that animals behave differently in captivity than in the wild. (Aldrich, 2015) By the same token, from the small studies done on homeschooled children, we know that children educated at home behave differently than those educated in the school system. Anecdotally, home-educated children are very close to siblings, parents, and extended family. Children educated at home do not display the typical developmental markers such as rebellion, separation, and argumentation that are considered normal tween and teen behavior. Homeschooled kids get a lot more sleep and have a lot less stress; this affects their moods as well as their cognitive development. They feel a sense of belonging to their communities and certainly to their families.

Education begins with the brain

The brain's most rapid development occurs during the first six years of a child's life. The child's experiences effect his social, emotional, physical, and cognitive health. Unlike the human heart and lungs, the brain is not fully formed at birth, that is, all its 100 billion brain cells, called neurons, are in place but are only about 60 percent developed. At birth, a very limited number of neurons are connected to each other—just enough for the infant's brain to send messages to the body to perform the basic functions of keeping the heart pumping and the lungs working. The vast majority of neuron connections—pathways formed over the synapses (gaps between cells)—are made as the child grows, through experiences and interactions with people and the environment; they peak at the age of three years but continue to form until the age of six.

How does the brain form pathways for the cells to connect with each other? Neurons are nerve cells consisting of a cell body, axons, and dendrites. The axons deliver signals from one cell to another; dendrites receive the signals. There are gaps between the cells' axons and neighboring cell's dendrites; and these gaps are called synapses. Signals are transmitted over the gaps by chemical and electrical messengers called neurotransmitters.

The neurotransmitters act like bridges over the neuron "land masses" in the brain. When two brain cells are connected by neurotransmitters, they are said to have formed a pathway. This is also called brain "wiring." These pathways are strengthened as the child's experiences are repeated because the same signals are sent between the two cells over and over again, making the pathways stronger and thicker. A pathway weakens if an experience is not repeated, while other pathways are formed by new experiences and strengthened by signal repetition. (Durrant, 2011) When a parent tells a toddler over and over not to bite his little friend, that signal is strengthening a specific brain pathway. Eventually, with increased executive function, or self-control, and language (use your words!) in the preschool years, the child stops biting.

These pathways shape feelings, thoughts, and eventually, behavior. By the time your child is three years old, the brain has made more connections than it needs to run efficiently, so it lets go of weak and unused connections. Thus, if a child is not read to or spoken to, the connections that are not reinforced will disappear.

At age 10, a child has about 500 trillion connections—about the same number as an adult. How do they retain connections? Use it or lose it—those connections that are frequently activated are reinforced.

Axons are covered with a coating called a myelin sheath, which is not fully developed until about age 25. However, we constantly learn and experience new things throughout our lives and this continues to shape the brain. This is brain "plasticity." (Durrant, 2011)

Because the brain is one of the least developed organs at birth, it needs good nutrition and good experiences to grow and develop. Proper nutrition provides proteins, sugars, fats (a good reason to give young children full-fat milk), and vitamins. The brain is the body's largest consumer of oxygen; it only constitutes two percent of human body weight but uses 20 percent of its oxygen. (Body Worlds, 2009)

The brain is not just kept in good shape by such physical care such as good nutrition, safety from injury, and early positive interactive experiences. A child's environment has an enormous impact on his developing brain. The field of epigenetics studies the brain's flexibility in allowing the human body to adapt to its environment while at the same time allowing the environment to impact the development of the brain. Children's brains can adapt to an ice-age environment with low technology, or an electronic environment with high technology. But it's a two-way street, in that quality of care, removal of stress, and positive stimulation affect the development of a young brain. The brain is a highly reactive organ, and adverse early experiences can harm the development of an average intelligent child and cause difficulties later in his childhood. Conversely, quality, loving, nurturing, attentive caregiving can temper a spirited, difficult child and promote intellect and emotional stability.

The child "loses" knowledge when pathways formed by learning are not reinforced through continued experience. A child who stops taking French immersion classes at age six will probably lose all the French he learned by age eight. Parents and teachers must continually reinforce the brain pathways they want the child to retain. Experiences such as reading, talking, speaking another language, traveling, and trying new experiences such as horseback riding or seeing a magic show build children's brain architecture no matter what the age. Getting out in the world and "doing" is much more educational than viewing the world on a screen.

Human beings need experiences that engage all five senses

Children need three-dimensional experiences that touch all five senses; for example, playing with play-dough—they can touch, smell, taste, see, and hear the play-dough as they manipulate it. This is far superior to simply looking up play-dough on a tablet, which stimulates only the two senses of sight and hearing. They cannot taste, smell, or touch play-dough on a screen—yet! Left to their own devices, all children love manipulating objects. If you put a big ball of play-dough out on a table with children around, I guarantee not one of them can leave it be. I've even done this with moms having tea at the kitchen table. Plunk down a big ball of play-dough and someone will pick it up and start creating.

Brain anatomy by age

The brain develops from the brain stem at the top of the spinal cord toward the back of the head, up to the top, and down toward the front. Its development starts at one month *in utero* and continues until about age 25. The cerebrum is divided into two halves, called the left and right hemispheres. Each hemisphere has four sections called lobes and each lobe controls particular body functions. The lobes develop and are particularly sensitive during different ages of childhood.

Baby brain development, ages 0 – 1

The brain stem is the most highly developed area of a baby's brain at birth. It regulates basic functions such as breathing, blood pressure, and heart rate, and controls the new-born's reflexes of crying and suckling; it also plays a part in handling some of the infant's emotions.

The **occipital lobe**, or visual cortex, sits at the back of the head and controls sight. The occipital lobe is one of the first parts of the brain to fully develop. (Covert, 2017)

Babies are hard-wired to love and to interact with people rather than toys or objects. They learn quickly that love and stress relief come from people. The interplay of attachment comes through the connection of at least one caring adult who relieves baby's stress by picking him up, changing his diaper, or feeding him when he crys. Attachment parenting is basically that—stress relief. Babies also have a high level of the chemicals that allow their brains to form connections easily. Dopamine and oxytocin help them form their attachments and trust parents and caregivers. Young children mostly develop their brain connections through their five senses: sight, hearing, smell, touch, and taste. The mouth is a major sensory organ, and until about the age of four, everything goes into a baby's mouth for him to explore. (Body Worlds, 2009)

Young children interact with the world through play with objects. Babies don't differentiate between a toy and a cardboard box. It's all the same to them, they love it all! The educational play and toy market for young children is a huge growth industry. Baby toys are labeled "early computer coding" as a marketing gimmick to make parents think they are giving their babies an edge. The market for toys and goods peddled to parents of babies under one year old is worth an astonishing $343 million per year in the US. (Wildman, 2009) Yet all babies need is adult interaction and a few objects to play with. They don't need so-called educational toys.

Toddler brain development, ages 1 – 2

A child's sense of self begins between the ages of one and two. He knows when he is apart from his caregivers and separation anxiety kicks in because he cannot stop his loved ones from leaving him. Toddlers need adults in order to thrive. At age two, the toddler's brain has double the number of synapses that an adult brain has.

He has likes and dislikes and wants what he wants, without understanding limits. He has very little self-control. Children this age need a structured, safe, and warm learning environment. Ninety percent of toddler actions are unconscious ones, performed out of routine and habit. They just "do" without thinking. They don't "think things through" and they certainly don't "know better!" Adults teach by repeating instructions over and over and over again. The repetition builds those pathways between neurons so that as the child grows, he will remember instructions with just a brief cue from adults.

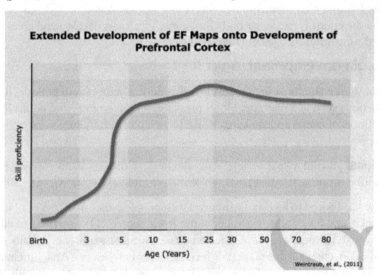

Executive function skills through the lifespan. (Palix, 2017)

From the graph, you see that toddlers have very little self-control, or what we call executive function. The big leap upwards occurs between five and six years of age. That is why a three-year-old can't play chess. He needs to have enough brain power to execute the four domains of executive function: working memory—the ability to remember that the queen moves all ways and the castle only two ways; focus—the ability to concentrate even among distractions; Plan B, or flexibility—the ability to find a new move when the other player takes out the Knight; and self-control—the ability to refrain from throwing the board across the room when he loses. These four executive function skills are almost non-existent in children under age three and it is the primary reason that young children "do not listen"—and this is not a discipline issue, but rather a development issue. It's why many children are not ready for structured learning and certainly not ready to sit and listen for mandatory school until at least age six.

Preschooler brain development, ages 3 – 5

The temporal and parietal lobes develop the most in toddlers and preschoolers. The **temporal lobe** is located at the sides of their heads, above the ears, and is the center of hearing and language processing. Its development begins before birth and peaks within the first year of life. This may explain why toddlers are subject to tantrums, because they hear and understand but they don't have the vocabulary to describe the volcano erupting inside of them. The temporal lobe also houses the amygdala, that little almond-shaped organ responsible for governing emotions. The hypothalamus governs thirst, hunger, and sexual impulses and is closely tied to emotions. The hippocampus forms long-term memory and as children acquire language, they also acquire their first memories. The thalamus is the control center for the limbic system. The actions of the amygdala, hypothalamus, and hippocampus are all relayed through the thalamus. (Body Worlds, 2009)

The **parietal lobe** is at the upper back of the head and processes the senses of touch, taste, and smell. It also contains the motor cortex, which governs motor coordination. Fine and gross motor skills become fine-tuned in the preschool years when children love to be active.

By the time children reach age three, they start pruning the lesser-used pathways to allow room for the more used ones to grow. Between the ages of three and six, a child's executive function skills take a huge leap, especially between four and five years of age. Children listen better to adults and although there is still great variation in their ability to sit still or refrain from talking, many children become easier to parent and teach. It's why some countries hold off formal education until age seven or eight. A study of parents found that 43 percent of them expected children to have self-control by age three when in fact, it does not exist reliably until age five or six. (Hawley, 2000)

School-age brain development, ages 6 – 12

As children move into school age, the **frontal lobe**, located behind the forehead, is the final part of the brain to develop. It is responsible for higher level functions such as cognitive reasoning. At this age, children begin to develop consequence thinking—that any action will have a reaction. They cannot yet think abstractly, but they can understand tangibles and concrete operations—objects and occurrences in their everyday lives. They can experience anything directly in their physical world. Problem solving, emotional processing, creativity, judgment, planning, decision making, and urge regulation all stem from this part of the brain. By age six, children's brains are about 90 percent of adult size. Experiential learning develops the brain best at this age because children still learn from touching and manipulation of physical objects in their environment. At this age, they no longer put things in their mouths; they use sight, hearing, smell and talking to learn. (Body Worlds, 2009)

Teen brain development, ages 13 – 17

Both gray and white matter undergo changes throughout adolescence. The prefrontal cortex experiences another major upswing in executive function—similar to the one from ages three to five, and the four executive function skills increase.

In the teen years, the amygdala is the gas pedal and the prefrontal cortex is the brakes. From age 12 on, the prefrontal cortex begins growing again; it is the last part of the brain to complete its development. Experiential learning in the teen years continues through the four senses of hearing, seeing, touching, and smelling.

The teen years may exhibit disrupted signals. The body is mature but the neural system is still developing. Teens crave that dopamine hit that anticipates reward or pleasure, and they get it from taking risks, "high adrenalin" activities, using substances, adolescent love, and winning at video games or other competitive activities. This could be the cause of poor decision making, bad problem solving, and lack of emotional control in the teen years. Teens' natural brain brakes don't always come through when teens need them, so trusted parents and caregivers still need to be their "external brains," contributing good risk analysis to point out to teens what they are missing and provide kind, safe limits and risk-preparedness. Non-punitive relationship building is very important in order to build trust and communication between parent and child.

Because of the intense craving for pleasure center stimulation, the regimen of formal school often takes a back seat to everything else kids want to do at this age.

Emerging adult brain development, ages 18 – 24

At this age, many children-adults become much more serious about their lives and their preparation for adulthood. At 18, they still have a few years of funded high school education to prepare themselves for further studies, if that is the direction they choose. Their executive function peaks to its optimum condition and this period is especially good for putting the past behind them and forging ahead with future plans. Their brains are still sensitive to new ways of thinking and cognitive behavior therapy is very effective in the treatment of addictions, formulation of new and helpful thought patterns, and working on a new lifestyle and new relationships.

Adult brain development, ages 25 – 50

By age 25, the brain's circuitry is mostly set, although we can certainly continue learning. Continued learning stimulates new pathways and strengthens existing ones. Brains can work for 100 years—although when neurons die, they are not replaced. The brain is at its most powerful between the ages of 25 and 50. After age 50, it no longer performs at its peak, but it certainly still serves most of us well! The key is to keep it active; keep challenging it with new learning and social connections.

Memory

The brain has a fascinating capacity!

There are three forms of memory. **Immediate memory** is great for instant use of information—remembering a phone number for long enough to dial it is an example. Then there is short-term memory, located in the prefrontal cortex. This holds the **working memory**—most adults can maintain their focus on an idea for about 20 minutes. Finally, the **long-term memory** involves the cerebral cortex. This impressive area creates memories by picking up information from the short-term and working memories and synthesizing the two.

The hippocampus and the amygdala color memories with emotion, which is why we remember data that has emotion attached to it: we remember favorite songs; the day a child was born; the day we got married or the first time we had our hearts broken—we remember these because major life events have intense emotion tied to them, be it joyous or painful. Children will not remember the years of patient parenting we gave them; they will remember the one time we lost it out of anger and screamed at them—because of the emotion of intense fear they attached to that experience. One time I was very angry at my partner and I threw a plant out the front door, pot and all. Although it was such an isolated incident, the kids still remember it. Usually, I am very calm! They remember it because their fear of my action was so strong.

People generally do not have memories from before the age of three. Preschoolers from ages three to six remember anomalies—isolated, out-of-the-ordinary incidents. School-age children remember ideas or people from emotions they associate with them. Teenagers have better memories, but only of their recent teen years. When my university kids were home for Christmas, I asked one son why he loved playing with Gordon the Big Engine from Thomas The Tank Engine train set, when he was five. He couldn't remember. I asked my 12-year-old son why he screamed for the first three years of life and he didn't know. The only memories of a trip to England with our 7-, 8-, and 9-year-old children were the three-wheeled cars they saw. When parents ask children to recall something they learned in school a year or two ago, the children rarely remember. The knowledge went into their short-term memory, stayed in the working memory for as long as they needed it—until they passed the test—and then got left behind. Unless the child is actively engaged, using the knowledge on a regular basis, or passionate about the topic, the learning gets dumped from their brains.

Dopamine connects the frontal lobe of the brain with the long-term memory in the back. Emotions and senses evoke memories because they result from dopamine release. Music inspires emotions. The pleasure of listening to music, eating chocolate, laughing, and feeling cuddled and loved increase the likelihood of making long-term memories. We connect the senses with the memories. So, if you really want your child to remember something, connect the learning with smells, tastes, music, emotions (hopefully laughter and not fear!), and love, and it will move into long-term memory. That is why cuddling up with children and reading to them lets them associate books and words with feelings of comfort and pleasure. And on the negative side, it is probably why I still remember the math teacher who embarrassed me so badly in front of my Grade 7 class. I remember nothing else from that year; how sad that that should be my take-away from an entire school year.

Although my children may not remember specific experiences, their brains developed because of them. Their brain cells made millions of pathways and connections, growing and developing their intelligence. I theorize that they probably developed many more pathways because of the increased interactional and experiential learning capacity of their unstructured days. School children spend roughly ten years in a classroom surrounded by books; unschooling children spend those same ten years outdoors, on field trips, traveling, doing chores, shopping, reading, and creating. It would be very interesting to see a comparison of their brains on MRI (Magnetic Resonance Imaging) scans.

As detailed above, emotional responses involve the thalamus, the amygdala, and the prefrontal cortex. There are six basic emotions that span all cultures: anger, joy, surprise, fear, distress, and disgust. The more that emotions are tied to learning, and the more the learning is embedded into stories, the longer we humans will retain the learning in our memories.

When a speaker tells an emotional story, the audience will remember it because he makes them share his emotions; if he tries to make the same point by reading from a bulleted list in a PowerPoint presentation, it will be completely lost. Stories always have an emotional hook—that is why people remember them. Storytelling was the way that people remembered and passed history through the generations long before it was recorded in books. We cannot dismiss the educational benefit or the teaching power of a heated family discussion on a social issue. School-age and teen children remember discussions far better than they remember facts from a book or information they read on a screen.

I say again: children need adults to provide the context and connections between facts and figures and emotions.

Creativity

The lack of prefrontal control in young children is helpful to them in their play and exploration. The prefrontal region inhibits irrelevant thoughts or actions; it is the self-control part of executive function, and self-control can limit our creativity by obstructing our "don't care what anyone else thinks" attitude. Being uninhibited allows children to play freely and explore without caution. They can be whimsical, creative, and flexible without having to plan or be logical. (Gopnik, 2004)

We know that the brain works best and creativity is heightened when the brain is at rest. That's why people get some of their best ideas while they are in the shower, or trying to fall asleep, or working out at the gym or going for a walk. Time away from distractions, whether background TV or phones or other people, helps to empty the mind so we can think, be inspired, or solve a problem. Downtime is essential for creativity. (Jeyanathan, 2014)

Stress

Stress affects the brain positively and negatively.

As discussed in Chapter 9, there are three kinds of stress: positive, tolerable and toxic. Every human being encounters stress, from infancy through old age. Positive stress is good for the brain. Tolerable stress is uncomfortable but essentially neutral, as it does not cause lasting damage. Toxic stress, however, is bad for the brain in that it causes an allostatic load, or wear-and-tear, caused by exposure to repeated or chronic stress, on the body and can damage childhood brain architecture.

Positive stress is induced by anticipating happy events like birthday parties, Christmas, weddings, vacations, and visiting relatives; or by the challenge of meeting a deadline, completing a project, or preparing for an interview. Positive stress motivates us to prepare; and successfully meeting the challenge is tremendously satisfying.

Tolerable stress comes from unpleasant experiences such as getting a speeding ticket, getting fired from a job, being bullied, divorce, or the death of a family member. This kind of stress is tolerable only if it is buffered by a support system of at least one caring, supportive person. Of course, healthy eating, exercise, sleep, and self-care help as well, but the one caring adult is the key factor. Tolerable stress subsides. It is not ongoing; it has a beginning and an end.

Toxic stress is continued, ongoing tolerable stress that has turned toxic because it is not buffered by a comforting, supportive human being. Babies left to cry for hours every night experience toxic stress, as they are not comforted. Colicky babies that are held and comforted while they scream experience tolerable stress rather than toxic, because they are physically supported by a loving, caring parent or caregiver.

Research does not yet give us insight on how much toxic stress will break us. It depends on the person. Some people can withstand immeasurable amounts of stress, as in a violent domestic situation; others will crumble under the same conditions. It is difficult to measure the emotional residue of toxic stress and the effects of the long-term release of stress hormones, and the resulting damage to a child's brain. There is, however, good research that documents the long-term effects of toxic stress from adverse childhood experiences, eventually increasing the risk of causing anxiety, depression, diabetes, addiction, heart attack, stroke, inflammation, and other afflictions.

Under either physical or psychological stress, the human body releases two stress hormones: adrenaline and cortisol. These hormones are good for us in the short term, as they enable us to focus, energize, and act—all of which are required for flight-or-fight reactions. We all need some of this positive stress to keep us in top shape. The release of these hormones can cause some side effects, however, such as dizziness, anxiety, and heart palpitations. But they have no long-term effect when released in small quantities.

Release of the same hormones over the long term can damage major organs and particularly, parts of the brain: the hippocampus, which houses emotions and long-term memory; and the prefrontal cortex, which controls executive function, or logic, planning, and working memory. Children living under toxic stress tend to have poor executive function skills. Their "air traffic control" of executive function cannot handle all the incoming sensory inputs and they often react spontaneously in socially unacceptable ways.

ACEs, or Adverse Childhood Experiences, trigger toxic stress that can accumulate and lead to a myriad of health problems and addictions later in life. About 60 percent of us do not experience any ACEs while growing up—or perhaps one, which should not lead to lasting problems. Another 20 percent experience one to two ACEs. The final 20 percent of the of the population, however, will experience three or more ACEs, and studies show that their risk of lifelong health, relationship, and employment problems increases with each additional ACE. (Palix, 2017) There are 10 types of ACEs, considered the 10 no-noes of parenting.

The 10 ACEs

1. Emotional abuse
2. Physical abuse
3. Sexual abuse
4. Witnessing abuse
5. Witnessing addictions
6. Witnessing untreated mental illness
7. Witnessing separation or divorce
8. Parental absence because of abandonment or imprisonment
9. Emotional non-attachment
10. Physical neglect

When children are soothed and comforted with hugs, touch, kind words, and listening, and given whatever help they need in the moment, their stress hormones are lowered and the damage is mitigated. By the same token, when they are on constant high alert because of stress factors, they cannot learn.

Children who are bullied are less likely to learn because of this. An isolated single incident of bullying can be a form of tolerable stress as long as the child is supported by a teacher, coach, parent, or another caring adult. But consistent, repeated bullying, especially without caring support, is a virulent form of toxic stress that can cause permanent damage to a child's brain architecture.

Technology and gaming addictions and the brain

Are addictions caused by nature or nurture? This question is asked by many parents who are concerned about their unschooled children playing video games all day. The answer is that addictions are influenced by both nature and nurture.

Addictions are the result of nature, or gene expression. Some people are predisposed to addictions. Their brains and genes have inborn fault lines that make an addiction *more likely* to develop under stressful conditions. In some people, those genes and fault lines are activated; in others, they are not. To date, research has not identified the triggers that would definitively activate such a gene.

Addictions are also affected by nurture, or environment. In a nurturing, warm, and structured childhood, most children will not experience ACEs or the resulting toxic stress that could activate the genes pre-disposed toward addiction. But if children experience three or more ACEs before the age of 18, it is more likely that addiction could be triggered.

So, children raised in a supportive, emotionally healthy, functioning, unschooling family, with caring, attentive adults will probably never fall into addiction, regardless of how many hours a day they play video games.

There are two main types of addictions, each with sub-categories.

Substance addictions are those in which substances are ingested or injected into the body to relieve stress. These substances can include alcohol, illegal drugs, non-prescription drugs, nicotine, caffeine, and food.

Process addictions are behaviors people engage in to relieve stress and release those feel-good dopamine chemicals in the brain. These behaviors include shopping, gambling, sex, pornography, exercise, and work. Although video gaming and internet addictions are not yet in the DSM-IV (Diagnostic Statistical Manual), because it is difficult to define diagnoses and treatment, they are very close in nature to a gambling addiction.

When vulnerable people suffer stress, they may turn to an addiction to relieve it. Parents can model healthy, non-destructive ways to relieve stress. Rather than grabbing a glass of wine or throwing a plant against the wall, they can practice deep breathing, get on a treadmill, drink water, have a good cry, or talk to a friend.

Because unschooling itself is relatively unstressful, it is highly unlikely that the unschooling environment will cause a video gaming addiction.

Children who are predisposed to addiction by their brain's fault lines and grow up in an environment filled with ACEs have a bigger risk of being consumed by addiction—any type of addiction—and it could be more than one.

The majority of children who spend a lot of time video gaming have a habit, not an addiction. Habits change when circumstances change. A child who plays video games all day at the age of 15 will leave that habit behind when he needs to: when it's time to enroll in postsecondary education, for example, or secure and hold a full-time job.

High school-age children in school coping with academic stress from parents and teachers and social stress from peers are vulnerable to substance and behavior addictions. They might turn to substances such as pot or alcohol, or obsessive behavior such as incessant talking or continuous mobile phone use. The substance or behavior releases the feel-good neurotransmitter chemicals of dopamine and oxytocin and feeds the pleasure centers of the brain. These unhealthy behaviors can consume a teenager, unless and until they are replaced with other, healthy, stress-reducing substances—such as drinking water, or behaviors—such as practicing yoga. Changing the way in which the brain processes thoughts and changing strategies for relieving stress helps reinforce new pathways in the brain.

Gender differences in the brain

As children, girls and boys have about the same amount of testosterone. After puberty, however, boys have more testosterone in the hypothalamus. They have more and longer neuron fibers and consequently are better at focus (ask any woman why men can't multitask!), spatial orientation, math, and physics. Generally, boys are more apt to play video games that demand these skills. Girls have more neuron cell bodies and are better at language, detail memory, and empathy. (Body Worlds, 2009)

Building healthy brain architecture

The following practices will help to build healthy brain architecture in children:

- Provide healthy nutrition, sleep, low stress, and adequate exercise to a mother during pregnancy and after birth.

- Provide children with a low stress environment; or, if the environment is unavoidably stressful, provide warm and nurturing comfort to ensure the stress is tolerable and not toxic.

- Provide human interaction including talking, singing, conversation, and reading. Responsive language in the form of conversation from an attentive adult provides children of all ages with much better education than screen learning.

- Prevent emotional abuse including criticism and bullying, sexual abuse, physical abuse including spanking and other corporal punishment, and physical, social and emotional neglect.

- As much as possible, prevent the child from witnessing emotional, sexual, and physical abuse, untreated mental illness, and parental conflict during separation or divorce.

- Provide a safe, rich, educational environment in which children can explore through all five senses.

At least one caring adult and a stimulating environment is all a child's brain needs to thrive throughout childhood. Unschooling provides that.

17

Babies, Toddlers, and Preschoolers Ages 0 – 5: Explore and Build the Bond

"Every child's an artist." — Pablo Picasso, Painter

Flash cards or cardboard boxes?

In mainstream parenting, some parents scramble to get their small children to baby swimming lessons, toddler storytime, daycare, and preschool. They buy flashcards, tablets, and DVDs to give them a head start before starting school. Some parents purchase elaborate, expensive "learning systems." Other parents sign up their tots for all-day preschool at age two or as soon as they are toilet trained, and definitely for Kindergarten (some full-day) at ages four and five, to give their children "an edge."

In contrast, unschooling parents plunk their kids down with unstructured playthings from cardboard boxes to Lego and let them play. They read to their children. They facilitate their interest in the world around them.

From birth to age six, all parents unconsciously unschool. They notice what their child is interested in and enroll her in activities accordingly or provide play objects to entertain the child and deepen her interest. Some may notice that their child loves to be at home, but buckle under peer pressure and sign her up for too many outside activities or for excessive stretches of time. Some parents might be homebodies themselves but notice that their child goes crazy cooped up at home when she really wants to participate in playgroups or activities. Either way, parents observe how their child learns and how much social activity is optimum for each unique personality.

Do children need people or stuff? There are two industries in which people will not spare spending: the funeral industry and the new parent industry. Who would not want to honor departed loved ones with the best? And what parent would deny spending money on products that could give their child an educational advantage? Educational products, enrichment activities, and schools and services can never, ever replace an attentive, nurturing parent, teacher, or caregiver. Ever. As my son says, "People are happier at airport arrivals than at the Tiffany diamonds store."

What we did

My children never went to preschool. We chose instead to take them to an unstructured "preschool" playgroup one morning per week. Volunteers set up play centers with play-dough, sand, water, painting, storytelling, puzzles, dress-up clothes, and crafts, and a snack area. The children played in whatever area they wanted to all morning, partaking in a single activity or sampling all of them. No constraints. The parents either stayed in the same room or visited together in the parents' coffee room down the hall. I loved the social aspect for me as well—I actually needed the mommy company more than my children needed their social time!

The rest of our days were spent at home. We did typical unschooling things: went to the park, the science center, the zoo, on nature walks, and on day trips, and played at home with many of the items listed under resources in Chapter 13. The children played with blocks, play-dough, stuffed animals, Lego, Playmobil, K'NEX, Meccano, dolls, and lots of toys. They made a lot of their own playthings.

There was no structure to the learning itself, although our weeks did have structure. On Tuesdays, we went to a Mom's Time-Out church group; on Wednesdays, to the unstructured playgroup; Mondays were for hanging around the house day while Mom did laundry—but Dad always took the kids to the library Monday evening; Thursdays were grocery-shopping days and Fridays were reserved for group field trips or play dates. Saturdays were for getting chores done and for parent date night; and Sunday was family activity day.

The oldest two children went from playgroup into the system for Kindergarten and Grade 1. We lasted three years in the school system before I pulled them out. I loved making new parent friends, as you do when your child enters the school system, but I had to admit that school did not work very well for our children. They hated anything too structured, even day camps or full-day field trips. I would have to make new mom friends in the homeschooling community!

Our home has always been heavy in literacy. Weekly trips to the library, about a thousand books on our shelves, and books in every corner of the home—including the bathroom—and car ensured that the children always had something to turn to if they got bored.

It is worth noting that we started homeschooling in the early nineties. Internet was still in the future. My husband and I loved to log into the BBS (Bulletin Board System), so we did have "interest groups" online, but the kids had access to only very elementary computer games for children. Our heaviest use of screen time was watching VHS videos, and we watched far more than today's recommended allotment of no more than two hours per day for young children. A typical Disney video is one-and-a-half hours, and the kids would want to watch the same video over and over again in a day. Some days, they watched the same video three times! I'm not proud of that, but on days when a parent is sick or tired, anything in the interest of sanity and a few peaceful moments!

The biggest difference between today and 20 years ago is that back then **screen time was only at home.** Videos were shown at home as a filler between other activities. So, children did not get used to being entertained or placated by screens in the car, at restaurants, in playgroups, at doctor's offices, at the beach, at theaters, at friends' homes, or while waiting in lines. Any idle time was filled with "language-rich parents-must-keep-kids-occupied" activities such as playing "I Spy," "tell a story," "rock, paper, scissors," "tell a joke or poem," "I'm going to Mars and I'm bringing..." games. Waiting rooms with children's books were favored and we read to the children while we waited. We used the same strategy as the kids got older, substituting dice and card games for books. I used to bring along a zippered lunch bag that we called the Busy Brain Kit. It was filled with paper, markers, dice, play-dough, pipe cleaners, bouncy balls, and a deck of cards to keep the kids busy on outings. Verbal language games built literacy and were great for getting the kids thinking and speaking.

We had a ton of toys around. The children filled their days with child-led play. By the time they grew into their teens, they had layers of experiential knowledge from which to draw background information.

What you can do

You do not have to enroll your child in preschool if you do not want to or cannot afford to. Even Kindergarten is voluntary in the province of Alberta. What young children need most during their formative years is a caring adult. Your time, interest, conversation, love, warmth, and undistracted attention, more than any activity or educational program, will develop your child's brain.

If the parent cannot fulfill this role full-time, many substitutes are available: preschools, daycares, dayhomes, educational programs, and summer camps. Companies vie for children's enrollment in their dance or art classes, sports, art, and other programs in the lucrative children's activity market. All of these can provide stimulation but not the love, nurturing, or caring that a loved one could. Activities are nice, but absolutely not necessary. Most parents can provide a stimulating, enriching environment at home without the need for outside services—and they add a big dollop of love and nurturing on top!

And parents can completely eliminate from the menu the baby learning DVDs, flashcards, toddler TV, and other commercial trappings of "education." A baby, toddler, or preschooler needs none of those things. They need a safe home full of play materials, unstructured time, and a willing, loving, responsive adult to supervise them—all the elements of an unschooling life.

If you have a precocious preschooler who is outgoing and extroverted, preschool might give you a bit of a break from being the only recipient of his social, in-your-face, exuberant personality. But don't think that you are giving him an edge. Most elementary school teachers cannot tell which kids come from preschool or which come from resource-enriched homes. It all evens out in the long run.

Cognitive development during this stage

> *Children under the age of five have very little executive function: self-control, planning, focus, or working memory*

Toddlers, ages 1 – 2

Children as toddlers:
- Recognize loved ones, logos, and pictures.

- Recognize themselves and others in photos and mirrors.

- Have a short attention span of just a few minutes.

- Master simple problem solving through trial and error: puzzles, shape-sorters.

- Point to and call common objects, body parts, animals, and people by name at two years of age.

- Understand simple directions but may be too engrossed in play to comply.

- Do not understand "tomorrow" and "yesterday"—they live in the moment.

- Do not understand "hurry."

- Do not understand ownership, money, or sharing.

- Have no conception of danger.

- Cannot identify which objects are breakable and which are not.

- Understand more words than they can speak.

- Understand that "no" is a powerful word, but do not understand the meaning of "not doing something."

- Cannot connect their actions with outcomes; they do not understand "consequences."

- Can make simple choices between two offerings.

- Can form two-word sentences: "more milk," "all gone," "me go."

- Can speak clearly enough for adults to understand most of their words.

- Confuse pronouns.

- At two, start making their earliest memories.

- Enjoy repetition of movies, books, rhymes, daily routines, habits.

Preschoolers, ages 3 – 5

Children as preschoolers:

- Know their name and age.

- May count and identify colors.

- Ask a lot of questions: they want to know how things work, including how babies are made; constantly ask "What's that?"

- Have an intense imagination; their thinking is magical.

- Need to play; they get lost in play and are not distracted from it.

- They practice animism: they may have imaginary friends or pets; stuffed animals are "real" to them.

- Manipulate objects to learn their characteristics.

- No longer put things in their mouths to explore.

- Can sing, rhyme, and tell jokes.

- Have a longer attention span of about 15 minutes.

- Can join in adult-guided problem solving.

- Can follow simple directions— "Put the toy in the box"—but may only comply 40 percent of the time.

- Can distinguish between edible and non-edible substances: candy, bread vs. dirt, shampoo.

- Have nightmares and night terrors.

- Begin gender role identification at five years of age.

- Understand 300 – 1000 words.

- Can form three-word sentences at age three, and complete stories at age five.

- Can speak clearly enough for adults to understand most of their speech.

- Can recite past experiences but not in the right order.

- Do not perceive lying as inappropriate, rather as wishful thinking; they tell tall tales.

- Have no time sense or ability to plan; they cannot understand adults' time schedules; they dawdle.

- Do not understand safety considerations or what causes death or injury; they are unaware of traffic dangers.

- At three and four years of age, cannot imagine the logical outcomes of certain actions on objects or people; they cannot foresee consequences.

- Begin to connect actions with consequences at five to six years.

- Cannot see others' points of view at three years but can at five years.

- Begin to develop executive function skills between three and six years of age.

Educational needs for this age

Children ages 0 – 5 need unstructured play, adult interaction, multi-sensory experiences, spontaneity, fun, physical movement, little to no screens, and child-centered activities that are supervised by an adult.

Technology for toddlers and preschoolers

Children don't *need* technology, but parents *love* it for the little mess and quiet surroundings it produces. That doesn't mean it is good for them! Young children do not require any screen time to develop their brains. The Canadian Pediatric Society recommends no screen time at all for toddlers under age two and a maximum of one hour per day under age five. (CPS, 2017)

Research has shown that the more the TV is on, even in the background, the more children lose language development. (Muscovitch, 2007) Children who have caregivers that talk to them learn about 300 more words by age two than those whose adults don't engage as much in the serve-and-return interaction. (Clyne, 2008)

Babies and toddlers hear words and form brain pathways on repetition. The more language is heard and repeated, the more pathways are formed. All young children need serve-and-return conversation with the loving adults that surround them.

The popular character Dora leaves a space for children to "talk" to her on a tablet, and then seems to answer back to the child, but it is stilted and not at all responsive in the way that a personalized adult response would be. Screens do not respond to a child's specific language or wording. Only humans can provide that individualized serve-and-return interaction. It's a conversation. Parents' and caregivers' heavy dependence on so-called interactive toys to keep children busy and occupied may stunt their language development.

In spite of the all the excellent research available on screens' effect on language development, parents want their babies, toddlers, and preschoolers exposed to technology as early as possible. They say that's where our society is right now and they want to give them a head start. Do children really need to learn technology so early? Will they be "behind"? My daughter was 17 when she got her first mobile phone and in no time, she caught up in texting speed. If 70-year-old people can master Facebook, e-readers and email, then any motivated person can learn anything.

How to build executive function in your child's brain without electronics

This is so easy—and yet so hard, when technology beckons! You can:

- Build focus and attention skills by reading or by telling stories. Give kids the time and the materials to color, paint, and build in response to the story.
- Use a timer to build impulse control skills. Play games like Simon Says or Bingo, in which they have to consciously restrict their actions.

- Encourage dramatic play with dress-up clothes and Barbies, Lego, or Playmobil. It helps to build working memory. Children have to remember the roles, voices and characteristics of their characters.

- Baking also helps build memory, as the child needs to remember which ingredients to use and in what quantities.

- To build planning ability, give children materials such as sheets, spare tables, and old sofa cushions to build obstacle courses. Have them plan a way to get across.

- Play games such as I Spy, I'm going on a picnic and I'm bringing..., and Hotter/ Colder to help develop logic and elimination skills.

Conversation promotes social and emotional development

Language is critical. American researcher Dr. Daniel Siegal says that when children have the language and words to express their feelings, they are much less likely to hit, throw, bite, melt down, and lash out. Toddlers express themselves in body language, or tantrums, because they don't have words. Preschoolers are better with both language and self-control and "use their words" with increasing competence. But they need to have many conversations with adults to improve on the verbalization of their feelings. (Siegal, 2012)

Emotional intelligence is needed even as children get older—indeed, throughout our lives. People are more often fired from their jobs not because of technical incompetence, but because they cannot get along with others in the workplace. Children need to recognize, name, and control their emotions, within themselves and with others. Parents can help build these skills by comforting their children, naming their feelings, and redirecting their expressions of anger in ways that won't hurt others or destroy things. Conversation helps to build self-control.

Play builds literacy in the "silent generation"

The more adults talk with their children, the larger their vocabulary will be. A child's vision and hearing are at an adult's capability in the first three years, so reading books appeals to their sight, and your speaking emotively appeals to their hearing and emotion. (Clyne, 2008) Reading also models a love and desire for books.

Allowing children to play is also critical for reading. "By age three, the brain naturally and biologically creates a scenario whereby a child can learn anything. That potential develops into competence through experience of different activities, which develops the existing synapses that form 'pathways' in the brain. If they don't have those experiences after about age 10, the brain prunes about 30,000 unused synapses a day. Parents worry that playing won't teach their children to read, when in fact, it happens most effectively in a properly developed play situation." If [children] can look at books and other printed materials, they will learn to read. (Clark, 2008)

Turn reading into fun! Have a regular reading time, usually just before bed, when the stresses of the day are put aside and you can snuggle up together. Try not to fall asleep! If your child wants you to read the same books over and over again, do it. They love repetition and it's good for them to hear the rhythm of words. Many families continue this ritual into the teen years.

Building numeracy

Count everything when shopping or driving. Skip-count on hopscotch playgrounds or trampolines. Make counting fun!

Preschool — is it necessary?

Depending on the child, preschool could be a nice enrichment, but it is certainly not necessary for beginning the pathway to university. From the Team of Thirty, eleven attended preschool and 19 did not.

The issue of preschool will probably come up by the time a child turns two. Should I, or shouldn't I? The peer pressure on moms to enroll their children in preschool is very strong, yet the attendance rate is only 50 percent, according to data from the Organization for Economic Co-operation and Development (OECD). That means that half of Canadian children do not attend preschool. They may go to a daycare, a dayhome, or stay at home. (OECD, 2013) Also, sometimes it's a matter of timing. Jenny's son Mark started preschool at age three but he clung to his mom; he hated the circle time and the structure. After discussing it with the teacher, Jenny pulled him out. She enrolled him again when he turned four, and he loved it!

Why do children need preschools? "The main purpose is to socialize the children to get them ready for their school years. To get them used to being away from their parents in an environment that is run by an early childhood educator who knows the developmentally appropriate practices to put in place with the children." (Cole, 2009) If you are not intending to educate your children in school, they don't need such "practice."

Homeschooling studies tell us that children do not need school or preschool to learn how to socialize. Right in their own homes, they learn the social conventions of taking turns, lining up, sitting quietly, and sharing if they have siblings; they participate in play-groups, library storytime sessions, and hobby or sports activities that provide opportunity for socialization.

Preschool is not necessary for intellectual development. The studies that show that preschool contributes significantly to a child's later success in school neglect to state that many of these studies are done on disadvantaged children. Children who lack a nurturing parent or an environment rich in books and toys will indeed benefit immensely from preschool.

Little is expected of children when they enter Grade 1, other than knowing how to write their names. The alphabet, colors, and numbers are all taught in Grade 1.

In fact, preschool may represent a disadvantage. Often, children who have logged several years in preschool and Kindergarten will be bored in Grade 1 because they already have this knowledge; they have already visited the zoo and the fire station, have already taken bike riding safety field trips in preschool and Kindergarten. One child exclaimed, "I've been to the fire station three times now,"—he'd gone with his summer day camp, his preschool, and his Kindergarten—and he refused to go again when he was in Grade 1.

As well, preschool is costly. At the average rate of $250 per month per child, a typical university course tuition at $600 for four months is actually cheaper than preschool!

A peer-focused environment can induce stress. More than five children per adult is considered peer-focused. Spending a significant amount of their time in a peer-oriented environment at such a young age deprives children of much of the warmth and nurturing of a loving parent that they need. In addition, groups of kids by nature are not nurturing. As Gordon Neufeld states in his book *Hold on to your Kids: Why Parents Need to Matter More Than Peers*, "As peer orientation increases, the teach ability of our students declines." [*sic*]

Another disadvantage of preschool is its rule-based environment. Too many rules and too much structure imposed on a child whose natural development of executive function is not yet in place can be harmful to that child's self-esteem. When a teacher continually admonishes an active child to sit down and be quiet when he really needs to move and socialize, it can set him up to think of himself as a poor learner.

The most important aspect of preschool is the break it gives to parents. Two hours twice or three times a week allows parents to run errands or concentrate on some work.

If you do choose preschool, be sure the one you choose is play-based and not academic-based. Some of the best preschools are the unstructured ones that do not mimic Kindergarten. If there is too much emphasis on rote learning of arithmetic and reading, the child will get bored if he can already do it or frustrated if he can't. Play should be the basis of all preschools—not worksheets. A preschool environment where children can move freely through play centers with many activities, and as little "sit-down" or "circle time" as possible, is best. Young children are developmentally designed to move; they do not have the self-control to sit or to focus their attention for any length of time.

Is preschool right for your child? Is your child ready? See if you can enroll temporarily instead of committing for a term or a year. Give it two or three weeks and see whether it's a good fit. If not, pull your child out and wait a few months or a year—or simply discard the idea.

Is your child potty-trained? Preschool is the most common reason for parents pushing potty-training on their child. Many are not developmentally ready for potty-training by age two or three when preschool starts, and most preschools will not accept children who are untrained. The whole potty-training process can erupt into a power struggle between parent and child and ultimately creates a setback.

Guide yourself by the maturity of your child, not his age, when you assess whether preschool is suitable for him. How social is your child? Does he separate easily from his parents? Maturity can't be taught nor hurried. Preschool is mostly about emotional and social development. It cannot be forced upon a child and may in fact set him back in terms of social growth. Let the child lead.

Playgroups instead of preschool

If your child is not ready for preschool or doesn't want to go, what can you do instead? Arrange a lot of play dates with other children. Join playgroups, parent time-out groups, pre-homeschooling groups, and "Mommy (or Daddy) and Me" classes. Many children love the social aspect of getting together with other children but need the security of having a parent close by. That's okay. It won't always be that way. They will eventually learn to separate when their need for security is replaced by self-confidence. And playgroups are way cheaper than preschool!

Kindergarten

In most provinces, Kindergarten, like preschool, is still voluntary. Grade 1 is mandatory. What do children do in Kindergarten? They have circle time with the teacher for about 15 minutes to share news, talk about the weather, the day, the date, and any special occasion related to the day. Sitting and listening develops the executive function skill of impulse control. But much of this time is taken up by the teacher shushing the children and reminding them to sit, take turns, be quiet, and listen—which is useless if the child is not developmentally ready.

Given that Kindergarten requires the teacher to exercise this much reinforcement of impulse control, it seems to me that children still may not be ready because they are simply too young. If children were to start school at age eight, their brains would have developed these skills naturally and school would not feel like such a corrective environment.

Some countries are pushing for all-day Kindergarten. Certainly, this would provide parents with relief from daycare costs, but is it really good for the children? Some studies clearly show that children do not benefit from Kindergarten, unless they come from disadvantaged homes. (Eisen, 2010) The Government of Quebec brought in $7-a-day government-run daycare plan to allow parents to return to paid work full-time and give children the opportunity to benefit from an equal, institutionalized "learning environment." Proponents of non-home learning espoused that a formal learning environment would enhance children's academic edge and produce better-educated children. After several years, studies emerged that refuted this. Instead of proving children to be further ahead academically than home-educated peers, the system only demonstrated more negative socializing effects such as aggressiveness and bullying. (Maclean's, 2014)

If we look at countries like Finland, whose children do not even start school until age seven or eight but consistently appear at the top of the PISA results, we note that children do not need full-day Kindergarten. What a child needs most in those early years is physical toys—not a tablet—that stimulate all five senses, a parent that reads to her, a house full of books from the library, perhaps a grandparent willing to take her to parks, the zoo, and the science center, and caring adults that will patiently answer her thousands of questions.

Parents and adult caregivers who provide loving attention are the best "curriculum" for the early years. Preschool and Kindergarten, as with school, are not necessary.

Instead of taxpayer funding for government-provided Kindergarten, which has no measured outcomes, funding would be better applied to two initiatives: stay-at-home parent tax deductions for those who choose it, and caregiver education on the positive effects of reading and conversing with children.

18

Elementary Ages 6 – 11: Play, Read, and Learn Together

"The earlier you hand over a child's education to her, the sooner she takes it on."

Soccer practice or family dinners?

In mainstream parenting, three words describe the lifestyle you have with a school-age child: schedule, school, and stress. Every day, some parents scramble to get their kids to school and back, and then to after-school art, drama, sports, music, and enrichment activities. They fret over homework not getting done and they sign up the child for summer school to improve their previous year's grades or prepare the child for the next year's curriculum. Some parents sign their kids up for extra school on Saturdays and Sundays because "more school is a better thing." At the very least, they hire a tutor to help with learning gaps. They may even pay big bucks for private school. They battle daily to motivate their child. They wonder why little Justin is already getting disengaged in Grade 6 and aligning more and more with his peers, who also hate school.

Unschooling parents introduce their children to anything under the sun—from cardboard boxes to Lego—and let them at it. They strew and then get out of the way. They provide structured classes, sports, art, music, and enrichment activities only if their child chooses them after being introduced to a variety of topics. They don't stress over homework, tutors, activities' demands on their time, fundraising duties; they also don't stress over report cards—there are none. Their children's love of learning flourishes because they are not coerced into learning anything they don't want to. They play, they learn, and they acquire an education.

What we did

In Alberta, children must be registered in an educational program by September 1 of year they turn six. Grades 1 to 6 normally include children aged 6 through 11 and is called elementary school; Grades 7 to 9, or ages 12 - 14, is junior high school. High school, or secondary school, consists of Grades 10 to 12, or ages 15 - 18. Postsecondary school includes colleges, universities, and trade, art, and technical schools.

Because we were not yet convinced that home education was the best thing ever, we sent our oldest two children to Kindergarten and Grade 1 in a French immersion school. When the school expressed concern about one son not reading in Grade 1, we switched them to an English school for the next grade. Then the English school closed and we finally decided to try homeschooling to better meet their needs. Our third child went to Kindergarten for the first year that the boys homeschooled, then decided to home-school for Grade 1 because she could see that they were at home and having fun! The two younger children never attended any school during their elementary years, choosing to stay home and play. The kids had play dates, sleepovers, went on field trips, traveled, volunteered, and had some structured lessons and homeschooling classes, but most of the time, they stayed home and created their own learning from play and fun.

What you can do

If you choose school, don't worry about homework getting done, tutoring, summer school, full-day Kindergarten, or too many after-school activities. During these years, kids need to enjoy learning rather than dread it; they need to develop their passions. Put your efforts into enjoying the relationship with your children. Let them play and explore.

If you choose to homeschool, don't engage in power struggles over "doing the work" because you could turn your child off of learning and he could develop a complex about math, science, or English, and develop low self-esteem if he perceives himself as a poor learner.

Simply put, in either case, this is not the time to stress over education.

Cognitive development during this stage

In general, girls are more developmentally ready for "school" than boys. School demands sitting still, paying attention, and cooperation, skills that girls come by faster. Boys thrive on competition, roughhousing, and building—the very skills that some schools have banned because of self-esteem and liability issues. New York City's Aviation High School has a mostly male student population; students spend half the day studying core subjects and the other half working on hands-on subjects, learning about aircraft engines and aviation hydraulics. They wear workwear and practice on real airplanes. The graduation rate is very high at this school of mostly minority and low-income boys because they are up and moving around, using all their five senses to learn, and studying interesting material. (Wente, 2013)

Young children, ages 6 – 9

- Are copycats—they love to imitate others.

- Are logical—they understand that actions have positive or negative outcomes.

- Comprehend logical and natural consequences.

- Understand that "no" means "don't do."

- Are questioning: they ask why and what if?

- Experiment by trying on behaviors from outside the family.

- Are rule-focused; they love rules and making sure everyone abides by them.

- Are negotiators; they love to make deals.

- Are Concrete Learners; they understand what they have personally experienced.

- Are black-and-white thinkers; they do not consider gray areas.

- Can cooperate on group projects.

- Can recognize ads from the media; can separate reality from fantasy.

- Understand money as a symbol for exchange and can handle an allowance.

- Are not yet good enough problem solvers to stay home alone.

- Love new experiences and places, field trips, travel.

- Understand jokes; love potty humor.

- Start reading and writing.

- Are creative in arts and crafts.

- Begin to understand time and the relationships of time.

- Can understand the basic mechanics of sexual intercourse and reproduction.

- Are rapidly increasing their executive function skills.

Tweens, ages 10 – 12

- Are outgrowing childhood toys.

- Can use a debit card to make their own purchases.

- Need reminders.

- Can cross a street alone and judge traffic timing.

- Can stay home alone briefly if they are good problem solvers.

- Remember where they left items.

- Are beginning to resist being controlled by others.

- Are still black-and-white thinkers.

- Have an increasing sense of right and wrong; their moral development is progressing.

- Have an attention span of one to two hours.

- Know the difference between real and imaginary in both digital and physical worlds.

Educational needs for this age

In this age group, children need experiences beyond the classroom. They need to learn reading, writing, and numeracy not as isolated subjects, but in terms relevant to their daily life and their own problems. They need to explore the real world, facilitated by a mentor, and have conversations about learning, ideas, insights, reflections, and observations. (Armstrong, 2006)

Learning without bribery and punishment

It's rare to find a democratic philosophy in education. Kids are forced to learn by the authoritarian methods of bribery and punishment. Yet motivation to learn is intrinsic.

Elementary schools rely heavily on the use of bribery and rewards to coax kids into learning. Bribery can come in the form of pizza coupons for the most prolific reader, prizes for the best fundraiser, and a "Best Kid of the Day" award for the most obedient child. Then there are the marks—the most common form of bribery and punishment. Bonus marks are given to children for handing work in early, or to encourage further learning. "I know I entered school with a lot of talent and a real zest for learning and when I got out 12 years later, I couldn't wait to get out of that classroom and away from books and 'learning.' Now I realize that I hated being forced to learn." (Lynnette P, 1999)

The system also uses punishments such as detentions, where kids are sent to a classroom to sit, or to write sentences on paper; extra homework; bad grades; time-out boxes; chores such as washing the blackboard; and removal of privileges such as recess, dances, and lunch hour or hall passes. Many schools in the US still use the strap to inflict physical punishment, although this practice is banned in Canada.

Parents are motivated by rewards too, and sometimes cannot imagine a world in which kids can be motivated without imposing bribery or punishment. One school abolished their awards night where they traditionally handed out awards to children who earned the highest marks, because the same kids were always getting the same awards. The school implemented a more broad-based model of acknowledgement in which effort and achievement in both academic and non-academic areas would be recognized. Parental reaction was highly negative—they asked how kids would be motivated if awards and trophies to the "high achievers" were eliminated? They actually circulated petitions against the innovative changes.

Some of us homeschoolers are not much better! I've known parents who keep their children away from fun outings, play dates, sleepovers, activities, and especially, computer and video game time, because the children didn't do their seatwork at home. I know, because I was one of them! The first year that I did school-replicated-at-home homeschooling, I would threaten and bribe all the time. I used to tell the kids that I would send them back to school. I remember a friend telling me:

Homeschool rule #1: We stop if somebody cries.

Homeschool rule #2: We never even try it again if Mommy is the one crying! (Melody W, 2001)

There is plenty of research showing that bribery has the opposite of its desired effect: it unmotivates children. They work only for the reward and once it is achieved, their performance drops off. The act of learning becomes something the child does for somebody else and not for himself. (Kohn, 2003) Research also shows that punishment often works against motivation. (Gordon, 2000) Never being recognized for effort often drives kids to drop out of school.

Both bribery and punishment foster cheating, because the reward for accomplishment or the avoidance of punishment is achieved at the expense of integrity. Seventy-three percent of university kids said that they cheated at least once, on written work, at some point in their time at school. (CBC, 2016) Are these the ethics we reward as a society? Do we want cheaters working as our professionals?

As a family life educator, I have been teaching parents about the negative effects of bribery and punishments throughout my career. You can read more about this in my two books, *Discipline Without Distress* and *Parenting With Patience*. Following are things you should know about using bribery or punishments in the educational setting:

The case against using bribery to get kids to learn

Some children, regardless of their efforts, will never win prizes for work that is evaluated on natural ability—there are children who could easily win a prize with almost no effort at all. When the end product is rewarded with no recognition of effort, children mistakenly judge themselves harshly and feel bad.

- Bribes can lose their value; the reward may be too small or too distant.

- Unacceptable behavior can inadvertently be rewarded; for example, class clowns get peer and teacher attention instead of hard workers.

- Bribes must be consistent to work and we know that humans are rarely impeccably consistent; a missed or forgotten prize or praise feels like punishment.

- Acceptable behavior should be expected and not rewarded. Children may start working only for the prize, but the prize may lose its attractiveness over time.

- Creativity declines when more emphasis is placed on the prize than on the effort.

- Bribes foster competition and cheating.

- Those who never attain the rewards can begin to alienate the habitual "winners."

- Giving prizes for reading may prompt children to ask, "If this book is so good, why did they have to bribe me to read it?" We want them to think, "Reading is the basis for all other learning, so I need to learn to read." Learning is a personal accomplishment, which is rewarding in itself. Appreciation for learning is intrinsic; it cannot be forced.

- Effort does not always equal achievement. Bribes change motivation from internal to external by focusing on an end result and ignoring process. Inner motivation to read and write, for example, is its own reward. External motivators are seldom effective - true self-esteem comes from one's achievement and is not influenced by others' perception.

- Prizes such as junk food are inherently bad for children; they can contribute to risk factors for emotional eating.

- Marks are often defended as necessary to provide a measuring stick for achievement. It doesn't always follow. Would you rather have brain surgery performed by the doctor who scored 95 percent or the one who scored 45 percent? I would pick the one who scored 45 percent because he probably didn't pass the first time and had to learn the same material twice, absorbing and internalizing it better than his colleague.

- The child may feel manipulated; the parent may feel used.

- An alternative to outright bribery might be for children to set their own rewards. For this to work, the goal must be challenging but attainable. This rewards each according to his own ability and motivation.

The case against using punishment to get kids to learn

- Punishment is not a deterrent; it can be inconsistent, delayed, or too mild. Repeated exposure to punishments lessens its impact.

- Severe punishment is abusive; the danger is that children actually adapt to increasingly intense punishments.

- There is no evidence-based research showing punishment as a successful tool; there are no studies indicating that punishment helps to connect, preserve, enhance, or nurture loving parent-child bonds or life-long learning.

- Punishment, or the threat of punishment, creates a power struggle between parent and child; sometimes children resent this to the extent that that they purposely repeat the misbehavior as a means of exerting their own power or to getting back at the parent—the power struggle escalates.

- It is exhausting; parents run out of energy to enforce a punishment; if punishment is used, it must always be carried out.

- Parents must stay calm when issuing a punishment, or children will associate it as an acceptable way of resolving anger issues.

- Punishment can foster aggression, anger, fear, humiliation, and retaliation—all of which interfere with the learning process.

- A child who obeys out of fear will only obey as long as that fear is present; it generally dissipates.

- Punishment can discourage a child to the point of giving up.

- Adults eventually run out of workable punishments; when children—especially early teens—realize that, the adults are effectively disarmed.

- Punishment fosters fear and anger that interferes with the trust process in the parent-child relationship; the punished distance themselves from the punisher both physically and emotionally. There is no room for punishment in a loving relationship.

- Children receive negative attention from the punisher but sympathy attention from onlookers, often serving to intensify or justify the bad behavior.

- Punishment teaches that those with strength and power can control those who are weaker or disadvantaged, or who are perceived as such.

- Not all children respond to punishment, especially strong-willed children.

- Punishment focuses on what will happen to the children, rather than showing them how their behavior affects other people.

- Punishment operates on the misguided theory that we must hurt children when they behave inappropriately in order to teach them responsibility.

- Punishment kills the very thing we are trying to teach—positive motivation.

- Punishment tends to benefit the punisher by providing a release of anger and frustration; there is rarely a satisfactory corresponding benefit to the child.

- Self-punishment is often even more severe, if children are encouraged to judge themselves harshly; this truly will damage their self-esteem.

Given all these drawbacks to using reward and punishment as incentives, and the damaging effect on the learning process, why do schools still resort to them? Because they are the tools of control. Schools have no other way of coercing kids to learn their program. Going up a few levels, even governments punish schools by withholding funding or accreditation, or threatening audits when schools complain about policies.

The biggest benefit of self-directed education is that there is absolutely no need to motivate the learner. Neither bribery nor punishment is useful in the learning process. Learning occurs naturally, entirely for its own sake.

If you have offered something educational to your child and he is resisting, there could be several reasons for it: Perhaps he is not physically, cognitively, emotionally, or socially ready for the challenge. So, let it go. It may be that the opportunity was not presented in the child's learning style. Find one that is. He may still be digesting other learning and is not ready for a new project, or he has been too busy and needs some downtime. Whatever the case, let go of your agenda and see where he wants to go. Opportunities present themselves constantly.

Motivation comes from belonging, choice, and autonomy

How do you motivate children without reward or punishment? Many parents struggle with getting children to help out around the house since they are at home so much. It's simple; just appeal to their five basic human desires:

1. **Affiliation**: Children are part of a larger entity: a family. "Membership" implies both rights and responsibilities. Taking part in both gives a child self-worth and a sense of contribution.

2. **Appreciation**: Everyone likes someone to notice what they do. Giving positive feedback is very encouraging, but it should always be a reflection of appreciation and not praise.

3. **Fulfilling contribution**: Work must be meaningful. Children need to see that their work really does make a difference and is not just busy work to "keep them occupied and out of someone's hair." Like adults, kids need to feel needed.

4. **Status and respect**: Children must feel that the work they do is recognized as valuable and is a respected contribution to a whole.

5. **Autonomy and choice**: Children need to have control over their learning and their activities. The more individualized control a child has, the better he will feel about himself, his abilities, and his work.

Your relationship with your child and her innate love of learning are so much more important than mastering long division or getting the house vacuumed.

The more parents back off, the more children will take up. The summer my son Neil chose not to go to university was a difficult one for us in terms of letting go of our own agenda. He had the brains and the Grade 12 course marks, but not the desire to enter postsecondary. We supported his decision. He was the first of our children who was eligible to go to university, and he chose not to. Until July. Then he decided that he did want to go! He brought out a big map, closed his eyes, and blindly put his finger on the map. It landed on Newfoundland, and that is where he applied for September entrance. It took him seven years to finish that degree, at more than one institution. Along the way, he struggled with health issues and each time the medical professional asked him, "Are you sure you like school? Do you want to quit?" He admitted his struggles, and many obstacles were thrown in his path—like courses that didn't transfer and he had to take over again—but he wanted to continue. The motivation came from him.

If an unschooler wants to go to postsecondary, he will do it. You cannot stop him. A question on an online group forum captures the essence of a parent's worries: "My biggest worry about unschooling, and I'm being completely honest here, is that even if my daughter really wants to go into nursing and doesn't have the discipline to finish the course in physics that she needs as a prerequisite, she will forgo the nursing idea. Whereas, if she is forced to take physics in high school then she would have more doors open for her. I've talked to so many adults that were thankful their parents pushed them in music. How do you instill that discipline to finish something without forcing them to do it?" Another mom replied, "If your daughter doesn't have the discipline to finish the course in physics, I would wonder if she has the discipline to handle nursing school. If she feels a vocation to become a nurse, that isn't something that will go away on a whim. And there are just as many adults who are so glad they are old enough and can finally say 'No' to music lessons."

Discipline imposed from the outside will not help a child develop self-discipline; it will only impose upon him someone else's idea of discipline. There is nothing wrong with a young person going out to work for a while and making life-altering decisions later, when they are certain of the path they wish to pursue.

Mathew finished his high school diploma with no Math or Science beyond Grade 11. He decided to pursue a career in STEM and had to pick up two math, two chemistry, and two biology courses of high school level before applying to university. At age 19, he had finished all six courses in adult education within a year and a half, self-motivated to work hard and get good marks. At age 21, he entered university to study his chosen field.

A friend's son dropped out of high school to start a mechanics apprenticeship at a local garage and got his mechanics ticket; later he decided to become a pilot and entered college. He now flies for a corporate airline. He never did complete his high school diploma.

All children are responsible for their own education, especially as they reach the teen years. "If they choose to go to school, there is nothing you could do to prevent them from doing so. If they prefer not to, it's their choice too. They can't blame you for messing up their life if what you have provided is support for their decisions. Education is not your job. It is theirs." Moreover, education is never finished. If they decide at age 18 that they really want a traditional school education, they still have three funded years to get it. After age 20, they would have to pay, but it is still attainable. The years they spend as an unschooler are never wasted. It is simply a different, valuable experience. (Louise A, 2000)

Non-coercive parenting and education produce cooperative kids

Children innately want be successful adults and live as competent, contributing citizens. They are raised in that environment and want to emulate it. They are wired to learn from the adults around them. (Liedloff, 1940) Watch a child try to make a bed like Mommy does or bake a cake like Daddy. Watch young children want to play soccer because their older siblings do. Even kids who smoke or drink do so because it makes them feel more grown up.

We might want to raise kids who:

- Share their thoughts, feelings, problems, and worries with us in a real, meaningful conversation, without attitude or sarcasm.

- Do chores and pitch in on family projects without being asked.

- Enjoy family activities and spend time with parents and siblings.

- Are responsible and accountable to their studies, relationships, and jobs.

- Solve their problems through discussion rather than avoiding them by turning to drinking, sex, gambling, or drugs.

- Care about our feelings, needs, and worries, and modify their behavior in response if necessary.

- Become interdependent adults who enjoy being with people but can live independently.

- Make a contribution, participate in society, vote, volunteer and do service work, and leave the world a better place—because they can.

When kids want to take a course or sign up for an activity, it is a good idea to outline the course expectations with them so they know what they are getting into. When my son Mathew signed up for a group homeschool co-op at age 13, there were parameters he was expected to follow. I tried to make him understand them as much as possible before we plunked the money down. He really, really wanted to do this, so the motivation was internal and he fit himself beautifully into all the parameters. He took care of all the logistics. He did all the homework and assignments without being prompted. He even begged me to put aside some time to help him with essay writing, as he had never written one before. He packed his own lunches and snacks and got his clothes ready. He developed an organization system for keeping track of due dates. He said, "Hello," and "Goodbye," to his teachers every day. In their words, "He treats us like human beings, instead of... well... teachers!"

It's very hard to let go of our children's education. But we must. The sooner we let go, the sooner they will claim it for themselves.

Things kids do without being asked

Some parents complain, "Kids just won't listen to me. I have to get them to do things by offering a reward or threatening them with punishment." Earlier in this chapter, we discussed the futility of these strategies.

I respond to such comments by saying that our culture has taught parents that there is no other alternative. But when a parent has a close, mutually respectful relationship with a child, the child will want to do things to please the parent. Children under age six are egocentric but become more others-oriented as they grow. By the school-age years, most children have enough self-control to put their own needs aside and think of others. They are influenced by their love and caring for the parent and want to help and contribute. Following are some examples from our own family life.

At age five, Ryan and Anna could help bring in groceries and get the mail. At age seven, Anna could empty the dishwasher and take out the garbage. At nine, Sophie could sew on her guide badges, read and write stories, bake, wrap gifts, decorate the house, and play with siblings. Eleven-year-old Neil could water trees, make breakfast in bed for Mom, weed and tend his garden, clean his room, and play with siblings. Ryan, at 11, would bring in groceries, answer the phone, vacuum the house, recycle and take out the garbage, and feed his pets. At age 12, Mathew would make coffee, shovel the walk, look after his siblings' pets, clean up the playroom, and make cards for family and friends' birthdays. When Mathew was 18, Neil 17, and Sophie 15, they assumed all pet care, cleaned up the main areas of the house, did yard work, did their own laundry and bedding changes, made meals, shopped and put away groceries, answered the phone and took messages, set their own alarms to get up for classes and jobs, packed and unpacked for trips, helped out with home repairs and renovations, kept track of their own deadlines, did their own banking and taxes, and babysat siblings. Basically, by age 13, kids can do everything an adult can do.

Attachment to parents is still important

Continued attachment is possible when you raise your child outside of a peer group. I often hear teens in school complain that all their friends talk about is how drunk they got, how fat they are, how badly their girlfriends or boyfriends treat them, how wronged they feel by their parents' treatment of them, and how they cut themselves or go on extreme diets just to "feel."

Dr. Stanley Greenspan, Clinical Professor of Psychiatry and Pediatrics at George Washington University Medical School and one of the world's most influential authorities on development, says, "Our society doesn't tell parents that the most important gift they can give their children is not a good education, elaborate educational toys, or summer camps, but time—regular, substantial chunks of it—spent together doing things that are emotionally and developmentally meaningful for the child." In his book, co-authored by T. Berry Brazelton, Clinical Professor of Pediatrics Emeritus at Harvard Medical School, called *The Irreducible Needs of Children*, they advocate for parents to learn their important roles in protecting the attachment process, which is critical for the child's future psychological, intellectual, and moral well-being. Research in the field of neurobiology, the study of the mechanisms by which human relationships shape brain structure and function, confirms through brain imaging (MRI) and genetic code mapping what attachment theorists such as John Bowlby have been seeing for the past 50 years. A child's brain is shaped by relationships. And this shaping does not end when the child turns five or six and heads off to school. Primary attachments will always be important within the family, even in the teen years. (Brazelton, 2009)

Children who are held, cuddled, listened to, played with, taught, read to, fed, and helped through their difficulties build a healthy attachment to the parent who consistently provides for their needs. That bond grows a child's self-esteem, independence, and academic, social, and emotional intelligence.

Human contact cannot be replaced by technology. In their teens, my kids didn't really care about or need mobile phones. Their attachment was mostly with family, not with peers or electronic devices. True friendships are chosen, not melded by the simple coincidence of sharing a classroom.

That is not to say that non-homeschooling parents cannot remain attached to their children through the school years. But it is more difficult; they constantly battle against the impact of peer relationships. Through the years, my five children have had many friends that were in school and whose parents I got to know. Parents must make a conscious effort to maintain the attachment with their kids. Some ways of doing this are protecting family-centered time such as meals, vacations, rituals, and celebrations and not letting homework, soccer practice, or friends supersede or dilute family time; going on one-on-one "dates" with each child; and using problem solving instead of punishment to resolve conflicts. The best way to remain attached is to listen to children and be willing to compromise. Maintaining a close attachment with children is easier when they are not peer-focused, but it is not impossible, even when they go to school.

Homework eats into quality family time

"Every parent homeschools. It's called Homework."

According to education futurist Alfie Kohn, there is no study that affirms that homework helps kids succeed in elementary and junior high. There is a modest correlation, not causal, showing that homework does improve test and quiz scores in high school. It is unclear whether homework helps to make good students or whether good students like doing homework and consequently do better. So why do schools still assign homework? Here are some of the reasons:

1. **Time crunch**: Teachers have too many curriculum outcomes to teach, so homework is assigned in order to cover what they cannot address in class. Responsibility for covering these themes moves from the school and the teacher to the home and the parent, and a parent may not be equipped to help the child or may simply disagree with the idea of homework. This causes undue stress. If there really is not enough time to cover all the outcomes during school hours, the obvious solution is to modify the expected outcomes.

2. **Instill discipline and a work ethic:** School is not the only place to learn good habits. Volunteer work, family chores, church activities, computer game guilds, and part-time jobs all teach discipline and a good work ethic. Parents indeed must scaffold good work habits in their children for success in postsecondary education and the working world, but why start so early? Teen children have the executive function to impose self-discipline. It will happen naturally.

3. **More academics are better for all students:** Many parents from various cultures believe that education is better than free play and that children should spend their free time "wisely"—that is, studying and not having idle downtime. Vera Goodman, author of *Simply Too Much Homework,* says that schools could assign homework "for further learning" that would not be marked but would satisfy parents who want their children to always be working; in turn, this would not penalize the parents who want no part of homework for their children. (Goodman, 2007) It may even help parents of students who are struggling, but more worksheets being shoved at a student rarely help them "get" a concept. Rather, it is likely that the student needs a different learning technique. For example, a student who cannot understand division of fractions on a worksheet may benefit from the exercise of dividing a recipe in thirds while baking—that type of experiential learning could be far more productive. On the other hand, students who catch on to a concept quickly should not need to waste time reinforcing knowledge.

4. **Kids might get bored:** We know that kids need downtime, but that may create work for us. Society, parents, and school administrators, love homework because it relieves them of finding things for the kids to do—useful things, not "wasting time with video games." They could spend time outdoors or with friends and family, participate in sports, music, or the arts, or yes—even play video games! Alfie Kohn, author of *The Homework Myth,* says, "It's arrogant of the school to promote academic development over social, moral, physical, emotional, and (artistic) development." (Kohn, 2009) Parents need to protect their children's time for free play. When do children have time to discover their true passions if they have homework, jobs, and extracurricular activities every night? Perhaps that is why so many kids enter university without real direction.

5. **Parents feel involved:** In my parenting classes, I've discovered there is a big difference between parents being involved in their child's education and taking on the responsibility for it. Most parents do the latter, adding to their stress load. Being "involved" means being informed of what the child is doing in school and then supplementing it. For example, if your child is studying wetlands at school—and you know about this, because you read the newsletter coming home—you could take your child to the local wetlands on a fun picnic and frog hunt the following Sunday. You enjoy each other and reinforce learning in the process of play. Being "responsible" means that your child has a report due on wetlands and you spend Sunday nagging him to write it; when he doesn't, you assume the responsibility and do it for him. In the latter case, homework clearly does not have the intended result.

6. **Practice makes perfect:** Just like when they are learning to play a musical instrument, children must practice to perfect a skill. But schools should build practice

time into instruction time. In adult education, we realize that adults never do homework. Their lives are already too full and too busy. So, we never assign it. What doesn't get done in class doesn't get done.

Work-life balance must be learned early. We need to say "No" to encroachments on our time. If schools do not want parents telling them how to run their classes, schools must not dictate to parents how to spend family time in the home.

Our family homework policy letter

My daughter chose to try out school in Grade 10. She had to spend six hours of her day in school. She wanted time to write in her off-school hours, to learn character and plot development on her own, and to pursue her interest in learning Latin. I agreed to support her decision and send the following letter, providing she committed to working diligently during class time.

Fall 20_____

Dear Teacher:

Thank you for teaching our child this year. As a family, we strive to live a balanced life that includes a variety of activities. Those activities include volunteering in the community, family social time, rituals and celebrations, part-time jobs, music and art lessons, sports, fellowship clubs, church, and much-needed downtime. We value those activities as much as we do academic learning in school.

In order to make time for these activities, we need to establish boundaries that will provide a fair division between school instructional time and homework that encroaches upon family time. Therefore, our family homework policy is as follows:

_____ [Your Family Name Here] _____ Family Homework Policy:

The school assignments that are not given adequate instructional class time to complete during school hours will not be completed at home. We do not expect grades on uncompleted homework assignments.

We expect our children to make their best efforts and concentrate fully during the instructional class time mandated by the government and provided by the school, in order for them to complete the required credits and attain acceptable marks. They may also use any of their school spares to complete school work between the hours of 9 a.m. and 3:30 p.m. We expect the school to provide adequate time and instruction in class for the student to complete the government outcome requirements of the entire course.

We do not expect our children to be socially penalized within the classroom for our implementation of the Family Homework Policy, nor academically penalized in terms of marks for work that cannot be completed within the allotted school time. The current available research supports our belief that supplemental homework is not required for adequate mastery of the subject matter. We appreciate that you respect our decision on how to spend our time at home as much as we respect your decisions regarding your time and curriculum management at school.

Thank you for your cooperation in this matter.

Sincerely, Your Name

The first round of parent-teacher interviews was held in October. When her teachers reported marks of 90% for the in-class assignments she submitted and 0% for the homework assignments she did not turn in, we faced a dilemma. The teachers' reactions varied. The newly minted, fresh-out-of-university teacher could not believe that a parent would support a no-homework rule. The more seasoned teachers took it in their stride and agreed to make adjustments. Clearly, if my daughter was getting marks in the 90s, she knew the topic and homework would be superfluous. However, in spite of lip service to personalized learning for every student, the administration was reluctant to grant my daughter any leeway and would not remove the zeros because "then we would have to do it for everybody"—this being the public school system's response to any personal request. We decided to pull her out of school to take some courses online from home so that she could finish high school in two hours per day and have the rest of the day to write and pursue other interests. We were tired of battling the bureaucracy. At least the homework letter provided a point of conversation at the parent-teacher interview regarding home and school boundaries.

What if they play video games all day?

Some of the best learning tools for both adults and children are group games, board games, and video and computer games. I will outline our family's bias right away—although I'm not one, I live with a husband and five kids who are all avid gamers!

Schools frequently use video games as a teaching tool, but at home, many parents still use video games as a reward to the child once homework or seatwork is done. "Gaming is being used more and more in all levels of education, all the way from primary to postsecondary. Then, in the academic world at the university, we use our game collection to support teaching, learning and research. It spans the whole spectrum. I think we have somewhere around 2000 game titles..." says Dylan Tetrault, manager of the University of Calgary's digital commons with the university's libraries and cultural resources. (Nelson, 2015)

In some areas, such as South Korea, Europe, and the US, competitive video gaming called e-sports raises the skills, education, and engagement that video games demand and gives it a public forum, much like the Olympics does for sports. In Los Angeles in 2013, Riot Games hosted an online arena for a League of Legends Tournament, in which some 7,000 fans watched their favorite teams battle it out for $10 million in prize money. Similar Olympic-type competitions such as the World Cyber Games and Major League Gaming have been around for 15 years. Due to crowdfunding, Dota 2 had almost $25 million in prize money for their tournament in 2017. (Reddit, 2017) Video games are a national pastime in many countries, much like hockey is in Canada and basketball in the US. Unfortunately, there are very few women competing individually or as a team—another reason to get girls excited about STEM early in their education.

Many new thinkers are trying to decide what the role of video games in elementary schools should be. They have discovered that gaming is more about the "doing" in the learning than about the "being told." In gaming, kids don't need prizes or punishments. They are swept away in time and are completely engaged because the content is fascinating, compelling, and challenging. The graphics in school videos are not even marginally as good as those in video games. Many organizations now actively integrate video gaming into the classroom setting.

The Team of Thirty includes many kids who were active video-gamers. I know, because they played at my house! Most of the kids' knowledge of reading, writing, math, science, history, arts, health, and religious studies was self-learned through computer exploration on the internet and through computer games, video games and movies. They would encounter a word, topic, or name in a game and then spend time researching it. This was supplemented with family discussions.

Research on screen time for older children

The research on screen time for young children under the age of six is still heavily negative, in that language development is impaired; consequently, social and emotional development lags in children of this age who log a lot of screen time. There is very little research on children aged seven and up. The smartphone came out in 2007 and the tablet in 2010, and there are still very few long-term studies on the effects of screen time on those two devices. Best practice advice is to use it moderation. Bottom line advice is that as long as children are getting daily exercise and face-to-face socialization, there are probably no long-term harmful effects related to significant screen time.

The effect of screen time depends on 3 factors

Content: Is the content age-appropriate? Is the game focused on the competition or the violence? What is the ERSB rating? Developmentally, children up to the age of seven are still in the murky power-fantasy-reality jumble and have a hard time distinguishing between reality and fantasy. Teens know the difference. Younger children may not. For this reason, violent games are not recommended for anyone younger than 14.

Context: For young children, should the parent sitting beside them monitor the content? For older children, is the child playing in a home or family environment that is violent? Or does the peace and kindness in a family setting provide the model for appropriate behavior? Do children see repeated violence outside the home in their (real) physical world? Is a caring adult around to offer explanation of content that is puzzling to the child? Human contact cannot be replaced by technology, so if a child is surrounded by an engaging family he can interact with, chances are the amount of technology will not be a harmful.

Child: Is the child particularly affected by the content according to her age, personality, temperament or gender? Is she a sensitive child? Some school-age children are bothered by even animated violence.

Video games are a significant part of a balanced life

Model a balanced life that incorporates the seven keys to health and happiness. Invite your child to participate with you in your pursuit of those seven keys. Parents are scaffolding when they build in unstructured time for non-screen pursuits and still allow time for video games and screen time. Many children will become active if the parents and the rest of the family are involved.

7 Keys to a Balanced Life:

1. **Social time:** time with friends, online or in-person.
2. **Physical activity time:** exercise, sports, active play.
3. **Mental exercise time:** watching documentaries, games, puzzles, reading, play.
4. **Spiritual time:** volunteering, meditating, solitude, church.
5. **Family time:** family projects, meals together, walks, sports.
6. **Financial time:** job.
7. **Hobby time:** leisure pursuits and projects.

Set limits or not?

Some unschooling families set time limits for screen time and other families do not; in between, there is every possible variation. We tended more toward the unlimited side of the continuum, and the parents of the Team of Thirty had varying levels of tolerance for screen time. It didn't seem to harm any of our children. All thirty developed good self-control skills. Some of our kids went away for postsecondary schooling and lived in residence, far away from parents' control. They had all learned to manage their time to accommodate their schedules and workloads.

When children first get computers, they love the novelty and never want to get off them. The applications and games are compelling. It takes time to set up, read, understand how a game is played, and hours to advance. Parents who never have played games often don't understand this.

In our house, with unrestricted screen time, the kids lived a self-imposed balanced life. They got fresh air, went to the park, rollerbladed, rode their bikes, and bounced on the trampoline. They read books for hours every day. They socialized with their sibs, parents, friends and people we met up with. They did art work, wrote stories, built things with Lego and K'NEX, and played computer and video games. As they got older, they would write, read novels, and play musical instruments. I believe there is plenty of room for video and computer games in a balanced family life.

Even with unrestricted gaming time, Mathew at age 15 spent two hours a day reading. He read 45 novels in one year! Neil, 14, read books on social issues and worked on high school physics and chemistry in his spare time. Sophie was 12 and read a 200-book series called *The Babysitters Club*, while writing her first novel and attempting a Grade 7 Math workbook. She also came to me one day and asked to restart piano lessons. She knitted, painted rocks, did chemistry experiments, and baked. One evening, she was babysitting her brother. We came home to a clean house—she had vacuumed, scrubbed the floors, and cleared the counters of dishes while we were gone, without being asked. The children could have all been playing computer games, but they chose to help her.

I did have my "worrisome" moments. When I complained that my children were not being productive enough, my son, 14, questioned my perception of "productivity." He wondered how anyone could judge the degree of productivity in what another person does in his leisure time. He asked, "Is gardening or golfing more productive than playing a computer game? Who judges that?"

Addressing concerns about screen time

Many parents express concerns about screen time based on their anecdotal experience of their children's behavior. Many experts' concerns are opinion based and lack reliable data. Let's examine them closely.

Addiction

Our children were on the computer by about age two, or as soon as they could use a mouse. Santa brought video games into our house when the kids were eight, seven, five, and one, and Nintendo 64 became our curriculum. The seven-year-old, Neil, was particularly enamored with the games, although Mathew and Sophie were thrilled too. Some days they would play for up to 16 hours, as I would not restrict them once they were over the age of six. Neil craved it and lived for it. This went on for months. I finally got worried and thought about starting to restrict their game time. If anyone had an addictive personality, it was Neil; pulling him away from the games was a constant struggle. But ironically, when I did make up my mind to interfere, the kids would self-regulate and play with something else before I said anything! I gradually gained confidence that the novelty of the games would run its course. This was one of the "waves and crests" of learning and interests. After acquiring 16 games, the kids discovered that they all had the same formula, with many variations on the theme. They eventually got bored and self-imposed a few months' break from gaming. I was impressed.

At the age of 16, Neil was the most self-motivated and self-regulated of the bunch. The year he tried out school, he went to bed every night at 10:30, knowing he had to get himself up in the early morning for school—his choice, not mine. He was in full control of his homework, tests, and assignments. He still leads a pretty balanced life, with friends, social and physical activity, homework, and gaming. At age 20, he wrote an excellent university essay on the traps embedded in video games that make them so compelling. In fact, of all the kids, he is the one who best monitors his game playing and gives himself healthy alternatives. He now works in the field of computers and engineering—I should have anticipated that from his early passion! —and takes frequent breaks from the computer. So, the moral of my anecdotal tale is that whatever your child is like, and what he needs or wants at a young age, may not be at all what he later turns out to be like or to want. Don't project! Every age of childhood is a stage.

Video games are very compelling but not addictive for the vast majority of children. About 0.05 percent of children have a gene predisposed to any type of addiction. Features embedded in video games mimic those in gambling. Games use casino tactics such as "random loot" and "pay-to-win" schemes that reinforce intermittent rewards and keep the player playing. Parents must be aware of the "hooks" and counter them with satisfying life experiences outside of gaming. (See Chapter 16)

Video games are structured to take an enormous amount of time to set up and play. It can be difficult for kids to concentrate and play a game in rations of 20-minute blocks. What parents see as an addictive desire to continue playing is in reality a concentrated effort to advance in the game. Games are very complex, and many things need to be done in the correct order to reach the next level. Not all levels are attained, nor is success guaranteed—and success takes a lot of time.

Some parents report that their child's personality is more argumentative after playing a video game. But are children snarky because of the game content and its modeling, or is it because of their frustration at having an enjoyable activity curtailed?

We do know that video games cause arousal in the brain. They awaken the flight-or-fight response, which stimulates the brain chemicals. Games are not the best activity for winding down before sleep, probably due to the complex brain processes required for playing. Again, moderation is the key. It might be helpful to have a two-hour window of non-screen time before bed to allow the brain to relax and de-stress before sleep.

Violence

I sometimes worried about my older sons when they were about 12 and 13 and took to violent first-person shooter games such as Half life, Counterstrike, Team Fortress, and Grand Theft Auto. They even begged their dad to take them on field trips to the rifle range. I was concerned that they were losing their empathy and becoming obsessed with violence. As it turned out, I didn't have to worry.

Some time later, Mathew went on a fishing trip and came home and adamantly swore he would never go fishing again because they had to kill the fish when he caught one and had to take the hook out! Neil is one of the most loving boys I know; he would be the first person to go and give his younger brother Ryan a hug when he was upset, sad, or hurt. Our family is very nurturing, and that helps to counter the violence they see on the screen. We have never spanked (well, ok, only once!) and we teach them daily how to resolve conflicts respectfully—that is, after all, my line of employment!

Eventually, even the girls would play the first person-shooter games. But they are all the most empathetic kids around. The older ones have come home from university at holidays and set up a robust round of Overwatch, and created League of Legends in our living room with five networked gaming computers. The played as a team and bonded together. I've come to the conclusion that if a child is raised in a non-violent, caring environment and is old enough to understand the difference between a screen and real life, which occurs around the age of nine, violent video games will not negatively affect him or her.

Aggression and Grumpiness

According to the Social Learning Theory of child development, children can copy the violent behavior they see on the screen, thinking it is acceptable and condoned in real life. But as long as they live in a family free from violence, they will clearly differentiate between violence on a screen and in real life.

Violent play is just another tool that children use to work through, express, and understand their emotions. Toys and play are and always have been children's means of expressing their developmental tasks and inner feelings. Playing video games is no different from playing with the toy guns, arrows, and knives our generation played with as kids. If anything, video games may be a healthy outlet for role-playing out feelings of violence, anger, and frustration. As my 14-year-old son says, "I can do things in the game that I would never do in real life. It's fantasy and I know the difference."

Isolation; no other interests

This is a huge concern for many unschooling parents, especially in the teen years. The new reality of socialization in our age of rapidly changing technology is that both children and adults socialize, not just face-to-face, but through in-game chats, text messages, and apps. Some parents work hard to arrange social clubs for their children. But all a home-schooled child needs is one good face-to-face friend, and often that friend is a sibling.

Screens turn the brain into mush

Seriously, they don't. I can't count the number of times parents have said this to me. And it has no biological basis. What they probably mean is that video games don't tax the imagination like books do. No, they don't, but they can be the catalysts for further expansion of the imagination. For example, when my children played the Mario, Zelda, Pokemon, and Kirby games, they would create Kirby stuffies and wooden Yoshi characters and Pokemon figures out of play dough. They would write their own storylines based on the characters. When they got older, they painted and drew beautiful, fantastical pictures resembling the settings in World of Warcraft. That requires imagination. Gaming is wonderful, but do have art supplies on hand and encourage artistic and literary expression inspired by the games to help your children have a more balanced experience and expand their imaginations.

Too much sedentary activity

A parent would never tell a child who is reading to put the book down and go outside and play. Yet reading books is also a sedentary activity. There is a definite societal bias against onscreen reading as compared to book reading. That being said, time spent indoors playing games instead of outdoors playing sports is a valid concern.

But rather than discriminate against one form of sedentary activity, parents need to look at their children's overall sedentary time and replace that with active time. Adults who spend 10 hours at a time scrap-booking, knitting, or watching movie fests tell their children to get outside and play. If we are truly going to address our children's lack of physical stimulation, we must look at the whole picture: our penchant for driving children everywhere instead of letting them walk or ride their bikes, and seldom going to the playground with them. Stranger-danger is no worse today than it was when we were children. Vending machines in schools, less physical education, frequent restaurant meals, parental modeling, and genes all play a part in our children's increasing waist-lines. Sure, talking forever on instant messaging is not physical activity, but neither was burning up the phone lines for hours at a time when we were teens. Many young people are foregoing TV for the internet—this trades an activity we engaged in as children for another activity that engages our own children now. It is not the sedentary nature that has changed, but the medium.

The epidemic of obesity in adults and children is increasing: nearly two-thirds of Canadian adults and about 28 percent of Canadian teens are overweight or obese. Two-thirds of Canadian children do not meet physical activity guidelines in spite of government-provided tax credits and mandated physical education classes in schools. (Statistics Canada, 2017) There are more dogs going out for walks with their dog walkers these days than there are kids going for walks. The single most important thing people can do to live longer is to exercise, yet kids hardly get any these days. Staying physically fit does not have to take a big effort. Ten minutes here and there add up. Build in small amounts of activity every day and your whole family will notice the difference in both physical health and emotional closeness. Parents cannot force their children to exercise but they can do lot to encourage and facilitate an active lifestyle.

How to get your screen zombie moving

1. **Set blackout periods**: Have specific times of the day or week during which no electricity is expended on machines. The children will find physically active things to do. Even more so if you send them outside to play. They may balk at first, but after a while they will be having so much fun outside, they will balk at coming back in!

2. **Get children involved in volunteering**: Many family volunteer jobs include physical activity, whether at the local food bank, shoveling the neighbors walk, or cleaning up city pathways or riverbanks. Many paid jobs for teens also involve lifting, moving, and carrying—good ways for them to get exercise.

3. **Do it with them**: Most children will get involved if Mom or Dad is also involved. Invite your children out for a bike ride, a rollerblade excursion, or some time at the basketball net. Driving them to the swimming pool and then texting on your smartphone in the viewing area sends them the wrong message. Get in the pool with them! Besides, most adults could use a little more activity in their life as well. It's good for everyone.

4. **Refuse to drive**: When children need to get somewhere, encourage them to bike, rollerblade, scooter, skateboard, walk along with their gang, or take the bus. Even when they use the transit system, they expand energy walking—or running if they are late—to and from the bus stop.

5. **Plan friend and family activity dates**: Rather than meeting friends or family members at a restaurant, plan to play a sport, walk, or do another physical activity for a playdate.

6. **Play active games**: Be open to providing funds to purchase active games such as video game dance mats or the get-fit video sports games on the market today. Also offer to pay for outdoor or indoor sports equipment, but not for sedentary video games. Put your money where your values are and your children will emulate them.

7. **Picnic, camp, or hike**: Get outdoors and the physical activity will happen. Bring Frisbees, balls, bikes, and other sports equipment to a local or out-of-town park for a day.

8. **Swim**: Most children love to swim; drop them off at the local pool for the afternoon along with some buddies.

9. **Fill a bin with outdoor toys** such as balls, a baseball bat, badminton rackets and birdies, skipping ropes, and Frisbees and keep it in the trunk of your vehicle. When there are waiting times while out and about, use the toys for getting some fresh air and exercise.

10. **Start a "playground swap."** Parents who work during the day could return the favor to those who walk their kids to school or to the bus, by offering to be the parent supervisor at the neighborhood playground after supper. Designate a time and place for all the participating children to meet up with one or two adults who will walk them to the playground, supervise them, and return them to the meeting spot at a designated time. Parents could rotate.

Games are just another food on the buffet of learning

In my parenting classes, parents often admit that withholding technology is one of the most popular punishments they use to try to control their children's behavior. They give their children mobile phones, laptops, and computers—then take them away when children misbehave. Yet these things provide such rich content. Children love their technology and parents know it. Research shows that punishment impairs the parent-child communication cycle because children do not easily share thoughts and feelings with their punishers.

If you treat screen time like any other educational tool, it will not be elevated to "treat" status in the eyes of the children, and they will naturally find a balance between that and other activities. Leave lots of other play options lying around. Everything kids are curious about is educational and contributes in some way to their development.

Educational benefits of video and computer games

Are video games educational? Of course, they are! Any kind of toy or game is educational in that it teaches children knowledge and competencies. Not every game has to be labeled "educational" to be educational. Other than volunteering, travel, and reading, video games have been the biggest "curriculum" in our home education and have been very valuable in keeping the children engaged in learning.

As a parent of five gamers of both genders, I learned early that my children hated the "educational games" that have primitive graphics, poor logic, clumsy interface, are non-multiplayer, and are just plain lame. These educational games seem to be marketed to parents who aim for productive use of time rather than plain fun. When my kids immersed themselves in games like World of Warcraft, Nox, Spore, Gizmos and Gadgets, Age of Empires, Graal, Lacuna Expanse, Civilization, Garry's Mod, Crusader Kings, Runescape, and League of Legends, they learned not only reading, writing, and math skills, but also social studies, mythology, history, and science. They learned the valuable social skills of cooperation and conflict resolution with other in-game players, and with buddies in the same room playing the same game. In WOW, League of Legends, and Overwatch, they learned the personal skills of resilience during adversity, perseverance and the commitment to continue and finish for the team, even when they were discouraged. They learned how to deal with challenges, problems, team members, and competitors under time pressure. They learned how to win gracefully, and how to face losing with dignity—and without throwing a keyboard across the room.

Indirectly, games and toys teach some academic concepts in ways that are compelling to children, aided by the focus that is essential for gaming success. Parents who don't play video games may not even realize how their children have learned these competencies. Have a look at the following impressive list of competencies that video games can help to develop:

Academic competencies

Executive function planning and working memory skills: Games teach critical thinking, analytical thinking, strategy, and problem-solving skills. Think about the scientific method. Most games give clues but not directions. So, a player has to hypothesize to find a strategy that might work. The game developers withhold critical information, so players must use trial and error to discover what they need to know. The games are giant puzzles that stretch executive function and working memory and develop skills. Further, gaming teaches problem solving under duress because many of the tasks they have to perform have time limits!

Multi-tasking: Players learn to manage many forms of information and options, usually under the stress of time limits and encroaching competitors. Just memorizing the number of items one can obtain in a game is an amazing feat. Some games make a player battle in order to stay alive, providing a great training ground for the workplace! When juggling competing interests, players also learn about time management and setting priorities.

Literacy: Games that require reading, writing, and spelling build literacy skills both on-screen and in game manuals that are often written at a high school level, telling gamers how to play and offering insights for getting over rough spots. Children who can't read certainly try to learn! Our kids learned to read, write and use grammar from playing

Graal, Animal Crossing, Sims, Sim City and many other games. Children who hate workbooks and seatwork can practice literacy skills in a format that really motivates them.

Math skills: Games develop pattern recognition and use math operations, reasoning, and logic to solve problems. The kids were motivated to learn how to tell time. They wanted to know exactly how long a half an hour was and how many more minutes until Neil gets off and they get their turn!

Computer programming skills: They learned coding, Perl, C++, CSS, HTML, scripts, and many other useful computer programming skills by playing user-modifiable games.

Art, History and Science: Games initiate interest in many topic areas in history, art, culture, and science that spur research and reading. My kids also learned much of elementary school Greek history from playing Age of Mythology, and science from Gizmos and Gadgets and Magic School Bus. Civilization and Crusader Kings were great for learning history. Kerbal Space Program was excellent for learning orbital mechanics, space travel, physics, and engineering.

Knowledge: Gaming allows the elderly, poor, isolated or confined person access to information and communication that might otherwise be inaccessible.

Creativity: During our children's heavy video game-playing years, they continued with their self-motivated art representations: they played mostly the Mario series, Donkey Kong, Zelda, Pokemon, and Kirby. They painted hundreds of pictures of the characters. In fact, the characters were represented in every medium possible—play-dough, Lego, wood, watercolor, markers, homemade costumes, stuffed figures, and many others. The handwritten stories of the adventures of Kirby and Mario, done by all the children, were equally impressive. They even made homemade board games featuring the characters. When Burger King ran a promotion handing out Pokeballs with characters inside along with their kids' meals, we ate at Burger King four nights a week and acquired an immense collection of figurines! Although they wouldn't touch those kids' meals today, the figurines still represent many cherished memories of their imaginary play in which they set up scenes, built habitats, and invented stories and games with each other and with their characters. I am still amazed at the creativity that those video and computer games inspired. As the kids got older, their creativity moved from physical objects to a screen. They generated art, music, writing, and videos onscreen. The creative process was still there; it just changed formats. Once children reach school-age, mainstream parents tend to get rid of traditional creative items such as arts and craft supplies, paints, dress-up clothes, and drama props because "the schools can deal with the mess." However, the schools become more academic from Grade 4 on, so very few children have creative outlets at home or at school. Hence the appeal of being creative on the computer, with games like the Sims, Sim Theme Park, and Animal Crossing, where children can create their own worlds. It's not the children's need for creativity that has changed, but the medium.

Social and emotional competencies

Connection: Children can easily stay in touch with family and friends around the world by playing games, talking, and socializing in real time over communication channels such as Discord or FaceTime. Grandparents love to connect with their grandchildren, regardless of how far apart they might be. My kids often would game with their siblings who were away at university or had moved to another city to work.

Entertainment: The internet and gaming provide limitless sources of entertainment in video and audio format. Name your genre and it's available.

De-stressing skills: Gaming helps players to zone out, de-stress, escape into fantasy worlds, and relax. My friend is 45 years old and works as a realtor. To de-stress, she comes home and plays computer games with her daughter.

Delayed gratification skills: Players have to work their way up by levels and cannot shortcut without others' help. Studies show that children who learn to appreciate delayed gratification at an early age tend to do better in life.

Executive function focus skills: Especially difficult in a background of music, noise, chattering, and distractions, gaming demands total focused concentration. This is a useful practice for many children. Often, children are diagnosed with attention deficits in school, yet can focus for hours on gaming.

Self-esteem: Games build self-esteem and confidence in skills that are admired by peers. This is especially important for children who don't excel in academics, sports, or the arts. Being accepted and respected for a special skill builds self-confidence in other areas of their lives.

Executive function inhibitory control: Games provide a method of teaching and practicing emotional intelligence. Games give children practice in handling anger, frustration, and setbacks—especially when they lose an acquired level because they forgot to save! It even teaches natural consequences and how to problem solve to fix a situation. Of course, children need an adult around to help them deal with those strong emotions, or else a controller will go flying against the wall!

Gender neutrality: The internet and gaming enable people to communicate without visual stereotypes. People are judged on their words and actions, not on age, gender, culture, or looks.

Commitment and work ethic: "My son doesn't commit to extracurricular activities, but he is persistent in mastering a game, committing to a team of five in a game, or learning coding," says Ellen, homeschooling mom of two.

Cooperation and collaboration: Multi-player games lend themselves to team building, cooperation, strategy formation, and group problem solving with other players both in the game and those watching the game. Players have to work together to develop a plan, achieve results, and cover each others' backs. They learn to negotiate, compromise, and practice fair play.

Encouragement: As well, when one child plays and another watches, they both learn how to encourage each other to take risks, try another solution, and keep going. It's wonderful to watch their "team approach," even if only one child is at the controls. Often, my kids played as a team against other teams in League of Legends and it was lovely to watch how they bonded.

Independence: In a world of helicopter parenting, gaming and social media provide a playground for children that is not micro-managed by adults. Children make the rules or the game makes the rules, but not the parents. When children get together face to face, they speak a gaming language that is not understood by adults, but that bonds them together in a secret world.

Conversations: When my kids would meet up face to face with their friends, they spent non-gaming time engrossed in conversations, bragging about games they had and which ones to go for next, which characters they wanted to play, and what levels they had achieved—much like we used to discuss hockey stats, car enhancements, and movie stars. Teens especially like to differentiate themselves from adults in their form of dress, hairstyles, music, and activities. Gaming is one more avenue that helps them do that.

Family closeness: Many parents play video games with their children from a young age until the kids move out—then come back for Sunday dinner and a round of League of Legends! As a non-gamer, I personally found that taking an interest in my children's gaming by sitting and watching them and listening to their descriptive adventures in the game brought us closer in communicating and sharing fun times.

Socialization: Minecraft Club! Computer Coding Club! Girls Who Game Club! As kids move into the teen years, they are not well practiced in initiating conversations because they are more self-conscious about what they say and do. They need an activity to focus on in order to relax. Gaming clubs provide that activity.

Social media benefits

Social: Kids can easily connect to other like-minded kids who share their interests.

Writing: They can flex their debating and persuasive writing skills on hot topics in discussion websites, with other really good debaters.

Research: They can learn about people with different backgrounds, religions, and cultures as they make online friends around the world.

Create: They can create and share musical, technical, and artistic projects with others by writing blogs and making websites, videos, memes, podcasts, and webinars.

Collaboration: They can collaborate on projects without ever meeting each other in person. Several books have been published with such collaboration.

Citizenship: They can organize, volunteer, raise collective consciousness, and raise funds for charitable organizations and worthy causes.

Entrepreneurship: They can start and grow a business.

Health: They can access health information on any topic from sexuality to depression and get answers to questions that they would be embarrassed to ask an adult.

Because of the proliferation of smartphones and video games, which 80 percent of Canadian kids play, children as a school cohort are dating at older ages, having sex later, driving later, and moving out later, and have little taste for alcohol and smoking. (McKnight, 2015) These are excellent trends. The trade-off is that they spend more time alone in their rooms, connected to their mobile phones. Thus, inter-personal and socialization skills can take a hit. Family can counteract that by spending time together and scheduling outside family social time. Declare some screen-free zones and times, like meal time, to gather together, socialize, and enjoy each other's company. Social media can also be brutal to children's self-esteem, so open communication with supportive parents and siblings is critical in keeping peer stress tolerable and not toxic. Screens have value, but children need face-to-face relationships in the three-dimensional, physical world. Balance is key.

Lessons, sports and activities: enrichment or overload?

"Healthy families need micro bedrooms and a macro kitchen."

The sun was shining on the brilliant green trees and the snow sparkled under the cloud-less blue sky. I was following my eight-year-old daughter down the slopes of the mountain ski trail. The previous year in her ski lessons, she mowed people over on the magic carpet lift because her body couldn't stop or turn. This year, she was skiing down the trail in perfect curves. What happened in between? Her body and her brain had matured. I mused on how wonderful it was that the last of my children could finally ski, skate, and swim independent of my help—what a day to celebrate after nineteen years of parenting and an aching back!

As a conscientious parent, I dutifully enrolled my first two children in formal lessons as soon as they reached the minimum age for an activity. Unparented lessons used to begin at the age four, but now they are often offered earlier, even as young as two years of age. Many days, I fought with my children to get them out of the house, causing power struggles, dawdling, and tantrums. When we got to the lessons I coaxed them to participate. Then they started having fun, and I went through the same all over again to get them back into the car! All the while, I had to entertain the younger sibs—I constantly looked for tips and tricks, and often resorted to giving them my mobile phone to amuse themselves. We would finally all head home—exhausted. Because the cost of the classes was significant, I insisted we go, even if the kids didn't want to. Was it worth it? No.

For the last two children, I simply got tired and didn't enroll them in anything. Every fall, I resisted the pressure from my fellow parents to fill up our schedule with activities, and refused to carve out huge chunks of our days to drive across the city for the practices, lessons, and classes that my kids were lukewarm about. Guess what? They still learned to ski, skate, swim, and play soccer—without lessons—and are pretty good at all of them!

I would say that if lessons involve "struggle," drop them! We struggled with lessons and practice when my kids were seven, eight, and nine years old, and then finally quit all that insanity. I took Linda C's advice and waited until they asked for lessons at least three times before I was convinced that they really wanted to enroll. They had to agree to be responsible for practicing, getting their gear ready, making their snacks, cleaning their uniforms, and anything else the activity demanded; only then would I write the checks and agree to drive them. I actually had a few uninterrupted, peaceful years when they didn't ask to be signed up for anything!

When they reached the teen years, at ages 14, 16, and 17, the begging began. They all decided to pick up an instrument. I think they even asked me more than three times each. We paid for violin, piano, and guitar lessons. I wrote the checks and drove them to lessons. They practiced as little or as much as they wanted, because their learning was between them and their respective teachers. I was amazed at how accomplished they became in a very short time. It's that self-motivation factor. They were motivated. The piano player took lessons for about a year; the violin and guitar players, two years each. They eventually decided to leave formal lessons and self-teach themselves further on their own time and schedules. Again—they are pretty good musicians now on their respective instruments.

I believe that waiting until their bodies matured enough to master the physical demands of the various sports really enhanced their enjoyment. The same with waiting until their executive function skills leaped at age 13 or14, giving them the cognitive development to sit still and pay attention to instruction and the executive function skill to endure practice, and move their bodies in response to the skills they learned. It seemed to all come together for them around the age of eight years for sports and 14 years for music and languages.

In retrospect, I regret starting children in lessons at age four. I have come to the conclusion that lessons for young children serve a single purpose—to give parents an hour's break. Unless the kids are truly keeners, most will quit after a year or two. I would wait until children are at least eight years old to expose them to new activities; lessons earlier than that just kill the fun for them and end in power struggles with the parents. Enrichment doesn't happen if everyone is in tears. Back off and wait a few years. Then they will beg you! Guaranteed!

As well, many lessons are scheduled either during the family dinner hour or during rush hour. Interrupting family time is not worth it. As previously mentioned, research shows that families who eat together suffer less stress and the kids perform better academically and are less likely to engage in undesirable peer behavior.

One of the beauties of unschooling and homeschooling is that many businesses now offer lessons and activities for individuals during the daytime hours to compete for homeschoolers' funding and fill an otherwise quiet time slot. This is great, as it leaves the evenings free for family time.

However, group sports and activities are generally not scheduled during the day. Teams need their school kids to be able to compete, so practices and games are held in the evenings. Keep in mind that team sports or organized extracurricular activities do not count as free play, which children need every day.

Many parents feel that their children's lives are enriched more by outside activities than by time spent with family. But hugs, conversation, interaction, and engagement with loved ones is more important for relieving stress, for learning, and for bonding, than any class, sport, or activity can be. Strong character development and emotional intelligence come from face-to-face relationships with family, not from learning new skills in a class. As Dr. Meg Meeker states, "The love-based, need-based connection that we have with our children is never reproduced in any of their activities. When was the last time you, as a parent, just sat on the couch with an empty lap, no book or electronics, and patted the seat beside you, motioning your child to come and cuddle and talk?" (Meeker, 2010)

Many families try the one-activity rule, where each child gets to choose a single activity. But signing your children up for activities does not make you a better mom or dad. Let go of the parent peer pressure. Repeat to yourself, over and over, "I'm giving my child a happier, relaxed childhood because we are less stressed and we are home together more." Even with the one-activity rule, two children means two activities—which may mean a commitment of up to four nights a week of driving, and almost certainly, losing family suppertime on at least some of those evenings.

One year, I did not sign up any of my children for anything. No activities. And they were all unschooling at home that year, no school either. It opened up so many possibilities for our family—discussions, impromptu games, walks, having friends drop by. We ate our dinner at a leisurely pace. We had more picnics in our beautiful parks. We were not driving across the city in rush hour or yelling at each other, "Get off the Wii and get ready now!" Or, "Mom, let's go! No more emails! Close that computer!"

"I think when you are trying to balance children's activities, it is important to realize that every time you add one, you lose something in exchange. The activity may promote the acquisition of skills or intelligence, but children always lose a little down time—and perhaps the chance to sit on the curb beside their bicycles and notice something about the way clouds move, or the opportunity to ask a question about the edge of the universe, or to linger over supper with Dad, or to browse through a book with a relaxed and receptive mind. Unstructured learning takes time. It can't be rushed and you can't schedule it. It, too, builds skills and intelligence, often with startling efficiency. Yet it is so easily squeezed out by scheduling enriching activities that turn out to be no more so than something that might occur naturally during unstructured time. 'Activities-based learning' is just so satisfyingly tangible, it's easy to get hung up on it." (Miranda H, 2000)

Before signing up for an activity, some important questions to ask, besides the cost, are:

- How will this affect the whole family? Is the enrichment worth the stress?

- Is my child super-excited or just lukewarm about the activity?

- What is the actual time involved for the participant and the parent, including preparation time, drop-off of siblings, practice time, fundraising, and driving time?

- Is it about winning, or is the emphasis on having fun?

- How will it impact holidays, vacations, dinnertime, bedtime, play time, and family time?

If the family decides against participating in activities, that is okay. There is no magic window for learning. A person can take up music or sports at age 8, 12, or 16—or 65. My kids pursued outside activities and interests during their university years and beyond. They enjoyed them much more because they themselves chose them, not me.

Just a note about parent participation. Many parents attend their children's activities and then spend all the time on their electronic devices. The main point of outside activities is to develop skills, which in turn build confidence and self-esteem. The joy on a child's face when he finally makes that goal or stops the ball in time to save the game is lost when they look up to see that their parents missed that magic moment because they were on their phones. I'm speaking from experience. If you are tagging along to watch—*watch*!

Elementary learning happens in waves

Most kids learn in spurts—uneven patches of interest. Like eating jags, they will devour one interest to the exclusion of all others and then suddenly move on to another interest or—gasp! — a dry spell of absolutely no apparent interest—*apparent* being the operative word.

Almost all homeschoolers who start with a schedule evolve into routines that become less and less like school as time goes on. Only in large groups of children in a structured program does learning seem to happen gradually and evenly; real, individual children learn in spurts and leaps and bounds—and plateaus. "Our daily schedule consists of collecting eggs, practicing violin and piano, and a bedtime story. Everything else happens in spurts. Math for hours every night for three weeks. Then reading with the same obsessive intensity. Then on to music theory. For a week after that, nothing but sewing and K'NEX. Another week—art history and origami." (Miranda H, 2000)

"Sometimes a little bit of learning can grow and develop 'in the dark,' to blossom later. I recall several occasions in which this happened with my daughters. One might struggle over a math concept where no explanation seemed to stick and the idea simply didn't get through. At this point, we just let it drop. Weeks or months later, the same math workbook would be revisited and whaddya know— 'Oh yeah, *now* I get it!'" (Diana S, 2001)

How do kids learn math?

Math is simply a tool to solve problems that exist all around us. That's why we teach it. But we often teach math processes independently of real problems. Children may be able to do math on paper but cannot apply it to real-life problems such as calculating a tip or counting out change to customers at their lemonade stand. In the school system, children start with paper math much too early and don't get enough practice in mental math, solving the problem in their heads. We can help children practice mental math if we hold back on giving them the answers and let them figure out a problem on their own. In school, teachers don't have enough time to do this. At home, we do.

A good example is a birthday half-cheesecake that we ordered for Sophie. It arrived and looked smaller than a half. We opened the box and immediately knew something was wrong. But we had to do the calculation on paper with Pi, to demonstrate to the store employees that they had made an error.

As a Humanities major, I used to be afraid of math, but no longer. Although my math proficiency ends at the Grade 8 level, I wanted to homeschool my five children through high school and into STEM career paths if they so desired. With great interest, I watched how their understanding of math changed with age.

Children aged 0 – 12 learn math through visualization and thinking. We call it "mental math" when they solve their everyday problems in their heads, using various strategies. You see this happen with babies using a shape sorter, toddlers sharing cookies, pre-schoolers sorting colored Lego pieces, or school-agers playing Battleship.

As unschoolers, we didn't use any math curriculum. The children experienced mental math through games, toys, and play. They started learning paper math at age 13, or Grade 8, when they took their first formal math courses, taught by a teacher, in preparation for entering STEM career paths. They didn't need to memorize the multiplication tables, as they had already been using their mental tools since a very early age.

At puberty, the children's brain development allowed them to understand abstract concepts such as "variables." Their brains had the computing power to work through eight grades of math in one year, by applying learned paper math solutions to experiential mental math problems. They learned the names of each math tool, such as fractions, decimals, variables, and addition, as well as when and how to apply each tool to solve everyday problems.

Ways to learn math without a workbook

Adding and subtracting: Play board games such as monopoly. Sell items and make change at a garage sale or lemonade stand. Pay for items in stores and count the change given back.

Multiplying and dividing: Cook, bake, sew, do workshop and art projects. Share food and objects among friends.

Greatest common multiples: Skip and count jumps on the sidewalk or trampoline. Learn about musical beats. Play Minecraft and Lego.

Fractions: Bake and cook from recipes. Divide up food with siblings. Decide on quantities of food to purchase per person when hosting dinners.

Decimals: Shop. Split restaurant checks.

Percentages: Calculate tips, taxes, and sale prices while shopping. Play League of Legends and calculate damage bonuses.

Estimating: Shop. Track travel miles.

Perimeter: Measure lengths for baseboards, or for framing pictures.

Area: Measure areas for carpet, paint, or screen sizes. Calculate fabric needed for sewing projects.

Volume: Measure parcels for the post office. Measure liquids or dry ingredients in the kitchen.

Circumference: Measure whether the half-cheesecake ordered really is half a cheesecake. One time we were ordering pizza in a restaurant and had to figure out whether one 12-inch pizza was better value than two 8-inch pizzas.

Least common factors: Lego pieces are named 2x2's or 2x8's; figure out how many pieces are needed to build a model.

Integers: Monitor temperature changes. Count money. Count zero pairs with red (negative integers) and green (positive pieces) Lego blocks.

Algebra: Computer games such as Graal, Minecraft, Zelda, etc. Count "debuffs" in video games such as World of Warcraft and League. Shop for packaged food items for a certain number of people. Figure out problems.

Variables: Decipher symbols that stand for concepts.

Place value: Sort and group toys and other items. Measure liquids, distances, and weight using the metric system based on 10. Count money in games such as Monopoly. Write checks. Cook.

Coordinates and ordered pairs: Play the Battleship game.

Rounding: Figure out how much allowance one needs to pay for something. Estimate the total bill when grocery shopping.

Angle properties: Make a sundial. Study astronomy. Visit historical sites where people made ancient contraptions to measure time and determine seasons. Calculate how far from the wall a ladder must be for safety.

Degrees: Format photos that are upside-down and sideways. Learn about astronomy to understand degrees related to a sphere. Question why the Xbox is a 360! Play hide-and-seek.

Temperature: Bake and cook. Monitor the weather.

Time: Study the clocks at hospitals and airports to learn the 24-hour clock.

Roman numerals: Read the *Asterix and Obelisk* books. Visit monuments.

Graphs, pie charts, and figures: Read newspapers and magazines such as The Economist, Time, and Maclean's, which include many charts and graphs. Discuss how the information is presented, and whether it is correct.

Even and odd numbers: Read maps and house numbers on a street. Divide groups based on birthdays.

Properties of geometric solids: Play with blocks and nets.

Slides, turns, rolls, and flips: Format photos on the computer. Play with blocks.

Symmetry: Play with mirrors, objects, and prisms.

Perfect squares and exponents: Examine a multiplication table and visually see the patterns. Make paper squares for cutting snowflakes and other paper projects. See how squares fit into other squares.

Executive function skills: Playing video games or chess helps children learn to take turns, plan the next moves, and tone working memory by holding multiple instructions in their heads, filtering distractions, and developing emotional self-control when they lose.

Math is fun! If you put a bag of jelly beans on a table in front of five seven-year-olds, they can't help but learn division without remainders. Cultivate a child's learning math tools through experience, and the mental concepts will stick when they finally learn paper math. Sometimes, Pi is better than cake!

By waiting until the teen years to do paper math, kids will not have developed the attitude of "I'm bad at math" because they couldn't get the right answer on their worksheets. They will embrace the logic and the fun of math because they are approaching it from a different mindset—solving the puzzle. Like the fun in video games is in solving the game, math can be fun in the exact same way. My friend's daughter loved math. At age 12, she picked up a Grade 11 algebra textbook and began working through its problems—just for fun.

$$X^2 + 4X + 3$$

Although my kids never saw a math workbook before age 13, we had a lot of math manipulatives around the house because they were fun toys. I had volume containers and nets—those little plastic things that fit inside the net and help children to learn surface area—that I would dump out on the table without saying a word. Each kid would walk by, glance at the container, intrigued—then sit down, take out the nets, and play with them. They would fill them, empty them, and rotate them. Same with fraction cubes that linked together. Same with algebra tiles. Same with fraction pizza pieces. They loved to play and made their own mental connections about the properties of math. They would sit in the sandbox with the volume containers and discover by pouring sand that three cones filled up a cylinder. It was hands-on math and it used several senses: sight, smell and taste (when I used real pizza), and touch (pouring sand). When they reached Grade 8 and learned how to calculate the volume of a cone in paper math, they had a broad, real-life experiential background to remember and base those abstract concepts on. Three cones of sand filled a cylinder the same size. Who knew?

None of my children ever memorized their multiplication tables. They learned them eventually, just by living life. For many years, we would skip-count on our backyard trampoline as a game. We would count one, two, and on three, we would have to land on our butts. Four, five, six, butt; seven, eight, nine, butt. This form of skip-counting reinforced the concept of greatest common multiples without even trying. One child learned the multiplication tables by repeated use of a laminated table in Grade 9, when they did paper math questions. Sometimes they needed paper and pencil to draw pictures of a concept to figure it out. If we buy five bags of hot dog buns and they are packed 12 to a bag, will we have enough buns for all 50 birthday party friends? Will some kids get two hot dogs in one bun? If so, how many kids would get two hot dogs in one bun?

Teachers would argue that math is important because unlike the other core subjects of English, Science and Social Studies, Math is built upon itself, concept by concept. One must learn in a linear way—first addition, then subtraction builds on addition, and so on. This is true, and it is why unschoolers have a difficult time leaving math skills to "chance." They want their children to have a strong math foundation to build on.

However, worksheets are not the best way for a child to learn math. Math is experiential; it is best learned by solving real problems. Kids cannot just learn the tools and solve abstract problems that have no relevance. Worksheets are irrelevant drills, and when children learn math by rote memory, they don't really understand the concepts behind the math. They know that 5 times 5 is 25 on paper, but what does it mean to be a perfect square? They know that 5 times 5 is not 5 exponent 5, but why? Early math education begins conceptually, not on paper, and children will learn even without being formally taught. They learn math concepts sequentially but based on their individual brain development timetable, not necessarily when it is first presented to them. Addition is always learned before division, whether on paper or in the mind. "Early childhood may simply be an inefficient period in which to try and teach skills that can be relatively quickly learned in adolescence." (Rohwer, 1971)

Clearly, none of our kids were hurt by a lack of formal paper math training before reaching their teen years. Three of them entered university in STEM streams and did quite well. The four kids' average mark in the Grade 12 Math diploma exams was 81%. Perhaps the boost in confidence as math learners helped because they didn't start paper math so early, and didn't stress over "not getting it," because by the time they tackled paper math, their brains were ready to handle abstract thinking.

It has been said that the adoption of discovery math in Canada's math classes has lowered the country's Math scores in the PISA results. "It just doesn't work," is a common retort from teachers when I discuss how discovery math works well in unschooling. They don't understand that although discovery math works well in the home, it does not work in a school. Unschoolers learn through discovery math all the time, but in school, "discovery math" is "forced discovery." It is giving a child a math problem in a workbook, and then teaching her five different ways of arriving at a prescribed answer. The five different ways must be documented line by line on paper, and the child is marked on how well she does that. So it is not enough that the child comes up with the correct answer. She must explain how she came up with it. In five different ways. This is a problem. Learning to calculate an answer in five different ways is very confusing to younger children. Some ways, such as visually demonstrating algebra with colored tiles, are so new that even professional engineering moms and dads cannot help their kids with their homework because they themselves didn't learn that way. As kids progress through to high school, many concepts are not even taught step by step. The kids are given a problem. The textbook does not give them step-by-step instructions. But the teacher needs an answer.

In unschooling, the child is encouraged to use whatever skills he has at his disposal to come to the correct answer. Since he is not forced to learn five different ways to solve a problem, the exercise is not confusing. The goal in unschooling is that the child learn the method that makes the most sense to him. The methods used in school can completely turn kids off math.

I'll insert one caveat here: discovery math does not work at a high school level for unschoolers who wish to pursue a STEM career. Unless a child is exceptionally bright, she will require direct step-by-step instruction in paper math for higher mathematical concepts such as polynomials, quadratic equations, and calculus. Unschoolers who know that they will want a STEM career often choose to take a direct-teaching math class in high school or self-teach from internet resources and textbooks. But the textbooks that work best are those that teach a single way to solve a problem—not five confusing ways.

How do kids learn to read?

The National Longitudinal Study on Children and Youth began in 1994 and follows 22,000 children across Canada, about 2000 children in each province. They check in every two years, with more major check-ins at 2, 8, 15, and 22 years of age.

On a reading scale of 1 - 7, most 15-year-olds in school were at level 3 - 4, but about 30 percent were only at level 2, which is a risk factor for future success. (Clyne, 2008) Why are 30 percent of 15-year-old school students reading only at level 2? Why do so many teens, especially teen boys, hate reading?

Before the advent of schools in the late 1800s, the most written words a child would have seen in one place might have been on storefront signs, or a newspaper if he was lucky. The average person now absorbs about 100,000 words per day from various media—television, radio, online, and print. (Laucius, 2012)

How could a child not learn to read? That's a 350 percent increase in the number of words! Opportunities to read are everywhere: billboards, menus, signs, brochures, comics, video games, recipes—everywhere!

Here is a secret: most children learn to read outside of school, or at the very least, through a combination of home, outside world, and school stimuli. "I have spoken with 10,000 home-educated kids over the past three years, and I can't remember a single instance of inability to read extending into the later teen years. All children learn to read." (Albert, 2003) Research shows that most kids crack the reading code around the age of seven. (Healthy Children, 2018)

I never taught any of my children to read, either. It was a skill, like toilet learning and talking, that they picked up on their own predetermined developmental schedule. When their brains were ready, they read—no hammering in phonics furthered them along. Every child is different.

My daughter Sophie, who devours three books a week and writes three novels a year, never, ever took a formal English course. The older boys started English classes in Grade 10, where they wrote their first essays. Sophie was an early reader at four years old, not surprising, given her intense love of reading. Neil read at five, Mathew at seven, Ryan at nine, and Anna at 10. All the children love books and reading and to this day, and you cannot tell who started reading when. The later readers were reading the entire 30-book Warrior series by Erin Hunter, the seven-book Harry Potter series by J.K. Rowling, Terry Pratchett's 40-book Discworld, and the 45-book Redwall series by Brian Jacques within a year of learning to read. From *Bob* books to *Discworld* in a year. When the brain is ready, skills advance remarkably quickly!

Our children now spend anywhere from one to four hours a day reading. All through university, they continued their reading for pleasure in addition to their required reading. Neil even entered the Ayn Rand essay contest after reading two of her books. In high school, kids have to read one novel per year. One! Mine read 20 - 30 novels because they had the free time to do so. My informal poll of the home education high school Facebook groups confirmed my theory. Home education kids love to read, because they have the time to read. The number of 300-plus-page books read per child per year was anywhere from 12 to over 100.

In an institutional environment like school, reading is a critical skill. If kids are not reading by the age of 8, it is much harder to catch up because they miss learning content that is primarily delivered by text. Unschooling children learn on their own pressure-free schedule. They don't see themselves as failures and they don't have any hang-ups about learning. In unschooling, you do not have to rely on printed materials. To learn about recycling, your child doesn't have to read a book. You can visit the plant and hear a docent talk about it. There are plenty of videos out there that impart information far better than a book can. Don't stress it if your child is not reading early. It will come.

We were pressured by several supervising school boards to meet the government mandate of having every child read by Grade 1. When we tried to teach phonics to our six- and seven-year-olds, they became anxious about reading. We would use the *Bob* books to teach phonics. They didn't get it. They stopped playing board games that required reading because they felt that they could not do what other kids their age could. Being labeled a "late" reader was beginning to damage their self-esteem.

All three of us became frustrated and disheartened by their lack of progress and their inability to read. My facilitator suggested they go on an IPP because they did not respond to phonics. But just like when my babies were overdue and the doctors threatened induction, I trusted my instincts and knew that they would be ready when they were ready. They would learn to read—on their own schedule and without any hang-ups—if we didn't make a big deal about it. If your children are not reading by age 12, they may need some intervention, but I wish I had relaxed and trusted my intuition more when my kids were younger. You know better than anyone else what your children need.

When we stopped pushing workbooks, exercises, and flash cards, the kids relaxed and so did we. At some point in time, the reading came. Ryan, who couldn't read anything at Christmas, read a few sentences of my parenting magazine over my shoulder by February. Big words! I looked at him and could not believe it. He just figured it out on his own.

Anna finally cracked the code by spring of her tenth year. She loved the Zelda video games but couldn't play them without sibling help because she couldn't read, and although she had the motivation, her brain wasn't developed enough. She finally did it all on her own, quickly advanced to reading big words, and then was incredibly motivated to read. Where months of attempting through workbooks resulted in failure and anxiety, her natural abilities kicked in when she was ready.

It is critically important to not create anxiety about reading. Let it come. If you do, your children—even teenage boys—will love to read. Our children's favorite books and authors were the Redwall series by Brian Jacques, all of Agatha Christie's novels, the Discworld series by Terry Pratchett, Jane Austen (yes, for teen boys!), The Hobbit, Lord of the Rings, Roald Dahl, Kenneth Oppel, the Harry Potter series, the Divergent Series, the Twilight series, the Eragon series, and many classics from John Steinbeck to John Grisham. Coincidently, many of the books they chose to check out of the library just happened to be on the government high school recommended reading list! We didn't discover the "official" list until high school, and were surprised by how the kids had come to age-graded genres naturally.

Facilitating literacy

Motivation to read does not come from receiving pizza coupons at school for each book read! Motivation should come from the pleasure of absorbing new ideas and being entertained. For my children, reading was motivated by being able to advance further in their video games—the cheat manuals are written at a Grade 11 level and contained valuable information. They also wanted to play board games but so many of them required reading cards. They wanted to use Facebook, but again, it required reading. Another motivation is a primal one: children truly want to be a part of society. They absorb the infinite messaging from street signage to pamphlets that understanding words, letters, and sentences is important in order to function in today's world; in their quest to be more like adults, they crack the code. I don't know any child who doesn't want to read.

A love of reading begins in the home. When children curl up in the lap of a loved one with a shared book, love of the printed word is nurtured. Peter would read all kinds of books out loud to the children every evening, even up to the teen years, and I would read age-appropriate books cuddled side-by-side with them during the day.

A home rich in literacy is one where books are everywhere: in every room, in the car, in the bathroom, on the bookshelves, and even in the kitchen. There should be cozy nooks and places to curl up and read a good book. In our last kitchen renovation, we built a huge window seat in our kitchen, big enough for at least five people to curl up with a book and read. It has been well used.

We go to the library once a week and sometimes more. The TV is never on in our house, not because of any rules but just because no one bothers to turn it on. All the children read avidly on the internet in addition to paper books.

Our home is full of every kind of book imaginable. We do not distinguish between comic books and English literature. We encourage Shakespeare, video game manuals, and Captain Underpants. Like video games, we believe that there is no such thing as junk or bad reading. Adults can grow a child's personal library by giving treasured books as Christmas and birthday presents, or even everyday pick-me-ups or treats. Having their own baskets or bookshelves of personal, beloved books is a fond childhood memory for many children.

The children's dad and I are voracious readers. In any spare time, we read newspapers, cereal boxes, blogs, library books, magazines—anything we can get our hands on. We read during waiting times. My daughter now carries at least one book in her purse for waiting times. When adults make time and space for children to read, write, and express themselves, the children will learn that literacy is enjoyable and useful in building a good life. Here are some age-appropriate ways to facilitate literacy.

The toddler years, ages 0 – 3: language learning

Note the following learning activities appropriate for toddlers:

* = suitable for all ages

- They can make their own books by choosing photographs and words and inserting them into adhesive photo albums.

- * Read. Children copy parents; the more they see parents reading, the more they will want to.

- * Read to them. But be sensitive to clues from your children. If you are reading and they get down from your lap, let them be. Don't force continued reading. If they have had enough, they have had enough.

- They love to play with board books. They explore with all five senses—and their mouths and teeth. They may chew, taste, and touch books as much as they will use their eyes to look at them. That's okay! You can buy the paper versions of favorite board books later when they are out of the oral toddler stage.

- It is okay to read the same books over and over again. Children love repetition at this age and their brains strengthen those neural pathways through repetitive action.

- * Make reading as interactive and animated as possible. Use character voices and vocal variety.

- Play rhymes, games, and songs with them. Musical voices and finger-plays such as *The Incy Wincy Spider* help children form valuable language skills with rhyme, timing, and cadence. It also exposes them to other languages.

- * Have a variety of books available. Story books are great for reading to toddlers, but they also need word-photo books where they can point to a picture and you can respond by saying the word.

- * Have plenty of markers, plain paper, crayons, and art supplies available for supervised free expression and writing. Coloring books are not recommended as they are too prescribed.

- Point out words whenever you see them, including signs when you are driving. Anna could point out the "bited ticket" Blockbusters Video logo and recognized both the logo and the word long before she could read.

The preschooler years, ages 3 – 5: reading readiness skills

Here are some hints to help your preschooler get reading-ready:

- Follow the text along with your finger so they can "see" the sounds of the letters.

- * Act while you read. Everyone loves to hear vocal variety—different voices for different characters. Make faces and use your body language!

- Start a sentence from a much-loved book and let them finish it. Many preschoolers will know the story by heart.

- Have them turn the page.

- Continue to point out words on street signs and buses or trucks.

- Start teaching the alphabet and letter sounds if they are interested. Don't just teach the letter names but sound them out. Say, "ssssss" when pointing to the letter S, not just "ess."

- * This is a good age to start visiting the library once a week and making it a treasured outing. It is easier to make it a habit if you do it on the same day every week. Don't limit the number of books they can take out. If they want it, get it! In our house, Monday was library day. As soon as we got home, the next three hours naturally became quiet time for the older kids as everyone tuckled down into their newly acquired books. One suggestion: do not shelve the library books, or you'll never find them when it's time to return them!

- * Leave books in all rooms of your home. If your child is bored and there are books available, the boredom won't last!

- * Make space for reading. Continue to use "nap time" as "quiet time" throughout the childhood years, to look at and read books. In this age of electronic saturation, children need a bit of guided scaffolding to help them carve out time for reading; all electronics should be turned off during this quiet time.

- * Make a cozy reading spot—a window seat, a favorite couch, or a loved one's lap!

Early childhood, ages 5 – 7: learning to read

The actual learning-to-read stage is very exciting:

- Two skills are involved in learning to read: word recognition and language comprehension.

- Help your children search out clues to figuring out a word, like beginning sounds and ending sounds.

- * Ask them questions like, "What happens next?"

- Help them find interest-based books on subjects you know they are curious about. Animals, space, places, and sports are good first subjects.

- * Have them read out loud to you. If they are self-conscious, have them read to a pet. The dog will love it!

- * Play word games such as "I spy" in the car, or "I'm going to Mars and I'm bringing…"

- For children who are struggling to read, choose the book version of a movie they have seen and enjoyed.

- * Encourage your children to help you write. Make lists, cards, and journals, or email friends and family. Spell out the letters for them to write.

- Help struggling readers by taking turns. My son and I used to read *Tintin* books together; he read the Tintin parts and I read the Captain Haddock parts. Or you could read the longer narrative parts and have children read the shorter dialog parts.

- * Focus on the meaning behind the words. After reading a section, ask questions and talk about the content.

- When children are done reading or they don't want to, don't force it. Nudge— never force!

- Scribe the storytelling. Let children draw the pictures and make their own picture books.

- Don't correct letter positioning in your child's writing. Kids will figure it out on their own eventually.

Childhood years, ages 8 – 12: reading to learn (in schools)

- Choose books at your children's reading level or slightly above, but not overly difficult. If they stumble over more than three words per page, the level is still a little beyond them.

- * Continue reading to them.

- Many parents separate fighting siblings, with one child on each side of them on the couch, and start reading. It helps children calm down and focus. Once everyone is calm, they can stop reading and problem solve the issue that caused the fighting.

- * Read everything: cereal boxes, bus ads, comic books, video game manuals, trading cards, internet sites, etc.

- * Encourage bedtime reading. Keep electronics out of the bedroom and plenty of books on the bedroom shelves. Offer children the choice of sleeping or reading. If you don't have to get them up in the morning, encourage them to read until they are sleepy, rather than forcing a pre-set bedtime. When they get sleepy, they will fall asleep, no matter how good the book is.

- * Find plenty of opportunities to talk with your children. Conversations help them pick up vocabulary, pronunciation, and grammar.

- * Play word games such as Boggle, Scrabble, Blurt, Hangman, crosswords, and hidden-word puzzles.

- Turn on the English subtitles for their favorite TV shows or movies.

- * Encourage writing by having them ask you for things in writing. Converse by email. Get them to do *your* writing—shopping lists and recipes, for example.

Young teens, ages 12 – 14:

- * Take books to places where there is not a lot to do: beach holidays, trips, Grandma's house, airports, or camping; get an electronic reader if books are too bulky or inconvenient.

- Before visiting places, have your children investigate interesting sites in guidebooks or on the internet.

- Encourage your children to read reviews of products that they want to purchase.

- Read what your children are reading; have discussions.

- Encourage your children to participate in gaming forums and websites where they can write. Don't worry that the language is casual. In some sites, they are even encouraged to write full sentences!

- * Continue library day and continue reading to them.

- * Encourage them to write wherever and whenever they want. Some children love keeping blogs and journals. But respect their privacy: diaries and journals are not places parents should ever visit without consent unless they are in a public forum—blogs, for example.

- Use writing in your own life and leave it out in plain sight. I often use mind mapping and make lists. Mind mapping involves drawing a center circle on a page and writing a main idea or theme inside it; then drawing spokes from the center circle to other smaller circles extending from it, in which you write secondary words and phrases.

- If your children are slower to read and write, have them say out loud what they want to express; help them scribe it into their own words.

- Help them edit by asking questions and letting them change the writing as needed.

- * Encourage your children to join book clubs.

Ages 15 – adult: continuing the love of reading

- * Protect unstructured time to read and write, for the whole family.

- Don't insist on a report or discussion. The biggest enjoyment killer is being asked to write about book that was read for pleasure.

- * Facilitate writing as much as possible, when it is appropriate.

- * Have lots of books around.

It can be tough to trust the motivation and learning desire of our children, but it will come for them when they want it. My husband, Peter, said that he was bored stiff with reading when he was 8 years old in an English school. Then he discovered a class reader about adventures for boys. That tipped off his love of reading. He went to the library as much as he could. Even now, he remembers one story about shipwrecked boats. He would remember that the worst cargo a boat could carry would be rice, because in a single day, the rice would soak up enough water to burst the boat.

How do kids learn to write?

Kids learn to write from reading and speaking. Good readers are good writers because they hear the sentence formation in their heads and are exposed to spelling and grammar conventions. Most of my kids were motivated to write by needing to input cheat codes to move up the levels in their video games. The video game *StarCraft* was a primary motivator at age six. When they started a new level, they would ask me every five minutes to spell "power overwhelming," or "Operation CWAL" until they had it memorized and could do it themselves. They would begin to write commands in games such as *Transformice*. Eventually those phrases turned into sentences. Then in their early teens they began to write in gaming forums like *Garry's Mod*. One internet forum would "fine" the kids for poor writing conventions, and they would have to use capital letters and proper punctuation or they would lose points.

The two components of writing are mental thought and physical act. The physical act can be writing by hand or typing on a computer. The mental part is harder. The child has to think of an idea, put it into words, and commit the words to paper. Young children can talk about their ideas and ask a parent to write them down. This is called scribing. We did this a lot when the kids told stories about their video game characters; I would write them as they narrated. They finished them off with beautiful pictures drawn on each page of their storybooks. We have so many homemade picture books about the adventures of their stuffed animals Lammie, Domas, and Panguey, and video game characters Zelda, Link, Yoshi, and Daisy.

I was the scribe for the children from about the age of three, and for the late readers, up to the age of 10. The early readers began writing around the age of four; they drew backwards and upside-down letters, with no punctuation or capitals. It was fine; I didn't correct any of it. I preferred that they got their ideas on paper. Editing can cripple emerging writers—that can come much later.

Video games were not the only catalysts for writing. The kids would make comic strips featuring their favorite pets—the gerbils and birds and guinea pigs. They would make recipe books featuring their made-up recipes. They would make lists of topics (complaints!) for discussion on the family meeting white board. They would make menus for our "restaurant," and theater tickets for the shows they presented. They made cat coupons (tickets that would allow the bearer to cuddle the cat for half an hour) to exchange for favors. They made signage everywhere including "Do not eat this or you will be in BIG trouble!," for their fridge treats. We would play word games of "I Spy," "I'm going on a picnic and I'm taking...," and Hangman during road trips. We would play video games of adlibs, in which they would write in the nouns, verbs, and adjectives, and the computer would spit out a hilarious story using those words. We would also play a lot of computer games like *Cluefinders* and *Reader Rabbit*, in which they had some fun rearranging paragraphs. None of these activities were forced; if the kids didn't like them, we didn't do them.

When the children reached 15 or 16, I taught some of them how to write paragraphs. Writing was never my strong point and I relied heavily on editors. I taught the kids the **PEE** method: how to make a **P**oint, **E**xplain it, and give an **E**xample. That is the simple structure for all writing. Then I taught them how to write the classic five-paragraph essay, with an attention-getting opening paragraph that included a rationale and a thesis statement. Three middle paragraphs explained three points and included three examples, and the concluding paragraph restated the thesis. This basic format came from the Toastmasters speechwriting techniques; from that, we went on to different types of essays: persuasive, comparison and contrast, chronological, and the research paper. It was so easy to teach them because they were eager to learn. Nothing was marked, but advice was given and well received.

Sophie, my linguistically intelligent child who read at age four, wrote at age five, and began writing novels at 15 after reading hundreds of them, checked many books out of the library to teach herself novel writing during her preteen years: books on character development, plot, elements of writing, researching different time periods and places, and much more. She never took any formal English classes before university, and she scored 84% on her government Grade 12 English exam.

The kids didn't need worksheets or workbooks to practice grammar, spelling, and punctuation. They practiced with the everyday writing that we all use, especially now with computers. They wrote proper, coherent emails and checked them for spelling. They wrote letters, resumes, thank-you notes, blog posts, reviews, essays, sibling contracts, and of course—stories.

The one difference between our writing and school writing is that our children's writing was totally motivated by their desire to create something. Writing must come from a passion to speak, inform, motivate, persuade, or entertain. When the kids really had something to say and were not just writing for a teacher's eyes or a mark, they were motivated to write well and intelligently. They never did book reports because they could not fathom why they would have to report on a book to someone. A review was different. If they thought a movie or book tanked, an online review would warn others of it; it had a larger purpose and hence was a huge motivator for them. Writing with a purpose for an audience of thousands had much more relevance than writing for a school assignment to gain nothing more than a decent mark.

Speaking and listening

Literacy means more than reading and writing the printed word. It might be a painting, a film, or a PowerPoint presentation. It includes speaking and listening. Children gets lots of practice in reading and writing in schools, but not much in speaking and listening. I've seen so many presenters and speakers who simply read their PowerPoint presentations, or read their speeches in monotone, never lifting their eyes to connect with the audience. I've met so many people who are afraid to speak up in a group or crowd. I have struggled with public speaking myself, as a public school graduate. In university, I used to choose the courses that didn't require an oral presentation in front of the class. When my husband announced that he was going to try Toastmasters, I decided to hire a babysitter for our three young children and accompany him. It was scary at first, but I loved it—learning effective ways to speak and present, and often wondered why we don't emphasize public speaking in schools.

I signed my children up for the Toastmasters eight-week Youth Leadership programs at age 12. They learned speaking, impromptu speaking, evaluation, and leadership skills. They learned how to write speeches—based on the same five-paragraph format as the essays—and how to speak without notes. It helped them make group presentations in university, and they were often the leaders that pulled together the group presentation. Neil did a presentation at university with no notes. He dominated the stage and addressed the audience with humor that had them clapping in delight. I was so proud of him! We also took the kids to Toastmasters contests, TEDx events, Optimist Speech contests, and Pecha Kucha nights. My daughter was the master of ceremonies for the homeschooler Christmas Pageant when she was 14, participated in the Optimist Speech contest at 15, and at 18 gave a speech at her graduation that she recited from her heart—not from a piece of paper.

Listening is another skill that is not taught in school. Sure, children are told to sit down and be quiet, and they learn to listen to a teacher, but they often do not learn about any other type of listening. Interpersonal communication listening involves both passive and active listening skills, including articulating an empathic response to what the speaker is saying. I have met so many nonstop talkers and people with verbal diarrhea, and I don't know how to tell them that a good conversation is divided into "parts," with each participant taking turns speaking for about 15 seconds, then waiting for the other to respond. Executive function inhibitory control in listening to another person speak without interrupting is a learned skill that gets better with practice. Effective listening is a skill that can garner much success in so many other areas of life. In this age of icons, listening may be more culturally important now than even writing.

But an artificial environment like school is the last place to learn effective real-world speaking and listening, because most communication is not conversational.

Red flags in literacy

Watch for the following red flags in your children:

- If children over the age of 10 have trouble paying attention when you read, it may be a sign that they have a learning disability. Keep in mind that it's okay for them to jump around or do something to physically occupy themselves while they are listening because some children are kinesthetic learners. If they can recite back what you have said, they are listening!

- Regression—if they have read well for their age at one point, and then start having problems.

- Signs of impaired vision or hearing.

- Totally shunning reading materials for a year or more may have an underlying cause that needs further exploration.

Social Studies and Science

In my experience in teaching adults, I have learned that people learn best through two vehicles: emotions and fun. Both of these are lacking in social studies and science textbooks. Social theories, history, geography, civics, and science are best taught in a humorous way and within context. Think of James Cameron's movie *Titanic*. Without the love story between Rose and Jack eliciting emotional responses from viewers, the movie would have been just a bunch of facts and figures about the tragedy of a sinking ship. *Stories* are how people remember facts and figures, and good history and science classrooms have books filled with stories. The Horrible Science book series is a good example of injecting humor into science, as is the Horrible Histories series for social studies. Movies are a great way to teach—they touch people's hearts and emotions. They may not be totally factual or accurate, but they give the viewer context that could lead him to research the true dates, the people characterized in the movie, and the true historical event. My kids have been spurred to research Pocohontas, Lincoln, Anastasia, and Apollo 13 by first experiencing the movie and then wanting to learn more. We would often watch a movie a day, then look it up on the timeline we had pasted in the hallway and the world map on the dining room wall. That would give us the when-and-where context. We used the internet to research the country, the period, the social milieu, the political times, and the true facts; we discussed it for the day. The next day, we started the same process over again. These were movies from Blockbuster or Netflix. They were not labeled "documentaries" or "educational." There were no writing assignments to ruin the enjoyment of the learning.

We didn't use any curriculum for social studies or science, so my kids missed the Grade 7 unit on Japan, the Grade 3 unit on Peru, the Grade 8 unit on Brazil, and so on. However, whenever we traveled as a family, we would make it a point to visit new places. When my son was 18 and went to university in Newfoundland, we visited. When he was 23 and worked in Germany, we visited, and when he was 25 and moved to Japan on a working visa for a year, the whole family descended upon him for a holiday—what better way to study about a country! We did the same in France, the US, Ireland, Italy, Australia, the Dominican Republic, Peru, Mexico, and England. We travel on the cheap by planning our own trips, not taking tours; taking trains; having picnics instead of eating in restaurants; and staying with relatives, friends, or fellow unschoolers. Airbnb allows for very inexpensive travel. We do our research on cultures by reading picture books that kids use in school. They are colorful and illustrate the land, its peoples, and its customs in a succinct way, whereas guidebooks simply list hotels and restaurants.

To learn science, TV shows such as Bill Nye the Science Guy (he does really funny math videos, too) and The Magic School Bus were fabulous for stimulating the funny bone. How Things Work and Mythbusters were great DVD series. The kids laughed and watched them over and over again. They learned most of the Grade 1 through 9 science topics through the medium videos.

Then they wanted to replicate some of the science in our own kitchen, workshop, and back yard. Kids are natural scientists. They love to combine things and see what happens. If you can tolerate some mess, let them conduct their own experiments. With light supervision for safety (my one son put foil in the microwave once), let them have at it. They will learn physical scientific concepts and methods that will allow them to make sense of the "textbook science" later.

If we want people to remember facts and figures for a few weeks, they need to memorize them and be drilled on them. If we want people to remember them for decades, on the other hand, we need to incorporate humor, stories, and emotion into the context. Teachers and parents are the best for providing this; they can stimulate discussion and ask probing questions. They can lead a child to think further about his own questions.

This is true learning.

Unschooling STEM education

Twelve of the Team of Thirty chose a STEM path at university, so clearly, unschooling math without textbooks in the early years had no negative effect on their grasp of calculus and linear methods later on.

276

Someone posed this question to me the other day: "My daughter is showing increased interest in math and science. Should I enroll her in STEM day camps, after-school classes, or extracurricular activities geared to STEM?" Which got me thinking, do children really need to be taught STEM learning, and do formal classes in STEM help or hurt children's curiosity?

When Neil was two years old, he loved those coiled metal rubber-tipped door stoppers that went twaaaannggg. He would play with them endlessly while lying on his belly on the cold floor, driving us crazy! But he needed to reinforce those learning pathways in his brain; he was accumulating experience with the way a door stopper worked, so that twenty years later in his engineering class, he would have the feel, or the "tangible connection" of sound oscillations and could relate and translate them into paper calculations.

As an unschooling mom to three children who chose STEM careers, I would say that you don't have to enroll them in anything. In fact, it may be harmful to do so, in that the lack of free experimentation could stunt their interest. Not all children take instruction well. Some children just want to experiment on their own. Instead of enrolling them in classes, here are some ways to encourage children who are interested in STEM:

1. Say "Yes!" as often as possible. If he wants to build a potato gun, say yes. If he wants to take apart an appliance or take the lid off the toilet to see how it works, say yes. If he wants to attend a Maker Fair, take him. If he wants to open up a potion shop in your kitchen, say yes. If he has seven train sets and wants more, get him more. If he wants to set up a workshop in your garage, say yes. If he wants yet another science or building kit, say yes.

2. Buy lots of Lego, K'NEX, Meccano, and blocks. Let him combine toys. Nullify your need to sort and categorize. If he wants to put the play-dough in sand or water to see what will happen, let him.

3. Let him spend as much time on the computer as possible. Kids need to play video games to learn to code them. Don't limit screen time. Getting to know a computer and all that software can do takes time.

4. Take him to science centers, zoos, and aquariums wherever you travel in the world. Buy season's passes to the local ones so he can go often.

5. Never shut down a question. Model "Let's find out!" and take the time to help him get what he needs in order to do so.

6. Host special interest clubs at your home. In a Minecraft club, coding club, or a Beakerhead or First Lego League project, kids can exchange knowledge, socialize, and have fun as well as learn.

7. Take him to Kids' Project Days at building supply stores; many stores offer them for free. But be sure to back off and let *him* build the project! Hammering nails in crooked is a great moment in learning physics and should not be taken over by the parent. STEM education embraces mistakes instead of avoiding them. Perfection is not important—the learning is in the process.

The only thing parents have to practice with their children is problem solving, because the world of STEM is all about solving problems creatively. This may involve risk and mess, but it is free and has unlimited possibilities. Don't limit your children, except in extremely risky situations; even then, use the opportunity to teach them about taking safety precautions and managing risk. Children are going to experiment with fire and water, and it is critical that you limit and supervise them. Better they do it while you are around and not behind your back. When my children wanted to play with fire, I showed them a safe place—the fire-pit—had a hose nearby and supervised them. We discussed what made fire dangerous as well as useful. We called it "the power plant." They poked at the fire with sticks and they burned things. Water and fire are natural kid magnets!

I am skeptical of the structured classes and extracurricular activities that involve very little creativity, popping up only to cash in on parents' homeschool funding or childcare budgets, or their anxiousness to do ever more to encourage their children's interests in STEM. Many of the extracurricular classes are just "more school." I was having a discussion recently with my engineering son and he said the one element that helped him further his interest in STEM was having the "control." In STEM classes, the students do not have the control; the teacher does. In order to experiment, kids need to be able to manipulate things, make hypotheses and plans, and especially, have and be able to carry out a Plan B. Lack of control is a big turn-off, and kids take back control by losing interest in formal structure.

As well, most classes are geared to underage kids, and liability issues will limit the cool stuff they want to try. In school, the most exciting experiment my kids ever did was making explosions with baking soda and vinegar. Boring. Parents, at home, can accept the responsibility and let their kids do so much more under their supervision.

As my friend Joanne said, "I couldn't agree more—my son, who is now headed off to study physics at university, hated his online high school physics courses, but he loves physics. I would like to think it might be because we owned balls and hot wheels and elastic and marbles and... and that I sat in the driveway as the safety monitor while he lit things and launched things and built things that rolled and put his little brother in them and pushed him down the hill and I let him jump in elevators and watch YouTube videos of other people doing crazy things for the first nine years of schooling. It made high school physics easy but dissatisfying. He is now looking forward to being able to study at a much higher level with people passionate about this area." (Joanne P, 2017)

If parents have a child geared to STEM, they will certainly know it! Sure, some classes might be fun, but find and fund what the child wants to do, not what some advertisement says he needs. This applies to any gender! If the class is awful, let him quit. You don't want to turn him off of a STEM interest with boring, limited, mediocre, controlled classes that will stunt him instead of empowering him. Get him access to what he needs, supervise the scary stuff, show him how to clean up, and get out of his way! Einstein didn't have STEM day camps and extracurricular classes!

Art, Health, Physical Education, Music, and languages

All kids love making art until about the age of 12, when the truly talented carry on with their art just for the fun or eventually start developing it into a career. Children don't need to be given art instruction—just give them the raw materials and lots of time. They will be creative. My kids have made reliefs, 3D paintings, rubbings, sculptures, puzzles, carvings, sculptures, ceramics, clothing, and many other things simply by being inspired by an idea. Give them any safe material and they will give you art made from wood, paper, soap, Lego, snow, clay, paint on canvas, metal, and much more. By age 12, most kids realize that they can't make realistic figures and they give up. But before then, they don't really care—they create for the love of it.

Performing arts is super easy for young children. Because of the lack of executive function inhibitory control in their brain development, they are natural performers. They just act—and often, don't care what people think of them! In school, we don't give them a chance to perform. We tell them to sit down and be quiet. At home, we can encourage children by excitedly watching their self-directed performances and clapping loudly!

Health is taught through good parenting. Modeling healthy habits in the home and being willing to answer questions about anything, including sex, will serve a child well.

Physical education is obtained through the love of playing games and trying different sports. We have a city program in which children from ages six to twelve can try out a sport for one day; they can choose from about 100 sports and venues. I wish it were offered more than once a year. It exposes children to so many different sports and gives them an idea of what they may like to try. They might try one, not enjoy it, and try another.

Like art, children are naturally drawn to music. They will tinker on strings or keys and experiment. They will make homemade instruments, like yogurt-carton rice shakers or homemade drums. Give them a how-to book and they will teach themselves, even setting their own timelines for practicing.

Languages can also be self-taught. My son taught himself German at age 22 before going to Germany for a university work term. He listened to YouTube videos toggled in German and used Duolingo. He practiced writing. After two years, he could speak comfortably and impressed many native speakers in Germany. At age 24, he learned Japanese in preparation for a year-long work opportunity there.

So, if you are worried that your 8-year-old wants to quit lessons and that she will blame you when she is 23 for letting her quit, that it's your fault she can't play an instrument now, you can tell her that brains keep on changing and it's her own fault that she didn't have the motivation to pick it up on her own! Just kidding. But don't feel bad about it. Anyone can learn anything with access to resources and a bit of motivation. No one can blame anyone else for not learning something. We all own our learning.

Will there be gaps?

Of course, there will be gaps. School has gaps. No one can possibly study every topic in the world. Schools pick and choose. French or Spanish? Othello or Macbeth? Peru or Brazil? Teachers pick and choose. There is no reason to think your child's learning choices are better or worse than theirs. In fact, the topics will be more current, as they won't have to wait years for curriculum revision and approval. Everyone needs literacy and numeracy, but beyond that, diversity is greatly appreciated. History, geography, social studies, and science topics are country-specific. "I have two older children educated in the system and their education was anything but rounded. It was canned, homogenized, and less than mediocre. Within the subjects where the kids showed aptitude, they were held back by an inflexible curriculum, and in the subjects where they needed support, they floundered, because the class had to move on." (Erin R, 1999)

Schools expose children to a lot of new topics. My son Mathew came home from his Grade 1 class one day and eagerly told me all about Terry Fox and his courageous run to raise money for cancer research. When that same son was 10, he had forgotten who Terry Fox was. Then, as a teen, he pulled that early learning from his memory and developed a more in-depth understanding when he came across a Terry Fox exhibition at a museum. So his exposure at age six was very limited; his understanding at 19 was deep. It is good to expose children to a lot of things, but schools are obligated to constantly prove they are doing that exposing—and that can get in the way of learning.

Sex education is not taught in all schools; where it is taught, it is not until at least 10 years of age. Often, it is not taught in homeschooling either. Yet pretty well every adult knows about sex. When humans want to know something because the need arises, they will learn!

And that's it for the elementary years. So play, read, live, and have fun!

19

Junior High Ages 12 – 14: Create, Experiment, and Travel

"If my kids learned one new thing, anything, each day, I considered us successful in meeting our goals."

Parties or projects?

In mainstream parenting, some parents begin to worry about streaming and their children's plans for the future. Parents are very concerned with academics as their emerging teens plunge head-on into hormonal chaos and the confusing social scene at school. Some hire tutors to help with learning gaps. They deal with daily battles over motivation and their children's increasing bonding with peers. Some parents do part of the homework, so their children will get a somewhat adequate mark. They release their children from chores so they can concentrate on the "real" work of school. The peer group can be a good thing or a bad thing, depending on the group dynamics. Inevitably, though, children start pulling away from family, parents, and home to integrate more fully into their peer society.

Unschooling parents free their children's interests by exposing them to more mature content. If an interest catches fire, they supplement it with activities, and let go of those that don't, regardless of their own desire for their children to love something they themselves enjoy. They continue to write the checks and drive the children to their activities, but they also relish the ability to leave them home alone, trusting that they will take care of the family home and keep themselves safe. These parents don't stress over homework, tutors, activities' demands on family time, financial commitments, or fundraising duties; nor do they stress over report cards, as there are none. They don't stress over negative peer pressure because there is very little of that in their children's lives. Their children's love of learning flourishes because they are not coerced into learning anything they don't want to. At this age, many children deepen their passions and go deep and narrow, instead of following the forced wide-and-shallow school curriculum. They don't cut off learning of other subjects, but they don't have to go deeply into a theme that doesn't interest them. Some children sign up for teacher-taught courses for knowledge and mentorship in specific subjects if they feel they need more of a subject matter expert than their parents or an online course. This exposure to formal, structured classes, in small amounts, gives them a taste of expectations and structures outside of the home. Because they have chosen it, they are more willing to dance through the requirements than children forced to "choose" it.

What we did

Junior high was as self-directed and just as much fun as elementary school. The children played and learned about whatever subjects interested them. They each took one or two online courses over the three years on one subject they wanted to know more about, but that they didn't want to self-teach—and I certainly couldn't teach them. In that course, they had their first taste of deadlines, exams, standards, and teachers. It was a learning curve, but they caught on quickly. They had one hour per week of live teacher instruction and one hour per week of assignments. That was it. Junior high in two hours per week.

If the kids didn't want to do any formal learning in those years, we didn't insist. In fact, our friends and I call the junior high years "the tunnel" because once the kids reached 13, they dropped some friends and some interests and didn't want to sign up for classes, lessons, or homeschooling and social events anymore unless we really coaxed them into it. But unschoolers don't bribe or coax! So they became hermits. As my friend Cathy said, "Those years at home during early teens are a safe place to take risks and explore who they are becoming." Many kids, especially boys, don't want to go out, or go on field trips, or even socialize with other homeschoolers. All my kids seemed to want to do was play video and computer games with other kids or siblings, all day, every day, for three years. With the first two children, I worried how this would affect their development. But when I asked around with my friends who had kids the same age, it seemed they were all going through the same stage.

As there is no mention of this in the development research, this is purely anecdotal evidence. We parents finally discovered that our children moved out of the hermit phase around 15 or 16 years of age, when they again became more interested in being with their friends and going to social events with adults. When they eventually got through the tunnel, they were more motivated to begin studying on their own. For all the kids, their first taste of a full load of five courses per semester was first-year university, and at age 18, they handled it very well. They didn't need years of practice to do what they needed to do, when they needed to do it.

What you can do

John Taylor Gatto once said that the entire elementary curriculum could be learned in a matter of months by a motivated child who was developmentally ready. The only reason school kids need to learn to read as early as they do is that there is so much reading involved in school. But reading is not the only way to learn things, and kids don't need to learn everything by reading. (Tia L, 1999)

Continue unschooling. Book work is still not necessary at this age. If your children wish, introduce them to the world of online classes or in-person classes on topics they love. Many children this age have defined interests and want to venture out of the home to access the services of a mentor, guide, teacher, or trade professional. Woodworking, metal works, sewing, cooking, auto mechanics, apps, and game and website building were several things that interested our children and although we could teach some, in many of these areas we had to seek outside mentorship and teaching.

Children have plenty of time to learn how to write exams, meet deadlines, write essays, complete lab reports, and practice discipline and test-taking skills. These are good skills, but not necessary ones at this age. They still have high school and university to perfect these skills. Rather, junior high is the time they should hone in on their true passions and explore those subject areas in greater depth. Don't worry about the hermit phase. It will pass. Waiting until they are motivated to learn avoids burnout and power struggles and prepares children to be successful learners for when their studies become more formal. Maintain your parent-child relationship by problem solving everything and keeping the lines of communication open.

Cognitive development during this stage

Junior high typically signals the onset of puberty and the much-dreaded "teen angst" in institutionally educated children, yet not many studies have been done on homeschooled junior high children. Do they suffer the same angst that institutional children do? Is angst a normal part of development or is it caused by peer pressure and judgment? Is it nature (genes) or nurture (environment)? Both. We found that our teens did demonstrate a bit of pushback and grumpiness on occasion, toward us parents and toward their siblings, but nowhere near to that demonstrated by our friends' kids in school. The Team of Thirty families had parents who had a democratic, mutually respectful parent-child relationship, and we all experienced mostly happy and well-adjusted kids.

The other major benefit of unschooling at this age is that children attach more firmly to family than do their institutionally educated peers. Although adolescents have friends and may wish to see them more frequently, family and siblings are still very much front and center in their lives. I had tea one day with two moms who have children spanning from 13 to 17 years of age. They said their kids were very peer-focused and they were getting normal hormonal backlash. I kept silent, all the while thinking, well, it might be normal in an institutional environment, but not in our unschooling home. It occurred to me that our children were not very peer-focused, and that distance naturally strengthens family ties. Humans are wired to connect, and if teens connect with siblings and parents as well as a few friends of the same age, their needs are met.

This is the stage in which children acquire their formal abstract thinking skills. When they have not had an institutional school experience, they have not yet experienced anxiety over studying, exams, teacher pressure, peer judgment, fashion problems, or consumerism and they enter the teens in a relatively calm state—yes, I did say the word "calm"—and yes, associated it with teens! They have lots of brain power, get lots of sleep, and their sharp minds easily remember relevant information. They are developing their critical thinking skills and are motivated to delve deep into their interests, which can range from world wars to World of Warcraft.

One of the biggest advantages to homeschooling at this age is children's ability to sleep in and take advantage of the body's natural circadian rhythm of later nights and mornings.

Teens naturally do not fall asleep early, and when they have to get up for school, they are cut short of the sleep they need. No wonder teen angst is at its worst during the junior high school years. Tired teens are grumpy teens. Because brains develop during sleep and while at rest, their growth will be hugely advantaged at this stage.

In the past twenty years, neuroscientists began to understand that teen rebellion, anger, defiance, and rejection were not personal failures, but the result of three or more adverse childhood experiences on the developing brain. At least one of every four children at a school has been impacted in this way. Such traumatized young teens have poor executive function skills and find it hard to pay attention, focus, and contain physical expressions of anger; they have trust, attachment, and other issues. Rather than blame the teen, trauma-informed education can reorganize brain pathways and help teens get a grip on anger, learn interpersonal socialization skills, and build strong, caring adult mentor relationships to compensate for their absence in the home. (Palix, 2017) Every teacher, principal, coach, and anyone who works with children should have the trauma-informed knowledge to help these kids. They need understanding, and kindness, and positive guidance. The problem is that school staff have too much curriculum to teach and not enough time to focus on building relationships with students. No wonder one in five kids does not finish high school. Many grandparents, relatives, and caregivers are taking on the homeschooling of challenging tweens and teens. They can produce amazing results by unschooling and building relationships rather than worrying about curriculum. It's like trying to teach a hungry child: the hunger need must be met before the learning happens. Relationships must take precedence over curriculum for many children.

Young teenagers, ages 12 – 14 years

This age group has the following attributes:

- Their attention span is the same as that of adults; they will enjoy attending museums, theaters, plays, and lectures.

- They are abstract learners; they understand intangible concepts such as algebra, religion, politics, theories, and death.

- They make decisions and mistakes and learn from them.

- They can make their own phone calls and appointments.

- They can get around the city alone on public transit.

- They may now want a smartphone; they are able to understand the rights and responsibilities of owning a smartphone or mobile phone.

- They understand the values and morals of sexual behavior.

- They need independence and they take control over their decisions.

- They demonstrate the executive function skills of self-control, planning, focusing, and working memory; this is the final sharp increase before age 25.

Educational needs for this age

Children in their early teen years need sensitivity and safety in their social interactions. They need personal adult relationships, positive role models, and expressive art activities. They need opportunities for decision making, and respect for their growing voices. They also need small learning communities and emotionally meaningful study. They still require physical activity and experiential learning activities. (Armstrong, 2006)

At this age, children just need to know how to read deeply, how to write freely, how to research a topic and establish credibility in sources, and how to use math to solve problems that they encounter. Everything else is driven by their interests. There is no need to force anything on them to ready themselves for high school, should they choose to go. In high school, kids will learn more essay-writing skills, scientific theories, math theorems, and social studies philosophies. Famous people, wars, accords, plant names, government regimes, and literary terms can all be researched online when necessary.

Travel

Children this age are a delight to travel with. They are strong enough to carry their own backpacks or drag a piece of carry-on luggage. They have enough brain power to understand travel logistics, such as acquiring passports, packing, going through security, booking Airbnbs and more. They are calm enough to enjoy visiting museums and can read the plaques and view the displays by themselves.

The beauty of traveling with children age 13 and over is that they remember their experiences. There is even a special term for nonstop travel and living in many places over the year with children of this age—some people call it worldschooling, and it is much cheaper than sending children to private school. Like everything else in our lives, we prefer to self-direct our travel adventures and have never booked a tour. Travel does not have to be expensive. Staying with friends or in rented apartments, using public transit, and enjoying picnics instead of restaurants can reduce travel costs to an affordable level. Even during university and jobs, our kids loved to join in the family holiday and even had the funds to pay their own way!

Volunteering

This is a great age to begin volunteering in a more formal way. Younger kids can bake cookies for sick friends, shovel neighbor walks, and create holiday hampers. But in the early teen years, kids can begin to volunteer at food banks, soup kitchens, and overnight shelters; participate in park clean-ups, disaster help, and in other places with their parents or an adult alongside.

Clubs and groups

Children from ages seven on find friends and form clubs, groups, or gatherings based on common interests. I know some friends who started a "Warriors" group for their children to read, discuss, and dress up in character. One of my friends mentored a

Youth Against Pollution club for about 12 kids in their early teens. They made displays, organized activism projects, and created plays. They did river clean-ups and arranged speaker nights and other events. They eventually morphed into a peace group; they examined the war in Iraq and brainstormed what they could do to help promote world peace. My other son joined a computer club; the kids met once a week, usually at someone's house, and set their own agenda. Many of the Team of Thirty friends came from the computer club and the environmental club. The general aim was to teach and support each other's programming and coding, yet some days they didn't code at all. They just played computer games and that was okay. My older daughter joined a girls' writing group when she was 12; they assigned themselves a writing project each week and then gathered to share, discuss, and critique each other's writing. One child had a bowling club. Our youngest had a Minecraft club. Parents would take turns dropping off the groups' snacks so the host only had to provide the space. The clubs held on Fridays would sometimes turn into sleepovers for the kids. One parent opened her home for family board game night at her house, and video gaming in the afternoon.

Sometimes the clubs were very unstructured with nothing pre-set except the meeting place and time. For years, the teens would meet for lunch at a public shopping mall food court. We would bring board games to the library and a group would show up at a scheduled time. The possibilities are endless.

Sometimes we would rent space, if a club had specific needs. For years, we rented the community center gym where the kids could get some exercise and play on the gymnastic equipment. There was no structure and no formal "plan." The children had a ball—they could set up their own games and make-believe scenarios. They made a ship from gymnastics mats and a climbing structure; they used pool noodles for paddles and role-played a captain and his crew. The parents let them be and the kids directed their own play. Parents had a chance to socialize with each other and the homeschoolers would join the unschoolers on a Friday afternoon as a treat after the week of homeschool seatwork was done. Other than to make sure no one hurt each other, and to help problem solve the odd squabble, parents gave the children free rein. The beauty of these unstructured groups was that children learned to socialize while parents were close by to guide them and help with tattling, bossiness, unfair play, and conflicts, which were actually very few. We had similar informal gatherings at swimming pools, arenas, baseball fields, soccer fields, and the science center or the community beach. New unschoolers would hear about these informal groups through social media groups.

Occasionally, a venue wanted to turn our free, unstructured time with access to their equipment into structured lessons; this happened particularly at gyms and science centers. Clearly, they saw an opportunity to capitalize on these groups of children by offering more "value" and, of course, charging for it. The idea was to help fill their venues during downtimes. They didn't see the value in free play. Whenever this happened, we unschoolers walked away with both feet and wallets, to find new places to gather.

"Homeschool Days" were offered by some venues to provide programs that met government curriculum outcomes. Some parents would buy the reduced-price tickets, ignore the classes, and roam around freely—in fact, our family did exactly that. My children hated listening to a tour guide and would fight with each other when they were supposed to be quiet and listen. It was embarrassing. I finally stopped taking our kids to group-organized prescribed homeschool field trips like these, going on our own instead and enjoying a leisurely pace. The teen years were better, in that I could ask the teens if they wanted to go on a group tour—which implied that they had to conform to the tours' rules. They could decide yes or no. Most times, they chose no.

The uniqueness of these groups was that other than providing the place and the transportation, parents were not involved. The kids led the groups and set the agendas. Even our unschooling Girl Guide troop had a campout that was totally self-directed. The Pathfinders decided what they wanted to do and planned accordingly. It was lovely. While our community-organized Brownie and Guide camps had every minute planned and accounted for and were wildly exciting, but a bit stressful for the leaders, the unschooling group had much more relaxed activities. The girls learned leadership skills and conflict resolution and made lifelong friendships. These opportunities are almost non-existent in a typical school child's day, where even the extracurricular activities are adult-directed.

Contact among groups' and clubs' members was through email, Skype, or online forums. The kids continued their sleepovers because they had homeschooling friends all over the city; for parents to avoid driving in rush-hour traffic, it was just easier to drop the kids off for a sleepover.

Planning clubs and outings is still the parents' job throughout the junior high age because many kids do not yet have the organizational skills to handle the logistics. However, consent is important. The kids must agree to participate, and they should be allowed to opt out. Around age 16, most kids start planning, organizing, and keeping track of their own outings. Even though I am an introvert, I do need more socialization than my kids do. Yet many times, I felt guilty leaving them at home—happily so—while I went out to socialize, especially at homeschooling events. Other parents would ask where my kids were and I had to say they didn't want to come, but that I did. I found that hosting clubs at our own home would enable me to socialize with other parents as they dropped off their kids, and still have my children enjoy some interaction, without having to drag them out anywhere. Again, consent is key.

Projects

Many kids get industrious and plan and carry out their own projects. Most of my kids built their own gaming computers at this age by consulting online reviews of products and watching YouTube videos to build their own. One child began sewing her own clothing. Another planted and tended a garden. One made a huge collection of wooden models that he carved and painted.

Pets were a project that featured prominently in our children's lives from their toddler through to their teen years. We had every kind of pet imaginable and the kids took good care of them—albeit sometimes after me nagging them.

Virtual schools

Online learning in the past decade has grown exponentially. Our entire education system seems to be moving toward digital teaching. However, I don't think it is the only way, nor best way, to go. Children should delay taking online courses for as long as they can, at least until the teen years, and continue instead to learn in the physical, real world. Currently, online learning takes place either in the home, where it is called distance education (not homeschooling, because it is not parent or self-directed), or in a school. (Alberta Education, 2013)

Face-to-face relationships are difficult to foster in the digital world, but are critically needed in the teaching-learning dynamic. In response to that need, a hybrid of online and face-to-face learning called "blended learning" is gaining popularity. All of blended learning is school directed, but some of the instruction takes place directly from a physical classroom, and some occurs through online content and/or correspondence.

Online education has some benefits, but more challenges. It certainly is not for everyone.

Disadvantages of online learning

There are numerous disadvantages to online learning.

1. Relationships are difficult to maintain

Online learning only delivers academic content. The physical, social, and emotional needs of the learner go undetected when there is no visual contact between the teacher and the student. Academic content is easy to find anywhere on the internet, but the best part of school is the teachers' relationships with students that is missing in online courses, especially when teachers have 300 – 800 students in their virtual classes. The teacher role is that of paid marker or accreditation conferrer, and many teachers have assistants who help with marking. The interaction is mostly one way. As mentioned before, it falls to the parent or even the at-home student to switch to the teaching role the moment the learner needs help. A 13-year-old at home can spend his whole "school day" on the computer and may learn the names of his teacher and his classmates, but he does not talk to anyone until his parents get home from work. This is isolating and lonely. Children need relationships.

2. Bussing

Bussing to a school in order to learn online is unnecessary, a waste of time for the student, and harmful to the environment. Children need adult attention daily, not peer attention.

3. Motivation needs monitoring

Successful online education needs structured parental oversight in the home, or daily interaction with a teacher, or an extremely self-motivated student. Very often none of these scenarios exist, and this is the reason online courses have such a high dropout rate.

Teachers are reduced to being pokers and prodders, trying to motivate learners who literally have to teach themselves the online content. This is degrading to the teaching profession.

4. The learner teaches himself but is constrained by the government agenda

Many online courses have no synchronous live instruction from a teacher, so the experience is no different than students self-teaching by reading text from a screen or a textbook. After reading the assigned screen text or book pages, they churn out short answers, essays, discussion comments, reviews, quizzes, and lab reports to "prove" they were engaged in the course. There are no oral responses because there is no synchronous interaction. If students have questions, a teacher's email response often comes far too late—and by that time, kids have often figured out the answer, or no longer care about it. Or they might search for the answer online. Or watch videos from the Kahn Academy, or from other online teachers not affiliated with a school. Or they ask a knowledgeable parent. In some cases, they acquire an external tutor. This is not online learning. Whoever is doing the personalized explaining is doing the teaching—and they should be giving the mark in the course, not the school. And if a student teaches himself, he should also mark himself, because he knows exactly what he has learned.

A true online course that is delivered by a teacher is one in which content is indeed read by the student, with the student then interacting with the teacher by phone or synchronous live video feed equal in time to at least half the number of regular classroom instructional hours. Anything less than this means the student is teaching himself, or the parent is teaching him, outside of the constraints of school.

5. The parent teaches the child but is constrained by the government agenda

I have learned so many new things by searching and finding answers together with my children. Kids today are products of the "instant gratification" generation. They want things right away. When my children took online courses, they didn't want to wait days for a teacher's answer, and they asked me. As noted in the previous section, whoever does the explaining is the de facto teacher, regardless of who does the marking. If a book or computer screen cannot adequately explain a concept to your child in a learning style they understand, and you have to supplement the written instructions with your own explanations, drawings, manipulatives, and further resources, then you are actively teaching the concept and the course. Schools conferring a mark and commenting on the output does not constitute true teaching. If the parent is explaining a concept in a way they know their child will understand, they should also be empowered to bestow the course marks. As the "explainer" I don't get paid to "teach" the course, but I do it because I hate to see my child driven to tears of frustration. As a byproduct, my unpaid labor subsidizes the education industry.

One parent describes this pretty well: "The course states, 'Online education works with students who can work independently without assistance.' This is the biggest misconception about online education. Those students that succeed have invisible support and assistance at home. I put my daughter in a Grade 7 English class to help her with accountability. While a teacher did the primary program delivery, I was still very much involved with helping to create schedules, identify deadlines, proofreading, ordering library books, helping with technology such as how PowerPoint worked, figuring out how to split files too big to upload as an attachment and other things. I found that I continued to play just as active a role in supporting my daughter as I did when I was delivering the subject under home education. Only, I couldn't give her the mark." (Colleen J, 2008) So if the parent is taking over many of the teacher's duties in a classroom, why not just have the student self-study from textbooks and from videos on the internet, and allow parents to assess the work and give the mark as they do in homeschooling?

6. Online learning only tickles two senses

Experiential learning encompasses sight, smell, touch, hearing, and taste, as well as talking and feeling, which embed learning in the long-term memory portion of the brain. Online learning and textbook learning, the economically efficient methods of delivery, are not the optimum methods for deep learning, because they only involve the sense of sight, and possibly, hearing.

Knowledge gained from online learning is present in the working memory but gets dumped soon after the final exam; it never moves to long-term memory. Pamela Gordon states that "Many studies show that we ignore, forget or misunderstand about 75 percent of all the words we hear." (Gordon, 2012) Anyone who sends an email and has it misread knows what I'm talking about. To get those ideas to stick, people need to make notes and talk to others about their impressions and reactions. That's why it is so important in adult education to get adults to write their own handouts or at least fill in the blanks—it helps them to remember key points. As the brain processes images better than words, it is often helpful to write notes with diagrams, mind maps, Prezi, or drawings rather than words. Talking about the concept moves information along neural pathways in the brain and takes it from short-term to long-term memory. That's why we often say you have to teach a concept to really learn it.

When Ryan was taking an online high school math course, he was having trouble self-teaching linear equations. Neither of his two older siblings who were attending university close by could help my son with his math. They had forgotten how to do these equations, even though they had taken the same math course less than two years before.

Schools try their best to help a child retain information by requiring a written "discussion" component from each online class. They require a learner to write at least one posting on a new topic and respond to three postings from other students to earn a certain percentage of the course mark. This type of discussion is not the least bit purposeful. Students hate it; they learn nothing because tone and intent is lost, so they do the minimum required, and check it off the list. And completely forget what they might have written. No learning occurs.

Now, even if online courses were adequate for visual and auditory learners, what about the majority of learners—the kinesthetic ones? Many children want to dissect a real frog, not a virtual one. Who doesn't remember forever the familiar smell of formaldehyde? Two of my children couldn't read well from a screen. Some children can't write on a keyboard either, especially for math problems. Many kids need a classroom, where the simple act of writing notes helps them remember, and a teacher to explain concepts live and in person on a visual board. Then the kids will get up and actively engage physically.

7. Children need to move

Excessive time spent sitting is not good. For many years, I felt bad that my children were on the computer as much as they were, playing video games and learning by reading. I thought that at least if kids went to school, they would move around in the classroom. Teachers soon quashed that notion! Children in classrooms spend a lot of time on their tablets or watching videos of a teacher explaining a concept. Hands-on learning is very much obsolete, especially in the junior high and high school years. Then they come home and spend an average of seven more hours a day online, according to the Vanier Institute. Where is the balance in their life when the majority of their school day is spent online—and then the majority of their off-time as well?

Increased screen time has detrimental health and social consequences. Continuous viewing causes eye strain and headaches. Even when children request a paper textbook, they often can't access one because schools will not pay for paper copies.

8. Online kids cannot handwrite

Many kids cannot handwrite anymore because of their ever-increasing reliance on key-boards. This handicaps children who use a computer all through their school years, but must write high-stakes exams with paper and pencil, slowing them down tremendously. Many professors at postsecondary institutions will not allow computers in their rooms for exams or even lectures. That means kids who never handwrite will be forced to do so for timed exams, and lose marks because of this physical "disability."

9. Virtual schools require technology support

It's not the role of parents or teachers to provide technology repair, upgrades, and computer trouble-shooting, but as more schools go digital, funding for the maintenance of technology becomes more important. Even internet access is now an essential service for educational institutions, and the debate rages on as to who should pay for it.

10. Technology creates errors

Computers are machines. They cannot use discretion when they mark online exams. Learners must get the short answer exactly correct with the right characters, capitalization, and spacing, as their work is computer marked and the program is designed to receive only a specific prescribed response. A teacher with 60 kids in her class cannot look for discretion in answers that are indeed correct but worded differently than what the computer is programmed to accept. Kids may never even know that a correct response was incorrectly marked wrong, as schools will not release marked exams to students to use as a learning tool. Schools are concerned that children will copy digital exams for their friends. This doesn't help a child learn.

11. **Parents are shut out of their child's education**

Of even more concern is the fact that ever more of their children's day will become invisible to parents. It's easy to open a textbook or binder to see what one's child is learning in school, but much harder to log into a website with the child's password—if the parent is lucky enough to have it, when the child can so easily change it. Many parents do not have the ability to navigate a website, and they remain locked out of their child's work and his marks. One school board I know of will not even allow their administrators to communicate with parents outside of their own website. The parent must log in to access the teacher and discuss their child's progress—the teachers are not allowed to send private emails to parents. This is wrong. Firewalls, compatible software, and passwords all contrive to isolate parents from their own child's education, in spite of all the research supporting the fact that that children do better academically when their parents are actively involved. (Olsen, 2010)

12. **Online education shifts costs from the school to the learner**

Many schools now require students to bring their own laptop to school. But the initial cost of the laptops is only the beginning. Kids will lose and damage memory sticks. The laptops will be dropped, lost, and stolen. They will get infected with viruses. Who pays for ongoing tech support when kids cannot load videos or exams because of incompatible software? Who pays for help in upgrading software? Or lost or damaged headphones and microphones? Who pays for technology trouble-shooting? Will the school offer orientation sessions to parents to support the learner with hardware, software, and networking?

And of course, textbook companies now want to provide online textbooks rather than printed ones. Think of their cost savings! As an ebook author, I know that printing is half the cost of book production; in addition, there are writing, editing, and layout costs. But the ebook cost savings are rarely passed on to the consumer; rather, the non-existent printing costs are still being passed on to you as parents! Just as businesses shift the cost of printing bills to consumers, charging them if they wish to receive a paper bill instead of an e-bill, parents are expected to bear the cost of the electronic tools to educate their children. If parents accept the financial burden of providing electronics, they should have choice in where the content comes from, and it may not be the government or the school.

13. **Poor content**

Even though there is no excuse for outdated content in digital courses, they are designed by humans and humans make errors. Factual errors, spelling errors, grammatical and editing errors.

14. **Online courses are designed to have a heavier student workload**

My children took Grade 10 Physical Education online. The course included 50 hours of writing assignments—three essays, ten quizzes, two projects, three discussions, and more. They had to log and prove 75 hours of physical activity. The kids learned all the vocabulary of soccer—but not how to actually play it. The school justified the excessive writing component by saying that they had to give more marked assignments because of the lack of face-to-face visual cues of absorption and feedback that they would receive from an in-person class. This lack of trust in online students contradicts the usefulness of such courses. Understandably, teachers need output to prove learning, but such excessive written output for a physical education course literally has no context or value.

15. Some components of learning are harder to accomplish on a screen

Math characters, for example. Unless one has a math keyboard, it takes so many more keystrokes to write exponents, fractions, and other characters. It is also harder to do group and collaborative work by computer than meeting in person to discuss the project and organize the workload.

16. Poorly organized courses

Course efficiency and organization depends on the learning style of the course developer. Some courses are structured in a very orderly, linear manner and come with clear instructions and checklists; the assignments are easy to navigate and the due dates are clear. Other courses are scattered and unorganized, with assignments here, additional links there, hidden labs elsewhere, and too much visual overload. My children took an art course that was so poorly outlined that they missed deadlines because links were hidden. It may have worked for the course developer's learning style, but it did not work for linear students. It is easy for a child to lose a vital bit of information such as an instruction to reprogram their graphing calculators because the test supervisors will clear it before your exam—and if you don't, your answers will be incorrect—because the notice is buried in "visual noise." As more and more of our lives are dictated by online instruction, we need more simplicity, not clutter. A book is linear. Online courses can be a scattered mess.

Advantages of online learning

And there are distinct advantages to online learning, as well, some of which I list below:

1. It is portable; the portal can be accessed and assignments submitted from anywhere in the world. Caution: learners must account for different time zones for live tutorials.

2. Text books can be outdated, while online content is easier to update and correct.

3. Videos and recorded webinars can be watched repeatedly.

4. Kids can ask questions anonymously. When they "raise their hand" virtually, classmates cannot see the hand nor hear the question, so it encourages children to ask questions without fear of embarrassment or ridicule from peers.

5. Students do not need to socialize with classmates. They avoid being subjected to bullying. This is a relief for introverts who just want to concentrate on the learning.

6. It is ideal for people with barriers that prevent physical participation: lack of child-care, mobility issues, transportation difficulties, and others.

7. It works for both visual and auditory learners.

8. Students can work ahead or fall slightly behind, within reason. Some teachers post the entire course at once, which is great for big-picture learners; however, many teachers will post the course in sections.

9. Learners do not have to sign up for the full-time school package to get teacher-directed content and personalized feedback on individual courses.

10. Learning is borderless. Learners can access courses that originate in other countries, if they feel they would be better served.

If kids are going to spend more of their time at school online, why not just stay home and pursue their own agenda on their own schedule? No matter what textbook learners read or which online course they take, they will learn enough math, biology, and literature to pass their exit exams, or postsecondary entrance exams, if they choose that direction.

If the internet were to become the main learner-centered educational hub, schools could provide valuable support as centers for teacher and tutorial help, supervised field trip coordination, technology support, and resource lending libraries. Postsecondary schools could provide the benchmark accreditation for getting accepted, and learners could learn anywhere.

Internet would be the "institution." Schools would be the support. Not the other way around.

Children with special needs and learning disabilities

"A learning disability is a neurological disorder based in a part of the brain that is involved in learning. It's wired differently than the usual way and thus, information is processed differently. This affects four basic functions of the brain: language skills, motor (muscle) skills, thinking (cognitive) skills and executive function (organizational skills)." (Learning Disabilities, 2018)

A mental health problem is a neurological disorder based in the part of the brain that controls function.

As children enter puberty, many experience depression and anxiety due to changes in their brain chemicals. Children who were happy-go-lucky during the young childhood years may have difficulty dealing with these mental health challenges. They may "cope" with mental health problems by manifesting undesirable behaviors such as drinking, taking drugs, cutting themselves, developing obsessive-compulsive or eating disorders, or by withdrawing and disengaging.

Parents should be the first to suspect that something is not quite right, and decide whether to take their child for a psycho-educational assessment. Such testing is controversial. Parents may feel that they have learned how to work with their child at home, and that testing will only label him and subject him to even more anxiety. Testing tends to happen more in institutionally educated children because the teacher needs to know how to adapt curriculum type, delivery, and assessment for the individual child, once a disability has been identified and diagnosed. This personalized program is known by various terms, for example, the Individual Program Plan (IPP). Some parents feel the testing process is a positive step toward finding out whether they are providing adequate support.

In an ideal world, every student should have an IPP. This occurs naturally in homeschooling and unschooling. In school, it takes extra work by the teacher and the teacher aides, extra funding for specialized resources and materials, and extra supervision because the classroom teaching is designed to deliver to the class average.

Often parents start homeschooling because they have kids with a learning disability. But critics of the institutional system theorize that in many cases, children do not have a problem with learning—they have a problem with the setting. That it is the classroom environment that is broken, not the child's aptitude. Children who cannot stand the noise, lights, and busyness of a classroom often do fine when they are moved to a quieter environment; those who cannot focus on curriculum in school do well when they are allowed to follow their interests.

Much of learning "disability" is simply learning "difference." Home education focuses on what a child can do individually, not what he can't do in a classroom. Will these children succeed in postsecondary education? Yes! As children age and become more aware of healthy coping strategies, they learn to adapt to new environments—when the time is right. They certainly do not have to begin in Grade 1. And perhaps they won't be ready for university at age 17, but they will be at 20. There is no rush. Each child is ready on their own timetable.

Thomas Armstrong, in his book on multiple intelligences, *In Their Own Way*, shows how labels that describe a person can switch from a negative to a positive connotation, simply by reframing and renaming the concept: change learning-disabled to learning differently, hyperactive to energetic, impulsive to spontaneous, phobic to cautious, daydreamer to imaginative, irritable to sensitive, scattered to divergent, stubborn to persistent, immature to late-bloomer. ADD (Attention Deficit Disorder) describes a bodily-kinesthetic learner, dyslexic a spatial learner.

The government provides additional funding to support children diagnosed with a learning disability. Unfortunately, many times such funding is not directed to the child it was meant to support. The funding earmarked for that child may be directed to the school's central operation fund, and get diverted to other, more general needs, such as a teacher's aide who supports the entire classroom instead of the individual learner. Funding tagged to buy special software that reads textbooks may be diverted to the purchase of more science textbooks for all the students. It is little wonder that parents get frustrated with the lack of assistance and support in the classroom and decide that they can do better at home, providing the specific resources that will directly help their child.

Unfortunately, parents are penalized when they pull their child out of school. In many countries, there is no extra funding for home educating a child with learning disabilities. It is a testament to parents' love and devotion that they will forego an income and pay thousands of dollars out of pocket for educational support and materials to help their child learn at home, while still having to pay the school taxes that their children will never benefit from.

When we enrolled our son in Grade 2, we discovered, through testing, that he had a learning disability. His working memory and auditory processing were delayed. Our school board provided an IPP and a code, but because his condition was labeled as mild, they did not commit any funding. I pulled him out of school in Grade 3, knowing he would thrive in an individual program at home. When he reached high school age, he decided to attend a regular high school for the last one and a half years. The school had a special wing with a homeroom class that provided support similar to homeschooling. It had a teacher, a guidance counselor, and a social worker to help kids problem solve, and it provided a haven away from the regular school's stressful hallways. It was a quiet place to rest, de-stress, chat with an adult, and write exams. This helped him get through Grade 12.

One of the advantages of having our child coded early with a learning disability was the record of required supports. But coding can also be done in the Grade 12 year, before exit exams are written. Postsecondary institutions usually want an up-to-date psycho-educational assessment completed during the past three years, in order to provide support and appropriate accommodation. We found that unlike grade school, postsecondary support really does go directly to the learner. At university, my son had a personal tutor, a learning strategist to help him with schedules and time management, software that would read his textbooks to him, extra time to write his exams, and a place to go when he needed help. This was doubly reassuring to me because it was his first time living away from home. Having the support of the accessibilities office to help him navigate independent living and a special homeroom to help him with academics provided him with the support and comfort of an "external family."

Experts' opinions on home educating children with learning disabilities are all over the map. Some professionals are very supportive. When my son was diagnosed with anxiety, they made it clear that it was a biological brain chemical problem—that his brain just did not produce enough serotonin—and that his condition was not "caused by homeschooling." Other professionals insist that a child needs "professional (read 'paid') therapists and teachers in a school setting," although there is very little scientific evidence to back that up. I am not aware of any studies that conclude that a child does worse academically at home than in school if he has a diagnosed learning disability or a mental health problem.

It is very difficult for parents to let go of notions that have been drilled into them for so many years, such as "learning issues need to be caught early," and "some kids need direct teaching," even if there is little evidence to support their credibility. Children grow and change and their brains develop, which is why an educational assessment is only good for two or three years. Children with learning disabilities or mental health problems do not *need* schools or teachers—that is only one of many options. What these children do need is patience, above all else; kindness, healthy role-modeling, encouragement, individualized attention, and the three mainstays of unschooling: an adult facilitator, rich resources, and unstructured time. They will learn in their own way. A home environment to learn and play in could be just what your child needs, supported by professionals when necessary—cognitive behavior therapy, specialized tutoring, or even medication.

Tutoring

Tutoring is a $1 billion-a-year business in Canada these days (Stockland, 2018) and many large companies are profiting hugely from parental anxiety. Parents worried about fierce competition to get into university are sending even early elementary children to tutoring companies after school and on weekends. Play falls to the wayside.

"Parents often enroll [their children] in tutoring services when: 1.Grades drop and teachers are concerned about academic performance. 2.The child develops low self-esteem about his academic performance and begins to resist school, homework and learning. 3.The child begins to act up in class or withdraw to cope." This text is captured from a tutoring company's brochure. But these outcomes occur in institutional school settings, not in home education.

The best tutoring companies encompass many learning styles and make it fun. The worst ones shove fun-sucking worksheets at children, drilling them on facts and forcing them to memorize information. Tutoring rarely teaches kids problem solving, critical thinking, or creative knowledge-seeking.

There is one instance in which tutoring is beneficial: when a teen is preparing for high-stakes exams such as university and college entrance exams. Tutoring can help the student brush up on study skills, build confidence, and impart useful knowledge at a time when he is most motivated to learn. Other than that, tutoring can do more harm than good by increasing the risk of education burnout, when used for younger children.

Leaving junior high

Through unschooling, most children, without any formal instruction, "learn" the four arithmetical operations of addition, subtraction, multiplication, and division; the multiplication tables; fractions, percentages, and decimals; and how to write the simple five-paragraph essay. These skills will help them get through either traditional high school, which is more paper based, or a less formal experiential learning experience. If children are missing some of these basic skills by the end of their junior high age, don't worry. They still have plenty of time to learn them during the next four years. And if they don't, they probably didn't need them to live a full and productive life in the first place!

20

High School Ages 15 – 18: Investigate, Problem Solve, and Explore Careers

"Choose a job you love and you will never work a day in your life."
- Confucius, Philosopher

Textbooks or travel?

In high school, some parents scramble to get their kids to school and talk to them about course choices, streaming options, marks, credits, and career plans. They may resort to nagging about homework or signing up for tutoring, weekend exam prep courses, or summer school to retake courses and improve their marks. In extreme cases, some parents will do the homework themselves—and look the other way when they find out that their child cheated. Some parents argue with teachers over their child's marks and go to great lengths to make sure their child has a transcript that will get him into the best universities. Courses are sometimes chosen for an easy mark and not because the child has any interest in the subject. Parents eliminate chores so the child can concentrate on school—although in reality, he is probably partying—and part-time jobs and volunteering are discouraged because there is no time left after academic pursuits, sports, and social activities.

Unschooling parents, on the other hand, empower their children with the right to determine their career pathways. Some kids want a formal high school experience and enroll for the first time; some don't. What if kids showed up to the first day of formal high school as eager to learn as kids on the first day of Kindergarten? This really does happen in home education!

Research shows that as home-educated teens age, they long for more social contact and may enroll in a regular high school to interact with peers on a daily basis. Most homeschooling parents can't teach high school level subjects; they don't want to first learn the content in order to teach and explain, or they may have gone back to paid work and don't wish to take responsibility for monitoring their child's progress in an online or in a correspondence course. That does not mean the child cannot continue to learn at home—there are still many options.

Some unschooling kids self-teach courses and challenge exams; some don't. Parents supplement their children's learning with mentorships, part-time jobs, volunteering, field trips, travel, and courses. They continue to write the checks but are thrilled when the child can drive himself to courses he decides to take. They encourage the child's efforts and offer help and guidance with the child's experiences in taking exams, writing longer essays, and taking study notes. They welcome the alleviation of their own stress when a child takes full responsibility for his own education.

What we did

The Team of Thirty approached high school in various ways. Some took regular government-school courses online, by correspondence, or in physical classrooms for their entire high school experience. Others did a self-directed high school program, the student deciding how each course would be accomplished. In courses where students were able to demonstrate sufficient knowledge, they received government-granted marks and credits. Outcomes were met, even though the learning methods might have been unconventional. Other students studied textbooks and self-taught material, sometimes with the help of a hired tutor, and wrote the final diploma exams. Some did a mix of online—which in my opinion, without a live teacher, is pretty well self-taught anyway—physical classroom, self-taught, and exam challenge courses to attain their marks and credits.

Some did not take any official high school courses, and simply wrote the final exams. Some skipped the exams entirely and applied directly to community colleges. Some completed the entire three years of high school courses, and some took only the final year. The children decided what they wanted to do for this stage of their education.

High school is where "the rubber meets the road," according to schools. Marks are allowed to be waived by schools in Grades 1 to 9, according to the government, but in Grades 10 through 12, marks are used to stream students.

In our family, we took the "buffet approach." Rather than ask the kids where they wanted to go to for high school, we looked at what courses they would need for the path that interested them, and then researched the learning method that would best prepare them. Online text-taught? Self-directed? Challenge the exam only? Correspondence? Classroom-taught, or online live teacher-taught? Some courses lent themselves better to one format. For example, Sophie was strong in English. She had read books on writing her whole life. To take a whole one-size-fits-all English course would be a waste of her time and efforts. We decided that she would self-direct her Grade 12 English. She wrote the two personal response essays and two critical analysis essays that were worth 50 percent of her final mark; then she wrote the government exam that was worth the remaining 50 percent. The government monitors the teacher/parent/student-assigned course mark to make sure it is in range with the required diploma exam mark. She self-taught the rest of her courses or took them online.

Mathew needed a classroom experience with teacher-taught math. He took Math and Science in an adult high school upgrading school and self-taught all his other courses or took them online.

Neil was strong in Science. He took Physics through a correspondence course that allowed him to breeze through the assignment books and hand them in for the course mark, without having to waste his time doing busy work. Because he so wanted to take welding at the local high school and proprietary rules prevented home educators from using high school facilities, he registered for the full Grade 11 school year just to be able to take the welding course—unfortunately, the public school system requires an all-or-nothing registration. In the end, he found the welding course very prescriptive; the kids could not decide on their own projects and had to make something chosen by the teacher. He got through the year, then decided that since creativity was not only discouraged in the welding class, but denied, it was not worth signing up for another whole year of school. For the next year, he self-directed in English and pure mathematics.

Ryan either took online text-taught courses or self-taught courses. In fact, most of the on-line classes were effectively self-taught, as he never reached out to a teacher for help. He read the text from a screen or textbook, worked out problems through trial and error, and wrote the exams. He got the course marks and credits.

Anna was not an online learner. She self-taught Physical Education, food studies, and Special Projects. We had a co-op group of eight kids who would work on social studies and English projects together, and we parent-guided those areas. For Math and Science, Anna went to an upgrading school to take those subjects in a classroom setting.

Each child is a unique learner. Fortunately, unschoolers are able to take the buffet approach to personalized learning; unfortunately, a physical high school is not set up to accommodate unschoolers in taking one or two high school courses that interest them. Unschoolers must piece together courses from the various delivery methods offered outside of formal high schools.

A common question is, "Don't teenagers miss daily contact with friends?" At this age, teens find their friendship groups either through clubs they form (like the weekly computer club on Friday afternoons at our house) or projects that bring them together (like volunteering), or activities they join. Teens are very particular about who they socialize with. Unlike the elementary years, a parent can't just throw kids together and assume they will all get along. Some teens prefer daily contact with various social groups (unlike school, which is always the *same* social group) and some teens are more introverted and welcome social events only once or twice a week. Many unschoolers have large families and circles of friends, and the social events just happen when friends are over constantly. For example, my 16-year-old might have all of the following activities in a single week: volunteering one afternoon at the food bank with a certain group of friends, video game playing another afternoon at someone's house with another group of friends, movie discussion group one afternoon at the library with a third group of friends, Minecraft club at someone's house, and family board game night at home. Throw in a lesson, a sports activity, and a part-time job, and that is at least one event per day, with different social groups at each event. This provides a level of socialization diversity that is far richer than any in a school.

What you can do

Unschooling allows children to continue their self-directed education through the late teen years if they so choose. If they choose to go to a school full time, or take online classes, or self-teach, they are still technically unschooling because they are choosing their learning format. Many children never set foot in a classroom or school or take an online course; they apply directly to college or university. And that is fine too.

As this chapter title implies, I'm going to focus on children who wish to self-direct their education and pursue postsecondary education.

The high school years, in an institutional school, are somewhat more buffet-structured than the earlier grades, which makes it easier to personalize a pathway. Courses are four-month, 125-hour packages of study. Much like universities, course offerings and facilities vary among schools. Children chase courses where they find them, and may not be able to take all of their courses from a single school. They might choose two core courses from their own school, another from an online school, and a couple of options from a work experience center. The public or private school that they are registered with reports all the student's marks and credits to the government for inclusion on a central document called a transcript. The transcript indicates the code of the school where each course credit was granted, and also records the course and diploma exam mark for the Grade 12 subjects.

Cognitive development during this stage
Older teenagers, ages 15 – 18

In their older adolescence, teenagers demonstrate the following aptitudes and abilities:

- They become more serious academically.
- They employ abstract thinking, empowering them to philosophize and theorize.
- They can obtain a first job, driver's license, and can stay home alone overnight.
- Their critical thinking blooms; they are interested in the world's social, political, and economic news
- They can understand finances; they can do their own banking and taxes.
- They have a sense of omnipotence and grandiosity; they believe nothing will hurt them.
- They can take full responsibility for their schooling, including their homework.
- They can start planning for their future.
- They demonstrate 90 percent compliance in a respectful parent-child relationship.

Educational needs for this age

Older teens require small learning communities and a focus on career choices. Jobs, internships, volunteering, and apprenticeships are great for learning about the world and oneself. Tolerance and diversity are learned in the community, not in the classroom. Classrooms are all about conformity for social survival in a hierarchical structure—much like jail! In contrast, democratic communities have kind, experienced adults willing to mentor the next generation. This is a great time to begin entrepreneurial pursuits, engage in philosophical discussions, continue experiential learning, and of course, engage in physical activity. (Armstrong, 2006)

In classrooms, serious learning starts in high school. We know that adults learn best by experiencing new concepts through all five senses, but the job of managing 40 to 60 kids in a classroom does not lend itself well to experiential learning; most high school courses are still taught through basic transmittal techniques such as lecturing, or having students read from a book or screen and writing a test. (See "Cone of Experience" in Chapter 7)

Is a diploma required?

A diploma is a nice way for schools to cap their students' 12 years of education and it allows them to produce statistics on how well they have delivered public education, simply by counting the number of "graduates." However, there are no statistics that capture the number of students who quit high school and still go on to attend or complete higher education. And there are many!

A diploma is useful if one is going into the world of work at age 16 or 17. Companies routinely ask to see a diploma as a demonstration of grit and commitment. The military often requests a copy of a high school diploma. For most universities and colleges, a diploma is not an entrance requirement. They do require certain course completions. Once higher education is attained, very few companies or institutions will ever ask to see a high school diploma. Many people leave it off their resume. When students are applying for jobs and post-graduate studies, they will be required to produce their most recent certification, such as a college diploma or a bachelor's degree parchment. Consequently, many unschoolers do not have a high school diploma because they do not see the value in wasting time working toward filler credits rather than concentrating on the core courses they need for admission to a postsecondary institution.

Happy teens

"Teens aren't developmentally grouchy, but circumstantially grouchy."

Seems like an oxymoron—teens and happiness in the same sentence! But our teens were generally very happy, and continue to be happy as young adults. How do I know that my kids are happy? They sing! Constantly. They come into the kitchen for a snack and they dance! When there is more than one, I will sing the first line of a song such as, "Do you hear the people sing!" and they will finish off the whole song from *Les Miserables*!

When I taught parenting classes I would ask my group to come up with behaviors of what they would consider "The Dream Teen." Here are some attributes they often came up with. This list describes the Team of Thirty and many other unschooling teens that I have had the pleasure to know. The Dream Teen:

* Doesn't do drugs, steal, engage in crime, or vandalize.

- Uses alcohol, caffeine, and prescription drugs responsibly.

- Doesn't swear at family members, friends, or others.

- Is polite to peers, and younger and older people.

- Does chores and volunteers or works.

- Takes care of his own pet, clothes, accommodations, meals, appointments, banking, and health care.

- Participates in adult discussions, storytelling, and joke-telling.

- Participates in family outings, holidays, dinners, game nights, and celebrations.

- Helps with household chores and maintenance.

- Goes to bed at a reasonable hour, eats healthy, and takes care of himself.

- Chips in on family expenses.

- Doesn't hang at the mall or neighborhood stores, or on the street corner with rotten kids.

- Shares feelings of joy as well as his gripes, challenges, and fears, with trusted loved ones.

- Has a sense of humor.

- Complies with reasonable requests.

- Attends classes and gets good grades when he is motivated to do so; he does his homework and gets up in time for the bus without parental coaxing.

Close siblings and parents

In some junior high and high schools, there are "awareness classes" that teach parents how to tell if their children are taking drugs, drinking alcohol, or having sex. This speaks to the underlying assumption that parents have been urged by society and the media to back off from their children's education and hence, their main social circles and personal lives for the previous eight years. It assumes that they no longer know their children or their activities and friends, and that communication has broken down. Parents can maintain close ties with their children through the school years, but like any relationship, it takes hard work, non-punitive parenting, listening, and lots of relaxed time connecting with each other. Close family relationships are easier when teens homeschool because of the lack of peer pressure and the increased time together as a family.

Sibling relationships are also close, even in the teen years. Of course, they will have the odd scrap over issues, like the time my older son threw the cat down the stairwell at his brother who was standing four steps below him. The cat bared his claws and scratched my younger son, who still has the scar on his cheek! The difference between them and many other children is that they have the time and the parental support to work things out between siblings. It warms my heart when I see my 18-year-old son offer his jacket to my 15-year-old daughter on a snowy day; when my 17- and 18-year-old sons spend half the night talking to each other about gaming; or when my husband and I go on vacation and the kids go out to dinner together without us. The 20-year-old helps the 12-year-old build a gaming computer. Another sibling tutors his brother in math. The whole family chats and posts on Discord so when one member is away in another city, we remain connected and are a big part of each others' lives. None of our five teens ever slammed a door in our house. Because they are not age-graded, they accept each other as people, not as lesser beings. Our teens would happily ski with their grandfather. My son would have lunch with my daughter during the one year they were in different grades at the same high school. They weren't at least the bit worried about what their "friends" would think.

Can teens be too "good"?

Many unschoolers who have close relationships with their teens, but hear about all the teenage angst and drama going on with their friends and their children, wonder if their family experience is "normal." Are their teens going to want to experiment later, when the consequences could be more dire? Will their teens miss the partying in high school, and engage in it at postsecondary instead? Parent Angie raised her concerns, "I'm in the thick of the teen years and am starting to feel unsecure when comparing my teens to others. (I know that we shouldn't compare, but I do.) They just seem so untypical of 'conventional' teens and I'm wondering if it's the homeschooling effect or the non-punitive parenting effect. Are there other teens out there like mine or are we really weird? My children are so unlike the typical development benchmarks that books, media and professionals deem normal such as angst, rebellion, battles, 'attitude' and eye-rolling. They don't drink, smoke, have sex, drugs, or indulge in consumerism. I mean, they don't even experiment! I wouldn't feel so bad if it was only one child of mine like this, but it's all three. Anyone else notice this?" Angie got many responses from other parents of teens.

Lynn says, "In our house, my teens don't feel they need a lot of peer contact. All have at least one good friend but they don't need hoards of them. They are perfectly happy to spend every weekend home with us, and we play board games, watch movies and they play video games with their siblings. Daughter occasionally goes to sleepovers, but as an introvert, she values her time at home doing what she wants to do. They are all very social participants when out at teen events, but all three prefer to stay home. We joke that 'grounding' them would be a reward, not a punishment. They have lots of interests other than staring at their phones. When my kids encounter groups of school kids, they were a bit put off by the immaturity of the kids. They thought the kids only talked about 'trivial' things such as boys, make-up, dating, who was gossiping about who, getting drunk, etc."

Marnie said, "I think we raise children who question how teens are treated in our society. Is it right that one has to ask for permission to go to the bathroom? Is it right that a student be humiliated in front of the class for not doing homework when they had to work to support the family? Is it right that stores limit the number of teens that can enter at one time? Are teens so ingrained in the system, they don't know when they are being abused? I don't know at what point kids get used to this, but I suspect it's very early. I have raised questioning, respectful, rebels and it has affected how they view institutions."

Gina said, "Isn't it so cool how taking institutional school and punitive, conventional parenting out of the equation throws the 'typical development benchmarks' completely out of whack? I am the one who feels the kids need more friends. It's my issue, not theirs. Both have stated they have no intention of wanting to date until they are way older. My daughter wants to see if she can go her whole life without drinking. What is so wrong with us being the main influence in our kids lives? It wasn't so long ago that parents were the kids biggest influences."

Jody adds a reply to the mom, "I just think kids grow up SO fast now, and your description of your home life with your kids sounds so, I don't know, back in time a little I guess, to where values were predominant, and relationships with family were key. I love it that they sound 'content.' I spent so much time being restless (and still do) that being content seems good enough to me. I think having one or two close friends is better than a horde that aren't that close. They've just had so much more settled, connection family time than the average teen, that it seems to me they are so much better prepared to be in the world - they know what matters to them, they call frivolousness where they see it, and they know who they want to spend time with."

Elisabeth said, "In my younger years, I worked for a non-profit in Chicago that served immigrants and refugees from dozens of cultures. Practically without exception, families I met had the kind of relationships you described—teens were relatively content, calm, focused, non-peer oriented, etc. This was even true for the families with especially hierarchical structures. At least until they acclimated to American culture and schools, anyway. I particularly remember chatting with a Vietnamese teenage girl who was so bewildered by how all the other girls at school hated their mothers. She loved her mother. She wanted to help her mother. Her mother was her closest confidant. She saw that these other girls had been nurtured by their mothers their whole lives—why didn't they want to return the favor? I didn't know what to tell her. But I wanted to be her."

Lucy said, "My daughter thanked me again last week for creating our unschooling lifestyle. She too doesn't enjoy hanging out with typical teens and with any free time at her outdoor group she can be found hanging with the leaders (who treat her as a responsible adult). Last week we were regaled with stories about a 'day-in-the-life of the typical parent-teen relationship' about that very day, from one of the leaders, while waiting for the meeting to start; All the other girls were gathered as far away as physically possible from the adults, in the far corner of the gym. It's that kind of environment that can easily push teens to escape home and look to their peers for direction, fun, and love. Those teen behaviors may be typical, but I don't think they are 'normal'; they are reactionary."

Pam said, "It's bad if children are forced into being too good, but most don't react that way - they rebel. Perhaps your children are choosing to behave this way because it is what feels right for 'them.' They already know they have control over their lives, they don't need to push to envelope to prove it to anyone. Sure, they may try different things later, but that will again be of their choosing, not in reaction to you. And, as Linda said, they love and respect their life 'now' and I don't see that changing in the future to such an extent that they'll go overboard and suffer harsh consequences. Why would they choose that? To prove what to whom? It certainly ain't fun if there's harsh consequences involved."

Cindy said, "I think that unschoolers have a selection of contented, settled and confident young people who will move organically and seamlessly into the rest of their lives just as they have always lived. Having close relationships is the chocolate of life. Talk with middle-aged parents whose young adult children haven't spoken to them in 5 years and who refuse to answer the phone or the door when they call to see if you'd prefer the alternative."

Rhonda said, "Will your kids, later on as a result of being free, supported, loved and cherished, move into self-destructive behaviors they are not currently 'experimenting' with? Why? I mean, for what possible purpose would they seek out that kind of thing? They clearly don't want it now, for reasons of their own. Why, when they're more mature and more self-aware, and more capable of understanding long-term effects and risk assessment... why would they do 'more' later? If you have never given your kids anything to rebel against, why would they? Even the TV parenting experts have it wrong, thinking that a necessary stage of development is alienation from the family. Yes, it is 'ordinary' for teens to rebel and engage in stupid and dangerous behavior -- but it's not necessary, however popular it might be."

Wendy said, "They are not typical teens. Typical teens are so peer identified that their lives are ruled by peers. One of my friends remarked to me recently that it was nice to see teenagers who still liked their mothers and obviously enjoyed my company, they laugh at your jokes, she told me. They listen when you speak. There is no rebellion at my house, no attitude, no slamming doors and screaming, 'I hate you!' We get along and when we do argue we work it out. I don't pull the power trip of 'I'm the adult; my house, my rules.' We are respectful of one another. I don't think the typical teen receives that." Unschooled teens are different but not in a bad way.

Personalized learning

One of the best offerings from the government, that very few homeschoolers know about, is the Special Projects course. The course is offered in Grades 10, 11 and 12 and is a shell course for whatever interest the child might have and want to learn more about. It is innovative and great, but Special Projects should not be limited to only 15 credits. I think that an entire self-directed high school program should be Special Projects if the child desires. We have taken full advantage of this option, as have many other homeschooling families. My children have used the following as their Special Projects:

- Helping Dad with a basement renovation
- Traveling to another country
- Writing a book
- Editing the aforementioned book

- Learning to code C++ programming and building a gaming computer
- Reading 42 novels from a favorite author
- Making woodworking projects
- Volunteering in community projects
- Starting a business
- Building a festival entry
- Reaching platinum level in League of Legends and applying the knowledge to game design and coding. (Yes, videogaming is educational and should count as learning for credits.)

Here is an example of a Special Projects Course Plan for those who have to submit proposals for government approval. The students give themselves the final mark based on their self-reflection.

Special Projects Grade 10 Title: Computer Project

Scope of project and objectives:

Time: 125 Hours   Credits: 5   Course Date: July 1 - December 31

Neil would like to continue designing websites and improve the design and implementation of the two websites he created. He will learn computer programming in Java and C++. He will explore possibilities for the future of the web.

Methods:

Neil will update the design continuously on two websites, attend computer camp for two weeks, and participate in a Homeschooling mentorship computer programming club.

Assessment:

Neil will provide:

- a certificate of completion of 80 hours (2 weeks) of Computer Camp. Neil will provide website addresses of two re-designed websites.
- a list of books and internet sites that provided advice and information on web design and development.
- a log of hours spent designing and updating websites.
- a log of time in the Homeschooling mentorship computer programming club.

Special Projects is not advertised to students in a physical high school because the school cannot finance a teacher to supervise an individual student or give marks or credit assessments, as there is no guide or rubric for marking. It would just be a headache for administration, especially with very little funding attached. It is just easier not to offer it to school students.

In fact, schools have no assessment process for any learning outside of their well-prescribed programs. My daughter's friend takes a lot of extracurricular dance lessons that she should receive in-curricular credit for, but does not. If a child takes a computer animation class from the local science center, or a continuing education jewelry-making class from a local college, or volunteers at the soup kitchen, he gets no credit. If he watches 20 TED Talks, or plays guitar in his church choir, or studies web coding from a free online website, he gets no credit. If he takes swimming lessons from the local pool or tutors junior high kids in math, or learns German by Duolingo, he gets no credit. If he reads 50 novels in addition to the single one he must read for Grade 11, he gets no credit. High schools can't possibly offer the array of learning that is now available, literally, at the child's fingertips.

Even option courses in a physical high school are government-prescribed. "Option courses offer competencies such as better critical thinking, problem solving, digital fluency, collaboration and leadership," says a government official. (Bolender, 2007) But many "options" could be undertaken at home in the kitchen, in daycares, in offices, in trade shops, and in small businesses much more effectively than by studying from a workbook or module book and filling out assignment sheets. Even video games offer the benefits just listed.

Right now, the system is still rigid. Kids basically have two choices. Sign up for a physical high school and do your three years of time, or consider one of many other ways to get to postsecondary, while studying your true passion.

Attending regular high school as an unschooler

Many children decide to quit their unstructured days and attend a physical high school as an unschooler. Three of my children decided at some point to do this to see what it was like. Two quit to return to unschooling at home.

In Grade 10, Neil entered high school at a private self-directed school with only 50 students. He would go for two days a week for certain subjects, and work at home for the rest of the week. He liked the friends, but he didn't like the busywork he had to do because the school was forced to use government curriculum. The next year, at 16, Neil went to a large public high school, with a student population of 2200 kids, for Grade 11. He made a few friends but hated going every day. He liked the discussions in Grade 12 Social Studies and liked the Science classes. He didn't like the disrespectful attitude of some of the students. He walked into the bathroom one day and saw poop smeared on the walls. At Halloween the teacher would hand out candy to the students and most of the wrappers would end up on the floor. He tallied the number of f-words that he heard in one day and counted about 30. He found it difficult to integrate into the cliques. His teacher said that he was the only person who said "thank you" after he got off the bus from a field trip. Neil's Biology teacher said to me in a parent-teacher interview that he was really mature and very ready for university. Neil didn't go back for Grade 12, choosing instead to self-teach and take online courses.

It was interesting to note that this school of 2200 kids needed to get parents out to the school council meetings. They managed to get eight parents on the school council. I joined too. Four of those eight parents were former homeschooling parents—I guess we like to stay involved in our kids' lives!

In Grade 11, Mathew entered a high school with a special program, after managing his anxiety during puberty. He was very mature and he tolerated the other students, but he was happy to get out of there. His teachers always said that he was polite, kind, and very conscientious. When he was 17, he actually got a Christmas present from his bus driver. I thought it would be the other way around!

Sophie entered Grade 10 at the same large high school for the purpose of enjoying the variety of options it offered, such as fashion, welding, and foods. Taking those courses in a school with a class was much more fun than taking them solo online. It was the same with social studies. She wanted a big classroom that would offer discussions on various topics. She found that going from three hours a week for online courses in math and three more in science, to 30 hours a week sitting in a building, plus five more hours for bussing every week, took a big chunk of her time. Then they applied homework. When she refused homework, her marks dropped and she left the school to self-study at home.

As a home-educated child who was used to having adults listen to her, Sophie felt very comfortable standing up against injustice. In one instance, when a fellow student was caught drawing on her desk, the Social Studies teacher punished that child by making her clean all the desks in the classroom. Sophie and another girl got up to help her clean.

Another aspect of school that the children disliked was not being allowed to have any spares. Free time was not allowed because statistically, "some students might get into trouble," and so no students were permitted free time! I personally think it is because the government funds the schools according to the number of students per course, so if students have a spare, they are not taking a course in that time slot, ergo the school misses out on that funding.

After being at home for Grade 11, Sophie decided to try a "self-directed" school for Grade 12 because I wanted her to have the "grad" experience. Unfortunately, her short-lived sojourn in the Grade 12 classroom deprived her of that!

In the end, Sophie did have the grad and prom experience after all—the very small school that supervised our home education program had a beautiful graduation ceremony for the three kids who were presented with diplomas. They were encouraged to make a speech, dress formally for the dinner, and invite all their family members attend. It was held in one of the banquet rooms of our beautiful zoo and it was so lovely and personal. Much better than the canned grads that high schools plan for 600 kids, where each child gets just a moment of stage time.

When I was feeling discouraged about how much my kids hated high school, and hence, I thought, would probably hate any future formal education (that old projection thing we parents do!), my husband would reply, "They are smart kids—they will figure it out!"

I worried about how Sophie would adjust to university life after that cozy online/self-directed high school experience she had, but she did just fine at university. She even spent two years in residence away from home, living and socializing. In her words, "University is *way* better than high school. In many more ways, they treat you as the adult you are."

I sat down with my friend, a high school math teacher, for tea the other day and discovered some interesting things about how high schools are run since Sophie's experience. She explained to me:

In regular high school classes, 25 percent of a class is expected to fail. The curriculum is too heavy and the teachers have no time to help the students. They are expected to present a new concept every day. About 25 percent of the top kids will "get it"—they are the ones who can naturally self-teach, or learn anything from a screen or correspondence course and easily understand new concepts. Teachers love those students because they are motivated to learn and they make teaching easy. That leaves 50 percent of the class that will take 100 percent of the teacher's time.

I used to think my kids were missing out on exciting high school science experiments. I remember dissecting a fetal pig and loving the experience. Now there are no science experiments in high school, because it's "too dangerous" to have 40 kids stuffed in a lab with glass instruments and Bunsen burners going! It's safer to show them a video of experiments, even though we all learn better through experience.

What do they do all day?

Even if kids follow a more structured self-directed plan, formal high school learning only takes two hours a day. What else do teens do? The bonus in many of the following activities is that they can be enjoyed with siblings or parents:

- Play board, computer, and video games.

- Read everything they can get their hands on and investigate topics on the internet.

- Read opinion forums such as Reddit and watch TED Talks on YouTube.

- Work, volunteer, travel, or start a business.

- Play a musical instrument and learn a language.

- Work on projects and renovations, fix household items or cars.

- Shop, do chores, cook dinner, drive siblings to their activities.

- Go out for lunch and to movies with their friends

- Go to the gym, ride bikes, go for a walk.

14 pathways into postsecondary institutions

"If you want to live in society, sometimes you have to play society's game of jumping through hoops. Life is more difficult if you don't. Figure out how to get what you need, but within hoops you can live with." — Paul Smith, Unschooling Dad

There are no shortcuts. One must be adequately educated to apply for postsecondary admittance, but school courses are not the only way to demonstrate competencies. Schools must expand beyond the traditional territorial control over conferring credentials and acknowledge that people can and do learn in unconventional ways.

The later teen years, from 15 - 18, are the home run of education. Teens learn the abstract ideas that will challenge their thinking and belief structure as adults. For many school children who have been coerced into learning and producing output, education is boring, irrelevant, and an impediment to living their daily lives in the way that they would like. They power down their efforts and enthusiasm. This is unfortunate, because these are the years that count—these final years of publicly funded education, when they should be powering up their efforts and increasing their knowledge base and critical thinking skills.

The 14 pathways into postsecondary institutions that I am about to discuss are based on Canadian requirements. They are considered general routes and are mirrored elsewhere, although specific requirements vary country to country. In this section, I'm going to use the term "postsecondary" to mean all postsecondary, or tertiary, educational institutions: universities, colleges, arts colleges, bible colleges, community colleges, trade schools, and technical schools.

In applying to postsecondary institutions in Canada, the Grade 12, or final year, marks are the most important set of grades. These are the ones that count. Most all postsecondary institutions now require aspirants to apply online, and there are no fields for inputting Grade 10 and 11 course marks—they are not interested in them. (They will, however, look at Grade 10 and 11 marks to assess applications for scholarships; see the Scholarship section.) Most universities want to see the course marks for English, Social Studies, Science, Math, and one option—Language or an extra Science—at the final year level. Of these five courses, only one is mandatory for university entrance in Canada and that is English, at the academic level for university entrance and at the applied level for entry into colleges, trade schools, and technology schools. The average mark of these five courses is the student's "competitive application average mark."

Most postsecondary institutions do not demand a high school diploma as an entrance requirement. They do require certain course completions. Neil was in his second year of university when he achieved his high school diploma. He had been missing one credit he picked it up with an option course while he was already at university.

Certain programs may require certain courses, whether they seem relevant or not. For example, one technology school required STEM math for a welding program—not because there was a lot of math required, but because the entry into the program was highly competitive, and the course requirement was a justifiable method of disqualifying some of the applicants.

Marks are also a good way to sort. Many STEM fields are very competitive now, and the schools base their cut-off competitive average mark on the number of applicants for a given term. If a school's engineering program entrance competitive average mark is 91%, then that will be the cut-off. Applicants with a competitive average lower than 91% will not likely be accepted. Timing is important as well; the following year, the cut-off might be 88%. External circumstances can also influence the cut-off mark. In the year that our province suffered a devastating flood, and in another year a disastrous fire, postsecondary institutions raised their target competitive averages because Grade 12 diploma exams—which often pull down a student's marks—were canceled in some areas. Volunteer work, leadership, and community engagement are generally not taken into account; often, application software does not even include fields to input them. They are, of course, considered when the application software includes these fields; and they are very important in scholarship applications. However, they will only supplement, and never replace, those five mandatory course marks.

The good news is that anyone can get into the postsecondary education system today if they so desire, regardless of their educational history. If students are motivated, they will succeed. Following are the 14 most common routes into a postsecondary institution. If your child has a goal in mind, I do urge you to work with him or her to investigate the specific requirements at the institutions they are considering.

1. Parent- or self-directed transcript and diploma

One route is to complete a traditional, "parent-directed," home education high school program with a parent-issued transcript. Keep in mind that governments do not recognize "student-led" under home education because students are considered minors, under the guardianship of a parent or caregiver, until age 16. Legally, a minor cannot be in charge of his own education so "unschooling" is officially labeled under "parent-directed" home education. Once a child reaches the age of 16, she can legally make the decision to quit school if she so desires; and if she does stay in school, she can be categorized as "student-directed" until government funding ends on September 1 of the year she turns 20.

Many families do not care whether their children's studies line up with the official government program of studies. If parents and students do not want or need any type of transcript, they simply follow the basic goals of education as described in the (*SOLO*), *Schedule of Learning Outcomes for Students Receiving Home Education Programs That Do Not Follow the Alberta Programs of Study*, just as for Grades 1 to 9.

Some parents issue marks for their child's self-directed work, and then devise a transcript and a diploma, calling it by a school name to represent their "family home school." As this document is not issued by the government, it may not be universally recognized. You must check the individual postsecondary institution's policy on accepting parent-issued transcripts and diplomas.

This route into postsecondary institutions may be the most difficult one, as it may also require an interview and the submission of a portfolio. Many institutions want credentials from a "recognized educational jurisdiction," or at least, to have the transcript evaluated by an independent recognized source. Contact your school board to find out if it is accredited to perform this evaluation.

All accredited schools have a school code, which appears next to each course on a government-issued transcript. This code will indicate to postsecondary institutions whether a parent-issued transcript has been vetted and approved by an accredited body. It is not worth pretending to be a school; this is considered fraudulent. It is better to be upfront and indicate that you are submitting a home education parent-issued transcript. On government-issued transcripts, all courses are school-coded, so a transcript that records a "buffet" education approach, as in our case, will have many different school codes recorded on it. One school supervised our self-taught food science courses; their school code is next to that course on the transcript. Another taught Biology online; their school code appears next to that course. When our child self-taught chemistry, the supervising school that evaluated and marked his work and issued the credit entered their school code next to the course.

If you are going to submit a parent issued transcript, you should:

- Contact the postsecondary school to find out how they assess home education students. They may require a portfolio, an interview, an essay, or references.

- Prepare a transcript listing at least five of the core subjects of Math, English, Biology, Chemistry, Physics, General Science, Social Studies, Geography, History, and options such as physical education, art, music, travel, or others. On the transcript, list what was studied in the past three high school years. For English, list the books read and the types of essays written. For Math, list the concepts completed, vectors, for example. List all the concepts covered under each subject.

- Assign a grade for each subject and indicate the grading rubric: for example, A = 80 percent of subject matter understood, B = 70 percent of subject matter understood, C = 60 percent of subject matter understood, D = 50 percent of subject matter understood; note that D is still a passing mark.

- Have the transcript validated by a recognized source. You will have to submit essays and work done, and perhaps exams, to support the mark on the transcript. Get a certificate of evaluation and an official signature. We are in an era of education assessment being about credential evaluation and not necessarily about teaching, because so many students can teach themselves.

Assembling a Portfolio

A student should begin assembling a portfolio at the Grade 9 level, or age 14. Here are some suggestions for a student on starting and maintaining a portfolio:

- First, research both general and home education admission policies at postsecondary institutions that could be of interest, to ensure your portfolio includes any specific requirements of those institutions.

- Visit university open houses, which provide great insight into what programs of interest might require of a prospective student, aiding in the content and organization of the portfolio.

- If possible at this stage, decide on your ultimate goal: would you be more interested in an arts, humanities, or a STEM program?

- Start a formal spreadsheet, or chart, and list all topics learned for each subject: English, Math, Social Studies (Geography, Sociology, History are all listed under Social Studies in Canada, but may be separate subjects in the US), Biology, Chemistry, Physics, and Earth Science. Keep records for Physical Education, Languages and Arts, Music, and special interests not included under the subjects listed.

- Consult government course descriptions for lists of curriculum topics by grade and level.

- Keep all work product. Arrange to have a teacher, tutor, or professor examine and evaluate it.

- Keep a list of all learning activities such as jobs, start-up businesses, travel, and volunteer work; and use education "lingo" to translate them into course names.

Following are areas to work on in order to amass a portfolio showcasing your knowledge and competencies. It's okay if you have no prior experience with them; you can begin studies in these areas can begin from age 14.

English Language Arts (reading, writing, speaking, viewing, presenting, and listening)

- For English, read anything and everything, but include more challenging texts as you progress. Read classic literature. Do close reading of both prose and poetry. Write reviews. Identify how the author conveys meaning and what observations he or she is making about life. Examine and explain tone, point of view, and bias. Using figurative language, analyze and comment on a book's setting, motivation, character development, conflict and resolution; and especially, its theme and thesis. Also read news and journal articles, studies, textbooks, reviews, and non-literature fiction and non-fiction.

- Reading helps you write. All university courses need strong writing skills, no matter what program you are entering. My son thought he had taken his last English class when he went into Science, but even scientists needs to write research and funding proposals! Practice different types of informal writing such as business emails, letters to newspapers and government representatives, book and film reviews, and blog postings. Practice writing formal essays and speeches. Write and analyze poetry; study its structure. Conduct analyses of various types of visual representations such as cartoons, films, photography, and presentations. Begin regular academic essay writing, paying attention to the different types: persuasive essays, research reports, comparison-and-contrast essays, personal response essays, and critical analysis essays. Learn different citation formats such as APA, MLA, and Chicago style. Learn how to write with structure, organization, style, and proper punctuation and grammar.

- Joining a club such as Toastmasters will teach you public speaking skills, impromptu speaking skills, presentation skills using PowerPoint and Prezi, speech-writing skills, and effective evaluation skills to give honest, constructive, and encouraging feedback. You will also learn valuable leadership and organizational skills, networking skills, effective meeting etiquette, and the basics of *Robert's Rules of Order.*

- Learn and practice interpersonal communication: active listening, assertiveness, problem solving in groups, conflict resolution, and reaching consensus.

- Look for other opportunities to present your learnings: volunteer groups, the Optimist Club, PechaKucha, and TEDx venues.

- Join a debate club to hone your listening and arguing skills.

- Join a book club for practicing listening and oral discussion.

- Document all of the above activity in the English section of your portfolio.

Mathematics

- Study a Math program beginning at a Grade 8 level that includes the topics currently required: basic arithmetic, exponents, algebra, order of operations, place value, decimals, fractions, integers, expressions, percentages, statistics, probability, geometry, measurement, rate and ratio, factoring, polynomials, linear and quadratic functions, systems of equations and higher order pre-calculus, calculus and linear algebra.

- Learn basic financial literacy: stocks, bonds, mutual funds, compound interest, credit card interest, and other terms and instruments.

- Continue studying Math from Grade 8 onward. For STEM programs, continue on to learning calculus at the Grade 12 level.

Science

- Focus on Earth and Environmental Sciences, Biology, Chemistry, and Physics.

- For sciences and maths, choose one type of curriculum to follow through Grades 10 to 12 to avoid gaps. Speed through the concepts that are easy for you and spend time on those that are not. Read textbooks, practice questions, and write the tests. Get a tutor to help; seek out resources on the internet. Get previous exams and practice writing them.

- Do labs and write reports.

Social Studies

- For Social Studies, read a national newspaper and magazines such as The Economist, Time, and Maclean's for current events. Read the news section as well as the opinion articles. Read academic journals. Watch controversial films and documentaries. Examine political cartoons and photo essays. Identify themes, bias, and beliefs and values. Have discussions at the dinner table on politics and social policies as well as world events.

- Know the types of political systems and their basic characteristics: democracy, liberalism, communism, totalitarianism, etc.

- Be sure you know where the continents, countries, and major cities are, and some basic characteristics of those countries such as economic and political systems, exports, ecosystems, habitat, culture, and religion.

- Follow politics. Be aware of North American political systems and the major parties. Be aware of the political, religious and economic history of other countries. Know the "isms" of social studies, such as feminism, nationalism, and patriotism.

- Attend seminars hosted by colleges, museums, libraries and speaker series. Identify their biases and the structure of their arguments.

- If so inclined, take a course in logic in order to understand effective argument.

Option Courses

- Get volunteer placements at companies and non-profits to build your skills and knowledge.

- Learn a second language.

- Seek internships and job shadowing opportunities.

- Take an adult-learning university course.

- Enter a competition in an area that interests you, for example, robotics or NaNoWriMo.

- Sign up for special camps and activities hosted by universities or community groups.

- Offer tutoring services to the public.

- Start a company.

- Complete a certification course in cooking, coding, horseback riding, Toast-masters, lifeguarding, coaching, etc.

- Log hours in lessons and practice for an art, sports, music, drama, language course; or for credit in option courses.

Essential Skills

- Develop the skill of learning independently from a textbook, or online text. Read closely and take notes. This is the most important skill one can practice for higher level formal learning.

- The second most important skill is learning how to take an exam.

For parents, this list must look formidable! What if your child doesn't want to do any of these? No problem. When children are motivated to apply to postsecondary schools, they often look for ways to improve their portfolio. If they don't, perhaps they are not ready yet. A motivated child can do most of the things listed above in one or two years. That's a very short time compared to 13 years of regular school! Be sure to document and save any proof of the child's work to turn into marks and credits when the time comes.

2. Submit student-directed coursework for a government-issued transcript and diploma

Under the same route but with a different twist is the traditional, parent-directed, student-led homeschooling high school program that meets the government outcomes and will be accredited with a government-issued transcript and diploma.

This is what we did for most of the English, social studies, physical education, and options course requirements. The school principal assesses the personalized work a child does in self-teaching high school level subjects; the school confers or validates the student's self-given marks and credits for completed work done and submits it to the government for an official transcript. Even though the work is personalized, for it to be government recognized it must demonstrate that the child has mastered the outcomes of the government programs of study in each course. The school may insist that the child write a school-supervised final exam worth 50 percent of the final mark and accept the parent- or student-assessed mark for the remaining 50 percent.

I think this is a nice balance between the objective measure of the exam and the daily observation and measurement from parent and student of how well he understood the course content. To those who question, "What if parents give a higher mark than the student deserved?" I suggest that nobody wins when cheating occurs. The child may finish the course but will not be successful in postsecondary if he lacks the knowledge and skills he should have learned in the course. And yes, that child may initially take a spot in university from someone more deserving, but he won't be there past Christmas of the first semester if he is not qualified. We must trust parents and students to self-mark appropriately, and studies show that they do. Alfie Kohn, in his talk in Calgary, stated that research shows that when students self-mark, they are even slightly harder on themselves than when teachers mark their work. (Kohn, 2009)

It has been my experience, in watching my kids apply to 12 different Canadian universities, that the schools all wanted "official" transcripts directly transferred from the government education department. Schools in our province pull them directly from the government website, where students upload their common government course code, and marks and evaluators verify them with the issuing school that supervised the home education program. Out-of-province and out-of-country schools wanted the transcripts mailed directly from the government. No photocopies were allowed, and the transcripts did not pass through either the parents' or the students' hands. Official copies of transcripts look like birth certificates. They have a standard color, type of paper, signature, and seal. Even scholarship applications will not accept photocopies; they want original, official transcripts.

To obtain a government-issued transcript

Students must prove that the course outcomes have been achieved. We are lucky in that our province's educational system is based on outcomes only. How students meet the outcomes is up to them. They can choose the resources, methods, and curriculum and personalize them. Be sure to keep essays, chapter questions and answers, exams, quizzes, and other course work to submit for outcome evaluation should it be required.

Have the course work accessed by someone familiar with self-taught learning and subject matter expertise. We had the same course evaluated by two different teachers at different schools; one teacher deemed it an academic course and another teacher deemed it a skills-level course because it was too personalized. Teachers have biases too, so get a second opinion if you or the student think the work is not assessed fairly. You have the right, as you are the one to witness the daily learning strengths and challenges of the student, not the school. Your "professional" opinion as a home education parent expert matters!

3. Write the SAT, ACT or Grade 12 equivalent exams

In our province of Alberta, we have mandatory Diploma Exams in Grade 12, for the core subjects of Math, English, Social Studies, Sciences and Languages. All students across the province who want a Grade 12 mark in a core subject must write the exam; and if they want a high school diploma, they must write the English and Social Studies exams. When my three oldest children wrote them, they were worth 50 percent of the final course mark; in 2015, the weighting was changed to 30 percent of the final course mark.

The exam questions go through a year of review by a committee, and then are field tested for bias, confusion, and discrimination. All students in the province write the exams at the same time on the same day. For example, all Alberta students write the Chemistry exam on June 25 from 9 a.m. to noon. To eliminate cheating, all students get the same essay question for English on Tuesday, June 13 from 9 a.m. to noon. Schools cannot unwrap the sealed exams before the time of writing, so even they do not know what is on the exam. The completed tests are sent to the government for the essays to be marked by two independent teachers not affiliated with the school; a computer marks the multiple-choice sections. If the two teachers' marks are too far apart, a third teacher will re-mark the exams. The Science and Math exams are multiple choice and short answer. The Social Studies and English exams are half multiple-choice and half essay questions.

These exams are the best quantitative research on the value of unschooling as an education alternative because children 19 years of age or older as of September 1 of the current school year are considered mature students and may challenge the government diploma exams without taking government prerequisite courses. The diploma exam mark will then stand for 100 percent of the final course mark and credits—without ever having taken the course. This allows every unschooler to bypass the Grade 1 - 12 education system.

If a mature student does take a Grade 12 course, the final course mark will be the better result of either 100 percent of the diploma exam mark, or the combination of course and exam mark. In certain instances, credits and marks may be awarded retroactively for grade 10 and 11. This proves the knowledge and competencies that have been obtained outside the school system. Any person aged 19 or older may demonstrate their knowledge acquired from any source, including unschooling, and apply to any postsecondary institution with recognized government credentials. Every country, province, and state should offer this ability to challenge the government exams in place.

Why do children have to wait until age 19 to demonstrate their self-directed knowledge? Why can they not write these exams at age 14 or 16? It's a question of job protection. First, if students don't need to take high school courses, the school doesn't get funded, and teachers don't get paid. So most parents and students do not even know that children can simply challenge exams. This policy is heavily influenced by teachers' unions and school board associations. The second reason is public perception. The government does not want to give children the opportunity to demonstrate their knowledge before the typical high school period, as it would beg the question, "What do we need schools for? Can kids learn without teachers? Can parents do just as good a job at high school level as teachers?" Home education parents know the answer to all three questions is a resounding yes, but the general public does not, because kids are not given the chance to prove it. At age 19, the government could say, "Oh, the student has been out of school for a year; they must have acquired their knowledge as a mature student." Age, antiquated policies, and job protection should not hold a child back from challenging the exams. The government must allow all children to demonstrate their knowledge and continue their educational path as they become ready and as they choose. Children's best interests must take precedence over all else.

The exams are the best objective indicator of whether the child knows the material well enough, regardless of by what means she acquired it, to continue on to postsecondary studies.

The average exam mark across all subjects and all students in Alberta is 65%. My unschooled children's average over a total of 20 diploma exams was 78%. One of my children had to write six exams because he took three science courses in addition to Math, English and Social Studies.

If a state, province, or country does not have final leaving, or diploma, exams to demonstrate acquired learning, students can write the SATs: Scholastic Aptitude Tests, or ACTs: American College Tests. If they have the knowledge, they should be given the opportunity to prove it. These exams originated in the US but can be written worldwide and are generally accepted by universities and colleges. The SATs and ACTs are scheduled several times a year.

4. High school Course Challenge

A child under the age of 19 cannot challenge the exam. They must prove that they have done some course work. The government calls this a Course Challenge. "A Course Challenge permits any senior high school student to challenge the outcomes of a course by participating in a formal assessment process in lieu of actually taking the course. The Course Challenge acknowledges that learning happens in a variety of settings, not just in schools. Students younger than age 19 on September 1 may challenge a Grade 12 level course on the recommendation of a parent and the supervising school board. There is flexibility in course work for high school subjects. Discuss the degree of flexibility allowed with your prospective school board." (Alberta Education, 2016) In my opinion, if a student has to jump through the hoops of a Course Challenge—and some of the challenge requirements that I have seen are as much work as actually taking the course—she should skip the challenge and simply write the diploma exam when she is older.

5. Complete only Grade 12 courses

Another route is to unschool for Grades 10 and 11 and then take the full formal Grade 12 level courses in a teacher-taught classroom, online, or self-taught. This would be Grade 12 Math, English, and Social Studies, plus a science or second language. Some courses build on previous levels; others do not and consist of stand-alone topics. If the government is funding courses, they insist that prerequisites must be met until a certain age. This is common to most provinces and countries.

At the age of 20 on September 1 of a given year, any student may take the Grade 12 level of any course without taking the Grade 10 and 11 prerequisites. The premise is that once a child is no longer government funded, she can gamble her own money—$600—on purchasing a Grade 12 course, hoping she can pass it. This is pretty easy to do as Social Studies, English, and Biology are stand-alone topics. English topics build competencies, so skipping Grade 10 and 11 will not affect a child's performance if she has good essay-writing skills and reads a lot. Math and sciences are more difficult courses to take without prerequisites, but if a student has taught herself the skills and knowledge leading up to the Grade 12 course, she will do fine. Many workbooks and online videos are available to teach the course and when motivated, kids can work through them pretty quickly. Textbooks can be purchased from Amazon. As the final Grade 12 diploma exams are based on government outcomes, it might be best to work with government-approved textbooks and learning guides, supplemented with resources from the internet. My kids used the official textbooks and relied heavily on Kahn Academy videos to help them through Math and Science.

6. Complete the five core subjects in Grade 10, 11, and 12, but no diploma filler courses

Not all children fare well on exams, and they may want to do the course work in all the grades of high school, not just Grade 12. Some may need a good foundation in Math or English and would benefit from a full-course approach—teacher-, parent-, or self-taught. They might take the Grade 10, 11, and 12 course progression in Math, English and Social Studies, plus sciences and one option. This will net them about 75 credits. This is not enough for a high school diploma, but they will save time and effort by concentrating on getting the best possible marks in the cores. They will not have to waste time acquiring 100 credits for a diploma by taking the mandatory filler courses such as career and life management, physical education, or career and technology "taster" option courses that are necessary to get the diploma.

Unschooler's interests may be in anything from cooking to fashion design, writing, hockey, family law—anything, really—and if they prove to a supervisor that they learned something, they can get marks and credits for the interest rather than having to take a school options course. This may complete enough credits for them to get a high school diploma without any effort that isn't already being expended in simply exploring and enjoying the interest. The key is to find a supervisor who understands the philosophy of self-directed education and will grant credits for education outside of rigid prescribed courses. Unschoolers aren't looking for shortcuts. They just want credits and marks for activities they are already doing and that they naturally enjoy.

If a child is not planning for postsecondary education, this might be a good way to fulfill the high school diploma requirements that some employers still require.

7. Get the GED — General Educational Development Diploma, or high school equivalent

Any student 18 years of age or older can apply to get credits for the GED. Fewer core courses are required at the Grade 10 and 11 levels, but all are required at the Grade 12 level and although the 100 credits can be attained through filler courses, travel, reading, or study, there seem to be more options than those offered by a regular high school diploma. But this route seems like a lot of work for a GED-designated diploma, which is still often stigmatized as being less worthy than a traditional high school diploma.

The other way to get a GED is to pass five tests in the four core subjects (English has two tests). The GED tests are not the same as the diploma exams, which measure specific Grade 12 topics and course material. "The GED tests measure your ability to understand and reason rather than how well you recall facts. The emphasis in the GED tests is on comprehension, application, analysis, and evaluation of reading material and data. Through an accumulation of education, work, travel, reading, and other life experiences, some people may have sufficient knowledge to pass the GED tests without special preparation." (Alberta Education, 2016)

8. Adult high school upgrading

Students are granted only three years' attendance in a government-funded high school because of space limitations. Although children are entitled to a funded education in most provinces until age 20, between the years of 18 and 20 they must attend special adult schools to pick up high school courses that cannot obtained in a high school. Many students who partied, or dropped out, or just want to get a better mark by taking the course again with a more mature brain, attend adult upgrading classes. These are designed for adults aged 18 – 100, although some will allow unschooling or home-educated children as young as 15. They do, however, discourage the younger ages because the classes are serious and full of focused adults who do not want class clowns disrupting their valuable teacher access time. However, if maturity can be proven, the kids that are allowed in do very well.

These schools recognize that adults have busy lives and limited time to study, so they teach the minimum needed in order to pass the course. This benefits the students in that homework is limited or non-existent, as adult students often have jobs and families. Many high school courses are offered in a single fast-track block, such as Chemistry Grade 11/12, resulting in students getting their marks and credits in one semester rather than over a full year.

Another benefit is that with mostly adult students, schools' liability policies allow really cool science experiments such as dissecting an eye, and field trips that are considered too dangerous for children under age 18. When my kids needed a classroom teacher but didn't want the full-time school experience, they picked up a class here and there from upgrading schools. There were no bullies or cliques; the teachers were experienced and kind, and the students were treated as adults. The classes only took a few hours per week and were funded until the child reached age 20.

Students get full course marks and credits at the high school level, which qualify for many high school-to-university scholarships such as the Alexander Rutherford Scholarship. If the same course is taken at a postsecondary, it is considered a university upgrading course rather than a high school course and is not eligible for inclusion in a scholarship application.

9. Apply to community colleges

Many colleges do not have prerequisites and children can apply at any age. A good example is Athabasca University, where a child of 16 can apply with no educational background. While they offer four-year degree programs, a child can also take a full first year and then transfer to another university for a degree program not offered at Athabasca. Many unschoolers take this pathway—they do a year or two at a community college, get good marks, acquire some option and humanity courses, and then transfer to the university program they want, either in a STEM or an Arts or Humanities field.

10. Challenge individual university entrance exams for a degree program

Many universities have their own entrance exams and may require home-educated or high school diploma students to write them. If students pass with flying colors, they might be accepted into the first-year courses in a degree program. If they do not pass them, they could either take adult upgrading at an adult center, upgrade at the same university under Open Studies, or take a high school course remedial class. Many universities do have entrance exams to ensure a standard of knowledge and skill acquisition because some provinces do not have Grade 12 diploma or final year high school leaving exams.

11. Universities Open Studies programs

Kids can apply to these programs at any age. Open Studies programs at universities allow students to choose from a decent selection of undergraduate courses with few or no educational prerequisites. Some schools may want demonstrated proficiency in writing and will require a test or a high school English course. Students can complete an entire 10-course year (five courses per semester) in Open Studies by taking first-year university courses, or upgrade by taking the final year high school courses to get the qualifications for a desired program. After the first year, students can transfer into a degree program at the same university or apply to transfer to another university's degree program. If the degree program they really want is too competitive, they may consider finishing a less competitive four-year degree and at the end of it, decide whether they still wish to pursue the original program. By already holding a degree, they will be better able to compete for a spot. If they wish to pursue a professional degree such as law, medicine, pharmacy, or teaching, these are usually taken after a general four-year undergraduate degree in any case, and it will not matter where the first degree came from.

Be sure to check out the admission policy for home education applicants in Open Studies. Unschoolers may have to present a portfolio, their SAT or ACT scores, some high school credits, a resume, an essay, letters of reference or another method of assessment, or attend an interview.

Another idea is to apply to enter in the Winter semester rather than the Fall. Winter admissions number about one-fifth those of Fall admissions and there is much less competition for seats. Many Fall-admitted students have dropped out or failed by Christmas, leaving a seat available for mid-year entry.

Transferring to another university or degree program from Open Studies

When transferring from one school to another, if the student has done less than seven single-semester university courses, usually both the high school transcript and the university transcript will be required and entrance will be granted based on the average of the two, but each school has its own calculation formula. If the student has completed one or two years of college-level courses, the receiving school may just ask for the previous university records and not the high school records. Still, check the admission guidelines to see how they evaluate prospective students.

The university grants course credits once the student has been accepted. The student must submit course outlines and should keep them from both high school and postsecondary courses to ensure that the outcomes are in line with university course code requirements. Sometimes a student may meet only half of the requirements of a particular course and will need to take another half or full course to make up the shortfall. They could also lose some course credits if the admitting school does not recognize the vigor of the textbooks assigned, the scope of topics, or the depth of the instruction.

Canadian universities do not have uniform curriculum for degrees. A five-year Engineering undergraduate degree at Memorial University does not align with the four-year requirements at the University of Calgary, or the program at the University of Saskatchewan, or the University of Waterloo. Some degree programs have mandatory internship or co-op programs; others offer them as an option. It is recommended that a student apply for transfer to at least three and up to five universities, allowing for course alignments at various institutions. Then the student can accept the offer that grants the most credit for the courses he has taken. Always accept that some courses or credits might be lost when transferring.

Universities only have a certain number of seats for transfer students, so marks do count. In many postsecondary and transfer programs, the competitive GPA required is a moving target. While my son was looking to transfer from one university to another, the entrance requirement changed. In six months the GPA required to get into the transfer program at one university jumped from 2.7 at Christmastime to 3.7 when he applied the following August. The transfer cut-off was based on the overall GPA average of the applications that year. Students who banked on getting into the faculty at 2.7 had no chance to redo courses nor even try to bring up their GPA for a September entry.

Only take this route if the student is extremely conscientious and aware of the risks. Poor first-semester marks can hamper efforts to transfer to another institution. Marks at postsecondary schools are cumulative and affect the average each semester. A bad mark will not roll off the 10-course average until nine more courses are taken. Even marks for failed courses that are successfully repeated remain permanently on transcripts; nothing will wipe out the original failed course mark. If the student is not sure very about attending, encourage him to work or travel before he commits.

My best recommendation for unschoolers taking this route is to do at least two full years in Open Studies at a university and get good marks, then transfer out if a specific degree is sought. Many of the courses will fulfill option requirements in Humanities and Social Sciences even for the STEM degrees, so they are never wasted. They will count.

12. University in-house upgrading

Every university offers high school equivalent courses but the downside is that they cost as much as regular university classes. If a child is under the age of 20, it is far less expensive to take the course under the funded high school system rather than in the postsecondary system that charges up to $600 per course. Some older students aged 23 and up may not like the stigma of "high school adult upgrading" and may prefer to take the equivalents at the university. Taking these upgrading courses also makes them feel more like university students and prepares them for the degree course experience to follow.

13. Apply as a mature student

Most universities consider students over 21 "mature." This might suit a lot of kids. For mature status in many programs in Humanities, Arts and Social Science streams, all that is required is the final Grade 12 course for English or an equivalency. Of course, STEM careers require Grade 12 Math and Science course marks.

This is often an ideal time to apply for postsecondary. Children's brains are more mature, and they have some work and life experience, contributing to the richness of class discussions and papers. They may be able to apply for government low-income adult student grants because they have been out of "high school" for several years. They are still young enough to take advantage of their parents' RESP (Registered Education Savings Program) savings because they have not yet reached the 25-year-old age ceiling; also, they can still be covered under parents' employee medical programs and qualify for bank discounts because they are full-time students.

If your high school aged unschooler is taking courses and hates them, consider pulling her out for a while to develop her passions. There is always time to retake the course with a different teacher and different assignments when she knows for sure that she really needs it and wants to take it. There are also alternative ways of completing the same course, such as correspondence courses or an adult classroom, which may have fewer assignments. In most places, adult students face fewer requirements than students fresh out of high school.

Many postsecondaries now offer first-year students "success" courses or videos about studying, exams, research, presentation, and writing skills. Many unschooled postsecondary students go through a stiff learning curve the first semester, and learn the different types of writing required in university by taking a first-year "how to write" course; they can do this rather proficiently when they need to, and with practice.

14. Attend a regular high school

Many unschoolers do not mind attending a physical or virtual school to get all their high school boxes checked off. This is an option.

Other less conventional ways to get into postsecondary institutions

"In every case, the route has turned out to be the right one for the person, and it continues to evolve. The factor seems to be 'unschooled,'—it appears to be a powerful input into a young person's life in terms of the capacity for self-direction and the ability to make an honest appraisal of what is important and what is not." (Stephanie J, 2002)

I have no personal experience with the following methods of entering postsecondary, but I have friends who have known people who started their postsecondary education in these ways. Linda C, a homeschooling Mom, suggests the following:

- Write the professional exams and begin at the professional level. If a student wants a professional degree in Medicine, Law, or Management, they can write the MCAT (Medical College Admission Test), LSAT (Law School Admission Test), or GMAT (Graduate Management Admission Test) exams. They may actually be able to start at a Master's level degree, or do a Bachelor's degree, skip the Master's and go straight to doctorate or PhD level studies.

- Get invited in by the head of department by making yourself known to him or her; then commenting on journal articles, writing to ask for more information, and cultivating acquaintances at open houses, public lectures, industry and field events such as conferences and seminars.

- Enroll to audit one course "for fun"—particularly a third- or fourth-year course—with the head of department; look keen and energetic.

- Take any course at all at the local community college; once you have a student number, enrolling in other programs or institutions is much simpler; and then add a few "serious" courses.

- Write a 200-page book and publish it. Writing and publishing a book is equivalent to a degree.

- Become famous by doing something spectacular at a corporation, in sports, the arts, government, or a non-profit organization. Many institutions confer honorary degrees.

Scholarships

Applying for and obtaining scholarships has a different set of requirements than applying for admission into postsecondary institutions. Scholarships are based on course averages. Most scholarships will not accept a parent-issued transcript. If a student has no marks for Grade 10 and 11 courses, they cannot get scholarships based on those grades. Often, a child who takes only the Grade 12 course will just have a credit or a pass/fail for Grades 10 and 11, and that factors in to scholarship determination.

Documentation for scholarships requires a government transcript, a resume, sometimes an essay, and proof that the applicant qualifies for the specific intent of the scholarship, for example, the scholarship could be specifically offered to those with a learning disability; it could be offered for a specific gender; or it could be based on proof of low income. One scholarship donor stated, "Home school grades will only be accepted if they have been validated through a recognized independent evaluation process." Scholarships can be hard to find. It takes close reading to discover whether the award fits. If a student is from a moderate-income family, has good but not necessarily excellent marks, and has no special status such as coming from single-parent, Indigenous, or Military background, there are slim scholarship pickings.

Scholarships can be difficult to apply for. Many are judged on how well the reference letters are written and the quality of the documentation sent. This puts a hardship on busy friends who are asked to write an acceptable letter. Essays are also judged. Many scholarships are overly complicated and bureaucratic. For example, one scholarship for students with ADD or learning disabilities required completion of an eight-page detailed application plus 15 attachments of various documents and proof of condition. Perhaps the donors forgot who would be applying for this scholarship, and what their limitations might be! Applying for scholarships can be time-consuming for no guaranteed benefit so students must weigh the time and effort against the potential benefit. I asked my daughter, who was entering third year at her university, "Can you apply for any scholarships?" She replied, "No, I don't qualify for anything. I'm too average." I asked, "What if I cut off your arm... would you qualify for a category then?" She replied with a twinkle in her eye, "Probably not, but there is a scholarship for orphans!"

Motivation for high school work

"When the student is ready, the teacher appears." — Anonymous

Streaming kids demotivates them. If students believe they can handle a course subject, they should be able to challenge any level of math or English. Teachers, principals, and school staff should not be in the position to stream kids into an academic or vocational route. Kids channeled into the lower streams begin to think of themselves as dummies. Parents often have to step in and advocate for the child, as they have the ultimate legal right to say where the child is placed.

"Today, my oldest son is writing his Grade 12 Pure Math (the type of math needed for STEM) diploma exam. This is the child who painstakingly didn't 'get' fractions, or long division, or many other math concepts in elementary and junior high. He took Math 8, Math 9, and Math 10 prep. His teacher at the time recommended that he take Lifeskills Math 14, the lowest possible level of math. We felt differently and knew he could handle at least the university Humanities stream of Math. So he took Applied Math that he needed for Arts and did well because he was motivated. When he decided to take a STEM career that required pure math, he took Bridging to Pure Math 30 and then Pure Math 30 itself. Not being naturally inclined in math, he worked very hard. He did every problem over and over. He persevered. Inner motivation fueled his efforts, in spite of education professionals' opinions that he would go nowhere in math. His course mark was 76%. He took seven Math courses in total for junior and senior high school. When kids are motivated to reach a goal, they will step up to the plate." So says a homeschooling dad. Believe in your kids.

I did not find motivation problems in homeschooling high school kids. When they want to learn and study more, they do their own research. Not research mandated by school, but research that answers their own questions. Many times, kids this age want the high school marks and credits and are willing to jump through the hoops to get them. My kids would take responsibility for all their courses and how well they did. Contrary to the popular opinion that not forcing kids to work would create lazy children, the opposite happened. The work in high school was novel and new and the kids embraced it with gusto. They were not burned out from having been in formal education from the age of two. Working hard at something that exhilarated them, instead of plodding through a standard government curriculum, was incredibly motivating. The key was flexibility and adult encouragement—something that only home education could provide.

What do most kids want from their education experience? Our provincial education department's Speak Out Survey of children's opinion of schools listed the following desirables.

- Teachers to provide more time to help them individually and smaller class sizes.

- More learning outside the classroom and hands-on experiments

- Working at their own pace.

- Less "drama" between students.

- More challenging material.

Out of the 56 forums held province wide, only three percent of students ranked up-to-date technology as the primary reason they learned best. Clearly, kids want an adult's presence, care, and knowledge more than they want the latest gadgets. (Cuthbertson, 2012)

Over half a million Canadian students participated in the national study, What Did You Do In School Today? The study showed that adult attention does make a difference and overcomes socio-economic factors in student engagement. A school system student's interest and motivation reach a low in Grade 10, the same age at which many unschoolers are just gearing up for formal learning. Homework completion and school attendance both drop significantly, to around 60 percent engagement by the time a student reaches Grade 12. (Friesen, 2009) Caring adults mitigate that drop.

Don't universities love homeschoolers?

Many homeschoolers think that universities are throwing open the welcome mat for students. In reality, many are trying to determine standards to measure homeschoolers against schoolers. Canada is lucky to have several paths into university without a diploma and home education is one of them, but rarely can an unschooler or homeschooler simply present a parent-directed portfolio that has not been assessed by an approved source.

Admissions departments use several criteria to sort out who to accept and who to reject. They may require courses that are not really relevant to the program but are academic enough to separate the wheat from the chaff. They have to have a clear, unbiased method to determine admittance, and the clean number that marks provide removes ambiguity and gives them the tool they need. Volunteering and community leadership are nice, but how does an institution measure one student's achievement over the other's? One of my children needed Pure Math to get into a health field. It was a sorting requirement. Once he got to university, he didn't need to know any more than volume and mass conversions for his courses.

If it weren't for those pesky application fees, I would undertake a research project to apply to every university and community college in Canada with only home education credentials and see how many would let me in. Anecdotal stories from homeschoolers are encouraging, but I would like to know the real numbers of how many home-educated students were accepted at universities all over Canada, this year, without five Grade 12 subject marks or previous university courses.

One university states on its website: "Homeschooling Students — It is an admission requirement to be a secondary school graduate. Therefore, homeschool applicants must be able to present a proof of completion of a program that has met graduation from a recognized educational jurisdiction and also faculty specific minimum subject and academic average requirements." There goes the parent transcript.

Are there other ways? Linda C, a long-time unschooler, professes: "The more intrinsically interested the student is, the easier it is to get in. There is nothing like making a name for yourself in the field, around people in the biz, to get you in faster than normal—and sometimes sideways, too. The first thing you need to know for sure: there is not an admissions office in a university or college on the planet that will ever admit there is any way in except 'do all the prerequisites, get great grades and apply with the form.' Their job is gatekeeping, and stopping anyone weaseling around them. Fundamentally, all schools are businesses, and they're in the business of paying themselves with tuition money—which they need in great gobs every year." I agree, but not all kids have the initiative and people skills to work past the gatekeepers. The parents have years of experience navigating gatekeepers, but in this age of privacy, it must be the kids who push.

High school graduation

If we value lifelong learning, why do we put such an emphasis on graduation? Graduation is the end of formal school and we celebrate it hugely. Instead of graduation, I would like to see "Welcome to Adulthood" celebrations to commemorate not the end of learning but the beginning of a new life stage of rights and responsibilities. Learning continues. It is never done.

From unschooling to university

Getting into postsecondary is half the challenge. Staying in is the other half. Many universities offer online degrees, but not everyone learns from a screen. Many people still prefer a live classroom experience. The next chapter focuses on success in moving from unstructured learning to a more formal learning environment.

21

Postsecondary School Ages 18 – 25: Follow Passions

"I don't know one single unschooled kid who would be stopped at anything for lack of a university degree. If they really needed one and didn't have it, they would just go get one!" — Stephanie J.

Gap year or first day of school?

At this age, many parents scramble to get their kids into university, checking out schools' offerings even when their child is ambivalent about attending. They urge the child to register and attend orientation sessions; they pay for tuition, books, residence, and living allowance. They discourage jobs and volunteering because it might interfere with academics. They strive to be on a first-name basis with the profs, the registration office, and the appeals committee. Many parents still try to control their adult children's academic progress by dangling or withholding electronics, cars, and beer money as rewards or punishments. If the child wants to drop out, parents insist it will be for a gap year only and they often encourage the child to go back.

"Eighty percent of the parents of Grade 10 students think their children will go on to university. By the time those children are in Grade 12, it is 40 percent of parents," says a school superintendent. (Faber, 2007)

Unschooling parents truly let their children decide whether they are going to attend university, college, or tech schools—or start a business, or work for an employer. Whatever their children choose to do with their own lives, once they are 18 or 19, is fine with the parents—as it should be. Parents can offer advice, information, financial help, and encouragement, but the learner must make the decision. The biggest gift parents can give is acceptance of their children's choices.

All parents eventually get to the stage of acceptance in which they realize they have no control over their child. How much grief and stress they endure on the journey to get there depends on how much interdependence is present in the parent-child relationship. When parents let go early, children take on education early and decide what to do with it.

University and college is where real school begins. It's as much a time for personal growth and life learning as it is for academics, especially for kids who live in residence or away from home. They quickly learn valuable life lessons—money management, for example, when they must choose whether to buy toilet paper or beer with their last $20! Learning about honesty, friendship, time management, responsibility, resource management, and problem solving really comes into play when Mom or Dad are not around to fix things at the residence.

What we did

One child applied to a local city university but wanted to experience residence life, so lived in residence accommodation for the first two years and then chose to live at home for the final two years. Another child applied to an out-of-town, but in-province, university and spent three years living in residence and one year in shared housing. He came home for holidays. The third child applied to an out-of-province university because we didn't want to pay a huge sum for him to attend a university in Europe, especially the first year, which is an "adjustment year." He transferred among three Canadian universities for various reasons and took more courses than he needed because universities across Canada do not necessarily have similar requirements or may not accept other universities' courses. He lived in residence the first two years, then switched to shared accommodations for the remaining five years. In addition to learning academics, the kids learned about living on their own, and quite a lot about who they are as people. All three adjusted well to a full course load, exams, essays, early mornings, and expectations when they needed to. Most of all, they were motivated to attend. The fourth child lived at home and attended a local university, as will our fifth child—if she decides to go. If not, or if she tries it and decides not to finish, we are fine with that as well.

Unschooling success comes in many forms. Those who do not choose to enter a postsecondary institution are highly successful, by virtue of knowing and understanding themselves and following their passions.

What you can do

Sorry. You can't unschool university! Universities won't let kids challenge exams with what they already know. At this age, when kids finally attend a formal structured school, the parents' job is to help them navigate the system for the first year—and then bow out. Many unschoolers, having no experience with registration, classrooms, clubs, and university rules and policies need an adult's help to explain the fine print and help them organize themselves. Some kids will grasp organizational skills right away and some will continue to need their parents' coaching for a while. Parents should help their children find the university, college, technical, or trade schools that fit them in terms of location, specialty, class size, prerequisites the student has completed, and the cost; then help them apply for entrance, residence, and scholarships or loans. Then—relax! The children will do just fine. They often have far more skills, knowledge, and competencies than their parents think they do, and with a little help, will step up to the plate of postsecondary demands even if they have never before set foot in a school.

Cognitive development during this stage
Emerging adults, ages 18 – 25

The prefrontal cortex completes its development; this part of the brain controls adult abilities to plan, make decisions, and think critically.

The executive functions of self-control, planning, focus, and working memory are fully developed. The child has common sense.

When children reach this age, they should be able to do most of the administrative tasks with the postsecondary institution. Privacy laws and regulations no longer permit the institution's staff to speak with you on behalf of your child. I once accidently paid the wrong university—I had three kids going to three different ones! —and the university would not return the funds to me, even though I had sent the e-payment. They would deal only with the student. In order to help your child during the first year, he or she may wish to sign a "Third Party Authorization and Consent" form, authorizing the school to speak with you about your child's academic and financial concerns and giving you access to his affairs while you help him navigate the system. I did this for some of my children who initially needed my assistance with loans, financing, and other concerns. Since it is often an unschooler's first exposure to administrative tasks, this is not considered helicopter parenting but rather good parental scaffolding, helping a child to perform the tasks he will eventually need to do on his own.

Essential college skills

This section is written for the new student.

Essays, group work, presentation skills, research papers, PowerPoint skills, notetaking, study skills, exam taking—and most of all, responsibility—are the skills required for success in postsecondary schools. One of the biggest success factors is to show up when you promise to and fulfill your obligations, even when you are sick, have a death in the family, or have another personal emergency. Universities do not take absences lightly! My son witnessed a girl get kicked out of the program for two absences that she did not let her professor know about in advance. Grit and determination are key to staying on course.

Figure on putting in three hours of study and work for every hour in lectures. Assignments are also fewer but more heavily weighted. In high school, you may have to turn in up to 45 assessed items per course, where postsecondary schools may require only two essays, each worth 30 percent of the final mark, and a final exam worth the remaining 40 percent. In universities, the academic year runs from September to April, with two four-month terms. Some programs may run spring/summer terms in May and June, or from May to August. The following tips may help you prepare for your university career:

- Practice taking tests and exams under time limits. These are high stakes in postsecondary, where a final exam can account for up to 90 percent of the final course mark. Average weighting of final exams is usually at least 50 percent because essays and reports are cheatable. Exams are harder to cheat on, so are more heavily weighted.

- Practice taking notes from lectures. You might do this weekly by listening to some of the many lectures available online, such as the TED Talks.

- Be sure to work on *formal* writing skills: practice writing essays with a formal academic voice, avoiding use of the first person.

- Practice writing research papers. Learn how to discern whether sources are trustworthy, how to avoid plagiarism, and how to correctly cite your sources.

- Practice presenting your learning; get together with other home-educated students and have each person prepare a presentation for the group.

- Practice working with others; group work is necessary in many classes. Learn delegation and leadership skills to prod others into doing their share. Practice with siblings.

- Practice good time management skills to balance fun and work.

- Set up good organizational systems to manage the business end of going to university such as paying rent, managing credit card deadlines, paying taxes, handling emails, and submitting scholarship applications; as well as doing such household chores as laundry, cleaning, and grocery shopping.

Which postsecondary school is right for you?

Degrees are four-year programs, associate degrees are three-year programs, diplomas are two-year programs, and certificates are one-year programs. Research schools by criteria important to you:

- Which schools offer what programs?

- What is the competitive average in schools of interest?

- How much is the yearly tuition?

- Is it close to home or far away?

- Are co-ops or internships offered? What is the size of campus?

- What does the city or town offer?

Tips for applying to postsecondary schools, for students and parents

Applications

Postsecondary open houses begin in October of the previous year as many schools' application deadlines are in February or March of the year of entry.

Apply early. For many programs, you can apply beginning from December 1 of your Grade 12 year. However, admission is still contingent on final June marks, so don't slack off! Many scholarships have early deadlines as well, so do your research and do apply early.

Apply to at least three schools and up to five, in case you don't get admitted to your first choice. Kiss the application fee money goodbye. If you only apply to one school, you may get rejected and have to waste a year. Many students apply to five institutions and at the last minute pull out of four of them, opening up spots during the first week of September. That's why postsecondaries charge non-refundable application fees! And why they carry waiting lists of up to 300 people that actually do have a possibility of getting in!

Some institutions will happily take your money before telling you that you are number 330 on the waiting list for a program; some will not even do you the courtesy of sending you a letter—they may email you a rejection or a waitlist notice—or not even that. Some may lose your application. The same applies for applications to residence. Parents, teach your child to stay on top of his various applications and follow up regularly by phone or email to check on the progress of his application.

For highly competitive programs, some admission decisions do not come until late August, as universities wait for all the applications to come in order to set their cut-off competitive average. Have your Plan B ready—applications to other programs or institutions.

Admission acceptance letters are usually mailed in bulky 8x10-inch envelopes; rejection letters come in thin business-size envelopes. So rejoice if you see a big package in the mail—and double rejoice if it comes with confetti inside!

Even when you apply well before the deadline date, if you are a transfer student, the university may not confirm acceptance or rejection of your application until late August. If you are accepted at the eleventh hour, you may have to scramble to find a place to live. One institution's tardiness in offering admission can affect four other institutions' seats and housing availability. You may have to juggle each offer's deadlines. In some countries, the UK for example, all universities have a common deadline for notifying applicants of acceptance—such a system would be of tremendous help to students for planning.

Paperwork

Make a Word file with your prospective institution's residence address, and your academic (or student center) and residence portal user names, passwords, and IDs. Parents: you also need this information in order to access the sites and assist or remind your children of deadlines or payments. By the second year, they should take the responsibility of doing this on their own.

Residence

Apply early. As soon as you receive an offer of admission, book the residence to avoid disappointment. Although you may lose the deposit, you can always pull out.

Parents: if possible, encourage your child to get a single bedroom with a door. Then the student can choose how much social interaction she wants by closing the door or leaving it open to the main suite or hall. It is worth the extra cost for peace and quiet and a better quality of study surroundings that can result in better marks!

Sign up for the lowest food plan available. Many places where kids like to hang out and meet their friends do not accept food plan cards, so they will have to pay extra for their meals at those places. Sometimes the dining hall is inconvenient, or is closed by the time your child can get there. Your child will grab food where it is handy, and that is often not at the dining center.

Do not buy a fridge, hotplate, bookcase, or bedding until your child has moved in and lived in the room for a week or more to see what is needed. And remember that most school and dorm supplies are on sale up to 90 percent off by the last week of September.

Take photographs of damage or dirt at the time when completing the rental report, and get receipts for everything.

Academic

Find out about book return policies before purchasing. Like gaming and video purchases, shrink-wrapped books that have been unwrapped may not be returnable. Do not buy books unless the class has started and the instructor confirms that they really are needed. So many textbooks are purchased and never even cracked open.

Find out how to sell used books at the end of the term or year.

Warn your child that unlike high school, university marks are cumulative. Make sure they know the deadline date to drop a course without academic penalty. My son did not know that and paid an academic penalty for three years for a course he left but didn't drop. It took nine more courses before that monkey of a mark was no longer included in his cumulative average. It can affect future transfers, entrance into different faculties, scholarships, and even institution admission decisions.

Let go of monitoring their marks and due dates. This is now their job! Your job is to coach them from home on the bureaucratic business and on how to assert themselves with the other new adults in their lives. Coach only—don't do it for them!

Encourage your child to get to know the Academic Advising department. These advisors are his new best friends for program planning.

Students, be sure to attend orientation week. It's lots of fun, and everyone looks lost—not just you! Parents, there are activities organized just for you as well. This is one parenting class that most parents attend, and all parents should!

Health

Monitor your children for signs of depression, anxiety, and stress. Trust your gut instinct. Talk to them about how they are feeling and encourage them to use the campus health clinic or wellness center. Encourage them to get flu shots, now that they are immersed in a far bigger pool of germs than they were exposed to in home education.

Send care packages of cookies, stuffies, and notes from home. They are probably home-sick.

Anything your child needs to do, but you haven't taught them, they can look up on You-Tube—how to sew a button, how to write an essay, how birth control works!

Text them as much as you need to! They love to hear your encouragement and love. They can choose not to answer. Remember, you are their roots as they try out their wings!

Parents, happy launching! Students, happy flying!

You are in; now, how to get courses

If you have been accepted into a program, it is easy to use the institution's software to register for courses. If you cannot get the course you need or want, keep trying. There is a lot of movement in and out of courses during the first two weeks of school as students cancel registrations. Get on the waiting list for any course or program you really want, then show up for every single class for a month. Buy the books and do the assignments. Make yourself known, in a good way, to the professor. Bums-in-seats get into the course before people on the top of the enrolment list, if they even show up at all. There is so much shuffling during the first month of any course, and often, if you're there, you're in.

The 5 critical rules for students

1. Drop courses that you are failing before the penalty deadline. Averages are cumulative.

2. Keep your GPA at least above 2.0

3. Organize yourself with a system, either paper or digital. Exams, essay and project deadlines, contact info, and work plans, as well as paper items such as articles and receipts, all need to be kept in a place where they can be easily referenced.

4. Learn how to learn if you haven't done so by now. Take advantage of the university's free courses on taking notes, writing essays and lab reports, prepping for exams, and handling stress.

5. Ask for help. Get to know Academic Advising, the health clinic, and your residence resource person. They are your new family and are invaluable for dispensing information and advice.

Massive Open Online Courses (MOOC)

ClevrU is a new kind of university that delivers video lectures that can be translated into any language. These types of online university classes are growing. They remove the barriers to higher education, as many people in third-world countries have smartphones but not desktops or laptops or access to traditional postsecondary schooling.

My daughter's first-year sociology class of 400 students was crowded into a single lecture hall; many of the students sat in the aisles because there were not enough seats. In such cases, many students cannot hear the professor or see the PowerPoint, and often the professor cannot speak English well enough for clarity.

336

Internet courses may be the answer if they are offered at a reasonable cost and can be accessed at any time. However, many do not yet offer credentials. The future may hold free access for all to university via online delivery, but at least for now, payment is required for learning assessment and conferring of credentials.

Credentials

We live in a world that operates on the basis of credentials. Credentials are meant to demonstrate evidence-based achievement of a certain level of competence in a field. I wish we didn't have to base our first judgment on them, but we do. We can work to change that, but at the same time, we must prepare our children for the world in which they will compete.

I disliked public school enormously. It seemed more like a maze to me, having to navigate intense social constructs, avoid bullying, try to fit in with peers, and mollify the teacher's wrath. I never thought of it as a place of learning. I never fit in very well, but I did my best to "get through it."

I did not think I would go to university, but at 25, I decided to give it an honest go. What a surprise! University was totally different from high school. And the reason for the difference was control: I could control what I wore because there was no peer pressure to dress a certain way. I could control whether I attended or not, what courses to take according to my interests, and what mark I wanted to earn with my efforts. I could drop courses and register for new ones. I could eat in class, smoke outside it (OK, it was the '80s) and go to the bathroom when I wanted. I was treated like a customer, not like a child. I loved it because I loved learning.

As a parent in an unschooling family, I am dismayed to hear from others that postsecondary education is overrated. It certainly may not be for everyone. And today, when knowledge can be gained from so many sources, I believe that some rules in university must change, like the ability to challenge courses in which learners already have self-taught knowledge. But I do believe in postsecondary education as one of many ways to learn, and it should not be discouraged. Here is why:

1. Our world lives by credentials. We all have varying stages of learning, but the working world needs a benchmark—a standard that recognizes a certain level of skills and knowledge in a given field. I want the pilot who is flying the plane I travel on to have a minimum amount of experience in landing the plane safely. I want the financial advisor I hire to have the expertise to guide me in planning a retirement that won't depend on cat food for meals. I want my son's neurosurgeon to be competent enough to ensure there will be no brain damage after surgery. I understand and acknowledge that people get their education through various means, but we do need a standard way to measure the levels of knowledge and skills necessary for public safety. I'm all for people challenging those standardized measurements—whether it is an exam, landing a plane, or practicing surgery. A university degree is one standard measurement. We can get our information anywhere, but we need to prove a level of competency.

2. Postsecondary education is the new high school, thanks to credential creep. More and more people are choosing higher studies, and postsecondary education is becoming the norm. But a degree no longer makes one stand out; if anything, it makes one blend in. Nowadays, people get a degree to conform to the norm. Master's degrees and doctorates are now what a bachelor's degree was 30 years ago.

3. A degree may not always constitute practical knowledge, but the one thing it does demonstrate is that the holder has the initiative, drive, and determination to finish something, despite personal, academic, and financial obstacles. That is a big deal to prospective employers and can open doors to careers that may not even be related to a person's degree. Yes, there are many other ways to prove grit, but this is one that should not be discounted.

4. Many university professors have worked in the real world. They are the most interesting coaches because they are real. They impart knowledge that they have gained through their unique experiences, hardships, joys, and failures. I agree that perhaps not much is learned from a professor who translates his knowledge through books alone and has not truly experienced his field, having lived in the sheltered ivory towers of academia during his whole career. But those kinds of professors are ever fewer and further between.

5. A degree is a sorting hat. Sad, but true. If two people have equal knowledge and skills to do a particular job, accountability to one's boss, shareholders, company, and the public at large demands that the person with the parchment—degree, diploma, or certificate—get the job.

6. Many practical skills are now taught in a degree. Mandatory work terms, co-ops, projects, and practicums in many courses allow learners to obtain skills through hands-on experience. The days of just writing, reading, and bookwork are gone. It would be even more personalized if self-directed learners could challenge university exams the same way they can challenge high school exams. And further, if they didn't have to pay an arm and a leg for the qualification assessment of such challenges.

7. A degree costs about $40,000 in Canada. This cost can be offset by loans, scholarships, grants, and income earned from part-time employment. Research shows that over a lifetime, the average person with a degree makes $1 million more than a person with just a high school diploma. That's a pretty good return on investment.

8. A degree can be earned while being employed. I personally finished a degree in eight years while working full-time, and graduated debt free. It took sacrifices, but it opened doors in areas I hadn't even imagined then. I got a job teaching Mom and Baby classes for our government health organization. They would not hire anyone without a degree—it could have been a degree in geology, engineering, teaching, or basket-weaving—but it had to be a degree.

9. Lastly, but most importantly, if we embrace unschooling, our children will determine their own learning goals and paths. If a child wants to get a degree, are

we truly supporting her learning by denigrating her educational goals? We must suspend our own agendas and support her. That is what self-directed learning is all about.

10. Moms and dads cry when they see their child walk the stage at graduation; she has reached her goals and they are so proud. But they must be the child's goals, not the parents'.

In this age, when many required core high school courses can be attained by writing exams to demonstrate self-directed knowledge, there is no barrier to postsecondary education. Loans, grants, scholarships, and part-time jobs can help.

There are benefits to postsecondary education. Don't rule them out!

If kids get lost at university

When children get lost at university, it may be because they are not ready. They may only be going because their friends are going; for the most part, they are going for the wrong reasons. When this happens, it's better to have them quit for a while—or forever—rather than waste time and money.

Will they get their passions back? Yes! The less parents do to control the child's future, the easier it is for the child to get on with the business of deciding what is right for him. This may be hard for the parent. But remember that influence is stronger and more powerful than control.

I have two children yet that may not graduate university and that is okay. We want them to be happy and find whatever fuels their souls. We will encourage whatever pathway they want to pursue.

One homeschooling mom said, "My fear is that my son misses the application deadlines and he is upset that he didn't act, seeing that planning was needed to keep himself on track, and I feel like I dropped the ball when he needed me to keep it in the air. So my question is—how much encouragement should I offer and when does that turn into nagging? Should kids do all the research and applications alone or should the parents bring in menus all the time?" I would say it's a delicate balance. Parents can encourage their children to apply, but need to clearly see and heed the signs if the child does not want to go. If a child resists researching opportunities, that is a good sign he is not interested. Research is the child's job, not the parents'. If the child really wants to go, he will research the possibilities.

My son Neil missed university application deadlines because he was not too sure he wanted to go, and it caused him all kinds of problems and put a lot of barriers in his way. However, the bright side was that the experience provided incredible life lessons. When he finally decided to go, the motivation came from him alone; he did the research and overcame the barriers. If a child wants to go badly enough, he will do whatever it takes to get in.

When children leave home for college, it is they who must overcome barriers and challenges, not the parents. And all students will have days when they will question how much longer they will stay. They will have bad days, bad marks, and conflicts with professors and other students. They will get sick and face the pressures of deadlines and commitments. Getting a college degree is not so much about the learning as it is a demonstration of initiative, persistence, grit when the grind gets unbearable, and putting up with an incredible amount of frustrating bureaucracy. But kids have to manage it, and they do. Our role is to empathize with our children's feelings of frustration and give them the encouragement they need to keep going when they feel like giving up.

Letting go: trusting your child's work ethic and your own parenting

Many parents insist on telling their children what to study. Today's over-involved parents feel they have a right to do so because they have over-invested in their children, and that this gives them the right to heavily influence their children's career choices. In response, many children decide not to pursue postsecondary simply because it's what their parents want. Parents need to know how to support effectively—when to offer advice and when to back off. When parents try to prevent their children's pain, they rob them of the confidence that comes from making it through on their own; of acquiring feelings of competence and well-being. Parents must accept who their children are without imposing upon them their own aspirations. As Sir Ken Robinson once said in a talk, "As soon as kids enter university, back off. Don't say anything. Let the children explore and go where they will go. Let them discover their own insights. They will learn things about themselves." (Robinson, 2013)

As parents, you have done all you can do. The rest is up to your children. Do they have an intrinsic work ethic or not? One of my biggest revelations was in learning not to judge how children will perform at university based on their performance in the years leading up to it. As I counsel parents of toddlers who hit, I assure them that they will not be seeing that behavior when the children reach their teens. Children change as they go through each stage of brain development; they grow up and become wonderful people.

My three older children were 12, 14, and 15 when they complained profusely about getting up before noon to attend a homeschooling event. It was horrible dealing with their pushback. I wondered where I had gone wrong. Should I have been stricter in instilling a work ethic and a schedule for them, so they would be better adults? I worried. Fast-forward seven years. It was Easter weekend and all three university students were home. Two of them were very sick with sore throats, conjunctivitis, and coughs. They had two more weeks of classes; assignments, essays, and lab reports needed to be turned in and exams studied for. Sophie studied all weekend for her exam on the Monday—even though she was sick. Neil pulled an all-nighter to finish a lab report worth five percent of the course mark—even though he was sick. On Monday, he took the train in to deliver it; then came home shivering with fever. Mathew was tempted to cut class on the Thursday afternoon, when I was able pick him up at his out-of-town university. He decided that he didn't want to miss the class and returned by bus on Friday. Less than half of his classmates showed up on the Thursday; for those that did, the professor gave them a bonus of five percent on their final exam for showing responsibility. I can't say the kids had that kind of work ethic in their early teens, but there is a time and season for everything and they certainly have it as young adults, when it counts.

I can laugh now at the naysayers who witnessed my younger teens sleeping in every day until 1 p.m. and questioned what kind of work ethic they would have once they got "into the real world." But kids will step up to the plate. All three kids' first job evaluations stated that they exceeded expectations in both work ethic and punctuality. Don't project. Change happens organically. When they need to make an 8 a.m. class or 7 a.m. job start, they will.

Don't project either that postsecondary education is off the table simply because school didn't work for your child. My daughter tried a year of Kindergarten but refused to go to school for Grade 1. Then she wanted to try Grade 3 in a school—it was too boring and she quit after three months. She tried Grade 9 in a school; too cliquey, so she quit after three days. She started Grade 10 at a high school and quit after two months because of the homework fiasco. She started Grade 12 at a "self-directed" school that many homeschoolers go to; she quit after two weeks because it took too much of her time.

When she signed up for university, including residence, I thought, here we go again—only now it's really going to cost us a lot of money that will be wasted. She was sad for the first month and came home every weekend. Then, everything seemed to click for her. She loved the people, the independence, the challenge, and the way kids were treated like adults. She graduated in four years with a degree in English, as well as participating in NaNoWriMo every year and writing six novels in her spare time. I've learned to have faith in teens' ability to know what is right for them.

Biggest unschooling regrets from the Team of Thirty

Lynn: I wouldn't have let myself panic when my son hadn't learned to read by the end of my comfort zone. I definitely would not have insisted that he do phonics with me every day, which I now believe only delayed his literacy.

Sharon: I would have gotten over my fear of rejection enough to continue offering lots of interesting things to do and places to go, even when they were initially refused.

Anne: Biggest mistake was that I ever put them in school in the first place! Biggest fear was that he would have a poor work ethic. I wondered if he'd do anything by choice! Also, that the kids would miss out on something they "had to know" which didn't happen.

Amy: Biggest fear was that I didn't know anyone who was doing it and my parents were against it, so we were heading into the unknown.

Karen: I didn't unschool and allow him to follow his passions right from the beginning. Biggest fear was concerns over how well they would be prepared for postsecondary - that is, until my oldest went to university.

Marie and Jill: None.

Melody: Geographical limitations (rural living) prevented her having access to social outlets for her math and science interests that were social and goal-orientated.

Annie: When my son went to high school from unschooling, there were some adjustment issues - he had to learn that he couldn't just get up and leave to use the washroom or get a drink, or just go do something else because he was bored. He felt that listening to a lecture on something he already had read was a waste of time. He did understand that he was responsible for his education, so he worked hard enough to get scholarships and graduate with distinction. One of the biggest lessons was how to jump through hoops to achieve his goals.

Olivia: Not unschooling longer when they were junior high age. It shouldn't be horrifying! Not taking enough time for myself.

Biggest unschooling bonuses from the Team of Thirty

Karen: Independent, confident adults.

Anne: Family closeness.

Amy: The kids are very close to each other and me. They spend a lot of time together. We have no regrets. Getting to be with them almost every day is amazing.

Marie: The girls really know themselves and are really confident in what they know they can do. The roundedness of their education, the work ethic they both have, and how settled they are in themselves.

Jill: Better relationship with my son.

Mabel: Homeschooling with my older brother made us grow inseparable. It allowed us to spend copious amounts of time together, which made us very good at conflict resolution. Since we learned this so young, we have all the tools necessary to sustain a healthy and close sibling relationship.

Olivia: Free schedule enables experiences outside of the school year.

Annie: My son has never waited for a teacher to spoon feed him, but has instead taken ownership of his learning. This benefit of unschooling really showed up in his final two years of university, when, having taken all the advanced courses in the subject he was passionate about, he approached a professor who had a keen interest in the same subject and the two of them designed and worked together, one on one, on several self-directed study courses - essentially unschooling at the university level. I would do it all again just for those years of family togetherness.

Melody: My son's work ethic, born of countless late-night hours problem solving his way through programming obstacles for fun. My daughter's confidence in her ability to independently overcome almost anything.

Helena: It didn't make sense to me that suddenly at the age of 5, I was no longer capable of providing a suitable learning environment for them. All three of our children are very close to both parents. There is a deep respect and love between us. We are so fortunate because we always treated them as equals and we bypassed a lot of the issues that other parents have with their kids. There was never any talking back, yelling at us, being mean to their siblings etc. We watched them grow into interesting, independent thinkers who have a love for learning. And for me, I got the bonus of having them around me every day.

Lifelong learning

My oldest three children have now graduated university and another is in postsecondary. In the summers and weekends that they came home from university, they still learned things they wanted to learn. They taught themselves languages, guitar, caligraphy, script coding, website coding, novel editing, building a 3D printer, baking, plant hydroponics, beer-making, wine-making, carving, sewing, costume-making for Comic-Con, violin, piano, painting, gardening, martial arts, candle-making, and the list goes on.

When Sophie was 19, she really wanted to learn Latin. She didn't have time or room to take classes in Latin at university so one year she spent the four summer months self-studying Latin in between working her retail job. She spent the summer between her first and second years of university reading the classics, including Homer's The Iliad and The Odyssey; The Time Machine; Madame Bovary; Frankenstein by Mary Shelley; Edgar Allan Poe's The Fall of the House of Usher; Ernest Hemingway's books; Agatha Christie's novels; and others.

Neil, at 20, spent the summer between his second and third years of university working for the local university's IT department and catching up on his reading: Ayn Rand's The Fountainhead and Atlas Shrugged; The Joy of X by Steven Strogatz; The Survivors Club by Ben Sherwood; Alif the Unseen by G. Willow Wilson; The Republic of Plato by Allan Bloom; Charisma Effect by Desmond Guilfoyle; The Shock Doctrine by Naomi Klein; The Moon Is a Harsh Mistress by Robert Heinlein; Flashman; How to Build a Time Machine; and books by Brian Clegg. He spent many hours at the local maker space to construct projects. To this day, he is a voracious reader and loves to create useful machines.

What do kids do when they come home from university on Christmas or summer break?

They continue learning and family living:

- They play Dungeons and Dragons and Settlers of Catan with their siblings.
- They go to dinner with their parents or friends.
- They do laundry, wash dishes, vacuum, shovel the walks, chip ice, clean up the yard, paint the deck, cook and bake.
- They drive siblings to and from outings and help them with their courses.

- They go to the gym; skating, swimming. They read novels.
- They catch up on dentist and doctors' visits, get haircuts, do banking.
- They join in family dinners and great discussions. They help host dinners and parties.
- They move computers into one room so they can game together and play as a team.
- They travel with parents and siblings to other countries (they even pay their own way!)

"Your time is limited, so don't waste it living someone else's life. Don't be trapped by dogma—which is living with the results of other people's thinking. Don't let the noise of others' opinions drown out your own inner voice. And most important, have the courage to follow your heart and intuition. They somehow already know what you truly want to become. Everything else is secondary." (Jobs, 2005)

Good citizens

Our four young adults vote in every election and make sure they understand each party's platform. They volunteer at the food bank and help the neighbors with lawn mowing, snow shoveling, gardening, and computer repairs, with no expectation of reward. They donate blood regularly. My 22-year-old son received his 10-time blood donation pin. They don't text or drink and drive. They didn't need a school to teach them good citizenship. They are not good citizens because they blindly follow rules, but because they have formed socially conscious convictions and follow them. That comes from living in an environment that welcomes critical thinking. The kids still seek our advice on matters and then make their own decisions.

Lifelong family bonds

Siblings are close even after leaving for university. There are 11 years between our oldest and youngest children but they still interact, chat with each other on a family discord channel, play video games as a team, build projects, volunteer together, go out together to social events, and participate in family outings. Most of all, they pitch in to help each other, even when it is inconvenient. They will go and dig their brother's car out of a snowdrift, fix their sister's website, build a server for a little brother's Minecraft group, or drive home a friend who had too much alcohol at a friend's party.

The three university siblings helped each other out during the school year by discussing course and professor issues and getting advice from each other. When we Skyped over family dinner on Sundays, we parents would leave the conversation to do the dishes while the kids stayed connected to each other online for hours to chat and play games.

When any one of the children comes home for Christmas, reading week, or summer break, and when we have to send that child off again, the whole family turns out at the airport or bus station to welcome them home or say a tearful goodbye. Our children are our best friends.

As a family, we all value relationships and give them priority over anything else. We live our life for two reasons: to spend time with and enjoy our loved ones, and to leave the world a better place because of our knowledge and efforts.

Unschooling does both. No school will ever love your child as much or as uniquely as you do. Enjoy your family and their education. You no longer have to choose between them.

References

Introduction

Gavel, Leslie, 2017, *Drop Out: How School Is Failing Our Kids (and What We Can Do about It)*, Page Two Strategies, Calgary, AB

Gavel, Leslie, 2014, *The Problem with Calgary Schools*, Article in Avenue magazine, Redpoint Media, Calgary, AB

Gray, Peter, 2014, *A Survey of Grown Unschoolers 1: Overview of Findings*, www.Psychology Today.com

Palix Foundation, 2017, *Young Children Develop in an Environment of Relationships*, Harvard Center for the Developing Child, Article in Working Papers, Cambridge, MA

PART 1: WHAT IS UNSCHOOLING?

Chapter 1 — Problem

Hildebrandt, Amber, 2014, *Back to School: 7 Million Students and 440,000 Educators Prepare for the New Year*, Retrieved August, 2014, http://www.cbc.ca/news/canada/

Harvaardsrud, Paul, 2013, *Most Likely to Succeed*, Article in Avenue magazine, Redpoint Media, Calgary, AB,

Gavel, Leslie, 2014, *The Problem with Calgary Schools*, Article in Avenue magazine, Redpoint Media, Calgary, AB

Hankivsky, Olena, 2008, *Cost Estimates of Dropping Out of High School in Canada*, Prepared for Canadian Council on Learning, http://citeseerx.ist.psu.edu/viewdoc/download?doi=10.t1.504.8760&rep=rep1&type=pdf

Miller, Lucy, 2013, *We Can't Afford to Ignore Low Graduation Rates*, Article in The Calgary Herald, Postmedia Network, Calgary, AB

Gatto, John Taylor, 2005, *Dumbing Us Down: 25 Anniversary Edition*, New Society Publishers, Gabriola Island, BC

Aldrich, Clark, 2010, *Unschooling Rules: 55 Ways to unlearn what we know about schools and rediscover education*, Greenleaf Book Group Press, Austin, TX

Aldrich, Clark, 2015, *Why All Education Needs Unschooling*, Session at the Unschooling Canada Association (UCA) First Annual Online Conference.

Sandy K, 2002, Homeschool Canada Yahoo Group Listserve

SAPTA, The Southern Alberta's Preschool Teachers Association, 2013, *Preschools Excluded from Pilot Program*, Canada's Education magazine, Calgary, AB

Chapter 2 — Solution

The Economist, July 26, 2014, *Choose Your Parents Wisely*, Article in The Economist magazine, The Economist Group, London, United Kingdom

Kidspot, 2016, *Children are Made Readers in the Laps of Their Parents*, News Life Media, www.kidspot.com.au

Yaniv, Hanan, 2011, *What Will the Classroom of the Future Look Like?*, Article in Avenue magazine, Redpoint Media, Calgary, AB

Farenga, Patrick, and John Holt, 2003, *Teach Your Own*, Holt Associates, Da Capo Press, Cambridge, MA

Shultz, Colin, 2014, *Unschooled Kids Do Just Fine in College*, Article in Smithsonian magazine, http://www.smithsonianmag.com/smart-news/unschooled-kids-have-few-problems-once-they-hit-college-180952613/?no-ist

Basham, Patrick, John Merrifield, and Claudia R. Hepburn, 2007, *Homeschooling: From the extreme to the mainstream,* 2 Ed., Publication for the Fraser Institute, Toronto, ON

Van Pelt, Deani, 2015, *Fraser Institute: Home Schooling in Canada: The Current Picture—2015,* Publication for the Fraser Institute, Toronto, ON

Martin-Chang, Sandra, Gould, Odette N., and Meuse, Reanne E., 2011, *The Impact of Schooling on Academic Achievement: Evidence from homeschooled and traditionally schooled students,* Journal article in Canadian Journal of Behavioral Science/Revue canadienne des sciences du comportement, Vol 43(3), 195-202, http://dx.doi.org/10.1037/a0022697

Helga R, Facebook

Van Pelt, Deani and Beth Greene, 2017, *Homeschooling's Lessons for Education,* Cardus Research, Retrieved April 2018 from https://www.convivium.ca/articles/home-schooling%E2%80%99s-lessons-for-education

Gray, Peter and Gina Riley, 2013, *The Challenges and Benefits of Unschooling, According to 232 Families Who Have Chosen that Route,* Journal of Unschooling and Alternative Learning, Vol. 7 Issue 14, North Bay, ON

Reeves, Richard and Kimberley Howard, 2013, *The Parenting Gap,* Brookings Institution, Retrieved Sept 13, 2014, http://www.brookings.edu/research/papers/2013/09/09-parenting-gap-social-mobility-wellbeing-reeves

The Economist, July 26, 2014, *Choose Your Parents Wisely,* Article in The Economist magazine, The Economist Group, London, United Kingdom

Gray, Peter, and Gina Riley, 2011, *A Survey of Grown Unschoolers 1: Overview of Findings,* www.Psychology Today.com

Ray, Brian D., PhD, 2009, *Home Education Reason and Research,* NHERI Publications, Salem, OR

Van Pelt, Deani, PhD, and Patricia A. Allison, MEd, and Derek J. Allison, PhD, 2009, *Fifteen Years Later: Home-Educated Canadian Adults; A Synopsis,* Publication for the CCHE (Canadian Center for Home Education), London, ON

Rothermel, Paula, 2005, *Home-Education: Comparison of Home- and School-Educated Children on PIPS Baseline Assessments,* Journal of Early Childhood Research, Vol. 2, pp. 273-99. U.K.

Home Education in Canada: A summary of the Pan-Canadian Study on Home Education 2003, CCHE, 2003 and

National Home Education Research Institute, 2003, *Survey of Adult Homeschoolers,* Published for NHERI, Salem, OR, https://www.nheri.org/

Moore, Raymond, 1999, *History, Research and Common Sense for Great Families and Schools,* Article for World Congress of Families 11, Retrieved July 31, 2014, http://worldcongress.org/wcf2_spkrs/wcf2_moore.htm

Gray, Peter, and David Chanoff, 1986, *Democratic Schooling: What happens to young people who have charge of their education?,* American Journal of Education, Volume 94, Number 2

Greenberg, Daniel and Mimsy Sadofsky, 1992, *Legacy of Trust: Life after the Sudbury Valley School Experience,* Sudbury Valley School Press, Framingham, MA, Retrieved April 2017 from the McGill Journal of Education, http://mje.mcgill.ca/article/view/8110/6038

Vangelova, Luba, 2013, *How do Unschoolers Turn Out?,* Retrieved Sept 13, 2014 http://blogs.kqed.org/mindshift/2014/09/how-do-unschoolers-turn-out/

Groeneveld, Nicolette, 2014, Founder and staff member of the *Indigo Sudbury Campus - a Sudbury School* which operated in Edmonton from 2002 to 2009, Retrieved in 2014 from the following blog: http://blog.play-i.com/sudbury-valley-school-part-1/#sthash.pOIKzPRO.dpuf

Lynn, May 2014, Receptionist at Summerhill School, UK, in a phone conversation

Chapter 3 — What Unschooling Is and Is Not

Tia L, 2003, Homeschool Canada Yahoo Group Listserve

Anna KB, 2000, Unschooling Canada Yahoo Group Listserve

Van Pelt, Deani, 2015, *Fraser Institute: Home Schooling in Canada: The Current Picture—2015,* Publication for the Fraser Institute, Toronto, ON

Armstrong, Thomas, 2006, *The Best Schools: How human development research should inform educational practice,* Association for Supervision, and Curriculum Development, Alexandria, VA

ADLC (Alberta Distance Learning Center) 2015, phone call

Kohn, Alfie, Feb 12, 2009, *The Schools Our Children Deserve,* Presentation at Banbury Crossroads School, Calgary, AB

Van Pelt, Deani and Sazid Hasan, and Derek J. Allison, 2017, *The Funding and Regulation of Independent Schools in Canada,* Fraser Institute, Barbara Mitchell Center, Toronto, ON

Wilder, Amanda, 2014, *Approaching the Elephant,* Documentary film about free schools in America

Johnson, Jeff, 2014, Feb 17, *Our Children, Our Future Symposium,* Minister of Education presentation, Calgary, AB

Miranda H, 2001, Homeschool Canada Yahoo Group Listserve

Chapter 4 — Play

Gotera, Adelina, 2012, *I will Play with You,* Trafford Publishing, Bloomington, IN

Brown, Stuart, 2010, *Play,* Penguin, New York, NY

Donaldson, Fred, 1993, *Playing by Heart: The vision and practice of belonging,* HCI, Deerfield Beach, FL

McDowall, Pamela, August 24, 2006, *Youngsters Learn Best in Fun Stress-Free Environments,* Article for The Calgary Herald, Postmedia Network Calgary, AB

Ginsberg, Kenneth R., 2007, *The Importance of Play in Promoting Healthy Child Development and Maintaining Strong Parent-Child Bonds,* Article for the American Academy of Pediatrics, Volume 119, Issue 1

Wenner, Melinda, 2009, *The Serious Need for Play,* Article for Scientific American magazine, Retrieved May 2018, https://www.scientificamerican.com/article/the-serious-need-for-play/

Shipley, Dale, 2008, *Empowering Children: Play-Based Curriculum for Lifelong Learning,* Nelson College Indigenous, 5th Ed., Toronto, ON

Klein, Diane, 2001, Teacher

Jensen, Eric, 1998, *Teaching with the Brain in Mind,* Association for Supervision and Curriculum Development, Alexandria, VA

Inspiring Education Conference, 2009, Alberta Education, Red Deer, AB

Bettleheim, Bruno, 1987, *A Good Enough Parent: A Book on Child-Rearing,* Vintage Books, New York, NY

EC Map Newsletter, 2011, *STEPS,* Published by Alberta Education, Edmonton, AB

Harper, Scott, 2011, *Lost Adventures of Childhood,* CTV Documentary film, Toronto, ON

Gray, Peter, 2011, *The Decline of Play and the Rise of Psychopathology in Children and Adolescents,* American Journal of Play, Retrieved May 2018 at http://www.journalofplay.org/sites/www.journalofplay.org/files/pdf-articles/3-4-article-gray-decline-of-play.pdf

Hoffman, John, 2005, *Daddy, Come Play With Me: A Father's guide to play with young children,* Dad Central Ontario, Toronto, ON

Brown, Stuart, 2010, IBID

Dunbar, Jean, 2013, Play therapist at Sheriff King, Calgary, AB

Hoffman, John, 2005, IBID

Gray, Peter, 2011, IBID

Building Blocks, Building Brains, 2011, PowerPoint presentation for trainers, Fraser Mustard Chair in Childhood Development, The University of Calgary, Calgary, AB

Wikipedia, 2018

Chapter 5 — Unschooling at School

Knowles, Malcolm, 1975, *Self-Directed Learning,* Association Press/Follett Publishing Company, Chicago, IL

Barer-Stein, Thelma, and James A. Draper, 1993, *The Craft of Teaching Adults,* Culture Concepts, Toronto, ON

Moore, Raymond, 1975, *Better Late Than Early,* The Moore Foundation, Camas, WA

McClure, Matt, Jan 30, 2012, *Teacher Budget Won't Cut Class Time,* Article for The Calgary Herald, Postmedia Network, Calgary, AB

Zwaagstra, Michael, July 18, 2009, *Alberta Education Not Broken, So Don't Fix It,* Article for The Calgary Herald, Postmedia Network, Calgary, AB

Fletcher, Robson, Feb 28, 2018, *How Much Funding Private and Public Schools Get In Alberta,* Article for CBC News, Retrieved May 2018 http://www.cbc.ca/news/canada/calgary/private-public-schools-funding-alberta-numbers-1.4553955

USC Rossier Online, Feb 9, 2011, *US Education Spending and Performance vs The World,* Retrieved Oct 5th, 2014, http://rossieronline.usc.edu/u-s-education-versus-the-world-infographic/

Moore, Michael, 2015, *Where to Invade Next?,* Documentary film, Michael Moore, Germany

Klassen, Karin, March 12, 2012, *Some Lessons for Teachers,* Article in The Calgary Herald, Calgary, AB

Pauli, Ken, 2012

National Governors Association Center for Best Practices, Council of Chief State School Officers, 2010, *Common Core State Standards,* National Governors Association Center for Best Practices, Council of Chief State School Officers, Washington, D.C.

PART 2: WHY UNSCHOOLING?

Chapter 6 — History

Winget, Larry, 2010, *Your Kids Are Your Own Fault,* Gotham Books, New York, NY

Canadian Encyclopedia, 2014, *The History of Education,* Retrieved May 2015, http://www.thecanadianencyclopedia.ca/en/article/history-of-education/

Education News, 2013, Retrieved Sept 2014, http://www.educationnews.org/education-policy-and-politics/american-public-education-an-origin-story/

Armstrong, Thomas, 2006, *The Best Schools: How Human Development Research Should Inform Educational Practice,* Association for Supervision, and Curriculum Development, Alexandria, VA

Wikipedia, Retrieved May 2013 https://en.wikipedia.org/wiki/Homeschooling_international_status_and_statistics

Maffin, Tod, Feb 15, 2008, *The Problem with Rock Tumblers,* Article in The Calgary Herald, Postmedia Network, Calgary, AB

Byfield, Ted, Editor, 1998, *Alberta in the 20ᵗʰ Century,* Multi-volume Series, United Western Communications Ltd., Edmonton, AB

Wikipedia, Retrieved May 2018, https://en.wikipedia.org/wiki/Alberta_Teachers%27_Association

Gibson, John, August 18, 2012, *Schools: A different style of education architecture,* article for The Calgary Herald, Postmedia Network, Calgary, AB

Holt, John, 1977, *Growing Without Schooling* magazine, Holt Associates, Boston, MA

Holt, John, 1989, *Learning All The Time,* Holt Associates, Harvard University Press, Cambridge, MA

Hildebrandt, Amber, 2014, *Back to School: 7 Million Students and 440,000 Educators Prepare for the New Year,* Retrieved August, 2014, http://www.cbc.ca/news/canada/

Roslin, Alex, April 5, 2010, *The New Homeschooling,* Today's Parent magazine, Rogers Media, Toronto, ON

Boesveld, Sarah, May 28, 2011, *The Politics of Unschooling: Raising independent trailblazers or lazy free-floaters?* Article for The National Post, Postmedia Network, Toronto, ON

Van Pelt, Deani, 2015, *Fraser Institute: Home Schooling in Canada: The Current Picture—2015,* Publication for the Fraser Institute, Toronto, ON

Martin, Jamie, 2012, *Homeschooling 101: What Is Homeschooling?* Article in Parents magazine, Meredith Corporation, Des Moines, IA

Van Pelt, Deani, 2015, IBID

Chapter 7 — Academic Benefits

Teghtmeyer, Jonathon, Jan 16, 2012, *Teachers: Lukaszuk's message was "pretty blunt."* Article in The Calgary Herald, Postmedia Network, Calgary, AB

Basham, Patrick, John Merrifield, and Claudia R. Hepburn, 2007, *Homeschooling: From the Extreme to the Mainstream,* 2 Ed., Publication for the Fraser Institute, Toronto, ON

EC Map Newsletter, 2014, *STEPS,* Published by Alberta Education, Edmonton, AB

Leman, Kevin, 2009, *The Birth Order Book,* Revell, Baker Publishing Group, Grand Rapids, MI

MacLean's, Sept 23, 2014, *Change to Quebec's 7 Dollar a Day Daycare Can't Come Soon Enough,* Article for Maclean's magazine, Retrieved May 2018, http://www.macleans.ca/news/canada/quebecs-plan-to-end-7-a-day-daycare-is-a-breakthrough-for-economic-fairness-and-common-sense/

Clyne, Graham, 2008, *Taking Stock,* Presentation at the Upstart Calgary conference, Calgary, AB

Mac, Amber and Michael Bazzell, 2016, *Outsmarting Your Kids Online,* Ambermac Media Inc.

Canadian Coalition of Self-Directed Learning, (CCSDL), *Fundamental Practices and Values,* Retrieved Feb 23, 2012 http://www.ccsdl.ca/blocks/page/view.php?id=2

Dale, Edgar, 1969, *Cone of Experience, Audio-Visual Methods in Teaching,* 3rd ed., Holt, Rinehart & Winston, New York, NY, p.108

Friesen, Joe, 2013, *French Immersion Enrollments Skyrockets as a New Linguistic Category Emerges, Article for The Globe and Mail, Retrieved Oct 14, 2014* http://www.theglobeandmail.com/news/national/education/french-immersion-enrolment-skyrockets-as-a-new-linguistic-category-emerges/article7935100/?page=all

Cuthbertson, Ruth, Aug 2, 2012, *Year Round Classrooms,* Article for The Calgary Herald, Postmedia Network, Calgary, AB

Tracy R, 2002, Homeschool Canada Yahoo Group Listserve

Satter, Ellyn, 2000, *Child of Mine: Feeding with Love and Good Sense,* Bull Publishing Co., Boulder, CO

Financial Post, May 2007, *The Skills Shortage Decoded,* Graph in the Financial Post Business magazine, Postmedia Network, Toronto, ON

Robinson, Sir Ken, Feb 14, 2013, Keynote at the Calgary Teachers Convention, Calgary, AB

Loney, Sydney, July 14, 2012, *Unleash the Power of Your Mind: Four Women Who've Done Just That,* Retrieved May 2018, https://www.chatelaine.com/health/wellness/unleash-the-power-of-your-mind-four-women-whove-done-just-that/

Gardner, Howard, 1983, *Frames of Mind: The Theory of Multiple Intelligences,* Basic Books, Perseus Books Group, New York, NY

Aziz-Zadeh, Lisa, and Sook-Lei Liew Francesco Dandekar, Feb 9, 2012, *Exploring the Neural Correlates of Visual Creativity,* abstract for Social Cognitive and Affective Neuroscience, Volume 8, Issue 4, 1 April 2013

Stephanie J, 2000, Homeschool Canada Yahoo Group Listserve

CBC, 2016, *Special Report: Campus Cheaters,* Retrieved May 2018 http://www.cbc.ca/manitoba/features/universities/

Huffington Post, November 27, 2012, *Cheating, Lying and Stealing Among High School Students Is On The Decline,* Retrieved July 2018, https://www.huffingtonpost.com/2012/11/27/for-the-first-time-in-a-d_n_2198714.html

Seaman, Andrew, Oct 16, 2012, *Extra Shut-eye May Improve Kids Conduct: study,* Reuters Health News, New York, NY

Rainey, Sarah, Sept 20, 2012, *Why Sleep Loss is a Nightmare,* Article for The Sydney Morning Herald, Fairfax Media, Sydney, Australia

Chapter 8 — Social Benefits

Press, Jordan, June 5, 2012, *Laws Won't Stop Cyberbullying,* Article for The Calgary Herald, Postmedia Network, Calgary, AB

Gavel, Leslie, 2017, *Drop Out: How School Is Failing Our Kids (and What We Can Do about It),* Page Two Strategies, Calgary, AB

Calgary Herald, Oct 25, 2012, *Minister Targets Teacher Workloads,* Article for The Calgary Herald, Postmedia Network, Calgary, AB

Neufeld, Gordon, PhD and Gabor Mate, MD, 2004, *Hold On To Your Kids: Why Parents Need to Matter More Than Peers,* Alfred A. Knopf Canada, Toronto, ON

Warren, Rachel, November 2017, *3 Ways to Raise a Healthy Eater,* Article for Consumer Report Magazine, Yonkers, NY

McMahon, Tamsin, Jan 12, 2015, *The Shrinking Teenage Brain,* Article for Maclean's Magazine, Rogers Media, Toronto, ON

Beilski, Zosia, Jan 30, 2015, *The Bystander Effect: Trying to turn witnesses into white knights,* Article for The Globe and Mail, Postmedia Network, Toronto, ON

Neufeld, Gordon, PhD and Gabor Mate, MD, 2004, *Hold On to Your Kids: Why Parents Need to Matter More Than Peers,* Alfred A. Knopf Canada, Toronto, ON

Cummings, Quinn, 2013, *The Year of Learning Dangerously: Adventures in Homeschooling,* Peragree, Penguin Group, New York, NY

Gray, Peter, 1994, *Psychology,* 2nd Edition, Worth Publishers, Boston College, MA

Kohn, Alfie, Feb 12, 2009, *The Schools Our Children Deserve,* Presentation at Banbury Crossroads School, Calgary, AB

Zou, Jie Jenny, 2017, *Pipeline To The Classroom: How big oil promotes fossil fuels to America's children,* Retrieved Feb 2018, https://www.theguardian.com/us-news/2017/jun/15/big-oil-classrooms-pipeline-oklahoma-education

Farenga, Patrick, 2017, *Education as a Family Enterprise,* Session at the Unschooling Canada Association (UCA) Second Annual Online Conference.

Chapter 9 — Emotional Benefits

Abeles, Vicki and Jessica Congdon, 2009, *Race to Nowhere*, Documentary film, United States

Grenier, Mike, Oct 29, 2012, *Why Pushy Parents Fail to Make the Grade*, Article for The Calgary Herald, Postmedia Network, Calgary, AB

Smith, Timothy, 2005, *Connecting With Your Kids: How Fast Families Can Move From Chaos to Closeness*, Bethany House, Minneapolis, MN

Hammer, Kate, Feb 12, 2013, *School Study Paints a Picture of Teens Under Pressure*, Article for The Globe and Mail, Phillip Crawley, Toronto, ON

Palix Foundation, 2017, *The Brain Core Story Certification Course*, Palix Foundation, Calgary, AB

Kohn, Alfie, Feb 12, 2009, *The Schools Our Children Deserve*, Presentation at Banbury Crossroads School, Calgary, AB

Arnall, Judy, 2007, *Discipline Without Distress: 135 tools for raising caring, responsible children without time-out, spanking, punishment or bribery*, Professional Parenting, Calgary, AB

Chan, Emily, Aug 30, 2014, *Edmonton Teacher Fired for Breaking 'No Zero' Grading Policy Wins Appeal*, Article for The Edmonton Journal, Postmedia Network, Edmonton, AB

Hatfield, Robert W., 2009, *Touch and Human Sexuality*, University of Cincinnati, Cincinnati, OH

Bodner, Nicole, July 26, 2009, *Eating together builds bonds with kids*, Article for The Calgary Herald, Postmedia Network, Calgary, AB

Lakritz, Naomi, May 2012, *Wheels Are Falling Off the Joys of Childhood*, Article for The Calgary Herald, Postmedia Network, Calgary, AB

Chapter 10 — Physical Benefits

Canadian Pediatric Society (CPS), 2016, *Sleep Guidelines*, Retrieved May 2018, https://www.cps.ca/en/documents/tag/sleep

Arnall, Judy, 2014, *Parenting With Patience: Turn frustration into connection with 3 easy steps*, Professional Parenting, Calgary, AB

Chapter 11 — Society Benefits

Macmillan, Amanda, Sept 4, 2017, *Teens May Do Better When School Starts Later*, Time Health, Retrieved May 2018, http://time.com/4741147/school-start-time/

Maclean's, Sept 23, 2014, *Change to Quebec's 7 Dollar a Day Daycare Can't Come Soon Enough*, Article for Maclean's magazine, Retrieved May 2018, http://www.macleans.ca/news/canada/quebecs-plan-to-end-7-a-day-daycare-is-a-breakthrough-for-economic-fairness-and-common-sense/

Retrieve.com, Nov 8, 2017, *The Decline of Memory Retention Over Time: The Forgetting Curve*, Retrieved May 2018, https://www.retrieve.com/blog/the-forgetting-curve

Ferguson, Eva, March 18, 2018, *CBE Class Sizes Not Meeting Guidelines, Even After Scathing Auditor General Report*, Article for The Calgary Herald, Postmedia Network, Calgary, AB

Labby, Bryan, Oct 3, 2017, *CBE Pays Absurd Rent for Admin Building Under Secret Contract*, CBC News, Retrieved May 2018, http://www.cbc.ca/news/canada/calgary/cbe-headquarters-lease-secrecy-election-board-education-1.4314396

Bieber, Sarah, March 25, 2017, *Our Students Deserve a Stronger Public Commitment to Their Education*, Article for The Calgary Herald, Postmedia Network, Calgary, AB

Van Pelt, Deani, 2015, Fraser Institute: *Home Schooling in Canada: The Current Picture—2015*, Publication for the Fraser Institute, Toronto, ON

Alberta Views, September 2013, *Jeff Johnson, Minister of Education*, An Exchange in the Legislature, November 26, 2012, Calgary, AB

PART THREE: HOW TO UNSCHOOL

Chapter 12 — Adult

Gavel, Leslie, 2014, *The Problem with Calgary Schools*, Article in Avenue magazine, Redpoint Media, Calgary, AB

Alberta Education, 2010, *Alberta Regulation 145.2006, School Act, Home Education Regulation: Schedule of Learning Outcomes for Students Receiving Home Education Programs That Do Not Follow the Alberta Programs of Study*, (SOLO) Queens Printer, Edmonton, AB

Nichols, F. and Humenick, S., 2000, Childbirth Education: Practice, Research and Theory, Second Edition, Saunders, Philadelphia, PA

Van Pelt, Deani, 2015, Fraser Institute: *Home Schooling in Canada: The Current Picture—2015*, Publication for the Fraser Institute, Toronto, ON

Kirschner, Paul A., and John Sweller, Richard E. Clark, 2006, *Why Minimal Guidance During Instruction Does Not Work: An Analysis of the Failure of Constructivist, Discovery, Problem-based, Experiential, and Inquiry-Based Teaching*, Educational Psychologist, 41(2), 75-76, Lawrence Erlbaum Associates, Inc., Mahwah, NJ

Angel, Gurria, 2018, *Pisa 2015: Results in Focus*, OECD, Organization for Economic Cooperation and Development, Paris, France

Friesen, Sharon, June 17, 2009, Presenter at *Inspiring Education: A dialogue with Albertans* Symposium, Calgary, AB

Gordon, Thomas, 2000, *P.E.T., Parent Effectiveness Training*, Three Rivers Press, Crown Publishing, Random House, New York, NY

Anielsky, Mark, June 17, 2009, Presenter at *Inspiring Education: A dialogue with Albertans* Symposium, Calgary, AB

StatsCan, 2004, 1994/1995, 2002/2003, *NLSCY - National Longitudinal Survey of Children and Youth*, On-Going study, Social Development Canada and Statistics Canada, Ottawa, ON

Arnall, Judy, 2013, *The Parenting Information Maze: How to find the advice that fits your family*, Professional Parenting, Calgary, AB

Arnall, Judy, 2014, *Parenting With Patience: Turn frustration into connection with 3 easy steps*, Professional Parenting, Calgary, AB

Baumrind, Diana, PhD, 1971, *Current Patterns of Parental Authority*, Developmental Psychology Monographs, 75, 1-103

Alter, Charlotte, August 24, 2016, *Secrets of Raising Super Siblings*, Article for Time Magazine, New York, NY

Bowlby, John, 1988, *A Secure Base: Parent-Child Attachment and Healthy Human Development*, Tavistock professional book, London, United Kingdom

Chapter 13 — Resources

Deborah S, 2004, Unschooling Canada Yahoo Group Listserve

Chapter 14 — Unstructured Time

Stephanie J, 2000, Homeschool Canada Yahoo Group Listserve

Linda C, 2000, Homeschool Canada Yahoo Group Listserve

Stephanie J, 2000, Homeschool Canada Yahoo Group Listserve

Chapter 15 — Assessment

CBE Learn, 2013, *Learning Plans*, Retrieved August 7, 2013, http://www.calgaryhomeschooling.com/documents/learningplan.pdf#5

McTighe, Jay and Grant Wiggins, 2005, *Understanding by Design, expanded 2nd Ed.*, Association for Supervision and Curriculum Development, Alexandria, VA

Alberta Assessment Consortium, *A Framework for Student Assessment* second ed. Retrieved August 7, 2013, http://www.calgaryhomeschooling.com/documents/learningplan.pdf#5

Martin-Chang, Sandra, Gould, Odette N., and Meuse, Reanne E., 2011, *The Impact of Schooling on Academic Achievement: Evidence from homeschooled and traditionally schooled students,* Journal article in Canadian Journal of Behavioral Science/Revue canadienne des sciences du comportement, Vol 43(3), 195-202, http://dx.doi.org/10.1037/a0022697

Diana, S, 1993, Homeschool Canada Yahoo Group Listserve

Ray, Brian, D., 2018, *The Relationship Between the Degree of State Regulation of Home Schooling and the Abuse of Homeschool Children (Students),* Research article for NHERI (National Home Education Research Institute,) Salem, OR, Retrieved May 2018, https://www.nheri.org/degree-of-homeschool-regulation-no-relationship-to-home-school-child-abuse/

Palix Foundation, 2017, *The Brain Core Story Certification Course,* Palix Foundation, Calgary, AB

PART FOUR: CHILD DEVELOPMENT STAGES

Chapter 16 — Brain Basics

Armstrong, Thomas, 2006, *The Best Schools: How human development research should inform educational practice,* Association for Supervision, and Curriculum Development, Alexandria, VA

Aldrich, Clark, 2015, *Why All Education Needs Unschooling,* Session at the Unschooling Canada Association (UCA) First Annual Online Conference

Durrant, Joan, PhD, 2011, *Positive Discipline in Everyday Parenting, 2 ed.,* Save The Children Sweden, Stockholm, Sweden

Calgary Science Center, 2009, *Body Worlds,* Exhibit, Calgary, AB

Covert, Denise M., *What the Different Parts of The Brain Do?* Healthfully.com, Ehow, Retrieved May 2017, https://healthfully.com/different-parts-brain-do-5393248.html#ixzz2muQbphP9

Wildman, Sarah, July 10, 2009, *No More Buy, Buy Baby,* Article for The Globe and Mail, Phillip Crawley, Toronto, ON

Hawley, Theresa, 2000, *Starting Smart: How early experiences affect brain development, 2nd Ed.,* Zero to Three Organization, Washington D.C. United States

Calgary Science Center, 2009, *Body Worlds,* Exhibit, Calgary, AB

Gopnik, Alison, 2004, *How Babies Think: The Science of Childhood,* Orion Books, United Kingdom

Jeyanathan, Joje, Winter 2014, *Train Your Brain,* Article for UMagazine, A publication of the University of Calgary, Calgary, AB

Palix Foundation, 2017, *The Brain Core Story Certification Course,* Palix Foundation, Calgary, AB

Calgary Science Center, 2009, *Body Worlds,* Exhibit, Calgary, AB

Chapter 17 — Babies, Toddlers, and Preschoolers

CPS, Nov 27, 2017, *Screen time and young children: Promoting health and development in a digital world,* CPS Canadian Pediatric Society, Retrieved May 2018, https://www.cps.ca/en/documents/position/screen-time-and-young-children

Muscovitch, Arlene, 2007, *Good Servant, Bad Master? Electronic Media and The Family,* The Vanier Institute of The Family, Ottawa, ON

Clyne, Graham, 2008, *Taking Stock,* Presentation at the Upstart Calgary conference, Calgary, AB

Siegal, Daniel J., MD, and Tina Payne Bryson, PhD, 2012, *The Whole Brain Child,* Bantam, New York, NY

Clark, Dawne, 2008, Professor, *Taking Stock,* Presentation at the Upstart Calgary conference, Calgary, AB

Enrollment in Childcare and Preschool, Oct 9, 2016, OECD, Organization for Economic Cooperation and Development, Paris, France, Retrieved May 2018, https://www.oecd.org/els/soc/PF3_2_Enrolment_childcare_preschool.pdf

Cole, Marjorie, 2009, *Alberta Preschool Association Conference,* Conversation with author.

Neufeld, Gordon, PhD and Gabor Mate, MD, 2004, *Hold On To Your Kids: Why Parents Need to Matter More Than Peers,* Alfred A. Knopf Canada, Toronto, ON

Eisen, Ben, Jan 2010, *Myths About Childcare Subsidies: A review of the empirical literature,* FCPP Frontier Center for Public Policy, Series #79, Retrieved May 2018, https://fcpp.org/files/1/PS79_MythsChildcare_F2JA28.pdf

Maclean's, Sept 23, 2014, *Change to Quebec's 7 Dollar a Day Daycare Can't Come Soon Enough,* Article for Maclean's magazine, Retrieved May 2018, http://www.macleans.ca/news/canada/quebecs-plan-to-end-7-a-day-daycare-is-a-breakthrough-for-economic-fairness-and-common-sense/

Chapter 18 — Elementary Years

Wente, Margaret, Feb 14, 2013, *Boys Will Be Boys: Schools need to understand that,* Article for The Globe and Mail, Phillip Crawley, Toronto, ON

Armstrong, Thomas, 2006, *The Best Schools: How human development research should inform educational practice,* Association for Supervision, and Curriculum Development, Alexandria, VA

Lynnette P, 1999, Unschooling Canada Yahoo Group Listserve

Melody W, 2001, Homeschooling Canada Yahoo Group Listserve

Kohn, Alfie, 2003, *Punished by Rewards,* Mariner Books, Houghton, Mifflin and Harcourt, Boston, MA

Gordon, Thomas, 2000, *P.E.T., Parent Effectiveness Training,* Three Rivers Press, Crown Publishing, Random House, New York, NY

CBC, 2016, *Special Report: Campus Cheaters,* Retrieved May 2018 http://www.cbc.ca/manitoba/features/universities/

Arnall, Judy, 2007, *Discipline Without Distress: 135 tools for raising caring, responsible children without time-out, spanking, punishment or bribery,* Professional Parenting, Calgary, AB

Arnall, Judy, 2014, *Parenting With Patience: Turn frustration into connection with 3 easy steps,* Professional Parenting, Calgary, AB

Louise A, 2000, Unschooling Canada Yahoo Group Listserve

Liedloff, Jean, 1940, *The Continuum Concept,* Da Capo Press, Cambridge, MA

Brazelton, T. Berry and Dr. Stanley, Greenspan, 2009, *The Irreducible Needs of Children,* Da Capo Lifelong books, Cambridge, MA

Goodman, Vera, 2007, *Simply Too Much Homework: What can we do?*, Reading Wings Inc., Calgary, AB

Kohn, Alfie, Feb 12, 2009, *The Schools Our Children Deserve*, Presentation at Banbury Crossroads School, Calgary, AB

Nelson, Chris, March 17, 2015, *Video games changing the way the world is learning*, Article for The Calgary Herald, Postmedia Network, Calgary, AB

Reddit, Sept 2017, Retrieved May 2018, https://www.reddit.com/r/leagueoflegends/comments/6x5h5f/riot_worlds_2017_prize_pool_fan_contribution_what/

Statistics Canada Publication, Oct 2017, *Physical Activity of Canadian Youth and Children*, Statistics Canada, Ottawa, ON

McKnight, Zoe, Aug 10, 2015, *Why Crime is Falling So Fast: How social media obsession, smartphone addiction, and even violent video games, have made the world a surprisingly safe place*, Article for Maclean's magazine, Rogers Media, Toronto, ON

Meeker, Meg, MC, 2010, *The 10 Habits of Happy Mothers: Reclaiming our passion, purpose and sanity*, Ballantine Books, Random House, New York, NY

Miranda H, 2000, Unschooling Canada Yahoo Group Listserve

Diana S, 2001, Homeschool Canada Yahoo Group Listserve

Bluedorn, Harvey, 2001, *Research on the Teaching of Math: Formal arithmetic at the age of ten, hurried or delayed*, Quote by William D., Rohwer, 1971, Retrieved June 2018, http://www.triviumpursuit.com/articles/research_on_teaching_math.php

Clyne, Graham, 2008, *Taking Stock*, Presentation at the Upstart Calgary conference, Calgary, AB

Laucius, Joanne, Jan 20, 2012, *The Need for Novelty*, Article for The Calgary Herald, Post Media Network, Calgary, AB

Albert, David, 1999, (Post in a homeschool newsletter 2003), *And the Skylark Sings With Me*, New Society Publishers, Gabriola Island, BC

HealthyChildren.Org, *Helping Your Child Learn to Read*, Retrieved May 2018, https://www.healthychildren.org/english/ages-stages/preschool/pages/helping-your-child-learn-to-read.aspx

Joanne P, 2017, Alberta Unschooling Families Facebook Group

Erin R, 1999, Homeschool Canada Yahoo Group Listserve

Chapter 19 — Junior High Years

Tia L, 1999, Unschooling Canada Yahoo Group Listserve

Palix Foundation, 2017, *The Prevalence of ACES in The Classroom*, A slide for *The Brain Core Story Certification Course*, Palix Foundation, Calgary, AB

Armstrong, Thomas, 2006, *The Best Schools: How human development research should inform educational practice*, Association for Supervision, and Curriculum Development, Alexandria, VA

Alberta Education, 2013, *Our Children, Our Future: Curriculum Shifts*, A presentation at the Inspiring Education symposium, Alberta Education, Edmonton, AB

Colleen J, 2008, Alberta Homeschooling Teens Facebook group

Gordon, Pamela, 2012, *Wake Up Your Brain*, Article for Speaker magazine, National Speakers Association, Tempe, AZ

Olsen, Glenn and Mary Lou Fuller, July 10, 2010, *The Benefits of Parental Involvement: What research has to say*, Pearson, Allen, Bacon, Prentice Hall, Retrieved May 2017, https://www.education.com/reference/article/benefits-parent-involvement-research/

Learning Disabilities Online.org, *What is a Learning Disability?*, Retrieved May 2018, http://www.ldonline.org/ldbasics/whatisld

Stockland, Peter, Jan 4, 2018, *Here Comes The 24/7 Classroom: Will private tutoring reconfigure learning?*, Convivian.ca, Retrieved May 2018, https://www.convivium.ca/articles/here-comes-the-24-7-classroom

Chapter 20 — High School Years

Armstrong, Thomas, 2006, *The Best Schools: How human development research should inform educational practice,* Association for Supervision, and Curriculum Development, Alexandria, VA

Bolender, Merla, 2007, Alberta Education, in a telephone conversation

Kohn, Alfie, Feb 12, 2009, *The Schools Our Children Deserve,* Presentation at Banbury Crossroads School, Calgary, AB

Alberta Education, 2016, *Ways to Obtain a Diploma Through GED,* Retrieved May 2018, https://education.alberta.ca/general-educational-development-ged/obtaining-a-diploma-through-ged/

Stephanie J, 2002, Unschooling Canada Yahoo Group Listserve

Cuthbertson, Richard, Nov 19, 2012, *Schools grappling with how to best use technology in the classroom,* Article for The Calgary Herald, Post Media Network, Calgary, AB

Friesen, Sharon, June 17, 2009, Presenter at *Inspiring Education: A dialogue with Albertans* Symposium, referencing a survey, *What Did You Do In School Today?,* Calgary, AB

University of Victoria, *Homeschooled Students Application,* Retrieved May 2018, https://www.uvic.ca/future-students/undergraduate/admissions/high-school/home-school/index.php

Linda C, 2002, Unschooling Canada Yahoo Group Listserve

Chapter 21 - Postsecondary Years

Stephanie J, 2002, Unschooling Canada Yahoo Group Listserve

Faber, Cathy, 2007, Calgary Board of Education CBE-Learn Parent Council Meeting, Calgary, AB

Robinson, Sir Ken, Feb 14, 2013, Presentation at *Calgary Teachers Convention,* Calgary, AB

Jobs, Steve, 2005, *How to Live Before You Die,* Retrieved May 2018, https://www.ted.com/talks/steve_jobs_how_to_live_before_you_die

About the Author

Judy Arnall, BA, DTM, CCFE
Conference Speaker, Trainer and Bestselling Author

Judy is an international award-winning professional speaker and a sought-after Canadian expert in non-punitive education and parenting practices. She regularly appears on television interviews on CBC, CTV, and Global as well as publications including Chatelaine, Today's Parent, Canadian Living, Parents magazine, The Globe and Mail, Metro and Postmedia News.

As a Certified Canadian Family Life Educator (CCFE), Judy teaches family communication and parenting leadership at the University of Calgary, Continuing Education, and has taught for Alberta Health Services for 13 years. Judy founded the non-profit organization, Unschooling Canada Association, which offers public information sessions across North America. Judy is an authorized facilitator of Parent Effectiveness Training (P.E.T.) Terrific Toddlers program, and Positive Discipline In Every Day Life.

Holding a Distinguished Toastmaster accreditation, Judy is a dynamic conference keynoter that engages audiences in interactive activities. Her keynote, "Play Is The Key To University" is popular with corporations, Teachers Conventions and associations.

As a specialist in child development, Judy is the author of the worldwide print bestseller, *Discipline Without Distress: 135 Tools for raising caring, responsible children without time-out, spanking, punishment or bribery*. As a parent of five children, Judy has a broad understanding of the issues facing families in the digital age and has authored a DVD titled *Plugged-In Parenting: Connecting with the digital generation for health, safety and love*. She is also the author of *Parenting With Patience: Turn frustration into connection with 3 easy steps*, and the parenting journal, *The Last Word on Parenting Advice*. Her latest book is *Attachment Parenting Tips Raising Toddlers To Teens*.

www.professionalparenting.ca

www.judyarnall.com

www.unschoolingtouniversity.com

@parentingexpert

jarnall@shaw.ca

Also by Judy Arnall
Specialist in Non-Punitive Parenting and Education Practices

Order the 440 page world-wide bestseller of tips and tools to raise caring children from babies to teenagers without any kind of physical or emotional punishment. Comes with a handy chart of common misbehaviours and matching strategies.

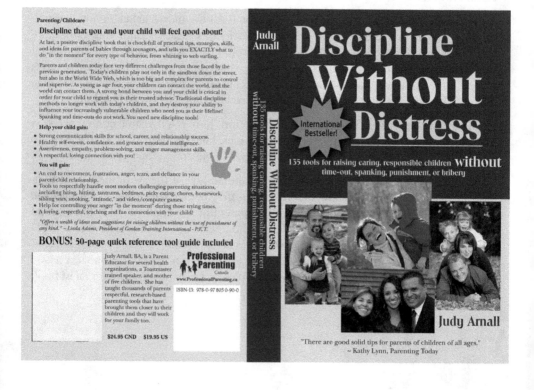

No parenting theory. No opinions. No judgement...

Just Solutions!

Attachment Parenting Tips is an easy-to-use reference book of ideas to solve every common parenting problem that arises while raising children from 0 to 13 years of age and beyond. Each tip is respectful, gentle, and non-punitive. Written by a certified parent educator and mother of five grown attachment-parented children, this book is bursting with over 3,000 practical tips tested by real parents. Every topic in parenting is covered from feeding and sleep, to bullying and homework, and the strategies can be put to use immediately.

Get helpful strategies on...

- The Baby Years: sleeping, breastfeeding, and crying.
- The Toddler Years: toilet training, hitting, picky eating, and sleeping.
- The Preschool Years: power struggles, not listening, and sibling jealousy.
- The School-aged Years: friends, school, screen time, and discipline.
- The Teen Years: the one tool that works for all teen issues.
- General AP Tips: more tools for babies to teens.

"A much needed reference book with no theory - just plenty of neuro-biologically informed, kind, and effective strategies for the everyday challenges parents face."
- **Lysa Parker, MS**, Cofounder of *Attachment Parenting International* and coauthor of *Attached at the Heart*.

"This book should be on every parent's phone or nightstand. It is a treasure chest of respectful tips and practical ideas to use for almost every common parenting issue."
- **Elizabeth Pantley**, Author of *The No-Cry Solution* series

Bonus! Every challenge includes a brain and child development tip for that age and issue.

Judy Arnall, BA, DTM, is a Certified Family Life Educator, Distinguished Toastmaster, interactive keynote speaker, and mother of five children.

She specializes in child development and non-punitive parenting/education practices.

Professional Parenting
"Savvy parenting for successful children"
www.professionalparenting.ca

Print: $24.95 USD
eBook: $9.99 USD

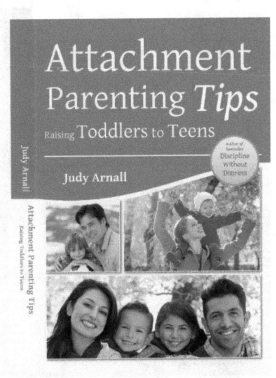

Attachment Parenting *Tips*

Raising Toddlers to Teens

Judy Arnall

Author of bestseller *Discipline Without Distress*

Judy Arnall · Attachment Parenting Tips · Raising Toddlers to Teens

---

Connect with your digital children while keeping them safe, healthy and happy!

Disc One - *Media is the Other Parent* : 74 minutes

Family Trends- The Generation Gap Widens
6 major changes to family lifestyle since the electronic revolution
What is "screen time?"

Parenting Pointers- Parents Matter Most
5 essential pointers to keep kids connected and safe

Balance and Health
7 keys for a balanced life
4 warning signs of obsession

Parents' Fears and Children's Needs
8 fears of parents and 8 needs of children

Safety First
Entertainment Software Ratings Board (ESRB) codes
14 cyber-safety recommendations

Benefits of Internet and Gaming
20 academic, social and life-skill benefits of internet and video/computer games

Disc Two - *Teaching Digital Intelligence*: 51 minutes

Babies and Toddlers 0-2yrs
Brain Development, Usage, Parents' Role, Safety Tips, How to Reduce Screen Time, and Experiential Learning

Preschoolers 3-5yrs
Development, Usage, Parents' Role, Safety Tips, How to Reduce Screen Time, Learning Styles, Acknowledging Feelings, Advertising, and Virtual Worlds

School-Agers 6-12yrs
Development, Usage, Parents' Role, Safety Tips, How to Reduce Screen Time, Sibling Fighting, Online Learning, Inactivity, Overeating, Cyber-bullying, Netiquette, Critical Thinking, Surveillance Programs and Luring Protection

Teenagers 13-19yrs
Development, Usage, Parents' Role, Safety Tips, How to Reduce Screen Time, One-time Consultation, Sharing Values, Boundaries, and Online Learning

Be a Part of Their World
The most important gift that children need and can't be provided virtually

Bonus! Includes 6 parenting vignettes showing problem-solving, acknowledging feelings and more!

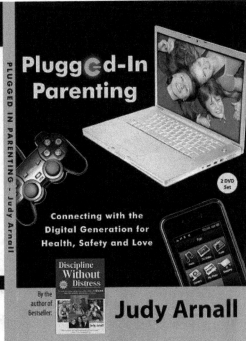

PLUGGED IN PARENTING - Judy Arnall

Plugged-In Parenting

Connecting with the Digital Generation for Health, Safety and Love

By the author of Bestseller: *Discipline Without Distress*

Judy Arnall

2 DVD Set

Parenting/Childcare

This is a quick book to read when you are calm, to use when you are not!

Positive discipline has to begin with positive stress management. All families have stress. Make it work for you!

- Learn how to embrace stress, manage it, and regain your patience before yelling.
- Learn why children have tantrums at all ages, and how to help them channel anger into lifelong skills for self-control and communication.
- Learn normal childhood development, capabilities and temperament, so you can respectfully and non-punitively resolve everyday family issues.

"Written in an easy conversational style, *Parenting With Patience* offers realistic advice for handling stress in parenting." - Dr. Christine Knight, Psychologist

"Every parent will benefit from the charts showing normal child age-capabilities and temperament characteristics. It's helpful to know the difference between a development issue that will reduce with age and a discipline issue that needs addressing." - Susanne Harach-Vatne, Parent Educator

"*Parenting With Patience* is full of compassionate and wise tools that parents can employ quickly when they need them the most." - Deborah Fannie Miller, Author of *Grappling with the Grumblies*

BONUS! Includes a handy section of calm-down tools to cut out and put on your fridge. Families can try a new one each week!

Judy Arnall, BA, DTM is a Certified Family Life Educator, Distinguished Toastmaster interactive keynote speaker, and mother of five children.

She specializes in child development, and non-punitive parenting and education practices which enhance family relationships.

Professional Parenting
Canada
"Savvy parenting for successful children"

www.ProfessionalParenting.ca

ISBN 978-097805095-5

5 1 6 9 5

9 780978 050955

$19.95 CND $16.95 US

Spine: Judy Arnall · Parenting With Patience

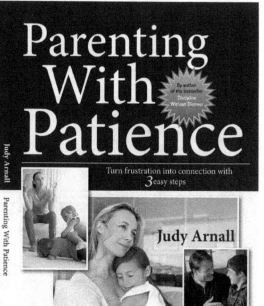

Parenting
With
Patience

By author of the bestseller *Discipline Without Distress*

Turn frustration into connection with *3* easy steps

Judy Arnall

"Every parent needs patience, and this book has simple, respectful ways to calm down and connect."
- Dr. William Sears and Martha Sears, RN, co-authors of *The Baby Book* and *The Discipline Book*

Parenting/ Childcare

Reclaim your parenting confidence!

This one-page parenting advice book is one of the most important pieces of advice that new and experienced parents will need in their parenting journey.

"Whenever I start doubting my parenting, I just open this book, and feel so much better." Maija Mills, BScPT

"This book is a wonderful tool to help parents trust their instincts and stay true to their own parenting beliefs!" Elizabeth Deneer-Roche, B.ChSt

"An essential gift for every new or experienced parent, for those times they feel judged, unappreciated or are just having a really bad day" Brenda Beatty, CBE, and mom of 5

"Finally, a book that tells you everything you REALLY need to know." Nicole Brouwer, BSc BEd, Parent Educator and mom of two

"My partner loved this gift." John Melisky

"A fantastic book that really encourages you to trust your instincts as a parent." Carolyn Campbell, Childbirth educator and mom of 4

"My Mother-in-law gave me this book when I became a new mom and I am forever grateful for this token of her support." Angela Farrell

Judy Arnall, BA, is a Parent Educator for several health organizations, a Toastmaster and professional speaker, and the best-selling author of "Discipline Without Distress: 35 Tools for Raising Caring, Responsible Children Without Time-out, Spanking, Punishment, or Bribery" and "Plugged-in Parenting: Connecting with the Digital Generation for Health, Safety and Love." As the mother of five children, Judy has taught thousands of parents non-punitive, research-based parenting tools and skills that have enabled parents and children to build caring, close, and respectful bonds.

Professional Parenting
www.professionalparenting.ca

9780978050924

$12.95 **$12.95**

Spine: The Last Word on Parenting Advice - Judy Arnall

The Last Word on Parenting Advice

"The secret to confident parenting – in just one page"
-Teresa Pitman

Judy Arnall